I0802329

Tableware Designs of Ben Seibel: 1940s-1980s

Richard G. Racheter

Schiffer Publishing Ltd

4880 Lower Valley Road, Atglen, PA 19310 USA

Dedication

For Shirley Walker Ohman: The finest lady I know.
and
My Grandmother, Charlotte Broking-Schoonmaker: Gone many years, but always remembered.

Library of Congress Cataloging-in-Publication Data

Racheter, Richard G.
Tableware designs of Ben Seibel, 1940s-1980s / Richard G. Racheter.
p. cm.
ISBN 0-7643-1603-6
1. Seibel, Ben--Catalogs. 2. Tableware--United States--Collectors and collecting. 3. Tableware--United States--History--20th century. I. Title.
NK8725.5.S45A4 2003
738'.092--dc21

2002156721
Copyright © 2003 by Richard G. Ratcheter

All rights reserved. No part of this work may be reproduced or used in any form or by any means—graphic, electronic, or mechanical, including photocopying or information storage and retrieval systems—without written permission from the publisher.

The scanning, uploading and distribution of this book or any part thereof via the Internet or via any other means without the permission of the publisher is illegal and punishable by law. Please purchase only authorized editions and do not participate in or encourage the electronic piracy of copyrighted materials.

"Schiffer," "Schiffer Publishing Ltd. & Design," and the "Design of pen and ink well" are registered trademarks of Schiffer Publishing Ltd.

Designed by Mark David Bowyer
Type set in Lydian BT/Lydian BT

ISBN: 0-7643-1603-6
Printed in Hong Kong
1 2 3 4

Published by Schiffer Publishing Ltd.
4880 Lower Valley Road
Atglen, PA 19310
Phone: (610) 593-1777; Fax: (610) 593-2002
E-mail: Info@schifferbooks.com
Please visit our web site catalog at **www.schifferbooks.com**
We are always looking for people to write books on new and related subjects. If you have an idea for a book please contact us at the above address.

This book may be purchased from the publisher.
Include $3.95 for shipping.
Please try your bookstore first.
You may write for a free catalog.

In Europe, Schiffer books are distributed by
Bushwood Books
6 Marksbury Ave.
Kew Gardens
Surrey TW9 4JF England
Phone: 44 (0)20-8392-8585
Fax: 44 (0)20-8392-9876
E-mail: Bushwd@aol.com
Free postage in the UK. Europe: air mail at cost

Contents

Acknowledgments

Fortunately a number of people, researchers, writers, collectors and dealers, were willing to share information. To bring together a book such as this requires substantial help from others. Rarely can an author "do it alone!" Those that share are the true friends of research, and the true supporters for the dissemination of Ben Seibel information.

Ann Kerr: Author and expert in many fields, Mrs. Kerr shared some personal recollections about Seibel and his work. Very sadly, Mrs. Kerr passed away on September 20, 2001. She will be missed.

Michael Pratt: This author and Mid-Century-Modern expert provided all the photographs of Seibel's glassware designs for Roseville. He continually has supported my efforts.

Jon Saffell: Former Director of Design at the Fostoria Company. Mr. Saffell hunted through his records and supplied invaluable information about Seibel's work for that company.

Emily Seate: An author and Fostoria expert, her insightful comments encouraged me to probe more deeply into Seibel's contributions to the glassware lines.

Polly Stetler: Special Projects Coordinator at the Pfaltzgraff Pottery Company: Ms. Stetler sorted through that company's archives for material on *County-Time*. Although she protested she could not find much, her information clarified some very vexing mysteries.

Eric Stevens: Although Mr. Stevens and I are no longer in touch, I still consider him a fine person whose knowledge in the area "Seilbel-esque" is quite outstanding.

Doug Way: This knowledgeable collector shared photographs of his *Universal Raymor* collection.

Sandi Woodward: A gracious dealer who sent me a series of photographs of *Raymor Modern Stoneware*—the expensive and difficult to locate pieces. She is acknowledged with thanks.

and finally, the late **Jonathan A. Perry**: He is quoted throughout this book.

Many others helped by providing various pieces of tableware—or in some cases, a much needed photograph: Edith Adam, Debi Bender, Dennis Bialek, Judy Byrd, Doug Cauble, Rick Crofton & Jeanette Nichols, Sarah Eury, Herb Fogliano, Natasha Greer, Shelly Long, Diana Molchan, Gail Pippin, Lee Russell, Catherine Sallustio, Terri Williams. Writing a book such as this depends upon many "building blocks."

Special thanks to Ms. Patti Baley, the smiling and ever-friendly lady to oversaw the developing of most of the photographs within this book.

And a very special, warmly felt thanks to the Librarians and Staff of the Department of Special Collections, Syracuse University Library, Syracuse, New York, for their continuing support and encouragement.

I wish also to mention those at Schiffer who worked on this book: Jeffrey Snyder, my editor; Mark David Bowyer, the designer.

Introduction

When I look back and try to remember a time when the name Ben Seibel was an unknown name, it seems as if that time never was. And yet, it has been only ten years (or so) since I held my first Seibel bowl and was told, quite confidently, "Ben Seibel will be well known some day!" The dealer who spoke these confiding words passed very quickly from my life, and, I confess, I no longer remember his name. Perhaps, but for him, I would not be writing this book. Since 1990, there has been an ebb and a flow in my Seibel interests, but in general there has been more flow than backsliding ebb. The first Seibel piece purchased was a spacious *Universal Raymor* individual salad bowl in the quite common Golden Burst design: I still own it.

By 1995, I had become familiar with the term Mid-Century-Modern, and in April of 1997, Michael Pratt sent me a list that he had compiled of the various line designed by Seibel. This list was crucially important because it gave the varied shapes and ensuing treatments. Since Mr. Pratt was delving in virgin territory, he never claimed the list was exhaustive, or complete, or correct. It was simply a beginning. In the presentation of the popular lines (the lines listed in the books of Harvey Duke), it was correct: accurate to a degree. The list faltered, as I discovered and Mr. Pratt acknowledged, in the dimly lit fields of Mikasa, Oneida and Fostoria, and surprisingly there was no mention of *Universal Raymor*.

Oh, yes, the date April 1997 is accurate! This list was such a watershed that I penciled across its top: "Received from M. Pratt, April 1997." This list is still with me, like that first *Universal Raymor* salad bowl, and I mark it as an additional thrust, a push coming to a shove, toward a desire to know more about Mr. Ben Seibel. Because it is so historically important to the understanding of Ben Seibel, Mr. Pratt's list is repeated here.[1]

STEUBENVILLE *CONTEMPORA*
- charcoal
- fawn
- mist gray
- sand white

ROSEVILLE *RAYMOR MODERN STONEWARE* (1952)
- autumn brown
- avocado green
- beach gray
- blue
- chartreuse
- contemporary white
- terra cotta

IROQUOIS *IMPROMPTU* (1956)
- Aztec
- Beige Rose
- Blue Doves
- Blue Vineyard
- Bridal White
- Chrysanthemums
- Colonial Blue
- Colonial Pink
- Country Garden
- El Camino
- Fiord
- Frolic
- Garland
- Grapes
- House of Flowers
- Jardinieres
- Luau
- Parasols
- Pins and Beads
- Pompom
- Pyramid
- Sleepy Hollow
- Spring Flowers
- Stellar
- Tiara
- Vision
- Wild Rose

IROQUOIS *INFORMAL* (1958)
- Blue Diamonds
- Bombay Blue
- Bombay Green
- Georgetown
- Harvest Time
- Lazy Daisy
- Old Orchard
- Rosemary

A sprig of white jasmine enhances a selection of Iroquois *Impromptu* Bridal White. From left to right: creamer, gravy and underplate, cereal bowl, sugar, individual compote, oil/vinegar. The stopper of the last named piece is difficult to find. For prices, see the section of *Impromptu*.

INHERITANCE (1959)
- Baroque
- Cotillion
- Dynasty
- Gold Band
- Grecian Gold
- Knollwood
- Medallion
- Platinum Band
- Su-Shi
- Teuton White
- Teuton Sheer White

INTAGLIO (1964)
- Blue Dahlia
- Blue Painted Daisy
- Diamond White
- Jade Rosette
- Old Englisah Pink
- Old English Blue
- Pink Painted Golden Dahlia
- Sun Rosette
- Woodale

FORUM INTERNATIONAL STONEWARE (1962)
- bone with yellow ochre motif
- chestnut with burnt ochre motif

FORUM INTERNATIONAL BUFFETWARE (1966)
- two motifs in:
- burnt orange
- moss or lime green

FORUM INTERNATIONAL IRONWARE (1962)

FORUM INTERNATIONAL WOOD FILAGREE (1962)

MIKASA (dates ??)
- *Casual Sophistication* (patterns?)
- Shannon
- *Couture* (patterns?)
- *Country Fresh* (3 patterns)
- *Duplex* (4 patterns +?)
- Juliet
- *Mexzicana* (9 patterns?)
- *Potter's Art* (8 patterns?)
- *Whole Wheat* (5 patterns?)
- *Studio Craft* (4 patterns?)

KASUGA VITRASTONE (date?) (patterns?)

HAEGAR POTTERY (1971) (patterns?)

PFALTZGRAFF *COUNTRY-TIME*

Imagine the excitement the collector to have suddenly before one a compilation where no compilation ever was before? It was a *Star Trek* tableware voyage to the unknown beyond. Now, does this sound a bit flamboyant, a tad effusive? Believe me, the simile is appropriate! Very few collectors knew anything about Ben Seibel—except a few expensively popular lines—and this list was a very special exciting and wondrous voyage for me. It was like a clean and clear Christmas tree—a basic structure upon which to place, like bright ornament, all the bits of information gathered surely and slowly over the years.

And remember, the year was 1997! Ben Seibel has come a long way since then, Baby!

My interest especially was stuck—like a bee in a pot of honey—to the Mikasa section. Little by little, this area was corrected, amended, changed: misunderstandings became understandable; names began to fit into their correct niches. Little by little more information was ferreted out and stored away. For example:

Shannon was not a shape, but a treatment of *Casual Sophistication.*

A grouping of *Couture* Homespun/Countryside. For a brief time, this Mikasa line was thought to have been designed by Ben Seibel. Prices are very modest: creamer and sugar set, $8-10; cup/saucer, $5; open vegetable, $5-6.

Casual Sophistication later was acknowledged as a full-fledged signed clone of *Duplex*.

Juliet became Juliette, a treatment on *Duplex*.

The changes were myriad, but these changes added little by little, bit by bit, as the information became known devalued this important list not one jot!

It is extremely difficult to believe that in such a short time,[2] so much knowledge was acquired. Seibel came tumbling riotously out of the woodwork. In a few short years, I acquired many individual pieces designed by this talented person. A number of fine and helpful acquaintanceships were made, and then, unfortunately, some of these friends drifted away—as often happens. This still saddens me, but I am old enough to realize this is a natural human condition. Surely, enemies were collected also. I remember after publishing my first Seibel article—on Iroquois' *Impromptu* and *Informal*[3]—one important Seibel expert boldly questioned the Russel Wright Discussion Board, "Who's this person anyway?" I never told him.

Again, so few years ago, those people who admired Ben Seibel and collected his work helped each other and shared bits of knowledge. Sharing was the watchword. When one young writer was fretfully composing a book on dinnerware, I took hundreds of photographs of my own colorware collection and sent them on. These appeared as the vast majority of illustrations in his book, yet very little acknowledgement was awarded. This event warned me of clouds beginning to shadow the researching horizon. Today, the world of the researcher is different. Some, in fact many, still help: men and women who are secure within their own strong niche, but there are those who hoard and accumulate and stifle progress. This is, naturally, their personal prerogative—they certainly have the right to do what they do, but it is a sad reflection weakly illuminating the world of Ben Seibel. When I questioned one person why he would not share a *Universal Raymor* brochure with me, the answer came tersely: "Because there is money to be made!" I never commented on this mistaken philosophy.

Despite this, collectors and researchers are fascinating people.

My approach to Ben Seibel, and my manner of writing, might irritate some readers. For this I apologize, but I really cannot change—even though I sometimes try. One snappy critic commented on a notable *Fiesta*™ message board that I tell stories! This is true! I do! Some readers enjoy this technique. Wrapping facts within narratives gives—according to my philosophy—these facts an immediacy that is, hopefully, direct and refreshing. I try to converse with the reader: having a personal discussion about a problem, an interpretation, an idea, a belief. Quite frankly, dishes and tableware are not all that important in the schemes of God and man, so I give the subject a little push. As I approach the end of my life, the shadow of the grave calms me down and things settle into proper perspective. I will never, however, completely (as Katherine Hepburn announced in the film *Lion in Winter*) "give up, give out, give in!" Or as Dylan Thomas suggested, I will "not go gentle into that good night."

So what is printed within the covers of this book is as honest and as truthful as possible. But since I am not a god, but very surely a man, mistakes will occur. Hopefully, readers will not fasten upon these mistakes with glee and chortle "who's this person anyway?" Researchers do need help, and depend upon knowledgeable collectors for help and support. Honest criticism and supportive suggestions are extremely welcome—and absolutely necessary if all of us are to better enjoy the creative work of Mr. Ben Seibel.

There has been absolutely no attempt within the covers of this book to comment upon the non-tableware designs of this great man—no discussion of the lamps, dividers, and furniture. One such line of furniture initially presented to New York City critics on December 6, 1966, was titled *Pivotal*. Did Seibel consciously transfer this name ten years later to one of the ceramic lines he created for Mikasa? The tables looked remarkably like the Iroquois *Informal* shakers and finials. There is fascinating delving to do and links to forge between Seibel's designs for the table and his other creations. Unfortunately, I am not vitally interested in furniture or lighting design: there are others vastly more talented possessing awesome expertise in these fields. I sincerely welcome a companion book on these Seibel non-ceramic subjects.

One certain point that collectors and readers must remember: Ben Seibel is a completely modern designer—and he is, in essence, still with us. Unlike Russel Wright and even Eva Zeisel, the judicious buyer can purchase original (not reproduction) pieces of Seibel dinnerware in the general marketplace. Or, to be absolutely correct, some of his creations for Mikasa were still available in 1997. In fact, Mrs. Seibel was still receiving royalties in that year for such Mikasa lines as *Bali Hai*, *Blue Eyes*, *Gracious*, *Maison Blanche*, *Southwest*, and *Sundance*. These items could be termed "genuine" Ben Seibel designs, for the Mikasa dinnerware represent some of the last work done by this talented man—work completed in the early 1980s just before his death, and, perhaps, serve as a bridge between Seibel and ourselves. Certainly it is too early to say how representative the prodigious work done for Mikasa will be in the complete *oeuvre* of Ben Seibel, and the complicated connection between American designer and Japanese manufacturer deserves careful and continuing study.

A Note on the Price Guide

Nothing so dates a book as the guide to prices. These fluctuate with abysmal regularity, and always cause some "experts" to fuss and fume: "too high, too low!" Yet they do have an importance. The idea of placing prices within the photographic captions is wise and economical. They are before the reader as he or she views the photographs. But be warned, the prices given are suggestions only and refer to pieces in mint condition. A "chigger" or a sand bubble can reduce the price some twenty percent while a prominent chip can pull down the original price over seventy percent. And yet, how many dedicated Seibel collectors will purchase a damaged, greatly desired piece and then, hopefully, replace it with a mint example at a later time.

There once was an elderly collector whom I admired many years ago. I am sure she is now no longer on this earth, but her philosophy was comfortable and sentimental. She told me once: "I always like and cherish dishes with nicks and chips because these show they were used and loved." A marvelous, simple approach to the furor of collecting, but how many of today's elite collectors would agree? Today, mint is *a la mode*!

So, I am sure, some of my pricing will be challenged. Remember, prices change from one section of the country to another: Manhattan, San Francisco, Los Angeles, and Seattle maintain brutal price levels. Besides condition, the factor of color can be important: some colors within certain of the Seibel lines demand higher prices. Too, the advent of the Internet makes the rare and the scarce instantly available through private dinnerware sites and through the various electronic auction houses. I have seen prices paid on eBay that are staggering! These anomalies must be taken into consideration. In the heat of a fiery lust to win, prices soar!

Thus, the prices quoted are what an average middle-America collector might consider paying. However, this is surely an oxymoron—for what collector is *average*?

Random Thoughts Regarding American Tableware

An Essay

Once encouraged, I can talk about dinnerware with complete abandon, and my thoughts wander here and there as new and old ideas merge, flowing in an almost endless river—sometimes turgid and murky, oft times bubbly and clear. My opinions are just that—opinions, and while I stand strongly behind them, "flexibility" is also a word I know and appreciate. Perhaps my thoughts are a little less than random: hopefully they will at least prove interesting and perhaps challenging.

There are a few collectors who move into the realm of the researcher, and this can be a double-edged Damoclean sword. Some researchers, when a new idea is discovered, become secretive, dogmatic, superior (I know of a number of these), but most are sharing, curious, inquisitive. These are the people who make dinnerware collecting and researching pleasurable and rewarding. Researchers, both sharing or secretive, belong to a strange breed of the human animal. Ferreting through the facts, researchers want to know, must know, all the "whys" and the "hows" and the "whens"! They become just as curious as experienced newspaper reporters hunting down a blockbuster story. Sometimes this curiosity hinders the simple joys of collecting; sometimes it enhances the entire process of acquisition. For example, the curious researcher is not just satisfied by knowing that pre-World War I dinnerware lines consisted of numerous pieces (some of them very ornate), he or she needs to know "why" and "how was this possible?" There were no dishwashers in 1910, so why did dinnerware lines consist of chowder bowls and spooners, very elaborate oyster plates, scrolled teapots, extended chocolate pots, *comportiers* and toast racks, massive tureens and small curved bone dishes! Even the mid-priced dinnerware made in America for Americans indulged in such fantastical delights. Why? How?

Alas, all this effulgent abundance depended upon the existence of a now extinct group of human beings: household help! The parlor maids, the cooks, the scullery maids, the footmen: those that did for those that had. Until the Civil War, some of these beings were slaves in the South, and in the North some women and men, boys and girls were no better than slaves, but not quite so tightly tied to their miserable destiny. Then there were indentured servants selling themselves for a specific time, or Swedish, Norwegian, and German immigrants, eager for a new life in America, forced (in most cases) to work for pittance wages in middle-class homes or cheap restaurants. Ten cents an hour was a "reasonable" wage, and deductions were made for a skimpy lunch. These were the people who made it possible to have tureens and delicate toast racks, finger bowls and immense platters. Every, or most all, middle-class homes had at least one of these helpers about the house.

The potteries poured their wares into the marketplace. Companies such as Homer Laughlin, Edwin Knowles, Pope-Gosser, Sebring, and others fed upon and grew prosperous upon the insatiable needs of the striving American middle-classes. Up until World War II the middle-class existed in a large but perilous group between the Upper classes and the Working classes. They were insecure and ambitious; they lacked the settled calm of the New England Brahmins, the Southern feudal plantation owners, the Hudson Valley patroons. Wealth really had little to do with class; it was how life was viewed, what priorities and standards were established, the way of "doing things" that settled where a family belonged. Some middle-classes strived to move upward—however none could contemplate slipping downward. Thus the middle-class aped their betters and detested (and feared) those beneath them. Today, naturally all this striving is basically finished in our so-called classless American society. Except for a few small groups floating above all the others in a haze of inviolable perpetual godhood, bushy presidential splendor or sanctimonious senatorial superiority, all American families consider themselves middle-class—and we all suffer from this democratic misconception.

What was one of the ways the middle-class attempted to impress and pull itself upward? Quite simply, living as lavishly as possible, but as inexpensively as possible! While these households, bolstered by a servant or two, and conscious of rank, could not quite afford imported Limoges, Minton, Wedgwood or Spode—at least not in the huge sets thought necessary for fine dining. Thus hostesses turned to American manufacturers.

A truly magnificent Limoges tureen with a detachable underplate. A grand piece like this would be the pride of any household, but few could afford a full set of this expensive imported ware. Suggested price: $200-250.

Of all foreign imports, Limoges maintains the highest desirability. Its name is known even among people who have little or no interest in fine porcelain. There are many different types of Limoges, but all project a delicate sense of detail: small touches as tiny decals within the bowls—floral sprays completely hidden when the bowl, tureen, casserole is filled. This sense of detail was copied by some American dinnerware manufacturers in an attempt to lure consumers from expensive imports.

Shown are four plates of varying sizes (see page 10). All are delicately made: all are old. Yet two are Limoges imports from France, and two are American products made in Newell, West Virginia. The latter were available through Sear & Roebuck catalogs and were deliberately meant to ape the expensive French lines. The back stamp of each plate is also given. How many readers can correctly match the plates with the correct back stamp?

One of the delicate touches of Limoges was the attention to detail. Deep within the tureen were several decorations—surely unseen when the piece was filled.

Here is the bottom of a *The Angelus* gravy boat. Homer Laughlin, competing with foreign imports, attempted to introduce the same kind of delicate detail. A gravy boat like this would be priced from $15-20.

Back stamp of Limoges tureen.

The Limoges 10" dinner plate, the 9" luncheon plate, and the butter pat. The dinner plates were always more expensive than the more common luncheon plate. Dinner plate, $18-20; luncheon plate, $10-12; butter pat, $3-4.

These manufacturers, Homer Laughlin for example, produced prodigiously huge sets reaching close to one-hundred items to be sold, not in fine urban department or specialty stores, but through catalog sales. *American Beauty*, considered the most extensive tableware line ever produced in America, was sold through the Sears, Roebuck & Company catalog. Just as the prosperous middle-class hostess aped her aristocratic neighbor who lived in a larger mansion on the hill, Homer Laughlin's *American Beauty* aped Limoges in both ornate style and amplitude of pieces.

This whole page:
Domestic dinnerware was designed to compete with French Limoges. Here are four plates of varying sizes, plus four marks. Can the reader combine the marks with the plates? Two are expensive imports from France, two were made by Homer Laughlin and available through the Sears, Roebuck catalog. [**Answers**: The plates (left to right) are: HLC *Colonial*; Limoges, France; Theodore Haviland, Limoges, France; HLC *Hudson*.]

A lovely *American Beauty* teapot (center) flanked by a creamer (left) and a rare and unusual spooner (right). Teapot, $100-125; creamer, $15-20; spooner, $40-50.

The mammoth *King Charles* round oyster tureen and the complete butter dish. It is very unusual to find the butter dish insert (right) for these pieces are often separated. Tureen, $75-85; butter dish (with insert), $50-60.

The low, flat-lidded *Seneca* covered vegetable is accompanied by the small *King Charles* jug. Notice the scroll work on these pieces—impossible to clean with a soft brush. Covered vegetable, $45-55; small jug, $10-12.

Hudson tureen, $30-40.

A selection of *The Angelus* dinnerware line. Bone dish (left) and 9" plate (rear) with three sizes of jugs. The large jug and the plate show the very desirable Majolica decoration. The "wavy" handles identify this shape. Large jug (Majolica), $25-35; 9" plate (Majolica), $7-9; bone dish, $3-4. Other jugs range from $8-15.

An assortment of highly ornate pickle dishes. Left to right: *The Angelus* "fish" pickle, *King Charles* "clam" pickle in the Arbutus pattern, and *American Beauty*'s scrolled small dish that is actually known as an olive dish. These range from $8-12 in price. Once scarce, they are becoming more easily found.

And who attended to this dinnerware, this *American Beauty*[1] or *King Charles*,[2] *Seneca*,[3] *Hudson*[4] or *The Angelus*?[5] Who but a humble and careful kitchen maid dutifully using a soft-bristled brush to clean all the embossed loops and curlicues, the peaked finials and narrow indentations making up sets of *Mount Vernon*,[6] *Lotus*,[7] or *Bristol*?[8] The girl was required to be gentle: a broken handle or chipped plate would call down the wrath of the cook and the angry wail of the mistress would sound throughout the house.

Now this discussion might seem to be of another world to any reader who does remember the Great Depression, and indeed, it is a world never to return. However, I most certainly believe, one cannot be a true collector of American dinnerware—even the modern twentieth century shapes—without knowing something of our past. Plates, and teacups, nappies and magnificent tureens did not exist without direct reference to how they were used, and who used them—and even those who cleared the table after the dinner was over!

When I was in the elementary grades, every lunch time after walking home from school, I had my soup and sandwich in the breakfast nook with my grandmother's Afro-American maid Margaret. For a while, Margaret was much more necessary to me than my rather cool and distracted mother. We lived in Rutherford, New Jersey, a community situated on a chalk cliff overlooking a rather pestilent salt march and the towers of Manhattan, ridged saw-toothed in the distance. The borough supplied the metropolis with white-collar workers. Margaret lived in Passaic, just to the west, arriving every morning and leaving after preparing the evening meal. On festive occasions, my grandmother would "borrow" the live-in maid of her sister-in-law, my formidable great aunt, Dr. Edith, a physician devoted to "women's problems." As a seven-year-old, I can actually remember sitting on the kitchen's shoeshine box watching the two busy women, one dark, one blond, preparing an important dinner. Margaret always served: it was "her house." My grandparents were not rich, merely "comfortable" and this was the standard of life for people of that class.

dollars stretch and living in a Los Angeles tract house—and the Chicano maid making coffee on the rather ramshackle gas stove.

Reality always comes late to Hollywood, and in some films "what was" is depicted as "what is." By 1957, very few struggling middle class households had a maid to make the coffee.

The time of change clearly can be pinpointed! The Second World War was the hammer that drove in the coffin nails, and when my grandfather died, life for the middle-classes in America relentlessly had changed forever.

At the same time, responding to the urgently and growing demand for simpler lifestyle, and the desire for acquisition which normally follows a devastating war, the ceramic designers began to create tableware less complex in appearance, and with fewer pieces.

And the designs themselves were drastically different.

There were, naturally, moments of splurge in the simplified '50s. Ben Seibel presented over fifty pieces in his 1952 work for Roseville Raymor, and Eva Zeisel created forty pieces of Hallcraft's *Tomorrow's Classic* (1953).

A *Hudson* spooner and sugar stand before two *King Charles* pieces: (left) the wide-edged rim soup and the 9" luncheon plate. The rim soup and plate can range from \$8-12. The *Hudson* sugar, \$10-15; the spooner, \$25-30.

Eva Zeisel designed two jugs for her 1954 line *Tomorrow's Classic*. Large jug (Pinecone), \$20-25; Medium jug (Studio 10), \$15-18; and the matching creamer in a rather rare treatment, Prairie Grass, \$8-10.

With a horrendous crash, amid the wailing of the European dying and dispossessed, all this lifestyle disappeared during World War II. My parents moved into their own smaller home just before the start of the war in Europe. It was here that we learned of the bombing of Pearl Harbor: in this house my mother never had domestic help—unless my grandmother, in a surge of not-too-well-appreciated generosity, sent Margaret to help with the spring house-cleaning.

Margaret disappeared from my grandparents' house, and from my life, soon after the United States entered the war. Like many others, she could earn much more in a factory. Yet she has always remained in my memories, and the last time I saw her was at the dinner given after my grandfather's funeral in February 1949. She, now gray-haired and solemn, cooked and served the "baked meats" of the dead.

Hollywood, the purveyor of dreams, the translator of wishes, the reflector of ambitions, the bellwether of American social needs, insisted that the average household had at least one, and perhaps two, domestic workers. We need only to remember *Mr. Blandings Builds His Dream House* (1948): Cary Grant and Myna Loy trapped with two daughters in a crowded West Side Manhattan apartment with the maid living in a closet-sized room off the kitchen. Or *Good Sam* (1948): Gary Cooper and Ann Sheridan quarreling because they are poor, and he always gives money away—and a maid in the kitchen trying to serve dinner. Or *Mildred Pierce* with Joan Crawford, hot and harried, making pies in her small kitchen in order to pay the bills or pay for Veda's piano lessons, and there is Butterfly McQueen wailing: "Ah don't knows how yuh does it Miz Pierce?" Or, finally, *Full of Life* (1957): Richard Conte as a harried writer and Judy Holiday as his pregnant wife struggling to make the

Tomorrow's Classic boasted of two types of candleholders. Here is the easily found low candleholder (Peach Blossom), \$30-35, and the very scarce tall example (Bouquet), \$70-75.

A quartet of lovely pieces: (front) eggcup in Caprice, $10-12; ashtray is the stunning Sascha Brastoff treatment known as Surf Ballet, $10-15; (rear, left) the oil/vinegar in the little seen Lyric design, $15-18; and finally, the rare vase in Fantasy, one of the most sought after and sophisticated of treatments, $100+.

This Zeisel shape, *Tomorrow's Classic*, is culturally unique: it straddled two worlds. In feeling it harkened back to a time—an older world—when dinnerware lines presented a variety of jugs; more than one covered casserole; candleholders; vases; eggcups and ashtrays; after-dinner coffee cups, saucers, sugars and creamers; covered onion soups and covered marmites. Yet in actual physical design it reached into a newer, lighter world where shapes turned upon a dime, and sculptural streamlined simplicity called out a new name: Mid-Century-Modern. The 1950s called forth a new breed of ceramic designer and these men and these women, in turn, brought forth a new concept for American dining. Wright, Seibel, and Don and Victor Schreckengost were exceptional talents, creative geniuses who swept the old concepts away and introduced crisp new elements of design. Yet Eva Zeisel literally bridged the gap between the two worlds, and only with her shape *Tomorrow's Classic*. This line of dinnerware must be recognized as the pivotal, the fulcrum, the single moment in the design of American tableware, where the old and new are joined, and, in a brief flash, recognize each other and accept each other as valid, albeit drastically different, interpretations of what is necessary on the dining table. A dining table itself radically changing, metaphorically changing, into the buffet board, the patio deck picnic, the snack stand ensconced before the flickering television. American eating habits changed. So too have the boundaries between the classes of American citizens become foggy and blurred; yet, no matter how much it is protested by misplaced liberalism, the "haves" have more, take more, and give less while the "have-nots" want more, demand more, and certainly have very little to give.

Polished tabletops proudly central in a room reserved for dining are no longer in the floor plan of every new house. The need for candleholders and candelabras, float bowls, ceramic toast racks, stately ocean-going tureens, and certainly eggcups and gravy boats have dwindled down to a trickle of nothing. The rusticity of the patio and picnic table, or the convenience of kitchen counter (where one perches precariously on tall stools), was becoming acceptable as all manner of Americans ceased to dine and began merely to eat!

Ben Seibel's early *Raymor Modern Stoneware* was created within the concept of informal eating. Although many advertisements depict the fluidly modern place setting settled on a gracious formal table, this tableware was not designed psychologically for the dining room table. Perhaps this is why Roseville Raymor did not succeed. It was too modern, offered too soon; available before the average American was really ready to abandon the dining room for the backyard grill? It was, after all, barely 1952. Television had not yet begun to dominate our lives.

When he designed for Iroquois, Seibel returned, in an effusive moment, to the concept of dining—but with the needed twist: vitrified china useful for preparing food, cooking food, and then serving it wherever dinner was being eaten that evening. The harried housewife, or even the new breed of househusband, could use *Informal* for both cooking and serving.

As the 1950s was opening up into the '60s, Seibel reverted even more dramatically to the concept of fine dining. For then he designed *Inheritance*—the true return to elegance and grace and aimed at the beauty of formal dining, but it was produced for only a few years. The wise and enlightened creative personality always remembers past beauty and successful designs and attempts to incorporate these successes within new and modern concepts. However, times had changed, and who had the time? *Inheritance* was the last truly, absolutely, dinnerware line aimed at formal adult dining. *Apres nous le deluge*!

The "winged" butter dish in the scarce Flair treatment, $30-35.

The tall coffee server in Hallcraft White, $125-135, and the more common, but still desirable teapot in Bouquet, $70-80.

Surely, *Tomorrow's Classic* must be one of the last lines to offer both a covered onion soup AND a covered marmite. The onion soup (left) appears in Buckingham, one of the few treatments with Mrs. Zeisel's approval, $20-25. The marmite wears Mulberry, a design not very popular with today's collectors, $10-12.

What a deluge it was! It rained melmac, a hurricane of stoneware, buffetware, and whirling tornadoes of snack sets and chip n'dip bowls dogged our desire for informal entertaining. America became devoted to informal eating. By the 1960s, everyone, from top to bottom, had become the "class in the middle" with a patio, a picnic table, and a grill. Here burly men performed for their pretty wives, squabbling children, perhaps a jealous neighbor or three. The patio, the grill, and Seibel's *Forum International Buffetware* was the rage! So be it!

Ben Seibel, wise as he was, followed the tendency for informal, although not necessarily simple, dining a.k.a. "eating." We have the extensive *Formal International* lines and then the seriously introspective Mikasa shapes he presented from the late 1960s, through the 1970s. Ben Seibel, cautious and curious, careful and clever, compelled Mikasa to produce some really outstanding tableware shapes. Floating on the top of the waves, Ben Seibel became the preeminent ceramic designer of late Mid-Century-Modern tableware. Sadly, he died too soon and with much still to be accomplished.

The collector has rarely seen the *Tomorrow's Classic* footed fruit bowl or centerpiece bowl. These are usually the highlight of any Zeisel collection, $100-125. The shaker appears in Surf Ballet, a recently discovered swirled treatment by Sascha Brastoff, $10-12.

Not only did Mrs. Zeisel design an AD cup and saucer for this very extensive line, but a matching AD sugar (left) and creamer (right.) The sugar is Holiday, $10-12; the creamer is Caprice, $12-15; the AD cup/saucer set in Satin Black and White, $20-25.

On Defining Terms

Before the main part of this book is broached, a brief discussion of "tableware" versus "dinnerware" might prove of some interest. I have maintained that Ben Seibel designed a number of tableware lines along with some purely dinnerware. While some use the two terms interchangeably, my personal view recognizes a difference. Readers might not agree with these definitions, but they will be used in this book. No offense is intended.

Naturally, we all realize that not all dinnerware or tableware is ceramic, but can be metallic, glass, wooden, plastic, and even paper.

A set of dinnerware contains items allowing people to dine—usually in a rather specific setting and in a widely varying degree of formality: lunch, dinner, supper, breakfast, brunch. Any of these can be served on the dining room table, or on a patio, picnic table or poolside. Dinnerware lines consist of various sized plates, platters, cups and saucers, bowls, and so on. The characteristic of dinnerware is that the pieces "come to you"—are passed about by other diners, or—now a rare occurrence—by servants. Dinnerware is moveable.

All dinnerware is also tableware, but tableware includes a wider spectrum of pieces. My conception of tableware is any item placed on any type of table to be used for dining or aides and enhances the same. Two categories that are not dinnerware, but are tableware, are silverware and stemware.

Tableware is usually stationary. The guest goes to it or simply admires it from some distance. Some tableware is simply too heavy to be moved easily: large beanpots, heavy casseroles and monumental tureens, complex divided serving dishes on heating stands, samovars, swinging coffee servers, mammoth bun warmers, lazy susans, huge trays piled with *crudités*, bubbling *bain-maries*, fondue pots, and elegant footed cake stands. All these pieces are securely settled on the table, sideboard, or rolling serving table and there they remain. This definition is arbitrary—especially when the term "stationary" is used. No piece of tableware is completely immovable. That would be silly and totally impractical. But what is meant is that a huge soup tureen is brought to the table or sideboard, placed conveniently, filled with tomato, turtle, or turbot soup and stays there until removed at the end of the course or the end of the meal. This is what I mean by "stationary."

Buffetware, like silver and glass, is a category of tableware, but instead of being identified by a material, buffetware is characterized by where and how the serving is handled. The careful reader will immediately recognize that dinnerware can be made from silver or from glass, but in general—to the ordinary understanding—the terms "glassware" means drinking utensils, and "silverware" means knives, forks, and spoons—even if these are NOT made of silver.

Other categories of tableware—if the reader will permit me—might be glamorous epergnes filled with flowers and fruit, candelabras and less ornate candleholders, nut and candy compotes, vases and float bowls, and those ashtrays that in a bygone time used to sit sedately at each table setting. In some cases lighters might be considered as tableware. In the past, these items need not have matched the dinnerware proper, or even match among themselves. One of the advertising tactics used by Iroquois China when it touted the new 1956 line *Impromptu* was that the service pieces matched the dinnerware. Service pieces—especially if overly large and awkwardly cumbersome—might be a synonymous term with tableware.

There is a tendency to regard "dinnerware" as having a better quality material, but this is not literally correct. It is not the material from which it is made that places a salad plate in the category of dinnerware: it is its use. Melamine, stoneware, clay, polished wood, sandwich glass, bone china, translucent porcelain, and rough thrown pottery, when formed into a plate and accompanied by other plates, cups, saucers, and soup and cereal bowls made from the same material, all become dinnerware.

When the same materials are formed into candleholders, napkin rings, large serving dishes on intricate stands, and bud vases, we suddenly are discussing tableware.

These definitions, naturally, have problems—and exceptions. What about kitchenware, cookware, and ovenware? When the hostess carefully cooks a pot roast in an *Informal* Dutch oven and brings it to the table, does it become "tableware"? No, it is the PRIMARY use of an item that categorizes it. One cooks in cookware, places ovenware in the oven, and prepares (chops, stirs, mixes, blends) food in kitchenware. If any of these bowls or pots end up on a trivet in the center of the table, they do not automatically then become tableware, and as well all know, and as I continually repeat, Ben Seibel was quite fond of trivets.

A trivet, by the way, is another example of tableware.

And the cautious cook must be aware there is a difference between ovenware and ovenproof. An ovenware casserole takes a great deal more in the way of heat than a casserole that is merely "ovenproof." The terms are not interchangeable—as I have learned to my misfortune.

In this book, I will occasionally use the term "dinnerware" when the correct term—according to my definitions—should be "tableware." This is done solely to avoid repetitious use of one or the other. Also—and again this is quite an arbitrary decision—if a line of china (see, I cannot really say either "dinnerware" or "tableware" so I beg the question) contains only one or two items of tableware, the entire line is termed "tableware." For example, *Pivotal*, one of Ben Seibel's most delicate and fragile lines must be termed, in my mind, tableware because it contains a huge tureen, and those three round jars whose true purpose has yet completely to be determined.

All designers must have firmly in mind the use to which their creations are to be put: formal dining, picnic barbeque, luncheon, buffet, or even that shadowy designation—for home entertaining . If the object is to create one or two pieces just for individual use, such as a wedding bowl, a bud vase, a fondue dish, a divided candy dish, or a martini mixer, then the term used is "casual ware."

As an exercise, let us place the Seibel shapes discussed in this book into one of the categories.

Jenfred items all belong in casual ware.
Contempora: dinnerware.
Raymor Modern Stoneware: tableware.
Country-Time: tableware.
Universal Raymor: dinnerware.
Impromptu: tableware.
Informal: tableware.
Inheritance: dinnerware.
Intaglio: tableware. [1]
Duplex: tableware.
Pivotal: tableware
Potter's Art: tableware.
Mexicana: tableware.
Kasuga *Vitrastone*: dinnerware.
Forum International Stoneware: buffetware.
Forum International Wood Filigree: casual ware; furniture accessories.
Forum International Ironware: cookware.
Forum International Buffetware: casual ware (despite the official name).
Oneida *Premium*: dinnerware.
Gilley: casual ware.
Haegar *Stoneware*: buffetware.
DeMaray: casual ware.
Gilley: casual ware.
Tempron: casual ware.
Fostoria *Facets*: casual ware.
Fostoria *Gourmet*: casual ware.
Fostoria *Precedence*: stemware.
Fostoria *Pebble Beach*: buffetware.
Fostoria *Module*: stemware.
Fostoria *Corsage Plum*: stemware.
Fostoria *Monarch*: barware. [2]
Fostoria *York*: barware. [2]

I would sincerely welcome any serious comments on the classifications outlined in this section.

A Note on Pronunciation

The name "Seibel" is often pronounced in two ways: SIGH bell and Suh BELL. The former with the accent on the first syllable; the latter with the accent on the last syllable. The correct pronunciation is:

Suh BELL

Color:
An Introduction

All tablewares—items of ceramic, glass, wood, or metal—that facilitate our dining or eating experiences depend upon three basic design attributes: texture, shape, and color.

Of these three, **color** is the first to be noticed, the first to catch the eye. Color surely must be one of God's greatest gifts to Mankind. It is a gift so wondrous, so seemingly simple, and it depends upon three natural phenomena: visual sensation, reflection or absorption of light rays, and the knowledge and expectations of the one who observes. It is absolutely dependent upon these three: light, air, and the eye. Enfolded, embedded in the cultures and mythologies of all men, color is everywhere, mysterious, omnipresent, and often under-appreciated. The understanding and appreciation of color can be basic and natural, Freudian or Jungian, simple or intricate.

Few humans can or will live without color!

Man's natural observations were responsible for the first attributes and associations attached to the various colors. Since blood is red, and since it gushed copiously when prehistoric Man hacked his way through a very short and violent life, red has come to symbolize war, death, destruction, and pain. Throughout the Western World red warns "no," "stop," "keep away," "danger." The red automobile gets more than its fair share of attention from state highway patrols. And Bette Davis, a New Orleans aristocrat with an independent streak in the film *Jezebel*, learned to her chagrin, young unmarried ladies do not wear red gowns to the Olympus Ball.

Red can also mean heat, warmth, flame. The raging red flames must devour the Phoenix in order that he may rise again from the smoldering ashes, as we learn in the second Harry Potter book. In the world of the Ganges and in the world of the far Orient, flaming pyres purify the corruptible human bodies and the purged souls float upward with the smoke into heaven. Red flames purify! Until the influence of Christianity, European cultures—Greek, Roman, Scandinavian, Celtic, and Saxon—sent their beloved dead into a new life by use of the flame. Red is the one—the most dynamic of the three primary colors. Primary colors are those that cannot be obtained by mixing or conjured by experiment.

Red is rarely used as the basic background color in dinnerware: it is too overpowering. But, and this is interesting, some of the rich browns used in Seibel's *Potter's Art* approach so close to the color red it is uncanny. Fusion, for example, is a modified brick red, and is one of the most popular of the *Potter's Art* treatments. It is also very interesting that Mikasa's *Duplex*, the most popular and available member of the Seibel/Mikasa connection, does not use red. While Mexicana, the most riotously colored of all Seibel Tableware, modifies its reds to rose and cranberry! Does this mean that wise dinnerware designers stay clear of this most strident of colors?

Blue is the second primary color: the color of the sky, the depths of the heavens, the shallows of the surging seas. It is the celestial color of the Greek god Zeus; his sister/wife Hera; Aphrodite, goddess of love—born from the foam of the sea. Blue is also the color of the Virgin Mary's robe.

Blue is the color of life, of hope. Since all waters are blue—reflected directly from the vault of heaven—and since most life rose from the warm nourishing primordial waters, humanity consciously or subconsciously, reveres blue.

Yet when we are sad, we are known to be "blue."

Due to its universal popularity, blue appears often in tableware decorative approaches. Mikasa *Duplex* makes a very favorable use of blue; *Pivotal* presents a lovely soft pastel blue for one of its hollowware color choices; and *Mexicana* utilizes some striking blues in a few of its flamboyant treatments.

Yellow, the most luminous and reflective of the triad of primary colors, is the most changeable. Add just a drop of black to the purest of yellows and it immediately loses its luminosity. Yellow is the color of the sun, or gold, it is the imperial color of the Chinese emperors, and yet yellow is the color or warnings, of quarantine flags, illness, or cowardice, and in sixteenth-century Spain, victims of the Inquisition were forced to wear yellow armbands—as were the Jews in Nazi Germany.

The three primary colors, Red, Blue, and Yellow, when mixed as pigments in equal amounts, create Black. For example, if one gallon of red paint, one gallon of blue paint, and one gallon of yellow paint are mixed together, the colorist will have three gallons of black paint. When the three primaries are mixed together as light—red light, blue light, yellow light—in equal proportions, the resultant light is White. Thus, if a brilliant red spotlight, another bright blue spotlight, and a third yellow spotlight are all three focused on an tall *Impromptu* coffee server, that server will be bathed in white light. Of course this is pure theory and might, in practice, be difficult to accomplish.

When only two primaries are mixed together in equal amounts, the resulting colors are titled Secondary Colors. All children learn—probably even before spending their first day at kindergarten—that red and yellow form orange, blue and yellow form green, and blue and red become purple.

Orange symbolizes fertility—as in orange blossoms. No tree is as fruitful as the orange. Saffron, a strong red/yellow has been utilized in the robes of Buddhist monks. In a practical use, orange (officially named tangerine) is used to mark pieces of machinery that might cause injury.

Green symbolizes nature and naiveté—as in "greenhorn." It is also the most ambivalent hue and yet appears everywhere.

Purple symbolizes majesty and lurid lushness—as in "purple prose." As purple orchid it calls attention to radiation hazards.

When a primary color—say blue—is mixed with its adjacent secondary color—green—the resultant color is referred to as a tertiary color. If blue and green are mixed in equal amounts the result is turquoise; but, if there is more green added, the color becomes teal. When the colorist deals with the tertiary colors it will be noted that many do not have well-known names.

The names of colors can be confusing unless the collector is aware there are two types: the first consists of official names established by semi-governmental color groups or associations within each country. The function of these national groups is to establish a unified nomenclature to accompany each known color. There always has been considerable attempt to "internationalize" a particular name. Thus the color known as "taupe" will be the same in the United States, the United Kingdom, or India. These official names can be simple or linguistically clever, i.e. sapphire, pearl, plum, toast, or as noted above, tangerine, saffron, orchid.

Color organizations abound to help both the professional designer and the amateur collector to become versed in the dynamism of color. **Pantone** **<http://www.pantone.com>** exists mainly for the professional, but its Internet color reports make interesting reading for anyone concerned vitally or peripherally in color trends. It is admitted some of the terminology is a little fanciful and the information geared for the "rich and the famous." Pantone, like most other professional color groups, relies on color numbers rather than easily confused names alone. For example, we read (in early 2002) that the future colors for the home will be:

PANTONE 19-2014 TC Prune
PANTONE 19-1663 TC Ribbon Red
PANTONE 18-2336 TC Very Berry
PANTONE 15-1242 TC Muskmelon
PANTONE 14-1113 TC Marzipan

The above are only five of the eighteen delicious sounding colors that will enhance our life in 2003. The numbers are the keys here, not the names. Pantone publishes *The Pantone Textile Color Guide*, which lists 1,757 colors in three distinct color palettes of bright, muted, and specialty shades with numbers and names—in six convenient languages.

A more seriously focused organization is the **IACC** (International Association of Color Consultants) **<http://www.iaccna.org>** operating from headquarters in San Diego, California. The IACC holds important seminars on color subjects. In the Fall of 2001, for example, a variety of lectures included such topics as Color as Information/Communication, Color Theory-Color Harmony, Color Environment and Human Reaction.

A final organizational example is my favorite: the **NCS** (The Natural Colour System), a Swedish based group. Approaching color as pure science, the NCS is a symbol-language for colors. With this system, every imaginable color can be described and notated, based on the way in which it is seen by human beings. The six color sensations which form the basis of man's inheritability to distinguish different colors are (1) pure white (W), (2) black (S), (3) yellow (Y), (4) red (R), (5) blue (B), and (6) green (G). These are the six elementary colors. NCS color notations are based on the degree of resemblance of a color to these elementary colors.

The NCS avoids completely the subject color name. No Foam Bisque, Gracious Green, or Plum Duff will be found here. Each of the over 2,000 colors is numbered as to its place within a nuance and hue. A brilliant scarlet is 1080-R10B, a pale chartreuse is 0060-G60Y. Scientific indeed! The collector, designer, or anyone simply interested in color would be wise to obtain the NCS indexes.

There are other organizations, of course—both domestic and foreign, but these three will serve the purpose as examples.

We have been discussing the official nomenclature of colors. The second class of names is troublesome. These names are attached to specific colors by the manufacturers or the retailer—there is no attempt at uniformity. Go into the paint department of a mega-store such as Wal-Mart, K-Mart, Home Depot and peruse the paint chips. Such names as Lemon Spritz™, Buttercup Petal™, Capri Grotto™, Confetti Fanfare™, and Sycamore Grove™ greet the eye. These are names chosen by people in charge of paint sales at corporate headquarters or the major distribution center for the store chain, and have no scientific base. These names are sometimes elaborate, sometimes cute and eye-catching, and often verbally give no idea regarding the major color group. Is Capri Gotto blue, green or purple? Is Confetti Fanfare a pink or green? And what about Sycamore Grove? If the interested collector went from Wal-Mart to Lowe's carrying a paint chip named Snapdragon™, no color by that name would be found. Snapdragon, and the recipe to produce it, belong to Wal-Mart. Yet Lowe's paint department could duplicate—to customer satisfaction—the color Wal-Mart entitled Snapdragon. I have tried this experiment with acceptable results.

The Wal-Mart names are particular to that store, not the actual color. Thus the colorist must distinguish between official terminology and distributor (store) terminology. This is vital.

For any collector determined to learn the rudiments of color, the knowledge of three terms is absolutely necessary. Not only is this knowledge helpful when discussing various dinnerware glazes; it also enhances the general enjoyment of life. To be precise in the naming of colors is to be precise in the approach to life. These three terms are: hue, intensity, and tone.

HUE: This term has two uses. It is (1) a synonym for the word "color," and (2) it also refers the special attribute of one color that distinguishes it from all other colors. Example: Emerald, Chartreuse, Teal are three separate colors, but because they are all greens they are similar in hue.

Black, White, and Gray possess no hue. These three in all of their many variations are colorless and are known as "Neutrals."

Black is the absence of light, and ranges from warm to cool. White is the presence of all kinds of light and is highly variable: yellowish as in white bread, or bluish as in milk white. White, in one of its many variations, is the ground glaze for a majority of dinnerware. Ben Seibel offered pure white lines in his Iroquois designs, and as foils in *Duplex*, *Pivotal*, and *Mexicana*. The pure, highly reflective bluish white of *Pivotal* is a complete contrast of the chalky matte white used as the background on *Mexicana* plates. Placed side-by-side, Black and White are pure drama, but this contrast is rarely dared by ceramic designers. Eva Zeisel dared once in her *Tomorrow's Classic* shape commissioned by Hallcraft. Mixed together in innumerable proportions, Black and White produce Gray, a neutral that encompasses wide ranges from moleskin to battleship gray, from charcoal to gun metal, from pearl to oyster gray. The neutrals are classic, sophisticated, glamorous, and bespeak of the rich and influential.

One of the most sophisticated ceramic uses of all three neutrals can be seen in the *Duplex* treatment named Casablanca.

INTENSITY: Another term for this attribute is **SATURATION**. When we are dealing with the purity, the brightness, the clean strength of a particular color, we are discussing how "intense" it is or how "saturated" it is, or how little it has been affected by another color. Add a dab of red to an intense green, and some of that intensity (purity, brightness) is lost.

TONE: There is also another word for this term: **VALUE**. Tone, or value, refers to the "lightness" or "darkness" of a particular color. When the colorist adds white to purple it becomes a "tint"—lavender. However when black is added to purple it becomes a "shade"—eggplant. Unfortunately, there are some collectors who use the term "shade" to refer to colors in general: pink is not a shade of red, it is a tint of red. Both "tint" and "shade" can be conveniently used as verbs: i.e. red tinted with white becomes pink, or red shaded with black becomes maroon.

Furthermore: the tint pink and the shade maroon are similar in hue: they are both reds. They also can be strongly saturated or weakly saturated: if pink is adulterated with a tiny drop of green, or blue, or yellow, it loses its intensity. Once red is tinted and becomes pink, this hue pink stands as an independent, separate color with its own value and saturation degree.

A final term should be understood: Complementary colors. These are found opposite each other on the color wheel. One complementary color will always be primary, i.e. red, blue, yellow. The second color will be the secondary color produced by mixing the two other primaries, i.e. green, orange, purple. These complementary colors can symbolize major holidays: Red and Green for Christmas, Yellow and Purple for Easter, and Blue and Orange is a favorite among university team sports! Complementary colors are absolutely harmonious.

All colors are affected by the finish or coating. A matte glaze will be much duller, softer, and seem retiring to the eye. High gloss finishes are more natural and brighter. In fact under some conditions a matte tone will look quite different from the same color with a high lacquer glaze. Eggplant fruits are quite shiny and bright, as are apples, plums, and blushing pears. Very few matte colors exist in nature.

Not all Seibel collectors will be interested in color to the same degree. Sadly, a few might not be interested at all. This is unfortunate because a number of Seibel lines depend almost entirely upon the sophisticated use of color—rather than the more common use of decal decorations: his early Raymor lines, the later *Potter's Art*, and the complementary addition of solid color hollowware. A good ceramic industrial designer should be a master colorist, and to properly and completely enjoy the work of such a person, the collector must also be aware and appreciative of the complex science of color.

Freelance Designers and Mid-Century-Modern

An Abbreviated Discussion

Before starting this section, an explanation must be given. The Mid-Century-Modern style plays a very important role in the history of American dinnerware. The number of produced designs within this category is not huge when all the thousands of individual lines are considered, but MCM's influence far outweighs its numbers: as a group, MCM is one of the dominant movements in industrial design. Regarding this general movement, my knowledge reflects only the proverbial tip of the iceberg. I am far removed from being an expert. Regard what is being written as random thoughts scattered into the winds of opinion.

Can the researcher ever capture—like sunfish in a seine—the definitive definition of the term Mid-Century-Modern? Or will we be, as are fanatical balletomanes arguing the merits of *Swan Lake* over those of *Sleeping Beauty*, hopelessly unable to reach an acceptable verdict?

There are, however, some salient points upon which most MCM critics agree: Mid-Century-Modern really has little to do with a specific space in time. The time is usually identified as running from about the early 1940s until the early 1970s—more or less. Michael Pratt states that appreciation for pure Mid-Century-Modern peaked in the late 1940s to early '50s, and even during this time, MCM's appeal never stole the show completely from other design styles. Once Mr. Pratt and I argued—discussed is the better word—about the role of *Fiesta* in the time warp of MCM. I posed the question and lost the friendly battle. Homer Laughlin *Fiesta* never was, never approached, and never aspired to being Mid-Century-Modern even if its production straddled the middle of the twentieth century!

In this case, a slice of time does not define. All tableware collectors accept this fact.

After World War II, as the century tumbled towards its midpoint, there arose a noticeable difference in the designer/manufacturer relationship. Dinnerware researchers seem to agree upon this point. The difference was the rise—like fresh sweet water bubbling up from a newly discovered spring—of the independent free-lancer. This term defined the man or woman who contracted for a specific ceramic project, and was not permanently employed by one producer. Not all potteries allowed such innovation to invade their art departments. Homer Laughlin China, for example, never subscribed to this mode of design: it was and is notoriously successful in maintaining the *status quo* with house designers. Once, some years ago during a telephone conversation, Eva Zeisel commented to me how she would welcome a design assignment from HLC. When I mentioned this fact to the late Jonathan O. Parry (then HLC Art Director), he replied briefly and succinctly: "Oh, no. Freelance designers are too much trouble!"

An observation possibly quite true—in some, but not necessarily all, cases.

While this class of creative artist was becoming a potent force in the 1950s and 1960s, some surely could be difficult. They were akin to great renowned sopranos engaged by smaller, provincial opera houses—engaged to enliven a production of Wagner's *Tristan und Isolde*, or to assume the tempestuous title role in Puccini's *Tosca*. These *prima donnas absoluta*,[1] acquired for their "dival" properties, sang magnificently, but they could cause a flurry of problems within the company. These glorious ladies, awesomely well known, had personal individual interpretations of their roles, and their forceful personalities overwhelmed the performance. In other words, there was little integration or balance, and after a performance or two, these great divas flew off with a flurry of press releases to another assignment.

The same general situations surrounded the hiring of the great free-lancers. These exceptional talents—officially titled "contract designers"—were engaged by Hall, or Iroquois, or Raymor to create one or more lines of dinnerware. With a signed contract carefully stipulating conditions, the designer clambered aboard for a month—or whatever time was necessary to complete the assignment. Some traveled to the pottery, some traveled at intervals between their studios and the plant, and a few stayed securely at the home studio and sent sketches or models. The ensuing creations were often beautiful to the extreme, and quite acclaimed by the critics, but frequently—when they were broaching new design concepts—not very well received by the paying public. Thus, many were not "consumer successes" at the time they were introduced; they languished and did not fulfill their anticipatory role.

Again, in the same manner as the great sopranos, after fulfilling each individual contract, the free-lancers left. Yes, perhaps they were demanding, artistically aloof, irritatingly aware of their special position, and unencumbered—unlike resident designers—with little emotional attachment or loyalty to the company. Yet, even if personality problems did occur, and even if the resultant tableware did not measure up to its messianic role, most of the designs, with the passage of years, have proved inordinately collectible.

Since I feel the necessity of continually explaining my comments, it must be noted that I am NOT saying only free-lance designers were uniquely talented. What I am saying is the contract designer's impermanent relationship with the manufacturer often was conducive to spectacularly imaginative ceramic creations. Many in-house designers were just as talented, but lacked conditions to allow the freedom to experiment with shape, texture, and color.

During the fifties and sixties much of free-lance tableware fit neatly into the category of Mid-Century-Modern. Perhaps there is really something inherently emancipative about being a free-lance contractor that releases one from conservative tendencies and allows or encourages the designer to "biomorphically soar"! Don Schreckengost was a master at ceramic design, but once he became enfolded in the Homer Laughlin China Company, his first concern had to be the company's policies and philosophies, not his own personal flights. The company rightfully expected such loyalty on Schreckengost's part, and he was absolutely willing to do so. Such is the give and take of full-time employment. Contract designers did not monopolize new and innovative modern ceramic masterpieces, and not all in-house artistic directors were shackled by conservatism. Yet this was the general tendency.

Here is a prime example of this tendency. It is accepted that Mr. Don Schreckengost was an innovative and talented ceramic designer, and he accepted the position of the Homer Laughlin Art Director in 1945—three years after the death of the former director Frederick Hurton Rhead. Schreckengost's first HLC shape was *Jubilee*, and this line led the way towards the establishment of a Mid-Century-Modern tendency at Homer Laughlin. In pale solid glazes, *Jubilee* never really was a powerful seller. Perhaps like Seibel's *Roseville Modern Stoneware*, *Jubilee* simply made it appearance too soon!

With *Rhythm* (1950) Schreckengost offered a clean design that pointed the way even more obviously toward a belief in MCM. It was smoothly simplified, gently curved, mildly couped—and it was extremely popular and is readily found today. The solid colored glazes are more in tune with the MCM ideologies. Woolworth's sold *Rhythm* glazed in yellow, soft gray, chartreuse, forest green, and a rich wine burgundy. It also existed in pure white—another MCM characteristic. For me, the *Rhythm* is a *tabula rasa*! With a push, a shove, an extended lip, a surprising lid, the next shape designed by Schreckengost could have been purely Mid-Century-Modern.

The next shape was a return to pure conservatism: in 1953, the rotund, pleasantly formal, and totally predictable *Cavalier*. Did Homer Laughlin deliberately step away from the Mid-Century-Modern concepts? Would that a true, honest answer might be known. In the mid-1950s, the Homer Laughlin Company was offering consumers quaint and charming *Cavalier* by Don Schrecakengost while Hall China was astounding both the consumers and the critics with *Hallcraft's Century* by Eva Zeisel.[2]

Michael Pratt supplied a marvelously concise definition of a Mid-Century-Modern piece. Often the collector hears of "biomorphism," "stretched extensions," "fluidity," but Mr. Pratt stresses one word—"surprise!" If a shape surprises, makes us look again, makes us catch our breath, then it is possibly belongs in the Mid-Century-Modern category! This surprise could be related by an off-center lid, a precariously extended teapot spout, or conversely, because of a "nubbined" spout of miniscule proportions. Surprise can come by way of an unusual glaze, or even a reverse embossment, such as appears on Seibel's *Intaglio* designed for Iroquois.

Surprise, not a place in time, defines Mid-Century-Modern!

Comments on Jenfred

The Jenfred line of products does not fit easily (or at all) into the category of "tableware," and yet a good number of Jenfred pieces can be used on the table. Thus, this short introductory commentary.

Jenfred came quite early in Ben Seibel's career—at a time when he was still involved in the Raymor Company guided, in part, by his good friend Irving Richards. Levco Metal Finishers of Long Island City, New York, produced the actual items. In the words of an advertising flyer:

> *This handsome group of smoking and serving accessories is hand-cast in an unbreakable metal alloy, then plated with a rich copper or a golden brass. As a final finish, a tarnish proof lacquer is applied to each piece.*

Three examples of Ben Seibel bookends. None are very heavy and thus will not support heavy books. They are, however, extremely decorative.

This is a clear and apt description of the extensive line of products sold under the general name Jenfred ware. Today when the collector talks of Ben Seibel and Jenfred, he usually is discussing one of the many varieties of bookends. To some Jenfred means bookends shaped as shells, arches, stirrups, and barbells. These items are very valued today.

Other items ranged from letter and magazine racks to lamps, from candle holders to salt and pepper shakers—all made in the manner described above. The smoking paraphernalia is, however, the true *raison d'etre* of Jenfred with over forty individual metallic ashtrays available to the Seibel collector. Serious smokers in the 1950s invested time and money in so-called vital adjuncts necessary to the smoking hobby. Lighters, cigarette boxes, pipe holders, and tobacco containers also fit into this category. Most formally set dinner tables provided between each pair of guests a small holder containing three of four cigarettes and a small individual ashtray. Smoking between courses was considered proper and oh-so sophisticated.

Jenfred also listed several sets of metal salt and pepper shakers. One set in plated silver (#5606) indicates how early Seibel was designing, in combination, the tall salt and the short pepper. They sold for $8.00 the pair. There were shakers the shape of cubes, the shape of brass flames, the shape of perfect balls perched on a raised foot. These were, as were the ashtrays, placed on the table to be shared by two diners.

A sampling of smoking accessories. The small silvery ashtray in front could certainly be used on the dining table.

There was also a considerable variety of metal bowls: extenuated and elegant candy bowls; large sleek fruit or salad bowls; copper trays; and sinuous brass nut dishes extremely usable on either the dining or the coffee table. These items would probably be better described as "casual ware."

There were also several kinds of candleholders: the most commonly available today being the swelling oval base with the small holder at the top. The collector will have little trouble adding one or more of these holders to a Seibel collection.

One of the most glamorous of the candleholders is in a modified boat shape, slightly curved in solid brass. It will support five candles: a pair would be a dramatic centerpiece for any table. Unfortunately this Mid-Century-Modern piece is difficult to locate and quite expensive, yet its solid brass beauty is well worth a concentrated effort to acquire.

Seibel designed Jenfred items, while not playing a major role in '50s dining, did add a golden gleam and a silvery sparkle to the tables and the buffets of the day.

An unusual "duck" ashtray—or candy dish—in front of the most commonly found candleholders. These are 6.50" tall, but the height and shape can vary slightly. Six to ten of these holders, topped with a variety of candles, would present a dramatic centerpiece.

Solid brass, this slightly crescent candelabra could have many uses on the modern table or buffet.

Contempora by Steubenville

Back stamp.

A Few Words About Dating

Unfortunately, sadly, but understandably, there is quite a raging controversy whipping about the dating of the first four Seibel tableware lines: *Contempora* by Steubenville, *Raymor Modern Stoneware (RMS)* by Roseville, *Country-Time* by Pfaltzgraff, and *Universal Raymor* by Universal Potteries. Actually, the tooth of the controversy concerns only the first two lines.

Researchers, in their eagerness to be correct and honest, fasten like barnacles on the bottom of a rowboat to the information they believe is true. All writers are prone to this disability—myself included. It cannot be escaped. There can be nothing reprehensible in believing in one's own convictions; however, reprehensibility comes to the fore when writers/researchers use guile and hypocrisy to promote their own opinions and squash the opinions of others. This power playing was not always so among those avidly interested in American dinnerware, but, again unfortunately, today it is nearly the norm.

The reader should remember that the four lines designed by Ben Seibel all appeared within a few years of each other, and when discussing *Contempora* and RMS we are concerned with only a short span of time—1950 to 1953.

The evidence to place one a year before or after the other is slim—needle eye slim—even slimmer than nineteen-year-old Lauren Bacall in *To Have and Have Not!* A most important writer bases his opinion mainly (but not solely) on a 1953 advertisement that hints, quite securely, that *Contempora* follows in the great Seibel tradition of *Raymor Modern Stoneware*.

My information conversely states that Seibel was invited to design RMS AFTER the modest consumer success of Steubenville's *Contempora*. Well, there you have it! Who is correct and who gets the black ball?

My contention basically is: WHO REALLY SHOULD CARE?

Advertising hoopla is known to be incorrect. What do we know? The Roseville Company was dying a very conspicuous death in the early 1950s, and we know that its last ditch effort was *Roseville Modern Stoneware* in 1953. This dinnerware, while striking different and beautiful, failed in its purpose and the Company died—not miserably, but the ending of a once powerful and productive institution is always painful. This is known as fact.

Now, by my reasoning—correct or incorrect—it seems impossible that Ben Seibel would have been asked to design a "savior" line of dinnerware as his first full tableware set. Would the powers at Roseville put their existence in a young and untried ceramic designer? Of course, Seibel had been working for Raymor in the Jenfred accessory line; but (and this I believe is true), he had no full dinnerware set to his credit at that time.

This is one reason—based on logic—that seems to support my contention that *Contempora* was the senior shape. Another reason touches on the *Contempora* shape itself. While stunning and quite novel, *Contempora* is not a finished line. I stress this in the following section. There are misjudgments and some outright mistakes. If a thoughtful person looks carefully at the gravy boats of both shapes—placed side-by-side and handled in turn—I can hardly believe Seibel reverted to the *Contempora* piece AFTER completing the RMS gravy. The first is a shadow of the second. The first is a proto-plan of the genius imbued within the second! Or so is my opinion: humble or not!

Thus I place *Contempora* first (1950-1951?) and RMS in its known position of 1952. But again, WHO REALLY CARES?

Ben Seibel's first four lines were closely involved with Richard Irving and the Raymor distributing company. (Note: To be truthful, the connection between Country-Time and Raymor is rather tenuous.) It could be said that Seibel concocted the shapes and Raymor found a pottery company to produce them. This seems logical. To what extent Seibel was controlled by Raymor is not really known—and should have no bearing on our discussion. What I am implying—quite strongly—is that Seibel surely could have created *Contempora* first and then completed RMS, but the two were reversed in production. So, which came first, the egg or the chicken? And again, who really can be concerned about such a minor point in the scheme of this surging world?

As has been stressed, when two or more tableware lines are produced in quick succession–A, B, and then C, it is entirely possible that line C was designed first, but produced last!

Enough said!

Thoughts and Reflections

Steubenville Pottery Company was officially organized on November 17, 1879, and existed as a rather important manufacturer until it closed during the last month of 1959. This Ohio based pottery was very similar to its sister company, Iroquois China. The reason for this is the two companies were not actually among the first rank in American dinnerware manufacturers; but, both had contracted major superstar designers, and this fact gave each of them a *cachet* of prestige. Steubenville and Iroquois produced dinnerware designed by Russel Wright and Ben Seibel–two influential and famous Mid-Century-Modern ceramic designers.

Some American dinnerware collectors insist that Russel Wright far outranks Ben Seibel and Eva Zeisel; but, as we move into the twenty-first century–the awesome Third Millennium–the ranking of these three design geniuses is beginning to draw closer and might very well mellow into an equality which will then be accepted by all collectors.

Of course, Wright's *American Modern* (introduced 1939) was the most popular dinnerware sold in America during the 1940s. Indeed, Steubenville Pottery was the first company to embrace and produce the new style of American dinnerware: a sinuous and sleek dinnerware beginning with Wright's *American* Modern and continuing with Seibel's *Contempora*. Here is a quote from *The Collector's Encyclopedia of Russel Wright Designs*, Ann Kerr's valued book.

> *The Ohio River potteries, all staggering from the assault of foreign competition felt this new ware [American Modern] to be too radical, too bold, too much of a departure, too costly to produce and since they felt that they knew the pottery market best, they felt they knew a loser when they saw one. One by one they refused to produce it. The Steubenville Pottery finally took a chance on a sure thing.*

Thus *American Modern* came into being and revolutionized the manner in which Americans dined.

As the1950s began, Wright's bold tableware was followed by yet another design just as bold, just as radical! Designed for Raymor by Ben Seibel, and manufactured by Steubenville, *Contempora* might have been planned as a second choice for those consumers who, for one reason or another, did not appreciate *American Modern*. The two shapes were similar in general creative approach, but were different enough to appeal to a variety of potential purchasers. While decorations were placed–albeit rarely–on *American Modern*, they never were used on *Contempora*.

In fact, only four solid colors were used on Seibel's dinnerware, in "rippling sgraffito textures," but this technique appeared only on the outside of the pieces. The term "sgraffito" simply means a decorating process whereby the surface of the ceramic was incised to reveal a different color lying just underneath. The word comes from the Italian *sgraffire* "to scratch," and this adequately describes the unusual surface ripple of *Contempora*. It looks scratched. True sgraffito could have been detected by touching the surface; this "incising" merely gave the appearance—a *faux* scratching.

The available four glaze colors were confined to neutrals: Charcoal, Mist Gray, Fawn (spelled "Faun"[1] in the original advertisements), and Sand White. The first two named being the most commonly seen and Sand White being the most elusive. According to advertising pamphlets, all four were meant to "mix and match" for formal entertaining and family dining; but even so mingled the general affect would be quiet and subtle.

The use of the word "Faun"–as in *Afternoon of A* ...– to designate a color was provocative. I have never seen a faun, nor do I know of anyone who has had the pleasure: these little rural goatish deities are rarely encountered today. Ever since Classical Rome capitulated to the power of St. Peter, fauns have retreated to the rugged bosky hills of Mt. Cavo to cavort with the dryads and naiads *a la* Walt Disney's *Fantasia*, and left humankind to its own devices. Thus I do not even know if a faun is fawn colored. The merchandising department at Steubenville or at Raymor must have a logical reason for using the name: it could not have been merely a mistake or a mythological whimsy.

Wright's *American Modern* could be viewed as the precursor of all Mid-Century-Modern design, and it definitely influenced Seibel when he came to create *Contempora* around 1950. During these exciting years, American design was being overwhelmed by what Ann Kerr called the new and the unusual. The Russel Wright approach to the design and manufacture of dinnerware, furniture, and fabrics filtered down and around like pure spring water, and both enticed and refreshed all manner of industrial designers. Thus *American Modern* exerted a direct influence on the young Ben Seibel. The earlier shape meshed perfectly with Seibel's concept for *Contempora*, even to some color choices. Seibel's Mist Gray[2] almost duplicates Wright's Granite Gray: only the sgraffito produces a noticeable difference.

Both designers approached their respective shapes with the same philosophy. This is NOT to imply Seibel copied Wright, but there are design similarities. For example, the gravy boats in both *American Modern* and *Contempora* are reasonably narrow, similarly long with inwardly overhung rims, and the pouring end is more blunt than the handle end. While the handle in the former, older shape is flattened and moves downward as an extended tab, the latter's handle flows upward, organically following the existing line of the body. Interestingly, both are awkward to use.

This awkwardness is found among other individual *Contempora* pieces. This attribute, at times, catches the potential collector off guard. Take for example the sugar and creamer set. The apple plump creamer possesses a neatly molded handle allowing for beautiful balance, and any liquid pours cleanly and precisely from the narrow pointed spout. Yet the creamer opening, over 4 inches long and shaped like a raindrop, is off center – at least in the good number of examples seen. However, the piece is a truly superb design, smoothly and gracefully composed–on the table and in the hand.

Alas, the accompanying sugar is not as balanced nor as graceful! The open upwardly angled handle appears stubby and can not bear comfortably the weight (13 oz.) of the sugar body: To hold and pass the sugar bowl by means of the handle simply does not work, and the width of the sugar's roundness (nearly 5.25 inches) precludes clutching the piece by the sides by anyone without Franz Liszt's hand spread. The two pieces do match if the collector remembers Seibel's design approach to the sugar/creamer set. In many of his dinnerware lines he matches a tall, elegant creamer with a low, round sugar. This concept might be called the "masculine" and the "feminine" aspects of tableware design. Thus in *Contempora*, if the Seibel penchant is recalled, it is not surprising that a shape disparity should exist. For a novice collector, however, such a match, or mismatch perhaps, can come as a surprise. But surprises abound in Mid-Century-Modern: unexpected surprises are part of the enchantment.

And, of course, *Contempora* is completely enmeshed within the Mid-Century-Modern ideals. The collector, either novice and experienced, is often caught off guard! One constantly must take another look: to consider and reconsider. Some round pieces are really not completely perfect—the plates for example. The teacup too fascinates. I have measured and re-measured and studied carefully from the top. Sometimes it looks perfectly round, yet turn it slightly so that the handle is at the clock's number 4 and the perfect circle seems to slightly swell. Totally an optical illusion, of course, and if planned by Ben Seibel, it is a masterful stroke. Perhaps the illusion is just because the rim undulates slightly or the rippling sgraffito lines affect what we think we see?

The teacup's handle is also of interest. Why is it applied when all the other handles are molded as part of the shape? As mentioned above, the handle of the creamer is near perfection both in style and function. Why was this type of molded, sculpted handle not used on the teacup? Probably a firing technicality!

One of the most popular pieces of the entire *Contempora* line is the nesting coffee pots. When Mr. Seibel was writing his column "From A Designer's Notebook" for *China, Glass and Decorative Accessories*, this delightful small pot often appeared as an example of a "space-saving" design. However, the "stackability" of the coffee pot–obviously meant for an individual serving–resulted in a near fatal problem: the pot's necessarily low table-top flat finial cannot be grasped at all. The lid has a deep flange and, for its size, is quite weighty. To try to lift the lid by means of the finial could result in a slip and a smash—breakage. While the pot is amusing and quaint, its functionality is questionable.

Since we are beginning to discuss the various items found in the *Contempora* shape, it would be wise to list them all.[3]

Ashtray	(401)
Bowl, salad, 11"	(416)
Bowl, soup, 6.25"	(406)
Bowl, vegetable, 9"	(415)
Bowl, vegetable, divided, 9"	(413)
Bun and muffin server	(429)
Casserole	(421)
Celery dish, 13.25"	(412)
Coaster	(430)
Coffee pot, nesting	(418)
Creamer	(408)
Cup	(403)
Dish, fruit, 6"	(405)
Gravy	
Jug	(417)
Pickle dish, 10.50"	(410)
Plate, 7"	
Plate, 8.25"	
Plate, 10.50"	(400)
Plate, chop, 14.25"	(414)
Plate, party, 10.50"	(427)
Platter, divided (food server), 3-section, 16.25"	(426)
Platter, oval, 14.50"	(409)
Saucer	(404)
Shakers	(422, 423)
Shaker server with handle	(424, 425)
Sugar	(407)
Teapot	(419)
Tureen	(420)

Thirty individual pieces were available in the *Contempora* line. The set was described as "a fourth dimension in dinnerware" and "gracefully sculptured." These phrases, meant to entice the prospective buyer, were reasonably correct–although one wonders how and why the advertising department inveigled Time as the fourth dimension into the selling scheme.

The number of pieces allows for the obvious ordinary items plus some unusual ones. Not all these special pieces could be called Seibel "signatures" although the tureen, massive and battleship big, appears in several lines. The jug went on to become quite an important piece in some Seibel lines of dinnerware. He liked jugs, just as he liked bean pots and warmers and outsized beverage servers; in his very first dinnerware line, an attractive jug lies at its center.

The bun and muffin warmer, a near perfect globe topped by a strong finial, is the most desired *Contempora* piece. Actually, the finial is hollow, allowing it to fit over a peg and permits the cover to move right or left reasonably well. The problem with this piece is its breakability: not only were they produced in limited numbers; the covers are also quite fragile. The *Contempora* bun warmer is a scarce item indeed! In Seibel's next tableware line, *Raymor Modern Stoneware*, the bun warmer returns, albeit heavier, flattened, and slightly deflated or crushed. During a time when the average bun, roll, or muffin warmer consisted of two impeccably clean (*a la* Julia Child) tea towels in a wicker basket or a utilitarian aluminum container, these ceramic warmers are unique—surprisingly and astoundingly so! A list of 1950s ceramic bun warmers conceived to share equal space on the family dining table would be a short list indeed.

Other tableware items fond to the heart of Ben Seibel were the miniscule coaster (a.k.a. butter pat or ashtray), the "party" plate, the divided platter, and anything that stacks. All these items, under various guises, appear and reappear in many of Seibel's dinnerware lines. They could be counted among his favorites.

For all its intrinsic charm and evident popularity, when I closely study or carefully handle specific *Contempora* items a flickering sense of dissatisfaction arises. Turning the pieces, one by one, this way and that, peering over and under, questions issue forth and disappointment tugs irritatingly. These feelings subvert pure esthetic enjoyment. There is an aura of the unfinished, the uncompleted, almost a rawness perhaps, as if someone left open a cellar window and a chilly, musty breeze is wafting disturbingly through an otherwise warmly safe and secure home.

Was *Contempora* designed in undue haste? Were the models or drawings shipped to Steubenville, then created and sent on to the kilns without careful reflections by all those concerned—a rare possibility to be sure. Yet there is, in my opinion, a lack of completeness, a sense that with a tuck here, or a tightening there, a strengthening or a straightening, a widening or a narrowing, miniscule manipulations of many of the individual pieces within the line, *Contempora* would have been raised to the same heights where resides Seibel's *Raymor Modern Stoneware*, once the hope of the Roseville Pottery Company.

Could it be conceivable that during the process of creating *Contempora* , Seibel considered it as a trial run, as a practice run, as a test run undertaken in 1950 to prepare the way for his ultimate 1952 masterwork–the mildly sinuous shape done for Roseville? While this conjecture is difficult to accept, the philosophic similarities between *Contempora* and *Modern Stoneware* are so evident, so patently clear as to make this supposition possible.

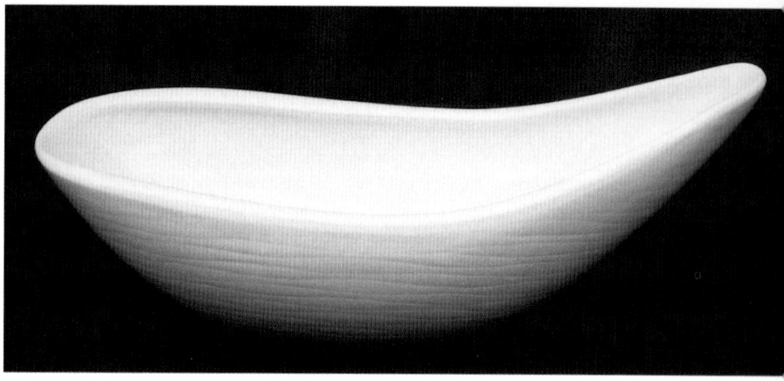

The gravy is Sand White. $30-35.

There is a philosophic similarity between Seibel's *Contempora* gravy (left) in a warmer Mist Gray and Wright's *American Modern* Granite Gray piece.

Was *Contempora*, sculptured, graceful, almost delicately conceived yet still immature, a beautiful "experimental" shape leading and guiding Ben Seibel to successfully accomplish the fantastically sophisticated richness and totally mastered maturity known as *Raymor Modern Stoneware*?

The "apple plump" creamer accompanied by the lower squat sugar bowl. $35-40 for the set.

Looking down on the creamer to note the slightly off center opening. One of the characteristics of *Contempora* is that many pieces are not centered.

The teacup with its saucer. $10-12.

The ceramic material used for *Contempora* is light, porous, and relatively thin.

Notice that the teacup handle is applied to the bowl—not modeled into it.

The nesting coffee server is a very popular piece, although more desirable in Faun and Sand White. Notice the low, rather awkward finial. $75.

The physically split divided bowl was one of Seibel's trademarks. While other ceramic designers of the 1950s used the same concept, none did it as well as Ben Seibel—except, perhaps Mrs. Eva Zeisel.

The 9" divided vegetable bowl. Note how reflective is the glaze. The divided bowl is harder to locate than the regular example. Seibel used the same approach to the indented bottom later in Iroquois *Impromptu*. $40.

The divided vegetable bowl is slightly larger than the undivided version. The latter is also usually priced slightly lower. Price: $28-32.

The long (13.25") and simplistic celery dish. $35.

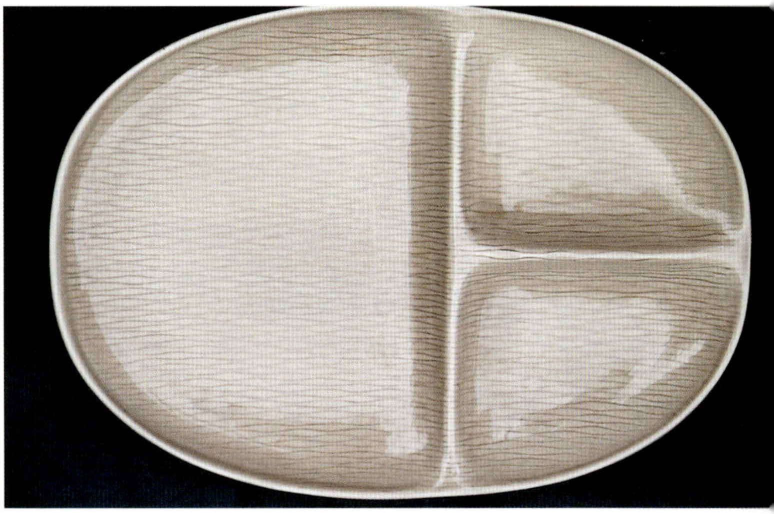

The large and impressive "food server" or three-sectioned platter. It is over 16" long and molded like sculpture. $50.

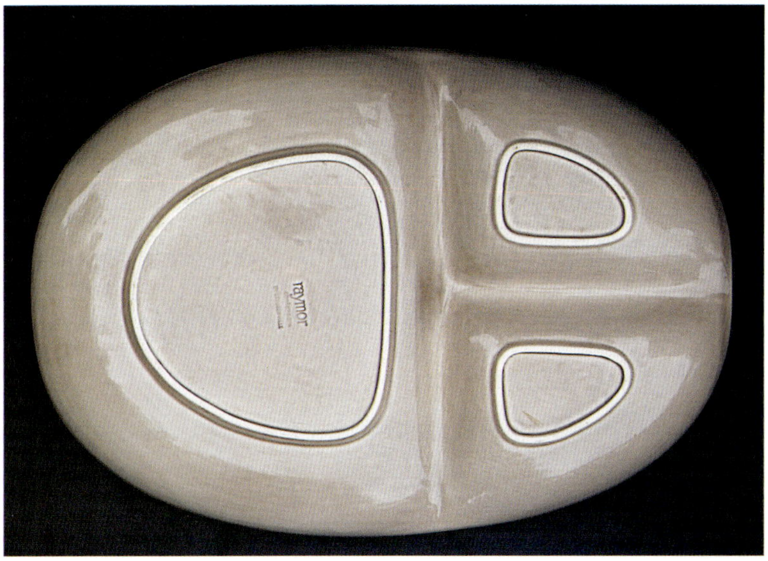

The reverse of the platter to show the three "feet" to allow it is stand firm on the tabletop.

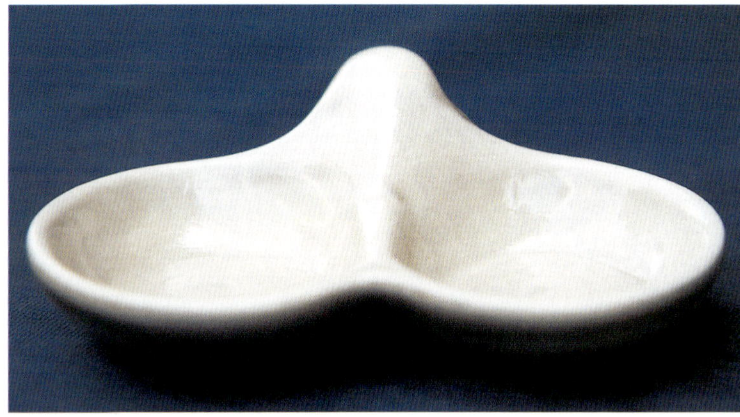

The handled shaker server. $15.

The closed bun warmer in Sand White. $135+.

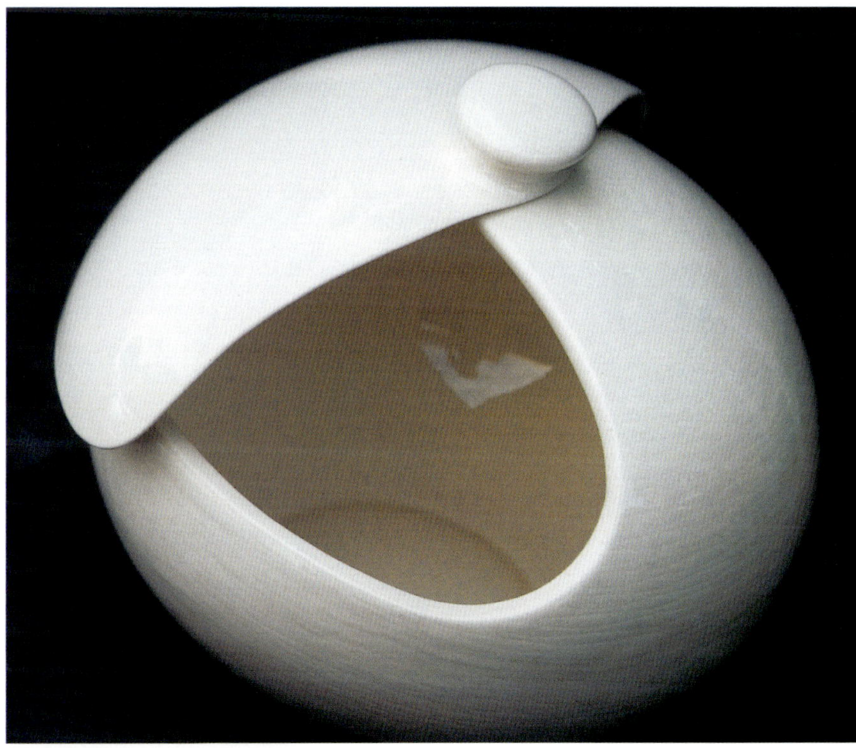

The bun warmer opened.

The bun warmer with the swivel top removed. Note the little peg over which the finial fits.

The cover propped up. Note the sculptural thinness of this piece.

The largest plate and the smallest: the chop plate (14.25") ($40) and the coaster (4") ($10).

The party plate (10.50") in Sand White. $35.

The dinner plate (10.50") ($10) with the saucer ($3). Note that the plates are not pure circles.

Even the small bowls are off center: the fruit dish (left) is 6" round while the soup bowl (right) is slightly larger (*6.25"). The former is priced at
$6; the latter, $12-15.

The casserole is low (3") and is 10.75" from handle to handle. In all the examples I have seen, the cover does not fit securely. $45-50.

The teapot is very desirable and popular with collectors. Luckily it is not too hard to find. The short spout can drip, but this attribute is wisely overlooked today. $70-80.

Sometimes dealers unwittingly confuse the lidded casserole with the *Contempora* tureen. This is understandable for those who have not seen the two together. The tureen (right) is quite spectacular.

Raymor Modern Stoneware

Reaching the Goal of New Perfection

If having completed the section on Steubenville's *Contempora*, any reader is under the impression my feelings for that shape are less than positive, I must apologize. Imperfections abound: *Contempora* is unabashedly juvenile, exuberantly youthful–as fresh as a gangly awkward fifteen-year-old boy waiting to grow, gain polish, and enter the so-called sophisticated world of the adult. Ben Seibel was young and he had imbued *Contempora* with the potential polish and hidden charm inherent in youth. Two years later in 1952, building upon his *Contempora* experiences, a still young Seibel enriched the world of American dinnerware by developing a line so unique, so simple, and yet so spectacular, so positively mature yet so redolent of enthusiastic youth that he, Ben Seibel, would forever be a powerful force in the design universe. This 1952 line of tableware was, of course, *Raymor Modern Stoneware*.

Roseville Raymor, as the shape is called informally, was to have saved the Roseville Pottery Company from the horrors of ruin and bankruptcy. It did not! The Wisconsin Pottery Association maintains an informative web site on Roseville Pottery. While skimming through its contents, I came across a clear and concise paragraph explaining this.

> *Roseville tried to offset its reduced artware sales by launching a dinnerware line in 1953. Roseville Raymor was well-designed by Ben Seibel, but the decoration was rather austere when compared to better-selling dinnerware, and the line was a commercial failure. Roseville Pottery closed in 1954.*[1]

Today's collectors, waxing ecstatic over the smooth richness of the glazes, would hardly agree with the word "austere."

Thus the failure to bolster the company's flagging finances implies that the dinnerware when first offered to a discerning '50s public was not accepted with enthusiasm. Perhaps, as the statement from the Wisconsin Pottery Association strongly implies, the relatively somber and neutral colors did not excite, did not inspire the consumers to purchase. Or perhaps the shape, ovoid, solid, sturdy, and spaceship (Buck Rogers) graceful would not translate to the ordinary household's fondness for the general run of rose or poppy or violet bouquet decals on ivory china. Even when—within a very short time—some pieces were restyled and bright blue and chartreuse glazes[2] were introduced, the line just did not—in the proverbial slang expression—"cut the mustard"! One wonders if Mr. Seibel agreed with these modifications. This practice of "modification" was quite common among manufacturers. Hall China, modified Eva Zeisel's concepts for *Hallcraft Century*—and greatly angered this redoubtable lady! The dinnerware was advertised by and sold at the best stories: B. Altman's for example. In one of the advertisements, it is stressed that "Raymor Modern oven-to-table stoneware makes the hostess a guest too." And it was made available with matching, newly designed Harmony tablecloths. A few prices were listed: the sugar bowl with cover and creamer with lid were offered at $2.25, and a sixteen pieces place setting for four was available at $8.95. Sounds fantastically cheap? I was curious, so some investigation was in order. What a single one dollar bill bought in 1950 would take $14.00 today (or so the reference section as the local library informed): $1.00 (1950) = $14.00 (present day). Thus the sixteen-piece starter set that cost $8.95 in 1950 would cost $126.00 today. Pure approximation, naturally, and seemingly over-priced, but it does give a sense that B. Altman's was not selling cut-rate goods. Whatever the reason—shape, glaze color, price—in the mid-1950s, this stoneware failed to create enough palpable interest to save the company.

The raised Roseville Raymor back mark. While there is no mention of Ben Seibel, each has an identifying number. Here #154 refers to the small plate. Suggested prices reflect collector color partiality.

Books used for intensive tableware research are valuable for both the inclusion and exclusion of information: what is written about and what is overlooked are equally important sides of the same coin. One of the most valuable of all references on American dinnerware and pottery is Lois Lehner's *Encyclopedia of U.S. Marks on Pottery, Porcelain & Clay*. It rests by the side of most men and women who write about or care about American ceramics, and bears the copyright date of 1988 – at least this is the date of my well-thumbed copy–not really many years ago. Yet, the name of Ben Seibel appears not in the index, and under the entries for Steubenville no mark is included for *Contempora*. The marks shown under Roseville Pottery Company fare slightly better. Mark 10 is "Raymor by Roseville USA Oven Proof. Pat.Pend." Since Seibel's name did not appear on this stoneware line there is no reference, and the accompanying note merely states:

> *Raymor used on dinnerware and some accessory pieces; made in later years before closing.*

Again there is no mention of the designer.

The *Official Identification and Price Guide to Pottery and Porcelain*, 7th edition (1989) was a major guide until the publication of Harvey Duke's even more comprehensive 8th edition (1995.) Yet, under Steubenville there is no entry for *Contempora* and the Roseville Pottery Company is not even mentioned. From both omissions, the researcher can conclude these two 1950s dinnerware lines—both similar in philosophy and approach—were not well known or deemed important in the late 1980s! Interest in Ben Seibel has come a LONG way in a few short years!

Roseville, Raymor, and Ben Seibel did not foresee possible public apathy in 1952, and thus with optimistic enthusiasm *Raymor Modern Stoneware* was introduced as an extensive line. It was well weighted with bean pots, casseroles, and trivets. It was also heavy with plates, platters, and trays. At the time of its launching, undoubtedly this wide variety was aimed at filling all the possible nooks, crannies, and niches demanded by a prospective purchasing public. Unfortunately, as mentioned before, the public did not purchase–at least in the amounts optimistically anticipated.

Fifty-four separate items were available, not counting the several restyled pieces. The former—the good majority—are known as the 100 series and so numbered: 155, 161, 198, and so on. The few restyled items, plus the ashtray, bun warmer, shirred egg dish, and the double-stacked warmer, belong to the 200 series.

A complete list of the *Modern Stoneware* follows:

Ashtray	(203)
Bean pot, individual	(195)
Bean pot, 2 quarts, 7"	(193)
Bean pot, 1 quart, 5"	(194)
Bean pot, 4 quarts, 8"	(187)
Bowl, fruit with handle (the "fruit basket")	(166)
Bowl, salad	(161)
Bowl, lug soup	(155)
Bowl, vegetable, 9.50" x 6"	(160)
Bowl, divided vegetable, 13" x 7"	(165)
Bun warmer	(202)
Butter dish	(181)
Casserole, individual	(199)
Casserole, medium, 10.50" x 8.50"	(183)
Casserole, large	(185)
Casserole, handled, 1.50 quart	(198)
Casserole, handled, 2.50 quarts	(197)
Casserole, handles, 4 quarts	(196)
Celery/olive, 15.50" x 6.50"	(177)
Cheese/relish set	(180)
Coffee pot	(176)
Ceramic stand for coffee pot	
Condiment stand	(173)
Corn server, 12.50"	(162)
Covered ramekin, 6.50" x 4.25"	(156)
Creamer with lid[3]	(158)
Cruet, oil or vinegar	(170, 171)
Cup	(150)
Dish, lug fruit, 5"	(192)
Gravy	(190)
Jam/relish	(172)
Spoon for above	
Jug, water	(189)
Mug[4]	(179)
Pickle dish, 9.50"	(191)
Plate[5], 6.25"	(154)
Plate, 8.25"	(153)
Plate, 10.25"	(152)
Plate, chop, 15.25"	(164)
Platter, 14"	(163)
Platter, steak with well, 20"	(178)
Relish and sandwich tray	(182)
Saucer	(151)
Shaker, salt	(168)
Shaker, pepper	(169)
Shirred egg dish, handled, two sections	(200)
Sugar with lid	(157)
Teapot	(174)
Tray for sugar and creamer	(159)
Trivet, bean pot	(188)
Trivet, casserole, medium, 6.75"	(184)
Trivet, casserole, large, 8.25"	(186)
Trivet, teapot, 5.50"	(175)
Warmer	(201)

Restyled pieces are not easy to find.[6]

Restyled Cup, round	
Restyled Plate, oval, 6.75" x 6"	(154A)
Restyled Plate, oval, 11" x 9.50"	(252R)
Restyled Saucer, round	

The restyled items are known in terra cotta but today are exceptionally valued in two new glazes: a pale chartreuse and a robin's egg blue – which were, as mentioned above, rather unstable. There was some "cross-over" use of the chartreuse and blue glaze: the originally designed plates, bowls, and individual casseroles have been located in blue. But, this blue is very dull and grayed. In fact, there is so much difference with the shiny, glistening, really "robin's egg" color (seen on coffee servers and celery dishes) and this dull version, it could be wondered if there were two blues—slate and robin's egg!

Was the introduction of a more traditional oval shape coated with more familiar colors a frantic last attempt to gather and hold the rapidly withering and tenuous halfhearted public interest?[7] Whatever the answer, the efforts were in vain. Public indifference and flagging sales were the result. Even though critics and professionals in the fields of ceramics, industrial design, and tableware design lauded Ben Seibel for his new and innovative dinnerware creations, the general public—the buying public—was indifferent and apathetic.

The shape fashioned by Seibel was in the pure Mid-Century Modern mold, but it presented a more thickened, heavy, and solid appearance than did *Contempora*. It depended more upon "surprises" than arching extenuations. Two of the most unusual pieces—really outstanding shapes for the early 1950s—were the divided vegetable (165) and the celery/olive (177). Both are fluidly conceived, femininely rounded yet still mesh very well with the more masculine angles seen in the plates and platters. The solid glazes knot the individual pieces together securely. I believe if the set was decorated with decals the variation in the physical shapes would be much more evident—perhaps even distracting.

For a young man, Ben Seibel evinced a secure and mature belief in his own ideals. A man less assured would not have mingled modified rectangles with ovals and circular shapes. There are, however, some very subtle similarities within the line itself. The curves and blunt squared ends of the plates are mirrored in the shape of the lidded casseroles and the covered ramekin. For example, place the ramekin in the center of the salad plate. This size of plate matches perfectly with the ramekin and, while not absolutely necessary, it is best to have them both in the same glaze—at least for this experiment. These two pieces reflect each other: the rounded swells of the plate are more evident and the tips more squared, but once the lid is removed the ends of the plate match perfectly with the ends of the lidless ramekin.

In the paragraph above, "rectangles" were mentioned and these refer to the platters and the pickle dishes. However the term must not be taken literally. The impression is rectangular, but the longer sides actually bulge slightly to soften the outline—and to echo the more pronounced curve in the plates. The butter dish (181) is also an example of the "rounded rectangle," and it is one of the most desirable pieces in the line.

At this point, a slight digression is inserted: this has to do with the butter dish—and other pieces in the same category. I speak of the very scarce, yet available pieces! In the *Raymor Modern Stoneware* line there are several pieces that are the stuff of dreams. Elusive, wished for, fantasized about, and yet rarely encountered or acquired. The handled bowl known as the fruit basket (166), the coffee pot swinging joyfully upon its ceramic stand, the double stacked warmer (201) in clean and pristine condition, the cheese/relish set (180), and the tiny spoon to insert in the jam/relish jar. These pieces are so unusual and so rarely found that they are deemed virtually impossible to obtain.[8] I tend to use the same outrageous analogy: these pieces are for the affluent collectors, or the ones willing to sell a troublesome maiden aunt into white slavery. Very few average collectors are able to pay $500+ for the fruit basket, or over $400 for the swinging coffee pot, or $400 for the bun warmer. Unless, of course, they live only for their Roseville Raymor collection or the maiden aunt is quietly sold for a pretty price! The average collector with the usual, ordinary, other financial commitments must pull back to the second rank of rarity—in which the butter dish resides and also perhaps the shirred egg dish. The ownership of a butter dish in reasonable condition[9] is the pride of any collection. In fact, its possession can raise a collection to more exceptional heights.

This philosophy is relevant in any line of dinnerware from the old to the most contemporary, the most modern. Pieces so rare as to be nearly nonexistent do not make the collector's heart flutter. Well, perhaps there is a flutter in the breast, but the brain keeps close tab on the checkbook! It is those pieces, rare, or perhaps "merely" very scarce, and yet accessible, which catch the heart and make the blood sing. The Roseville Raymor butter dish is one of these!

The original glazes to appear on this stoneware are subdued: subdued in the same manner as the glazes used on Seibel's *Contempora*, but with a difference. Whereas in the earlier line there were four (remember Charcoal, Faun, Mist Gray, and Sand White), Roseville dinnerware was slated to appear in the finer stores dressed in five named glazes with multiple "versions." As Harvey Duke explained, "a bit confusing."

One of *Contempora's* glazes—Sand White—was meant to match with Roseville Raymor's Contemporary White, but the latter is not as brilliant as Sand White and, in the matte version, can look quite grayed—until placed next to the real Beach Gray. Then came four rich, well-saturated colors—Autumn Brown, Terra Cotta, Beach Gray, and Avocado (browns, gray, and black)—all five glazes appearing in two versions. The first version exists in a matte finish, the second in a gloss finish. With due respect to Mr. Duke, these are listed below.

MATTE or Plain Finish
- Autumn Brown (known to collectors as Chocolate)
- Terra Cotta
- Beach Gray
- Avocado Green (known to collectors as Black)

GLOSSY or Mottled Finish
- Autumn Brown
- Terra Cotta
- Beach Gray
- Light Avocado Green
- Dark Avocado Green (known to collectors as "Frogskin")

Autumn Brown—in both versions—is the easiest to locate. But some dealers state Terra Cotta as the most "common" color variation. "Frogskin" is viewed as highly desirable by all collectors—beginning and advanced—and commands the highest prices. But, and this is a purely personal opinion, the matte Autumn Brown is deep and rich as dark Dutch chocolate. It is so perfectly saturated that it seems to seep through the entire body of the pieces so glazed. While matte Autumn Brown might seem to be the most "common" Roseville Raymor glaze, it is as satisfying as a double devil's food cake! The collector must play one glaze version against the other: the matte glazes are deeper, darker, and more intense; the glossy glazes shimmer and are highly reflective and seem to rest upon the surface of the piece.

Mr. Duke does not mention Contemporary White as having both the plain and mottled finishes, but I have a mug in mottled white. Actually this mug possesses white mottles on a light tan background. Perhaps it can be assumed the white mottled version is a little unusual.

Seibel's approach to color within the framework of both *Contempora* and *Raymor Modern Stoneware* was sophisticated, subtle, and mature. For a young man just embarking on a career in ceramics and design, his color palette was daring, controversial, but (according to today's collectors) absolutely perfect. Nearly all foods would appear to advantage on the browns, the grays, and the tinted whites he chose to wash over his early dinnerware. Seibel again returned to the browns late in his career when he created the masterful Mikasa line *Potter's Art*. The solid and reliable browns have always suggested security, love of home, safety, and maturity: brown eggs, brown bread, brown rice, brown sugar are "no-nonsense," true, and reliable. In Europe, restaurants that hope to cater to the solid middle-classes prefer to decorate using the settled and peaceful browns. At the beginning of his career and at the end, Ben Seibel stressed the warmth, comfort, and substantiality that intrinsically was present within the wide ranges of the color brown.

The 1950s decade was an enthusiastic, quite inquisitively seeking, creative period in the young life of Ben Seibel. His first two important ventures into tableware design could be termed as experimental: he was imbued with the philosophic genius of Russel Wright. Seibel, as did Wright, depended on pure shape washed with solid glazes. For some reason—perhaps a personal predilection—Seibel's color palette was more somber, deeper, and darker. Even the whites were muted and somber. He eschewed Wright's lighter, more fanciful glazes—cedar, cantaloupe, glacier blue and bean brown, coral and sea foam—and opted for neutrals and tones drawn from the earth. Although not quite stygian or tenebrific, Seibel did prefer the colors of the night as a background upon which to serve food. He esteemed also the *yin* and *yang* of Dark and Light: the conception of matching opposites—dark/light, feminine/masculine, short/tall reappears with regularity with Seibel's tableware, but never with over-emphasis or stressed in an obvious manner. This sense of contrast in color and form appears continually, but never blatantly, never obviously. Even as a young man, Seibel had a decorous, seemly, and subtle design sense. While Roseville's Contemporary White lacked the glimmer and ivory voluptuous of *Contempora's* Sand White it nevertheless contrasted somewhat starkly with the intense darkness of matte Avocado. Just as Cecil Beaton delighted film audiences with his memorable Black and White Ascot,[10] so did Ben Seibel permit the '50s hostess the delight of setting a black and white table: *Contempora's* Charcoal and Sand White, *Raymor Modern Stoneware's* Avocado and Contemporary White. True sophistication is reflected by less, not more!

The discussion of the Roseville Raymor line ends with a mention about Ben Seibel's fondness for stands, warmers, holders—especially when made with non-ceramic material. These could be considered among the "Seibel Signature Pieces!" As far as I know none existed originally in the *Contempora* line, but with the stoneware shape they did. Since the ceramic stand for the swinging coffee pot was so fragile—and it came under heavy use when allowing the pot to "swing"—that Seibel agreed on the substitution of a metal meshed-like cradle that replaced the ceramic. These are not very aesthetically attractive, but they are quite scarce. Being made late in the rather short and harried life of *Raymor Modern Stoneware*, they are most collectible. The iron stands for the medium and large casseroles are stark and quite bleak, but still interesting. A simple metal frame for holding four casseroles when serving a huge buffet becomes an impressive architectural centerpiece.[11] The presence of all these stands, coupled with the evident domination of serving pieces, neatly catapults—albeit gently—this line into the category of buffet ware.

The cup (#150) and saucer (#151) in Terra Cotta. $12-15.

Autumn Brown creamer (#158) without its lid. These lids are very desirable, but relatively scarce. Without lid: $14-16. With lid: $30+.

Autumn Brown sugar bowl (#157). The base of the sugar reflects the cup. $25-30.

Four-quart bean pot (8") (#187) in mottled brown with the individual casserole (#199). Price: $80-90 for bean pot; $20-25 for individual casserole.

Two bean pots in Avocado Green (black). Price: $45-50.

No matter, *Raymor Modern Stoneware*, even if it did not fulfill its stated and desired role, has become one of the most sought after, desirable, and collectible tableware lines in the United States.

Above and right:
Two views of the 2 1/2-quart handled casserole. Price for Terra Cotta example: $60-65. Add another thirty percent for frogskin.

The fabulous Terra Cotta bun warmer (202)—one of the exceptional Roseville Raymor pieces. Price: $300+.

Three trivets: top, 5.50"; middle, 6.75"; bottom, 8.50". Each: $45-50.

Top of the double stack warmer (#201). It is proportionally shallower than the regular bean pot and has a recessed base. These are not common. Price: $200.

View of the recessed base. This piece fits over the larger bean pots.

The shirred egg. This is the first of the 200 series. It is a very shallow piece: 6.25" round and nearly 10" to the tip of the handle. Price: $60-70.

Ashtray in mottled Autumn Brown. Price: $20-25.

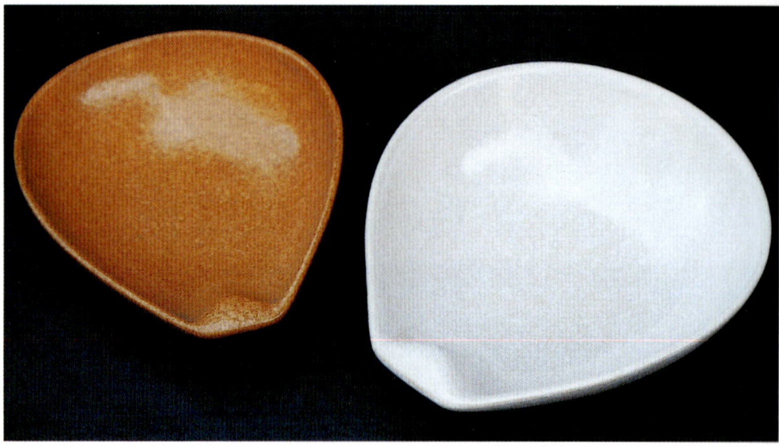

The fruit dish (5") (#192) in Terra Cotta, and the larger, but identically shaped, lug soup (#155) in Beach Gray. Both priced: $12-15.

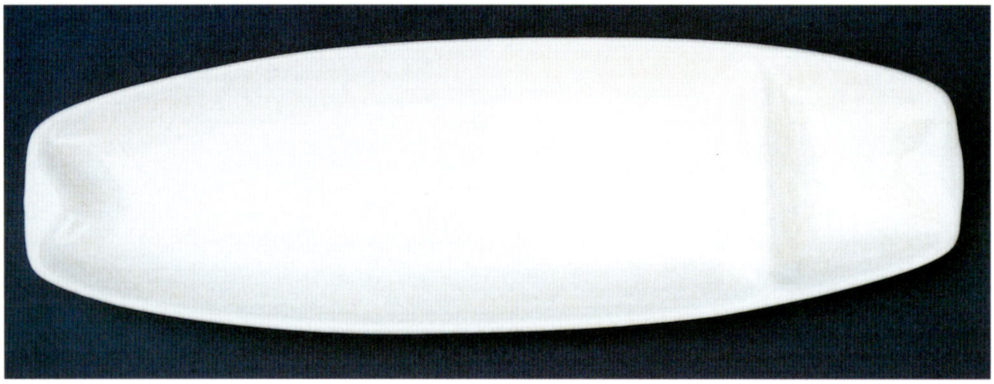

Individual Contemporary White corn server (#162) (12.50"). Some dealers label this item rare with prices to match, but while elusive, the price should never be over $30-35. Of course, to pay less is preferable.

The relish or jam pot (#172). This type of small covered pot or bowl, a.k.a. mustard, marmalade, or relish disappeared from most tableware lines in the 1950s. The coordinated items were replaced by jars of individual designs—in the shape of strawberries, oranges, even apples. My mother owned a jam pot in the shape of purple grapes. The spoon for the Roseville Raymor jam pot is one of the rarest of the line's pieces. Price for the pot alone: $40-50.

Notice how these three plates blend in both shape and color. The 8.50" salad plate (in Terra Cotta) is the hardest to find. Prices: Dinner (#152), $20-22; Salad (#153), $18-20; Bread & Butter (#154), $10-12.

Beach Gray teapot on a trivet. While the teapot and coffeepot are the same general shape, the collector can never be mislead: the coffee pot has two nubbin projections to allow it to hang and swing. Price: $120-140.

The "robin's egg blue" color of these two restyled plates is quite poor. These restyled pieces are not easy to locate, and they do not have the rich, distinctive qualities of the original plates. One should not pay top prices for such dulled versions. This dinner plate should be priced $10-12 and the bread & butter, $5-7.

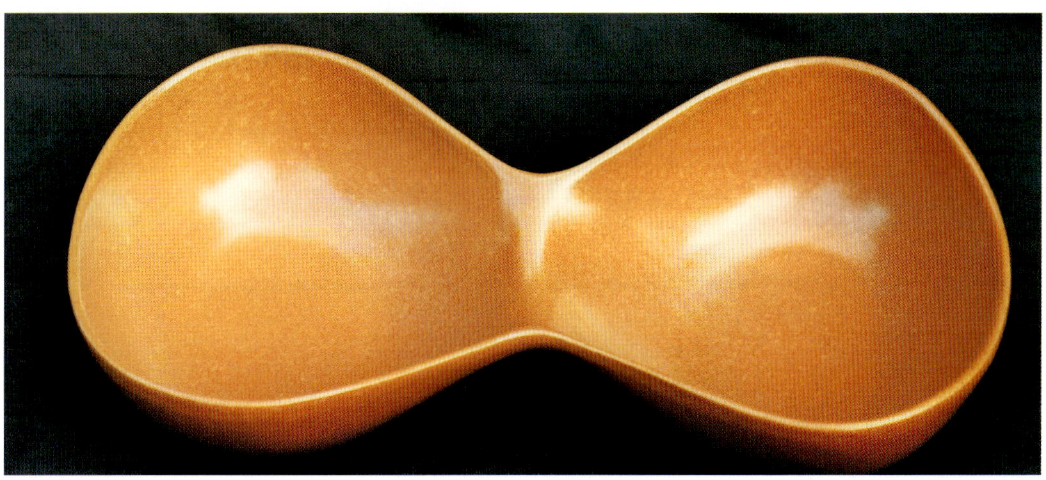

The very popular divided vegetable bowl (#165)—often jokingly called "the Amazon warrior's breastplate." An unusual design copied a few years later by Eva Zeisel in her Hallcraft Century. Price: $50-60.

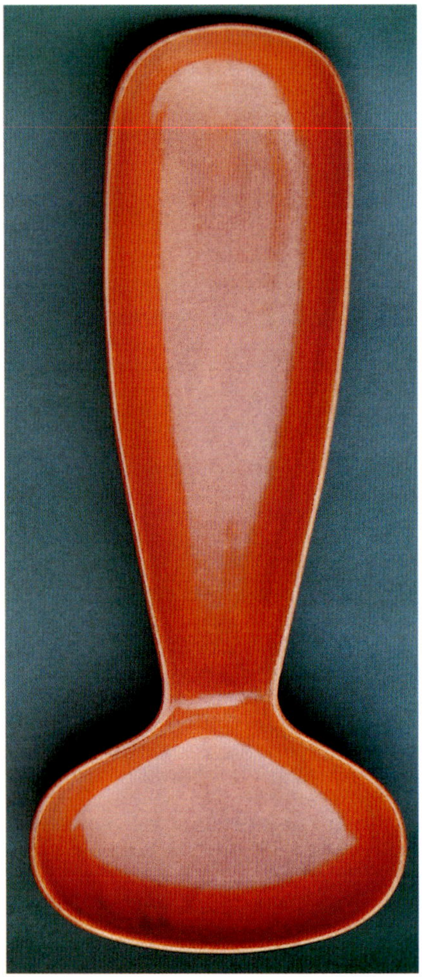

A second item extremely popular with collectors: the celery/olive—called the "exclamation point bowl!" Seibel was very inventive when designing this line. This particular bowl was purchased in the early 1990s for about $8.00. Today, one could scarcely hope to buy it for less than $40.

Above and below:
The individual casserole (#156) fits perfectly on the salad plate, but even more so when its lid is removed. Notice how the Terra Cotta glaze changes color under different lights. Hostesses can use this changeability to their advantage.

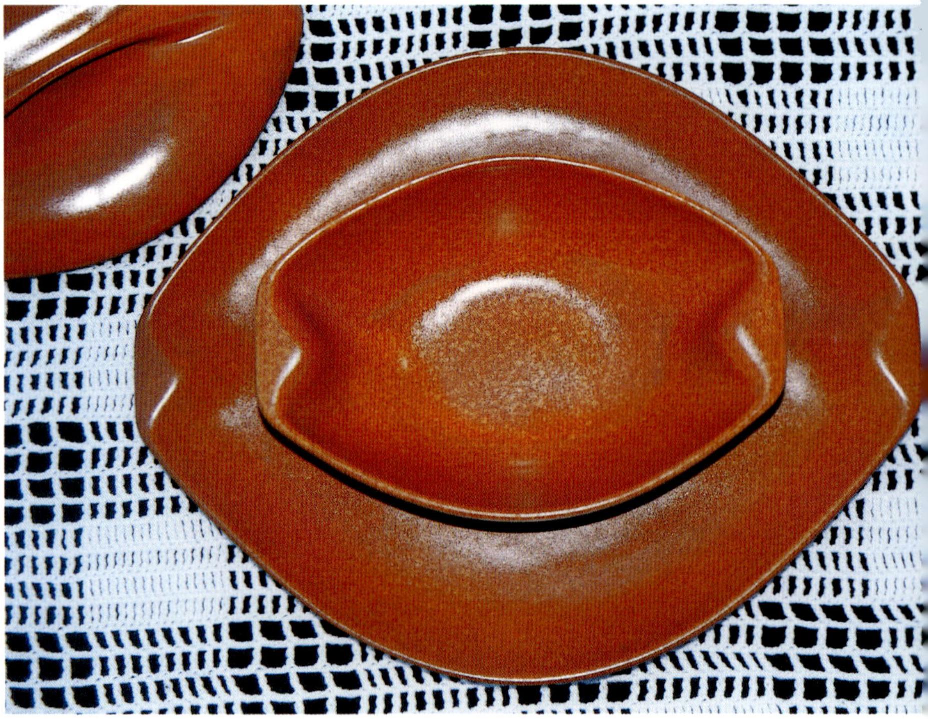

The sides of the pickle (9.50") (#191) swell to a great degree compared with the 14" platter (#163). Both are Beach Gray, but the pickle is slightly mottled. Prices: Platter, $25-30; pickle dish, $15-18.

The platter in Autumn Brown matte—a rich dark chocolate.

One of the Raymor Modern Stoneware's "glamour pieces," the handled fruit bowl (#166). Extremely rare and highly prized, the frogskin version can be priced as high as $800. Here it is in Avocado matte (black) and would cost about $600. Known to collectors as the "fruit basket," it is an exceptional item to possess.

The coffee pot (#176) in the ceramic stand. While not as rare as the fruit bowl, collectors do struggle to add one to their collections. The stands are very fragile. Prices: Coffee pot, $200+; stands, $100+.

When seen alone, Contemporary White can seem grayish, but when placed next to a Beach Gray piece, the difference can be seen quickly.

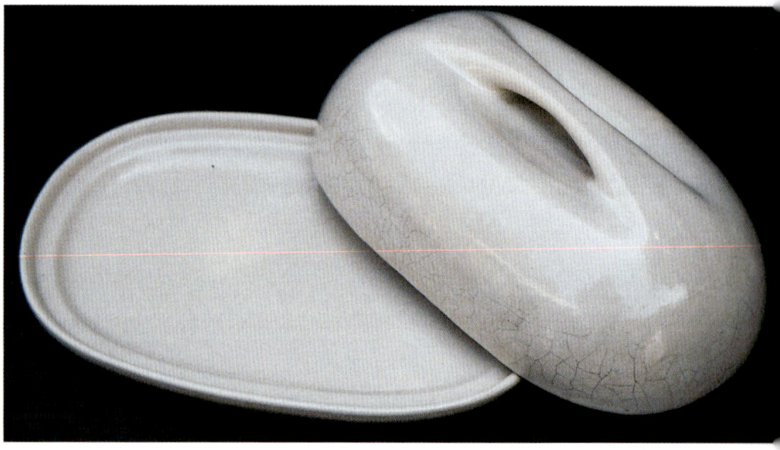

Above and below:
The high arched butter dish can be prone to crazing and staining. This one is in Contemporary White. If in very good condition: $65-70.

The Contemporary White mottled mug (#179)—short handled version. Price: $40-45.

Left and right:
A lovely example of Frogskin on an individual casserole. This color can vary widely in intensity. This is a good example. Price (for Frogskin): $40-50.

Close-up of the mottling—quite exceptional.

The shakers (#168) stands out starkly against the "black" bean pot. Quite a contrast. Price for shaker: $10-12.

Three mottled cups (#150): Contemporary White (top), Avocado Green (mild mottling), and Autumn Brown. Cups in all variations are quite easy to find. Price: $10-15.

The medium casserole (#183) measures 10.50" long and 8.750" wide. These do not seem to be as popular as the bean pots or handled casseroles. Price: $50-55.

Since the ceramic stand was very soon to be found fragile, Seibel designed a substitute stand in metal. They proved more sturdy, but not as attractive. Actually these are quite scarce because the entire line was being questioned regarding its viability. The coffee pot is in Frogskin—quite a stunning combination. Price (for set): $400+.

The water jug in Beach Gray accompanied by two long handled mugs. These mugs are more desirable than the short handled version. Prices: Water jug (#189), $85-95; Mug (#179), $55-60.

The Terra Cotta gravy (#190). The regular vegetable dish is a larger version. The gravy is really not hard to find. Price: $25-30.

Pfaltzgraff's *Country-Time*

The more common *Country-Time* back stamp.

"America's Most Complete Line of Serving Accessories"

Yes, this is how Ben Seibel's *Country-Time* was advertised! It was billed as having the most complete line of serving pieces. This, however, was not exactly true, for Pfaltzgraff's 1950 line *Gourmet* outdid the newer shape. *Country-Time* appeared around 1952. Later, in 1967 the *Yorktowne* shape (designed by Maury Mountain) put both to shame with its superabundance of oven-to-table pieces.

Still *Country-Time* was rich with accessories, extremely fanciful in shape, and displays a clever eccentricity that makes it attractive to both Seibel fans and the general collector. Just as Sister Margaretta said of Maria in the *Sound of Music*: "Maria makes me laugh!"—*Country-Time* makes me laugh! It is plumply amusing, Mid-Century-Modern 'quirky,' not quite serious, and certainly not staid or proper, yet still honest. Like Maria, *Country-Time* is a delight.

Country-Time is one of the most unusually designed American tableware lines.

As will be mentioned again, the criteria for a "dinnerware" line is that it contains a dinner plate, a cup, and a saucer. *Country-Time* does just this, so officially it ranks as dinnerware. Yet, Seibel strongly emphasized the accessories—the pots, bowls, trays—and it is these pieces that make the line sing!

Raymor executives must have been impressed with Seibel's work because this is the third time the young man was engaged to design a complete line of Raymor tableware. The time sequence[1] indicates that Seibel must have been working on the Roseville line at the same time he was developing *Country-Time* (or *visa versa*). In fact, his Roseville cup crossed over the bridge and shows up here among the *Country-Time* pieces. Three designs within just four years certainly proves Raymor found Seibel's work critically potable even if the average consumer preferred a more conservative dinnerware diet.[2]

However *Country-Time* departed drastically from the sleek and *soigné* elegance of *Contempora* and Roseville Raymor. There can be noted among the platters and plates, the peasant roundness of jugs, bowls, and pots, a certain Italian bumptiousness, a flavor of the sun-baked Italian hills, or the implied scent of olive oil, roasted tomatoes, basil, and softly plump purple olives. This was, no doubt, a planned concept as Raymor was intimately connected with colorful Italian craft designs—perhaps the company directly stipulated to Seibel what was desired in *Country-Time*: dinnerware to be used during a summer cavort in the country!

At this point, the reader will be tangentially led astray—but a point needs explanation. The company Raymor has been continually mentioned in the paragraphs above, and it has always been assumed that Raymor bore a vital and legitimate relationship with *Country-Time*—as it did with Roseville and *Contempora* before it and Universal after it. *Country-Time* was introduced in 1952—as mentioned above. Seibel also used the identical Roseville cup for *Country-Time*. The assumption regarding a Raymor/Pfaltsgraff connection was strongly based, but was it true?

Ms Polly Stetler, Special Projects Coordinator at the Susquehanna Pfaltzgraff Company (York, Pennsylvania), is a careful and dedicated researcher. During our exchange of e-mail information, Ms Stetler raised some intriguing questions. After I had explained my beliefs about Raymor and Pfaltzgraff she replied:

> *I did discuss the Raymor connection with David Walsh* [Pfaltzgraff's archivist] *and he was of the opinion that Seibel worked directly with Pfaltzgraff and that it was not a Raymor-driven product. He commented that all the Raymor lines that he is aware of have "Raymor" on them. What do you think?*

Ms. Stetler's comment sent me immediately to the shelf where a few of my *Country-Time* pieces were stored. Looking at three pieces, I saw the mark shown at the top of page 50. My reply elicited a quick response:

> *I'm afraid I haven't been able to come up with much for you. I took a look through our files and found nothing that related to Raymor/Ben Seibel/Pfaltzgraff. I asked* [a company executive] *about his recollection of the line, and* [he] *was aware of Raymor, but knew of no connection between Raymor and Pfaltzxgraff- but couldn't say there wasn't a connection either.*

Ms Stetler wrote later:

> *In looking at our* [the Pfaltzgraff archives] *Country-Time and Snowflake pieces, I found none that had "Raymor" on them, and our only catalogue folder does not mention Raymor. We have Country-Time pieces in blue on gray, brown on creamy white, and blue on yellow/gold. I wonder if this last colorway is the Saffron Yellow? We have no cobalt blue or teal blue, but I wonder if they are the color referred to, but crossed out* [in the advertising brochure] *Aztec Blue?... I am sending you a copy of the brochure under separate cover. ... I hope these help a little.*

When the brochure arrived it proved invaluable. Since I was given permission to use it, photographs of the pages appear on pages 50 to 52. But what have we learned? (1) That *Country-Time* bears two different back stamps: one with Raymor mentioned, one with no Raymor mentioned. (2) The pieces with Raymor in the back stamp seem to be confined to the solid blue or teal pieces and the Smoky Gray pieces. At least the five pieces of Smoky Gray in my personal collection mention Raymor. The Saffron Yellow pieces and the Natural Beige pieces bear the back stamp shown at the top of this section. (3) The Smoky Gray pieces in the Pfaltzgraff archives do NOT mention Raymor.

Seemingly a mystery! Could it be that Raymor was involved at the beginning of the negotiations between Seibel and Pfaltzgraff, but later ceased involvement? Some pieces might have been produced during this time—Aztec Blue and Smoky Gray—and bore the name "Raymor." When Raymor no longer was the "middle-man," its name was removed from the back stamp? This is the only answer I have at this time.

Two other persons had comments on the possible connection between Raymor and Pfaltzgraff. When asked directly, Mr. Walsh e-mailed his opinion.

> *At this time we have no information that links Pfaltzgraff with Raymor other than the backstamp that can be found on some Ben Seibel Country-Time product[s.] There are a couple of possibilities that could explain the two backstamps (with and without the name Raymor.)*
>
> *The first scenario would be that Pfaltzgraff commissioned Ben Seibel to design a new shape and decoration to be manufactured and distributed by Pfaltzgraff. At a later date foir one reason or another an arrangement was made for distribution through the Raymor organization.*
>
> *The second scenario which I believe more feasible is that Seibel designed the Country-Time shape and pattern for Raymor. Raymor had the product manufactured by Pfaltzgraff. When Raymor decided to no longer distribute the product, Pfaltzgraff negotiated the rights to continue producing and distributing the line. This could account for the number of Pfaltzgraff shapes (particularly from the Gourmet line) that can be found in the Country-Time pattern.*

Michael Pratt also added his opinion.

I also have pieces [of Country-Time] marked Raymor as well. I have an industry notice somewhere that states that Raymor was working with Pfaltzgraff on a line by a known designer, and somewhere ... I have more specific information. Just don't have time to track it down now. My off the record suspicion is that initially there may have been serious talks for Raymor to distribute, but this changed very quickly.

Obviously an area of Ben Seibel research eagerly awaiting in-depth study.

When Ms. Stetler's brochure was studied it was the first time I have had the good fortune to see the metal stands with the ceramic candleholders. These remind me somewhat of constructions I made as a child using my Erector Set. The Seibel designed stands for *Country-Time* look somewhat awkward on the tabletop. They must be considered quite rare.

There is surely a rusticity in the design and a semblance of earthenware. Surprises, yes! Sleekness, certainly not! The *Country-Time* would benefit from a large and tumbling bouquet of wild flowers—daisies, goldenrod, gentians, tansy, and German chamomile. While the two earlier Seibel designs (*Contempora* and Roseville Raymor) would exult in the stark formality of *cymbidiums* and *cattleyas*, *Country-Time* needs fieldfare.

There are thirty items belonging to the *Country-Time* tableware line, and while none of the pieces are easy to locate, some are more difficult than others. The divided casseroles, the fork and spoon, the tureen, the samovar all border on the very scarce. The accompanying metal stands with ceramic warmers are truly rare. These pieces, typically a Seibel signature, often were separated from the piece they served and once removed were hard to identify. The items were:

Bowl, individual salad, 6"	(135)[3]
Bowl, large salad, 10.50"	(134)
Butter warmer (S)[4]	(101)
Casserole/cover, individual, 12 ounce	(162)
Casserole/cover, 2 quart (S)	(165)
Casserole, divided, 2 covers	(185)
Casserole, rectangular 3 part, 3 covers, 21" x 6.50" (S)	(190)
Coffee pot, 10 cup (S)	(187)
Beverage samovar, 28 cup (S)	(197)
Creamer	(157)
Cruet, oil or vinegar	(132)
Cup, closed handle	(180)
Cup, open handle[5]	(180)
Gravy (S)	(102)
Jug, 2 quart	(186)
Meat board and platter[6]	(126)
Plate, 8.50"	(177)
Plate, 10"	(199)
Plate, grill[6], 11.50"	(188)
Platter, 11"	(128)
Platter, 12"	(129)
Platter, 13"	(130)
Saucer	(189)
Salt, 5 holes	(117)
Pepper, 3 holes	(118)
Sugar/cover	(156)
Tray, relish & cheese[7], 16" x 6.50"	(114)
Tureen, 6 quart (S)	(167)
Fork, wood handle	(134)
Spoon, wood handle	(135)

The Italianate roundness of covered casserole, individual salad bowl, and coffee server. All in Saffron Yellow, with the casserole bearing the fruit design, the other two the "snowflake. Prices: Casserole, $50-60; Salad bowl, $12-14; Coffee pot, $60-70.

The sugar bowl and the handle-less creamer are also roughly molded. The creamer stands 5.50", and would take a strong hand to grip it about the top. The sugar is 3" high and measures 7" to the tip of its handle. These are NOT delicate pieces. They are honest, earthy, and well worth collecting: Prices: Creamer, $10-12; Sugar, $15-18.

In *Country-Time*, Seibel introduced a new material—wood. The use of wood and metal was to become an important ingredient in his work. Unfortunately these wooden inserts, and also the metal/ceramic stands, rarely appear for sale with their companion pieces. This problem arises in most of the Seibel lines. Beware of "coat-hanger" substitute stands—these are all too common.

Seibel came close to adoration when dealing contemplating and with samovars or large beverage servers. These items appear over and over, even in lines with a conventional coffee server. The 28-cup swinging coffee samovar here in *Country-Time* reaches monumental proportions. Unfilled, this piece weighs eight pounds, is nearly 13 inches tall, 9 inches to the tip of the spout, and a substantial 11 inches round. The "roundness" is not perfect as there is a considerable bulge under the spout. As an experiment, one was filled with water and it became virtually impossible to lift: the only way coffee could be poured from this immensity would be by swinging it gently over a waiting cup! This samovar is really useless without a stand and swing.

The casseroles too are prodigious in size and complexity. There are three casseroles: four if the collector can accept the tureen as a casserole. One of my favorite pieces is the divided casserole with two lids (185). The base is divided in a manner Seibel used later in the *Impromptu* shape produced by Iroquois, and before in the *Contempora* divided vegetable. It presents a very unusual style, but the lids are creaking and problematic. They are charming, but still definitely difficult. The two lids do not seem to be interchangeable and take considerable maneuvering to replace them, or even—on my example—to open them. While not ergonomically correct, the design is appealing. Beware, however, and do not try to force the ceramic "pins" into place: they look highly vulnerable to breakage.

The creamer, looking straight down, and ironically, the opening is a perfect round.

The sugar from above, with the cover removed. It must be repeated, this is one of the largest and heaviest sugar bowls in American dinnerware. Seibel perhaps over emphasized the need for size in these two ordinary pieces, and collectors should be thankful he did: they are very primitive and very beautiful.

This cup was the first one used by Seibel and was taken directly from *Raymor Modern Stoneware*. It was soon replaced. Price: $12-14.

Two examples of the *Country-Time* back stamp mentioning Raymor. The one to the left was on an Aztec Blue grill plate, the one on the right appears on a Smoke Gray butter warmer.

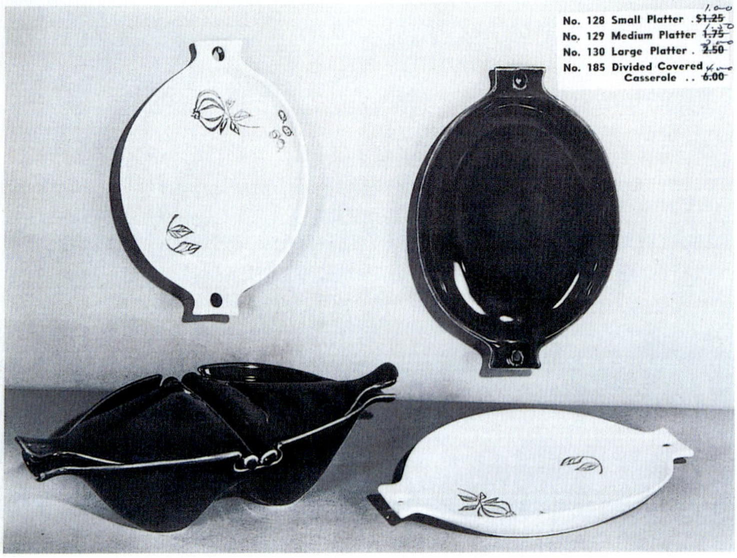

The platters were meant to hang on the kitchen wall. One platter (the medium) and the divided covered casserole appear in dark blue.

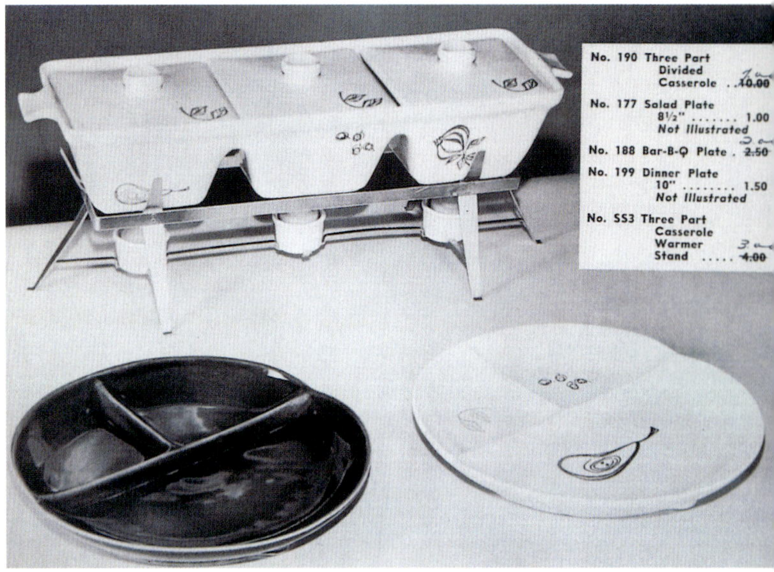

The three part divided casserole needed a great deal of room on the table: it was attractive in an awkward way. The price has been reduced from $10.00 to $7.00: today it would cost $100-110. This price includes the warmer. I have never seen this casserole offered for sale without the warmer. The grill plates were made in solid color and decorated as seen here.

The coffee pot with its stand and warmer, the cup/saucer set, and the blue creamer matched here not with the lower sugar but with the two-handled individual covered casserole. The "Roseville Raymor" cup is not shown in this brochure.

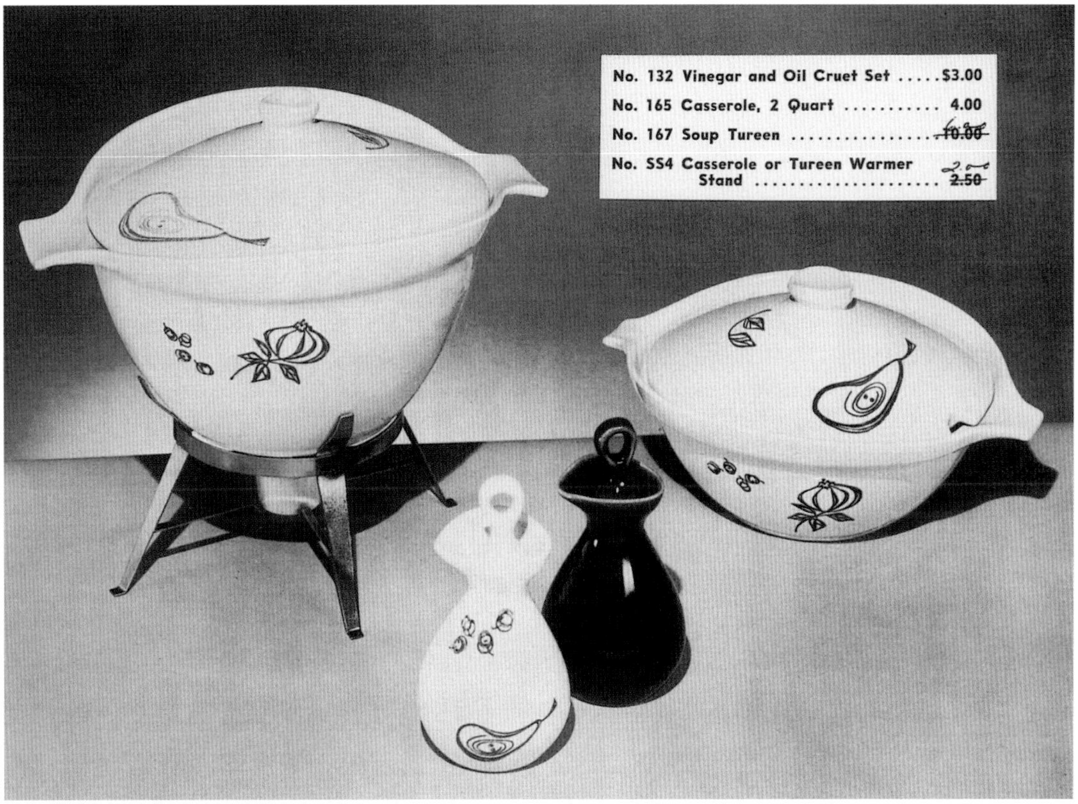

The huge soup tureen astride its warmer, which, by the way, also fits the casserole (right). Two cruets are in the center. Even though Aztec Blue was crossed out as a color choice in this brochure, the photographs still included this blue. Notice the prices in the box, and how some were reduced: the warmer stand from $2.50 to $2.00. This also means they were sold separately. Instead of being priced at $6.00, today's collector would have to pay from $85-90 for the tureen. Notice also, it seems that the photographer switched the interchangeable covers: the casserole cover has the opening meant for the tureen.

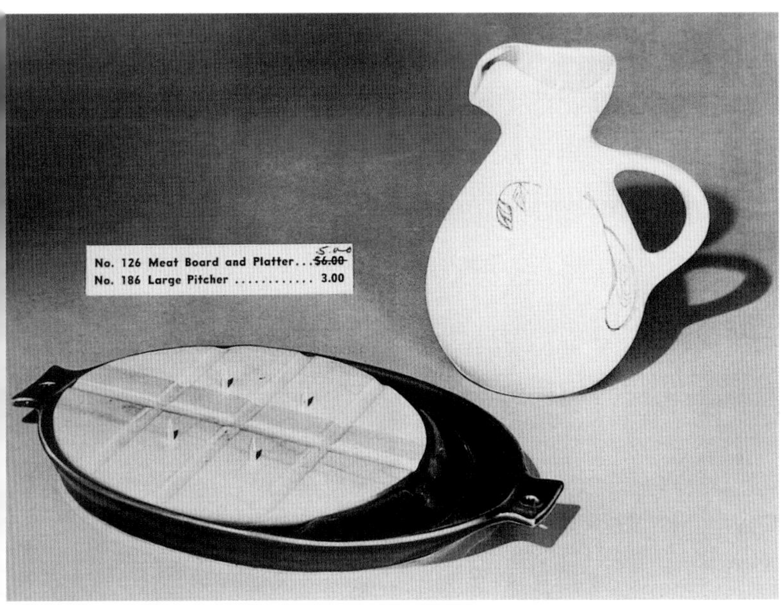

Look how neatly the wooden "spiked" insert fits within the meat platter. Called the meat board and platter, these are quite difficult to find intact in the collectible marketplace. Be prepared to pay $45-50 for one. Remember, without the wood insert pay no more than $25-30.

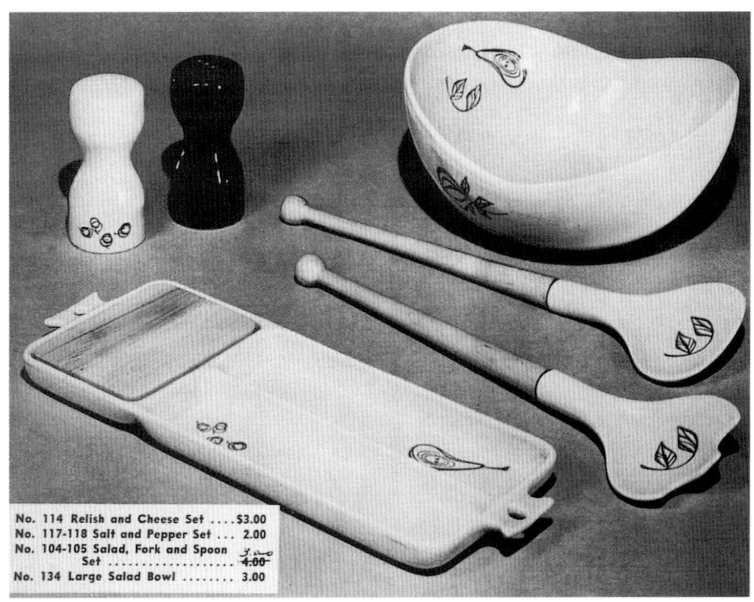

The cheese and relish tray also has a wooden insert—unfortunately it often has been separated from the tray. The spoon and fork are special treats to locate: they both have a wooden handle and are rarely seen. Price for either: $45-50.

The unusual butter warmer (left) and the slightly larger gravy (right)—both on their own stands. The sugar bowl stands between them. The gravy would be suitably priced today between $35-40.

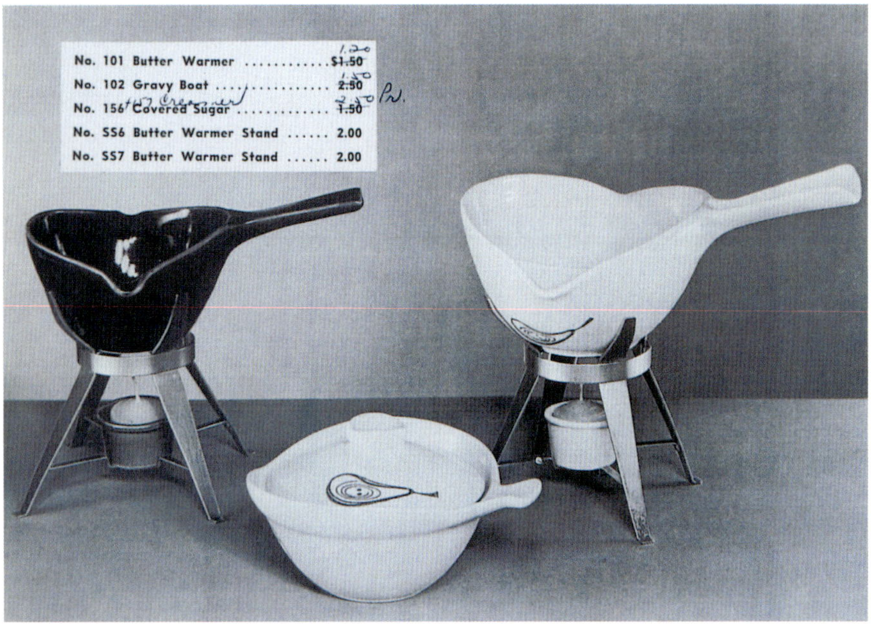

Another close-up—this time the open handled cup. This is sometimes called the "mug" and is easier to find than the Roseville "look-alike." Price: $8-10.

Notice the wide, sturdy stand to keep the samovar in place. It could hardly be called a graceful item. The samovar with all its parts could be priced as high as $125 and many *Country-Time* enthusiasts would not hesitate to pay the price.

The 10" dinner plate—not seen very often. The salad plate and the saucer are strangely difficult to locate. Prices: Dinner plate, $14-16; Salad plate, $10-12; Saucer, $5-6.

What of the treatments appearing on *Country-Time*? As usual with the work of Ben Seibel in the 1950s, the glazes and decorations were simple, forthright, and perhaps a tad bit naïve. First there were two solid glazes, and today both are quite scarce. A rich dark blue called Aztec Blue and a light warmer, slightly "greenish" blue called Teal Blue. The former is easier to locate than the latter, but probably not much of the solid glazes was produced. Researchers, at this time, are not even sure if all *Country-Time* items were available in the two solid blues. This would make an interesting project for a Pfaltzgraff enthusiast. And please remember, both these blues were penned out on the "Colors Available" page of the brochure/pamphlets found in the archives by Polly Stetler.

The Saffron Yellow cheese/relish with the wood insert in place. Price: $25-30.

A closer view of the cruet—either oil or vinegar. The stopper is elusive and is often missing. Price: $35-40.

In *Country-Time*, Seibel did not differentiate the salt from the pepper by size, but the salt had five holes, the pepper three. Price: $35-40 the pair.

The small platter in the Natural Beige glaze. This glaze is not seen as often as the yellow and the smoky blue. Price: $18-20.

The front and bottom views of the relish/cheese tray—without the wooden insert. Notice the underneath is also divided, and also please notice the stamp does not mention Raymor. Price (without the wood insert) runs from $18-20.

Notice that this cheese/relish has perforated handles. This was to allow it to be hung upon a kitchen wall. These are not more valuable, but were the original design.

Left and right:
Three views of the huge samovar without its handle and stand. Note the "knobs" which allow it to be "hung" on the stand. Stripped though it is, collectors would not mind paying from $50-60 for this piece.

Top view of the divided casserole. Even though the covers fit erratically (as easily seen) they fit no other way. Basically crude, this item is as delightful as a naughty child. Price: $75-80.

Above and below:
The same casserole with one lid lifted and then both removed. The lids seem to be quite fragile and will bear no forcing.

The individual covered casserole could also be called a "marmite." It is quite small in contrast with the other casseroles. These are priced in today's market at $35-40.

The grill plate is seen in the dark, rich Aztec Blue. This piece has Raymor mentioned in the stamp. Price: $22-25.

The coffee pot in Aztec Blue. While quite scarce, many collectors eschew the solid glazes. Thus both versions tend to be priced the same. $55-60.

The grill plate (or Bar-B-Q plate) in the more common Smoke Gray and the fruit/leaf design. Price: $18-20.

The decorative approaches were only two: a "snowflake" burst and a fruit/leaf design. These two decorations—widely scattered and really quite crude—appeared stamped[8] upon three glazes: a rather earthy (greenish?) yellow (officially called Saffron Yellow), a blue gray (called Smoke Gray), and a warm ivory (called Natural Beige). The last named is the most difficult to find and the decorations are usually in milk chocolate brown. Again, please remember, Natural Beige appears typed in on the "Colors Available" brochure page. It seems to have been a substitute for the removed blues.

When listening to a verbal description, the new collector can be excused for believing the butter warmer and the gravy are very similar. Actually these two are very different; one is simply not a larger version of the other. Notice how "tear-shaped" is the gravy—quite sharply pointed at its pouring end and including a barrier. I really do not think the infinitesimal "spout" at the round (right) end is actually usable. The butter warmer is rounder and easily pours from both spouts. I have seen photos of the gravy where the internal barrier is not seen—thus it pays to have a piece of china "in hand"—if possible. The butter warmer (without its stand) is nicely priced at $30-35; the gravy at $35-40.

The jug. Again it bears repeating that Ben Seibel liked jugs—all manner of jugs appear in his tableware lines. "Chunky" and loveable, this jug is priced at $40-45.

Michael Pratt, author and collector, is gratefully acknowledged as the source of this strikingly different Pfaltzgraff meat platter. It is missing the wooden insert, but it is the color that astounds: a rich and yet soft brown—not unlike the best of Dutch cocoa. To date, the platter is the only piece seen wearing this unusual glaze—hopefully more will come to light. I know Mike would want to share this treasure with readers. Price: NP (No Price).

Many collectors adore this shape, and an equal number regard it as unappealing. No matter, it was designed by Ben Seibel and produced by Pfaltzgraff, and had a connection, albeit tenuous, with Raymor. And it was labeled as a Seibel work. If a collector truly is interested in Ben Seibel, *Country-Time* cannot be overlooked. If an individual collector does not like the heaviness, the size, the pleasant crudity, the informality, the atmosphere of Italian peasantry, this certainly can be understood, but *Country-Time* is still the work of Ben Seibel, and must be accepted as a legitimate creation of the designer and a true product of the era.

Universal Raymor

Continuing the Connection

The name of the company that manufactured this ware, Universal Potteries, Inc., is not old. In fact, the Atlas-Globe China Company (Cambridge, Ohio, 1925-1932) reorganized and was renamed the Oxford Pottery Company. Another reorganization in 1934 brought about a new name: Universal Potteries. Producing semivitreous dinnerware until 1954, Universal ceased this type of ware and made tiles. Then in 1956 another renaming took place—this one permanent—and the company, quite successful, was known as the Oxford Tile Company. After twenty-years, the tile company ceased all production.

Since the pedigree of this company is complex, an outline might be useful:

Bradshaw China Company (1901-1921) sold to A.O.C. Ahrendis.
Crescent China Company that very soon became...
Atlas China Company (1920-1925), merged with Globe Pottery that was another plant owned by Mr. Ahrendis and became...
Atlas-Globe China (1925-1932)
Oxford Pottery (1932-1934)
Universal Potteries (1934-1956) (manufactured tiles only1954-1956)
Oxford Tile Company (1956-1976) (company ceased to exist).

Back stamp of *Universal Raymor*. This has been called the most attractive back stamp in American dinnerware. The stamp always mentions the name of the treatment.

This is the rather changeable career and name line of a company whose only real interest—and here it is hoped no reader is offended—to American dinnerware collectors spans the twenty years it was known as Universal Potteries: really only eighteen years since Universal was manufacturing tiles the last two years it was operating under that name.

Except for the popular line *Ballerina* and the decal known as Cattail, and perhaps the 1937 line called *UPICO*, Universal's contributions to the excitation of collectors was very limited. Thus, the introduction of an exciting new shape near the end of Universal's existence comes as a wondrous surprise.

While some researchers proclaim 1955 as the birth of *Universal Raymor*, this date must be accepted with some reservations. For all purposes, Universal is believed to have turned from dinnerware to tiles in 1954. This does not mean, however, there was not a last moment plunge to rally the company as a dinnerware producer—very similar perhaps to the Roseville situation—and here again Raymor's Irving Richards, as producer of hopeful miracles, probably turned to his good friend, designer Ben Seibel. The result was the graceful, pleasantly flowing line *Universal Raymor*. All conjecture, naturally, but with the strong possibility of certitude.

Other assumptions follow. Since Universal sailed into the solid, more profitable, sea of tile making, this fourth Raymor/Seibel connection seems not to have saved the situation. *Déjà vu* Roseville again! Except for glaze inconsistencies, few collectors complain about the physical production of *Raymor Modern Stoneware*. But in the case of *Universal Raymor*, the general consensus is that the line is not well made. This opinion is mildly and gentle spoken because collectors seem to harbor fond feelings for the shape despite any faults it might possess. We are NOT discussing the design, but the translation of that design into a product! The shape has all the characteristics of the Mid-Century-Modern style, but when production took over this shape, the result was a tad indifferent. We really cannot say slovenly or slipshod, but there is a careless, indifferent quality about the glaze, the decorations, the general manufacturing quality. Be aware, this is not the same case as Raymor's *Contempora* where the shape itself was a little insouciant or *degagé*—a product of a brilliant but still searching talent. *Contempora* was manufactured well; whatever faults it had—and there were really only a few—stemmed from the design itself. But with *Universal Raymor*, Seibel developed a fully mature, skillfully conceived shape. Seibel, no longer experimenting, knew exactly what he wanted and accomplished it superbly. It was the production, not the creation, that here can be faulted.

Notwithstanding the negative criticism, *Universal Raymor* is a shape of major importance and commands a vocal and wide appreciative following. If we can pursue the assumptions a little further, probably the line was not greeted enthusiastically in 1954-55, and the careless production soon stopped. Surely, Universal was not producing this Raymor dinnerware at the same time it was firing tiles. And beside, the name "Universal" ceased to exist in 1956. A very short time to flood the American market with a rather carelessly produced dinnerware line! No, this line lived a short, brittle life and disappeared into the dust very soon.

All this contributes to the relative scarcity of the pieces, and the high prices being paid by those collectors who madly are avid to acquire what is still wafting about waiting to be corralled and shelved. There is a "franticness" about some aspects of *Universal Raymor* information. A number of important researchers/collectors no longer will share material or information about this shape. Several times my queries have been countered with a firm (sharp?) NO! Fortunately, a few open and friendly people are willing to supply both information and photographs. Authors writing about collectibles depend upon those willing to share. Knowledge about *Universal Raymor* is scant, assumptive, and based a great deal upon conjecture—logical conjecture to be sure, but still conjecture.

The scant knowledge is the result of a dearth of paper material: brochures, price lists, advertising sheets. There are very few of these available to the general researcher and collector. What few paper items there are seem to be guarded deep within vaulted possession of those advanced collectors who wisely realized—a number of years ago—that interest in Ben Seibel and *Universal Raymor* would burgeon considerably. Interest has grown enormously, and those who appreciate this Seibel shape insist—and here I tend to agree—that even the back stamp is the most fascinating of its kind to appear on any American ceramic ware line.

Since very few official brochures are available, a list of individual items generally must be drawn from what the collector acquires piece by piece. This slow procedure can be rewarding, as each new item added to one's personal list becomes a personal triumph. This manner of acquiring knowledge is rather more satisfying than perusing a price list, albeit at times frustratingly slow.

- Plate, 10"
- Plate, salad, 8.50"
- Plate, bread & butter, 6.50"
- Bowl, large salad, 13" x 11.75"
- Bowl, vegetable, 9" x 8"
- Bowl, cereal, 7" x 6.50"
- Bowl, fruit, 6" x 5 50"
- Platter, handled, 15"
- Platter, handled, 13"
- Gravy
- Underliner for above
- Vegetable, divided, handled
- Cup
- Saucer
- Coffee pot
- Teapot
- Jug, 11"
- Shaker, salt
- Shaker, pepper
- Casserole/lid
- Sugar/lid
- Creamer
- Tray, TV
- Tureen w/underplate
- Tray, 3 part, 16" x 13" "meal server"
- Spaghetti bowl w/cover

Michael Pratt, one of the most knowledgeable of Mid-Century-Modern collector/researchers, states the last two items are to be considered the "most rare" pieces of this line. The three-part tray is identified as "a triply divided bowl with three separate lids and it is called the three-compartment covered food thermos." Mr. Pratt's opinion on *Universal Raymor* rarity affects my hasty comment (made below) that the salad plate is the most elusive.

Certainly this is a very respectable number of pieces—including some surprises. Ben Seibel liked "surprises"! The offering of a coffee server AND a teapot is very unusual in a line that encompasses only thirty items. In fact, such munificence was uncommon after World War II. Seibel rarely designed both. In fact in his later work included a "beverage server" of generic possibilities: coffee or tea. Often, if he felt the need for two beverage servers, the second one took upon itself the prepossessing grandeur of an impressive samovar—complete with warmer or holder. Seibel was tending, even in his younger days, to lean (or sway) toward buffet presentation. In this softly spoken line, the emphasis is on the typical dining table. Although, there are a few items—the divided and handled vegetable bowl (sometimes called a relish), for example—that bestride between the buffet and the formal table.

Certainly the scarcest of the *Universal Raymor* pieces are the last four on the list: TV tray, "meal server" tray, tureen with its underliner, and the covered spaghetti bowl. The tureen is not overly deep (6") but is a full 11" round and has the typical Universal double-lipped rim. The surprising item is the underliner: this piece has a raised well in the center and presages the trivet server in *Intaglio*. This fact reinforces the belief that ceramic designers often "reuse" their most creative ideas.

There is a seeming anomaly within this shape: the pieces most difficult to acquire are the dinner plates, the teacups and saucers. As stated above, the salad plate is most elusive. The collector must be aware, however, when "difficulty" is mentioned, we are really only mentioning those pieces that SHOULD BE quite easy to locate. We are not discussing those items—as the tri-covered food thermos and the lidded spaghetti bowl—which are virtually unknown with decades passing without their being found. Plates, cups, saucers, when first produced, are the most numerous, but over the years these "common" pieces are most often broken, replaced, and broken again. When the householder becomes tired of the set, the plates are given or thrown away while the large platters, large impressive bowls and casseroles are thought worthy of being placed in a china cabinet or relegated to the storage attic for a daughter's dowry. This predisposition is the cause of the existence of so many old covered casseroles: they were just too grandiose to be thrown into the dust bin!

Upon rereading, I wonder if what was stated in the preceding paragraph was completely true. Perhaps a more positive approach would be more helpful. What are the easiest pieces to find in this shape? Surely the creamer: found more often than the low sugar bowl. The gravy also appears readily in auctions, and the vegetable bowl. When the collector stops at these three pieces, a broad gap intervenes. In all my years of awareness regarding *Universal Raymor*, only two teapots have been seen—both Golden Burst—and only one coffee pot—also Golden Burst. Casseroles seem more available than those quaint divided and handled relishes, and I have never touched a T.V. tray or a meal server. These have only been seen in photographs. To be accurate, it would be best to admit the entire line is extremely difficult to locate, but with the creamer, the gravy, and the vegetable bowl a little less difficult. This statement better expresses my opinion.

Now what of the ceramic material from which this line was made? When the collector handles the various pieces, he/she—if at all discerning—immediately notices a "lightness," a sense of "porousness," even "sponginess" in the item's weight. The items look solid but they are truly like the bones of birds—light, delicate, almost as if there were air pockets within the ceramic. This ceramic airiness can also lend a quality of ethereality, of fragility to the shape—and not exactly in positive terms. Again, it cannot be assumed Seibel was given the right to choose the clay, just as he probably had no control of the production methods. These questions and their almost impossible answers merely add considerable mystery and interest to this shape.

Not only is the ceramic material composing this shape "light," the design itself eschewed any physical heaviness. With *Universal Raymor* Ben Seibel allowed no solidly and weighty behemoth casserole to float across the dinning table, no immense bean pot standing strict and tall on cast iron server legs. Here the approach was cautious, delicate—but not dainty—with upswept handles and small and curved finials. The curves were obvious. The largest piece is the tureen majestically, but not overpoweringly, ensconced on its liner, The salad bowl is also impressive with its substantial size, relatively low, the sides sweeping into an almost petal delicacy. The teapot is plump and round with a short full spout; the coffee pot (server) is taller, with a more curving spout. They are easily matched: the same lid fits both.

As said before, the creamer is easy to locate. It is an overtly charming item. One could make a modest little collection of these well-shaped creamers. They look beautiful artfully arranged together with the spouted rim looking ever so much like a mid-sixteenth century French high-standing collar. There are present some highly refined sculptural qualities.

The jug: oh, those wonderful Ben Seibel jugs! Here the collector looks forward to the Iroquois *Impromptu* water jug—the designer—even the genius—cannot escape personal inner conceptions and artistic approaches. Seibel simply loved water jugs and designed them with thoughtfulness and thoroughness. Sometimes these jugs repeated a certain design philosophy, and the viewer could say with certainty: "Oh, this jug looks as if it were designed by Ben Seibel!" But at other times, Seibel could surprise the viewer, the collector, and the gurus of research. Sometimes a jug, striking in concept, unusual in creation, would not look like a Seibel design AT ALL! Whatever the intention, these jugs were special!

However, it is not any individual item that garners most of the praise when pundits review this line: it is the handle. The handle that graces four pieces: the coffee pot, the teapot, the jug, and the creamer. Seibel wisely did not attach this handle to the teacup. The size of the handle differs with each of the four, but the style is duplicated: the space narrower at the top, more open towards the base. This allows for a firm levered hold—with no slippage allowed. To understand what I mean grasp the *Informal* jug as it arches high above the top of the jug itself, and then grasp the handle of the larger, but lighter, *Universal Raymor* jug. The difference in the balance between the two jugs can be perceived immediately. The handle is an example of model engineering.

Now, what about the treatments? As far as can be ascertained there are eight. All appear on the same satiny semi-glossy white, and all are quite modest: subtle, understated in both size and color, small and retiring in shape and placement. Of the eight, Golden Burst is—by far—the most common. In fact, fully eighty percent of the available treatments seem to turn up as Golden Burst. It is a pleasure to find a piece not wearing this treatment, and, unfortunately, this makes the collector tend to distain the treatment. Golden Burst is really quite beautiful. Look closely at the center of the "bursts" and one sees a series of delicate +: quite a special touch. I know of an entire collection made up entirely of Golden Burst, and the owner, Doug Way, is completely satisfied.

The treatments listed below are accompanied by official Universal descriptions.

Boutique White (Series 1100).

Festive Leaves (Series 2100). Four leaves and their shadows. Colors are olive green, russet brown, peacock blue.

San Souci (Series 2200). Full of light hearted charm, soft shades of blue, turquoise, lavender, outlines in charcoal gray.

Golden Burst (Series 3100). Antique gold bursts.

Cornucopia (Series 3200). Horn of plenty in warm gray line work splashed with ochre and rose.

Shandri-La (Series 3300). Subtle greens, blues, and gold against china white with a small leaf in repose.

Constellation (Series 3400). A starry display of rich gold yellow accented by muted green blues.

Choreography (Series 4100). Jeweled blues and greens.

Boutique White has no decals at all and represents Seibel's fondness of undecorated shapes, but with this line the decorations are so simple and retiring that none interfere with the enjoyment of the pure lines of each piece. Choreography is probably the most difficult of all: it is rarely seen, and should be purchased whenever possible. I have seen only two examples of Choreography: the creamer and the large salad bowl. Only the latter graces my collection.

So, with the 1954-1955 *Universal Raymor*, Seibel again attempted to salvage the finances of a floundering dinnerware manufacturer—or at least bolster the weakening company props. It is not exactly known how long this line was in production: perhaps it did continue for a while as Universal's only dinnerware line. Although Universal Potteries, Inc. did not totally flounder; it did cease to produce new items for the table in 1954, and turned to tile production. Also, this point seemed to mark the end of the very close and intimate relationship between Ben Seibel and Raymor. Up until this point, there was an almost exclusive connection between the man and the company. It was time Ben Seibel strode down a new path.

The large handled platter (15") behind the smaller example (13"). I have never seen these pieces in anything other than Golden Burst. Prices: Large platter, $18-20; small platter, $12-15.

The well-proportioned creamer: this beauty stands 5.75" tall and is the easiest piece to find. Price: $8-10.

The fruit (left) and the cereal bowl. They sport the same type of "handle" as do the platters. Prices: Fruit, $4-5; Cereal, $6-7.

The casserole is 9.25" round, but the handles (again similar to the platters) add .75" to the width at that point. The base is not really shallow (3") but the lack of any type of foot projects a "low" image. The split finial is molded to the convex cover, and is prone to glaze slips. Price: $25-30.

The creamer and sugar set in Shangri-La. Again Ben Seibel pairs a tall creamer with a lower sugar bowl. This was one of his design characteristics. Although much more available, the collector popularity of the creamer keeps its price higher than the sugar. Price: Creamer, $12-15; Sugar, $8-10.

One of Seibel's more unusual designs: the divided handled relish. It is substantially sized: 13.50" to the end of the handle, and 8.75" wide. Actually it could be a divided vegetable. A unique piece. Price: $15-18.

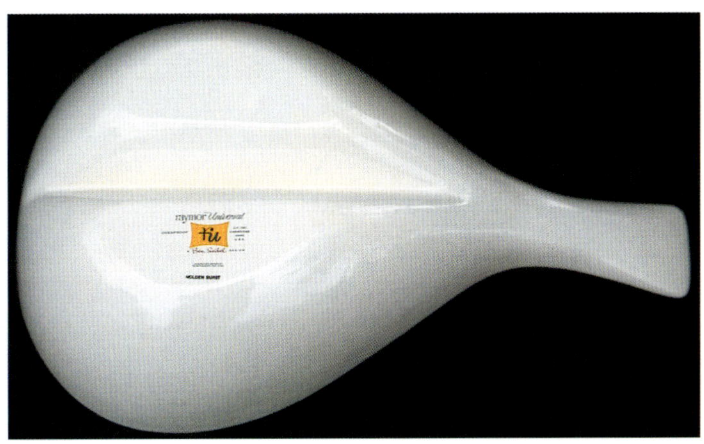

Underneath the divided relish.

The coffee pot. Although smaller, this pot is heavier than the jug. Not counting the lid, it rises to 9.25", Price: $25-30.

Although the teapot is considerably smaller (only 5.75" tall), the same lid fits both coffee and teapots. To many collectors this is exactly what a teapot should be: short and stout. It is a favorite piece, and this popularity is reflected in the price. Price: $40-45.

The dinner plate that I labeled very scarce. In fact, as I finally agreed, the entire line is scarce. Price: $10-12.

For years, while it was generally assumed *Universal Raymor* possessed plates other than the large dinner plate, there was little proof. Of course, some researchers know, but the information was not readily available. However in early 2002, the "assumption" was proven by the appearance of a 5-piece place setting in Festival Leaves: this included a 8.50" plate and a small 6.50" plate. Personally, these sizes are still considered scarce. The price for this set was $30.

Close-up of the Golden Burst treatment.

The low and wide 13" salad bowl with the open vegetable bowl inside. The vegetable bowl is relatively easy to find. Prices: Salad bowl, $25-30; Vegetable bowl, $10-12.

The magnificent jug. The grandest piece in the line! It is fully 11" tall and yet is surprisingly light. The top part is a reflection of the creamer. Price: $50-60.

Front view of the jug.

The teacup and saucer. I stated in the section on *Interplay* that the *Carrara Modern* teacup bears a marked resemblance to this piece. Seibel was known to reuse his cup shapes! Price: $8-12 the set.

Here is the huge salad bowl (13" x 11.75") in the rather difficult to find treatment Choreography. Advertising "hype" mentions "jeweled blues and greens," but while the delicate triangles are cleverly placed and delicately designed, they are not sparkling.

Close-up of the Chroeography treatment.

The gravy on its underplate. This gravy, a little over 9" long and 4" wide, bears some resemblance to the *Contempora* and *Raymore Modern Stoneware* gravy. At least the approach is the same. This general style of gravy is not easy to pour and, despite the spout, really requires a ladle. The underplate has no indented area for the gravy: the result, the latter slides about vigorously. Prices: Gravy, $12-15; Underplate, $8-10.

Close-up of the San Souci treatment.

The Cornucopia creamer. It is a very delicate treatment.

The reverse of the creamer to show additional decorations.

Close-up of Shangri-La.

The shaker set. Again Seibel call for physical differentiation between the two, and the pepper is smaller. Price: $12-15 the set.

General Comments on Decorative Treatments

This "preface" was the last to be written: all the other sections are awaiting shipment to the publisher. When the researcher or collector has spent months closely encountering a myriad of various treatments, the gray matter should begin to generate some thoughts and questions—and commentary is the result.

As mentioned in the section on free-lance designers, Jonathan Parry implied that contract designers could be troublesome because when they submitted any decorative suggestions it arrived on the dinner plate—nothing else. The impression given was that this was the general rule. Then the staff workers at the pottery had to adapt this plate decoration to fit all the other pieces. Mr. Parry was discussing free-lancers who had designed a line of tableware and were now submitting the decoration to appear on it. Of course, this is not always the case. Some contracts only allow the designer to create the shapes and what appears on those shapes is up to the manufacturer, or in some cases, the distributor. Milhurst (NYC) was such a distributor who frequently chose or modified treatemnts. What happens or does not happen, or how much control the creative artist has upon the future of his/her work is spelled out quite succinctly in the signed contract.

Of course, the term "decorative approaches" refers to any manner of decorating the complete line of tableware—be it decalcomania, free style hand-painted work, or the use of solid colors. Embossment or, in some cases, debossment, are integral parts of the physical design of the shape and, while "decorative," are not applied.

Thus it can be believed that Ben Seibel made the decision that *Potter's Art* would make use of color only, and it can also be assumed, he had the final choice of what colors. This would also be the case in *LifeStyle*: no doubt because the Seibel name appears in the *LifeStyle back stamp*. What control Mr. Seibel had on the decorations that appeared on the clonal shapes that did NOT bear his name is a matter of conjecture. Perhaps he did not care.

The assumption is that Seibel had considerable input on whether a decoration would appear on more than one tableware shape—as when Beige Rose appeared on both *Impromptu* and *Inheritance*. Assumptions can be dangerous and open to challenge but they are necessary to research if progress is to be made. Assumptions can always be withdrawn if proved unfounded and only the ego-bound researcher will refuse to do so.

Wise to state: the contract controls it all!

More blatant conjecture: if Mr. Parry' statement was generally true (a condition not only experienced at the Homer Laughlin offices)—and he certainly was a more than truthful person—then perhaps when submitting some Iroquois *Informal* treatments, Seibel sent the Teuton/Thane as it appears in Mr. Harvey Duke's *Official Price Guide to Pottery and Procelain*, 8th edition. This has been mentioned in the *Informal* section: the plate with the large central heraldic figure with smaller *fleur-de-lys* besprinkling the edge. How Mr. Duke acquired this *Inheritance* plate probably will never be known, but the staffers at Iroquois could immediately see such a treatment could not possibly translate to the other pieces, and Seibel was requested to change the design. He did so, and this is the present Teuton/Thane treatment. Pure conjecture, remember!

Thus we conclude (as the next logical step: if the above summations are true) that the treatments on the dinner plate are pure Seibel and the translations to the other pieces were the work of the Iroquois staff. Perhaps Siebel had final approval regarding this "translation," perhaps not. Again, the contract would tell all.

This commentary is using Iroquois China Company examples, yet these words can fit easily with any tableware shapes Seibel happened to create.

Since the use of solid colors to accompany decorated pieces appears over and over again within the Seibel's *oeuvre*, it is not hard to say this solid color suggestion came directly from the artist. If it is ever proved that Seibel was connected to *Interplay* (early 1950s), it started then and continued up to the end of his life.

The astute collector can quickly learn to divide all applied dinnerware decorations into separate groups.

The first two groups, it is believed, would present absolutely no problem to the staff worker designated to accomplish the "translating." The first would be any floral grouping containing one or more flowers (or leaves) in various sizes. Beige Rose is again the example: full bloom, smaller rose, tiny buds and budlets. Or the omnipresent Harvest Time would be another example. All the artisan would have to do is use a suitably sized decal on the appropriate piece. No problem here.

The second example is equally easy, but takes a little manipulation. These were extended or fluid designs that could be fragmented without problems: Vision and Jardinieres come to mind. Take one portion of the former, or one of the hanging basket/lamps in the latter and these would adequately grace the creamer, the sugar, or even (in extreme cases) the shakers. Some reduction might be necessary, but this was done with facility.

With the third category—the geometrical or mathematical—more work is required and the staffer has artistic decisions to make. What about those charming little triangles: Aztec, Fjord, and Pyramids? It might seem easy to merely lift the rim hugging triangular shapes directly from the plate and place them, in the same manner, on all the other pieces.

But wait! To have all the pieces bearing the same size triangles in the same encircling route on all the pieces would be, quite frankly, very boring. Since the original decoration was geometric, the rearrangement must be the same. Thus, no sprinkling of tiny triangles like pepper on the sides of the sugar or casserole. No, not suitable at all!

During times like this, the in-house artist must show great interpretative skill. Just look at how these three identical treatments were handled! Enlarged slightly and placed base-to-base and placed in a short row. How easily this fills the sides of the coffee pot, the sugar, and even the casserole, or the bottom of the bowls. Notice, moreover, the stroke of brilliance depicted on the sugar bowl cover: instead of completely running the figures about the edge, they are divided into three groups of four triangles each. These triangular figures are the same size as those on the plate. To further instill some interest, one of the four triangles is slightly separate from the other three. Without even being aware of the fact, the viewer (or collector) is saved from the sense of ennui.

There are two final degrees of adaptation—both more difficult.

Look at *Impromptu* Garland or Luau!—or any treatment incorporating solid color within the original design. What happens to the solid color? Now it must be acknowledged that Seibel (or any designer) might have known exactly what the result would be. The solid color (olive green, Wedgwood blue, rust brown, etc.) was used on the saucers, inside the casserole, and so on. Easy answer. And it reinforced Seibel's liking for color. The color can disappear entirely from most of the pieces—as it did in El Camino.

The final category is the most troublesome. Either the staff artist makes independent decisions or the creative designer helps with suggestions. What happens when the original plate treatment consists of a large heraldic or geometric design—a design like Thane or Teuton?

In these cases, the original device must be cut apart and reshaped slightly (without losing its true qualities) to fit on small and large lids. I speak of the marvelous adaptation on the sugar bowl lid. There would be many ways of handling this dilemma. Instead of running some small heraldic devices about the edge of the vegetable bowl, they could be placed in a row in the well. Someone had to make the final decision—it certainly could not happen by chance. Perhaps in these more difficult cases, examples were made of two or more variations and the department director (or the designer) made the final choice.

Thus the categories are:

A treatment consisting of flowers, leaves, or other shapes in various sizes, and the smaller decals can be used on the smaller dinnerware pieces.

A treatment consisting of a fluid, easily dissected design that can simply be split apart.

A mildly geometric treatment that can be pulled apart with care to keep the original mathematically squared flavor.

A treatment using a large amount of solid color that is then transferred by itself onto individual pieces.

A treatment consisting of rigidly heraldic or geometric devices that must be "sawed" apart and slightly reshaped to fit the other pieces.

There are variations of the above basic five. For example, instead of flowers in category one, the artist could be working with a group of figures: people, animals, fruit. Instead of a large heraldic device in category five, the treatment could consist of elaborate scene of cottages that would need to be pulled apart and reworked.

The simplest of all the approaches is the use of solid color. Perhaps this is why Seibel favored its use—either entirely (*Potter's Art*) or partially in *Informal*, *Duplex*, and *Pivotal*. The problem with this approach is that the solid color must be as perfect as possible—no *Fiesta* glaze skips allowed. It is best if the color seems to rise from within the piece, not to be merely applied. This can be technically difficult to accomplish.

Designing tableware is very similar to designing clothing. Some dress designers make a detailed sketch and simply pass it one to the pattern maker. This person, with a mathematical eye, translates the sketch into a viable pattern that allows the sketch to become reality. Some fashion designers, the late Erte for example, would sketch a series of elaborate women's dresses that simply could never be translated into patterns—and thus never produced—at least more than once. I am sure some ceramic designers have sketched an idea for a bowl or a teapot or a sauceboat that could never be molded. The molder in a pottery company is the pattern maker in a dress company. This person is the key, the fulcrum, the man (usually) or woman who makes the designer's concept a realization.

Only after these two processes—the design and the molding (pattern making)—does the designer's original creation pass to the decorator: the dinnerware uses decals, the clothing uses fabrics. Then at last, the customer views the finished product—sometimes unwittingly ignorant of the elaborate and involved processes that brought it finally to the retailer.

The back stamp of *Interplay*.

The Iroquois China Company/Ben Seibel Connection

The back stamp of *Carrara Modern*.

The fact bears repetition! The 1950s decade was a creative watershed for Ben Seibel: his designs flowed like honey sweetening the world of American ceramics. Preceded by his metal work designs for JenFred[1], he was swept into a flurry of ceramic designs for Raymor and these were manufactured by some of the most important American pottery companies. None of these designs were overwhelming public successes, but each one portrayed a different aspect of the genius within the young designer. Each proved that the 1950s just were not to be considered totally the decade of Russel Wright. Ben Seibel was a force recognized by industrial designers and critics, and it was soon understood the young man was both prodigiously talented and softly good-natured: an admired, well-liked individual.

In the year 1954, out of the kilns of The Iroquois China Company of Syracuse, New York, there flowed in substantial, yet not overwhelming, number of pieces of a new line of dinnerware. It was called *Interplay* and from that date until this date a controversy has raged. Here the word "raged" is used with literal deliberation, for few questions have caused such a polarization among researchers and collectors of American dinnerware as:

Was Ben Seibel the designer of *Interplay* or was he not?

The question is further complicated by the appearance in 1955 of another Iroquois line of dinnerware called *Carrara Modern*: a line bearing an exact spatial resemblance (except for the teacup) to *Interplay*. The questions regarding the creator of these two variations of one shape have never been satisfactorily resolved, nor probably will they ever be. The creator of *Interplay* forever might remain a mystery.

A few years ago—1995 to be exact—the controversy was considerably acerbated when Harvey Duke[2] accredited Ben Seibel with the creation of *Interplay* – and thus also *Carrara Modern*. Those who love Mid-twentieth-Century Modern American dinnerware immediately rattled the dice and entered the fray. Most railed against the idea that Seibel could have designed such a line of dinnerware; a scant few said he did; and some, perhaps the wisest of all, replied "maybe."

Oh, how the furor flew down the halls of American dinnerware academia. In my possession is a series of e-mail messages discussing[3] all the crackling and snapping reasons why Seibel did not, could not, would not, impossibly should not have designed *Interplay*. I dare not go into too much detail because some names are well known and some of the negative reasons given somewhat embarrassingly illogical and strangely convoluted. Yet all the statements are honest and true in so far as these commentators believed them to be honest and true. And indeed when the feathers settle they might be!

Incidentally, it must be mentioned at this point that I am not advocating Ben Seibel was the creator of *Interplay*. No, never would I dare to be so bold! Neither have I the ear of ranking researchers, nor would they confide in me if I did. My comments come from my own personal convictions. What I am saying is: two of the reasons given to negate the Seibel/*Interplay* connection seem weak and tenuous, and one reason, while very important and damagingly against any Seibel involvement, could have been the result of a contractual agreement. The three major reasons given to prove Ben Seibel did not design *Interplay* are:

Ben Seibel's name did not appear in the *Interplay* mark.
The *Interplay* shape does not look like Ben Seibel's work.
Iroquois has NEVER linked Ben Seibel with the *Interplay* line.

The first reason should be overlooked. There are a number of dinnerware lines designed by Ben Seibel that do not have his name in the mark or stamp. In fact, the name "BEN SEIBEL" does not appear either on his first dinnerware line: *Contempora* or his second dinnerware line: *Raymor Modern Stoneware*. And this same situation occurs later when the name Seibel had become more important than it was at the entangled beginnings of his design career. A number of Mikasa lines are known to be designed by Mr. Seibel and yet do not bear his name. The lack of designers' names on the back stamps of dinnerware, or written on paper labels is poor proof regarding any particular designer's creative involvement. Once, on the prestigious Russel Wright Message Board, an inquirer spoke of seeing an original sticker with the name "Russel Wright inked out—and he knew of several other collectors who had noted the same condition. A terse, but true (?) reply was forthcoming from a researcher with a prominent name: "Just Eva and Ben having some fun!!!!!!!!" A joke, of course, but it should make the sensible collector wary of the absolutist truth regarding the presence or absence of designer names!

The second reason is a little harder to explain away! Yet *Interplay* appeared in the early '50s when Ben Seibel was still experimenting, learning, and evolving his personal design style and philosophy. To say that a ceramic design does not look like the product of designers X or Y when X and Y have barely begun to design dinnerware is rather simplistic. If *Interplay* had appeared AFTER the Iroquois shapes *Impromptu* or *Informal* then perhaps the "does not look like" appeal might work. When *Interplay* first showed its unusual shape,[4] Ben Seibel had only *Contempora*, *Raymor Modern Stoneware*, and Pfaltzgraff's *Country-Time* barely behind him. *Universal Raymor* had probably been designed and modeled, but perhaps not yet in the stores. While these dinnerware lines are exceptionally collectible TODAY and highly revered TODAY, in 1954, the four shapes were of considerable disappointment to the manufacturers and might have been considered commercial disasters. Why would Ben Seibel have created *Interplay* to look like these four odd-ball commercial so-called failures?[5] To say that *Interplay* did not look like a Seibel design is, quite frankly, bordering on the ridiculous—when all is put into a logical time sequence. The time frame is essential to know, and assuredly the serious Seibel researchers and *aficionados* are well aware of what shapes appeared when! Could it simply be Seibel was attempting, early in his career, to create an utterly new design concept? Had he accomplished just that? If it were quickly known that *Raymor Modern Stoneware* was not a wildfire seller at the fine department stores, why would Seibel have tried to create another line that "looked like it?"

Once—and this was during the Spring-Summer 1997 e-mail discussions—I requested help from one of the best known Seibel enthusiasts. It might be interesting to include the entire short conversation. My comments are in italics, the expert's replies are in regular type.

Do you remember me…??? We had a brief mail correspondence a few months ago!!

Sorry, but I talk to so many people about Ben, RW and Eva that I forgot who I owe what to and who needs help :)

I have a very small set of Interplay. *Some 11 pieces I purchased through the mail and [over] the telephone from a Minnesota mall. Ten-inch plates, cups (no saucers) shakers, cream, sugar with lid. It is a pure white glaze with foliage in gray and deep orangy-yellow. The mark is* Interplay *(the INTER in yellow, the PLAY in gray) No mention of Seibel. But the plates*

LOOK like Seibel ... but I am a novice in all this.

All of this Ben stuff is confusing. I think once you see enough [of] his designs, you will be able to tell that *Interplay* and *Carrara Modern* are not Ben's designs. I think I know where some charcoal b&b's, small bowls and saucers are. If I recall the glaze was so dark that I couldn't read the mark. For a while there were plates too that were marked, but someone bought those.

It is understandable perhaps, but unintentionally rude, that an important personage would forget the name of a correspondent after only six or so weeks. Especially since we had planned to meet at the college library where I then worked to talk about Ben Seibel. However, the one most interesting comment was that after I "see enough of his designs, [I] will be able to tell that *Interplay* and *Carrara Modern* are not Ben's designs." Oh, I wanted to ask HOW? Tell me HOW to know! My correspondent was so sure, so positively sure, I wanted to share in his certitude. But I did not ask, and I was never told, and the brief moments of correspondence ended. However, I have not forgotten this gentleman as he has clearly forgotten me!

It is certainly conceivable that when it was completed, Seibel did not like the general sweep and ground-close heaviness of *Interplay* and decided—as far as he could—never to repeat any of its characteristics. But, and this is an important "but," there is an individual item and a glazing technique introduced within the *Interplay* line that appear later in known Seibel work—several times in fact: one is the presence of a small footed compote in place of a flat fruit dish, and another is the appearance of solidly glazed pieces (usually hollowware) to mingle in with the decorated items.

The third reason to protest the Seibel connection with *Interplay* is more problematic because it is true. The name of Ben Seibel has NEVER been linked with *Interplay*. Indeed, NO ONE person or NO GROUP of individuals has ever been officially linked with *Interplay*. This total silence regarding the creator(s) of this Iroquois shape is, to my mind, unnatural and symptomatic of a concerted cover-up. Never has the Iroquois China Company hinted, suggested, or even allowed to be hinted or suggested any name(s) that was (were) responsible for *Interplay*. Why? As the fifties faded into the sixties and the sixties swept into the seventies, no one ever came forward and claimed for himself or herself any connection with *Interplay*. Why? It seems impossible to believe that any designer—no matter how great or minor—would never, absolutely never, put in a legitimate claim as the creative power behind Iroquois' *Interplay*. Imagine, if you would, this scenario: you were a young, struggling house designer at the Iroquois China Company in 1952 to 1954, and the company's managers asked you to design or help design a new shape. You did so, and the shape (*Interplay*) was reasonably successful. Furthermore you were asked not to reveal your role, and modest and struggling as you were, you agreed! But time passes, and unless you were killed or incarcerated to keep the secret, why did you not let the fact be known years later? Thus the announcement: "YES, I, PAUL PETITFOUR, DESIGNED THE IROQUOIS SHAPE, *INTERPLAY*, AND NOW I WANT EVERYONE TO KNOW! It simply does not make logical sense that the innovative creator (or creators) has (have) never stepped out of the murky shadows and claimed a connection with *Interplay*. Why has not this one fact been questioned more precisely? Why all the secrecy unless the designer(s) never desired to be known! This mummery results in frustrating speculation and bumptious bungling. No one knows who was responsible for the heavy, vitreous, and beauteous dinnerware line *Interplay*. It is certainly somewhat rare, it does bear some philosophical resemblances[6] to later Seibel work, but these might be unconscious adaptations as opposed to conscious efforts to repeat a physical characteristic. Will it ever be known who actually was responsible for *Interplay*?

The very fact that there has been no claimant—officially or unofficially—to be the designer of *Interplay* goes a long way to prove some type of legal/contractual agreement. Silence in this case speaks loudly.

What is extremely mysterious is that the Iroquois China Company or any of its executives NEVER, even decades later, mentioned or wafted a public whisper about what went on in the Iroquois Design Department in the early 1950s! Did Russel Wright and Ben Seibel design it together as a merry lark? Yes, this suggestion has been seriously presented! The refusal to give any hint—Siebel or not—speaks clearly at some type of contractual situation or obligation, or as one important Mid-Century-Modern scholar has said: "I think it is fairly clear that a concerted effort was made not to mention a designer for *Interplay* and *Carrara Modern.*"

This is a correct assessment, but I add one more pebble to the beach. Again and again the question must ring out! WHY? Why was there such a concerted effort to keep the designer or designers of these two unusual shapes unknown?

In 1952, Ben Seibel was deeply indebted to Raymor and on very friendly terms with Irving Richards. As said before, Mr. Richards remained a personal friend of Mr. Seibel until the latter's death in 1985. Perhaps, just perhaps, Seibel did not want to jeopardize his business relationship with Raymor and did not want to disturb his close friendship with Irving Richards, and thus designed what might be considered an "experimental" line for Iroquois with the ABSOLUTE understanding he never be revealed as its creator?? Just perhaps! If this were true, it would also explain his successful flight to the Iroquois China Company in 1955.

Irving Richards remained close friends with Ben Seibel when connections with Raymor were severed. In the meantime, Seibel had already proved himself to the directors and managers of Iroquois, and they welcomed him earnestly and enthusiastically "back home"!

There have been several suppositions regarding a possible creator of these two Iroquois shapes. In one article, Russel Wright has been listed assuredly as the designer of *Carrara Modern*, and then, of course, Ben Seibel's name keeps rising to the top of the turgid waters. Guy Cowan, who was living in Syracuse in 1952, and whose *Shelledge* bears some slight resemblance to *Interplay*, has a few votes for the possible designer. Then, one of the most popular possibilities is the entire design staff at Iroquois! This group (who could certainly be identified) got together one chilly and boring winter day and their Leader spoke: "Hey, gang, let's spend some time, get together and design a dinnerware shape and call it *Interplay*?" Sounds reasonable? Or does it?

The readers, collectors, delvers into dinnerware dilemmas, researchers, and other interested creatures will just have to wait and wonder. There is no wrong answer, and no correct answer—just a "maybe!"

Review of statistics. There are two[7] known solid glazes that are used on some *Interplay* pieces: gold and dark brown. These can appear on the bowls, the saucers, and the smaller plates. There are three treatments all using the same gold, red, and black colors in a (1) delicate contained scroll unit (Arabesque), (2) a berry/foliage design, and (3) a *fleur de lys*.

Carrara Modern has three glaze treatments: no true applied design: (1) smoky charcoal gray with thin white lines, (2) pure white with thin dark gray lines, and (3) the rarest, a "fleshy" pink with a green drizzle.

Both lines are found in the following items:

- Dinner plate, 10"
- Salad plate, 7.50"
- Bread & butter plate, 6.50"
- Platter oval
- Platter, meat or "tree"
- Bowl, soup/cereal, 6.50"
- Bowl, open vegetable/salad, round, 9.75"
- Bowl, divided vegetable, oval, 9.75"
- Au gratin
- Comport, 4.36"
- Casserole with lid
- Tureen with lid, footed.
- Teacup[8]
- tea saucer
- A.D. cup
- A.D. saucer
- Jug/beverage server[9]
- Gravy
- Underplate
- Salt shaker
- Pepper shaker
- Creamer
- Sugar

A tantalizing early advertisement for Interplay stressing the solid color choice: dark brown and gold. The emphasis seems to be the solid color/pattern combo was a surprising event—guaranteed to create "the most unusual tables your guests have ever seen!" Are there only two solid colors and three patterns?

Twenty-three items in all, including both a lidded casserole and a lidded, footed tureen. The inclusion of two such pieces gives implied importance to the dual lines.

There is no mysterious confusion about the other four *Iroquois* shapes! All are neatly and clearly marked "Ben Seibel," and for this we must be thankful. Each of the four was designed to fill a specific niche in American dinnerware, and each was generally aimed for a particular type of consumer. This was the genius of Ben Seibel: he perfected the philosophy with Iroquois and accomplished it again with Mikasa in the mid- to late 1970s.

Impromptu (1956): Strong but graceful, and carrying the "cook, bake, and serve" guarantee, this line combines delicacy of outline with heavy utility. It was the most popular of the four shapes and was available in many patterns.

Informal (1958): Stronger, less graceful, more solid in appearance and usage, this line presented true cookware in the presence of Dutch oven, fry pan, and saucepan. It was the epitome of "stove to table" dinnerware. It did not reach the heights of popularity enjoyed by *Impromptu*, but many collectors consider it more distinctive in shape.

Inheritance (1959): had the quality of fine porcelain dinnerware. Thin with a fine translucency, clearly oriental and conservative in approach, this was the most formal, most elegant of the four lines. The consumer could easily purchase *Inheritance* for formal dining occasions and buy *Informal* for just that—informal dining. This was marketing mastery.

Intaglio (1964): The fourth in the Iroquois dining quartette, *Intaglio* possessed some clever design techniques. The presence of incised ovals placed in rings about the edges caught the light of candles or electricity and projected a shadow effect. It was not as pristinely delicate and conservative as *Inheritance* nor as "rough-and-tumble" as *Informal*. And it did not bear the elegant "up-lift" of *Impromptu*. It is hard to place the market niche of this shape, and it proves more popular as a collectible today than it was when it was offered in the finer stores of Manhattan.

Such a merry lark to be confronted with a unit of four different dinnerware lines designed by one creative personality, and in a relatively short span of time. The relationship between the Iroquois China Company and Ben Seibel must have been absolutely secure. It would be easy to imagine that during the years the Iroquois lines were being born that Seibel gave up his "contract" status and, temporarily of course, became an in-house designer. The fact that each line filled a special category seems to imply these four were created as a unit: each one carefully detailed to fulfill the needs of a specific designated customer. The designs tumbled forth in rushing abandon. One could have hardly been completed as another was being sketched upon the drawing boards. The first two are common, strong and utilitarian enough to still be used in today's dining rooms, breakfast rooms, and rustic patios. Yes, *Impromptu* and *Informal* are still pre-eminently usable today—competing with television and basketball games and dressed with food from the microwave, gas grill or stew pot. *Informal's* Harvest Time is one of the easiest treatment to find in any dinnerware—collectible or not! But *Intaglio*—and certainly *Inheritance*—should be carefully cherished. They are quite rare, hard to replace, and belong, most likely, safely in cabinets and china display closets. But, be my guest and live dangerously. Get out and carefully wash that small set of *Inheritance* Shu-shi. It would be perfect for an intimate dinner for two: the results might surprise!

This jug (right) won an award, and Russel Wright was one of the committee presenting the award. The example at the left is the smaller *Carrara Modern* jug. Exteriorly they are identical, but the spout arrangement is different. These "jugs" seemed to have acted as coffee or tea servers according to the advertising brochures seen. Jugs can range in price from $35-45.

Admittedly this *Interplay* gravy looks slightly awkward, yet I find it pours perfectly.

The small compote appeared in *Imperplay* (left). While differing in shape, the *Impromptu* fruit compote (right) continues the concept.

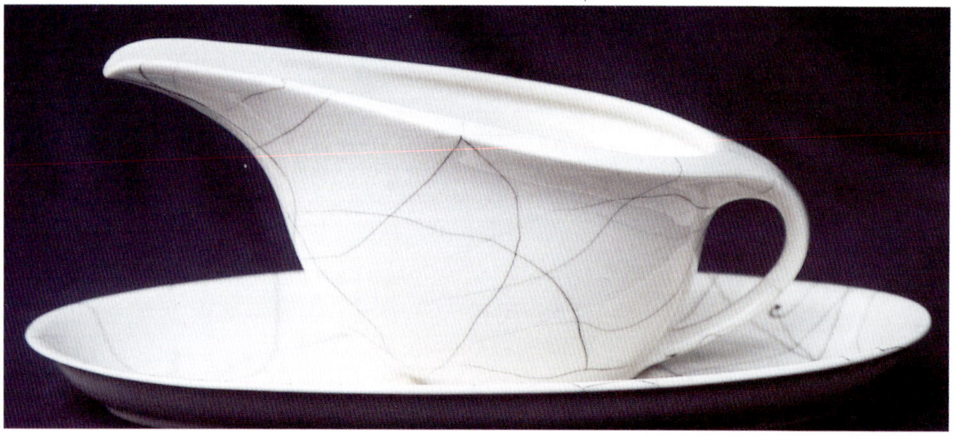

Here is the *Carrara Modern* gravy seated on the underplate. Notice how exactly the gravy fits the plate: any drips are caught by the projecting plate front. The placement was determined by the designer—there is a well into which the gravy settles. Nothing is left to chance. Price: $18-20 for the set.

The *Interplay* cereal bowl was available with the design and in a plain glaze. These were in golden ochre and deep chocolate. The idea continued throughout Seibel's career (if he did design this line). Over twenty years later, while working for Mikasa, the concept continued.

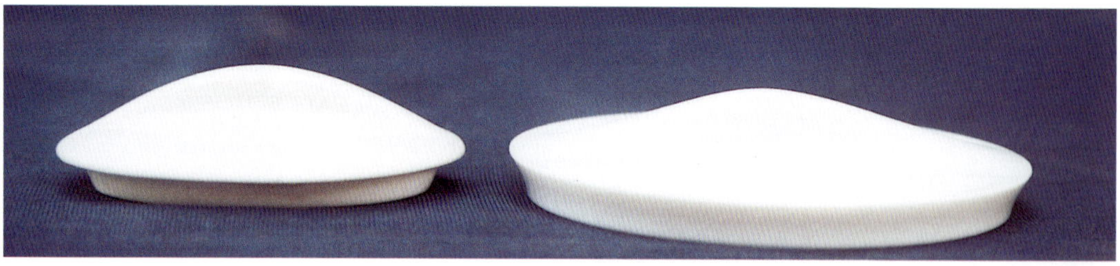

Above and right:
Notice the similarity between the finial of the *Interplay* sugar bowl (the smaller example) and the Oneida *Premier* sugar bowl (left photograph) and the Roseville Raymor bean pot lid. Granted the latter is opened, but the shape is the same.

The covered casserole is very solidly hewn to the tabletop.

Seibel always enjoyed designing the shakers, and he often (if not always) created them differently. What more simple difference than to raise a curved ceramic P and S? These two are just 4" high. If Seibel did have a hand in the *Interplay*, he was a young man with a young man's lack of experience. He wanted to show a difference between the two shakers. In *Impromptu* the difference between the shakers continued, and with *Informal* the design itself was striking along with the size. Intriguingly, with the last two Iroquois shapes—*Inheritance* and *Intaglio*—no shakers exist. Had Seibel, for a moment, run out of shaker ideas?

The tureen. The designer took the casserole, raised it upon a foot, and reshaped the handles. The result is a much lighter piece.

The *Interplay* teacup is vastly different from the *Carrara Modern* example. The latter is much more refined and balanced—another sign someone cared about these sister shapes! Price: $8-10 for the set.

The dark *Carrara Modern* teacup and saucer. The cup bears a slight bodily resemblance to the *Universal Raymor* piece. Price: $8-10 for the set.

The creamer and sugar are quite small: the former parrots the gravy, the latter a slimmer version of the casserole.

The large and graceful open vegetable. It is low but stretches to 10".

The *Carrara Modern* oval divided vegetable. It might look as if a lid was available, but none existed—or to be carefully cautious—no lid has ever been located.

The gold lines glitter (as all gold does) but only under certain circumstances. Price: NP.

The oval platter. In the *Interplay* line this piece was usually in solid color.

Intricate scrolls edge this 10" dinner plate. This treatment is often called Arabesque.

The dinner plate emphasizes the clean and stark "whiteness" of the basic glaze. There were (as far as is presently known) only three *Interplay* treatments. The third was the *fleur de lys* shown on the gravy boat. On the plates, this design marched sword-like point outward and near the center.

This whole page:
Impromptu creamers. Prices range from $6-10, depending upon the treatment.

Impromptu

The First Among Equals

In the mid-1950s, Ben Seibel commenced work on his monumental series of tableware lines for the Iroquois China Company. *Impromptu* was announced in January of 1956. Since the first work must have begun some months earlier, I believe—but am open to correction—that Seibel at the very beginning had contracted for the complete group. For how else could each have been planned so carefully to fill a certain niche in the world of dinnerware. The four shapes—*Impromptu, Informal, Inheritance, Intaglio*—were produced swiftly in sure and rapid succession: so rapidly, and with the names so beautifully in tune with each other, that Seibel and Iroquois must have regarded them as a unit. Each of the four lines was aimed at and appealed to an entirely different type of consumer: there was little overlap in philosophic intention. The contention can really never be proven—unless somewhere deep within the boxes or files of the Seibel Archives there exists a contract stating thus: a contract not yet known to the researchers.

Also I believe—and again expose myself to censure—that such an ambitious design plan of four separate major shapes within eight years (1956-1964) was agreed upon by Iroquois because of some previous connection between the company and the designer.

The first flowering of this agreement between Ben Seibel and the Iroquois China Company was *Impromptu*: airy, but with strong physical weight. Heavy, but still projecting a perception of lightness. It was the first and the best of Seibel's contributions to the House of Iroquois! Or certainly, it became the most popular! Also *Impromptu* was the first commercially successful tableware line designed by Ben Seibel. Now this statement too is open to controversy. But weigh the facts as they stood in the mid-1950s! *Contempora* (1950) is repeatedly touted as a very successful line, but was it? It was Seibel's first design for the table and bore the unmistakable signs of youthful experimentation. *Raymor Modern Stoneware* and *Universal Raymor* both failed to save the companies that so hopefully had manufactured them. And Pfaltzgraff's *Country-Time* is so beautifully awkward and deliciously cumbersome that it is wondered if the shape could have—at the time of its introduction—ever been rewardingly popular with the public? It is very easy to transfer present day collectors' wild enthusiasm back over the years to some fifty years ago.

Meanwhile *Impromptu* evinced all the typical signs of commercial success. Commencing with the offer of twenty-seven individual items appearing in seven patterns, pieces were added and deleted and patterns came and went—all the signs of a healthy, vigorous, and prosperous mercantile existence. The following information was taken from a press release written by Ms. Jane Scrivner, Publicity Director of Alfred Auerbach Association, East 53rd Street, New York. She wrote:

> *Iroquois introduces* Impromptu, *inspired new idiom in dinnerware. A study in sculptural curves and linear contrasts is presented in* Impromptu, *a spectacular new dinnerware collection designed for Iroquois China Company, Syracuse, New York, by Ben Seibel. Iroquois' famous "Replaced If It Breaks" warranty will be introduced at the Pittsburgh China, Glass & Gift Market (Suites 15-17-19, Hotel William Penn) January 11-18, 1956.*

If the collector is lucky and owns a few brochures or advertising sheets—and it is strongly suggested this be the case—the comings and goings of various *Impromptu* pieces can easily be studied. In 1956, the inaugural year, the following items were presented to the consumer:[1]

Dinner plate, 10"	(510)
Salad plate, 8"	(508)
Bread & butter plate, 6.50"	(507)
Cup	(580)
Saucer	(581)
Fruit compote	(502)
Soup[2]	(503)
Cream	(540)
Sugar/cover	(541)
Open vegetable	(560)
Small platter, 11"	(592)
Large platter, 13"	(593)
Salad bowl	(595)
Coffee pot with cover	(550)
Divided vegetable	(583)
Water pitcher	(550)
Gravy bowl	(590)
Gravy stand	(591)
Casserole with cover	(587)
Relish tray	(506)
Salt and pepper	(594)
Cruet with stopper	(570)
Mustard with cover	(571)
Condiment dish with brass	(572)
Centerpiece dish	(573)
Centerpiece insert	(574)

The list above was taken from a 1956 brochure and uses the exact descriptive words. On page 88 is shown the inside of a 1956 brochure. All the pieces available at that time are photographically portrayed and numbered—the number repeated in the listing at the right. Here we have exactly what was offered clearly identified. This fact is very important because some lists drawn up by a few commenting authors have confusing inclusions.

For example, the collector can be confused by a list that includes both a "celery, (15")" and a "relish tray, (11.25")." And then I have seen on one list (as mentioned in endnote 2) both a lug soup (14 oz.) and a coupe soup (7.25"). Here can be seen there was no piece known as a "celery," only a long, thin 15" relish tray, and the coupe soup just did not exist in the *Impromptu* line.[3]

The reverse of the brochure shown above names the Gift Sets.

> *Outstanding departure in the* Impromptu *collection is a series of "Gift Sets," an exciting new interpretation of serving accessories. Related to the dinnerware, yet elegantly appropriate as individual gifts, the companion units are imaginatively styles in china with golden brass accents. Serving with dramatic function, the "Gift Sets" include a handsome flared-round covered casserole with a tall, tapered covered coffee pot, each resting on its own gleaming brass warmer, perforated for flames to twinkle through. A condiment tray with a highly distinctive flare has a slender brass stem rising through the center, looped at the top to form a handle; ... A fourth set is a low, round centerpiece bowl, of magnificent proportions, with removable brass pinwheel candelabra unit on a flared china base.*

All the pieces that include metal (brass) were planned for the Gift Sets. The 1956 prices were Casserole Set (527), $9.95 to $11.95; Coffee Set (520), $9.50 to $10.95; Condiment Set (522), $14.95 to $16.95; and the Centerpiece Set (523), $14.95 to $16.95. A very good sign of customer popularity was that within a year the top prices of each set (in order) rose to $13.95, $11.95, $18.95, and $19.95. A company rarely raises the prices when items are selling poorly.

One final comment about this 1956 brochure: it shows the very scarce salad bowl (595). This rarely seen item looks as if it could be easily mistaken for the much more common open vegetable bowl.

In the list above, the eight pieces in *italics* (salad bowl, water pitcher, cruet, mustard, condiment dish, centerpiece dish, centerpiece insert) were no longer available in 1965 and this fact surely accounts for their scarcity in today's collector market.

The condiment dish with the brass handle is eagerly sought. The size is larger than might seem in a photograph: 9" round and nearly 10.50" from the table to the top of the curved handle. Seibel envisioned the dish as holding two cruets, the mustard, and the pair of shakers. Indeed with these pieces, the condiment dish was offered as the "condiment set" and became one of the *Impromptu* gift items. However I have seen this sturdy round dish used in a variety of manners: for *crudities*, olives or pickles, anything to be handed easefully about the table. Technically all the pieces in the condiment set should match—wear the same treatment—but collectors are rarely fussy when adding a scarce piece and one sees many "mix-and-match" condiment groupings: rather like the song *Anything Goes!*

Recently a four page1958 advertising pamphlet was located. Not only are we told that during this year two new *Impromptu* treatments were introduced (Wild Rose and Spring Flowers), but much more exciting, an absolutely new item was added to the line's listing: the martini set—available only in Bridal White. (Please see page 88.)

The "martini shaker" is simply the original water jug, and since this item disappeared from the 1965 *Impromptu* list, it can reasonably be assumed the "martini" concept was an attempt to save the jug from oblivion. Unfortunately, it did not!

This martini set sold for $14.95 and consisted of the "shaker," glass stirrer, and six china martini cups. The existence of the "cups" might be confusing until one realizes these are tall teacup *sans* the handle—and they do make for a very graceful presentation. This concept cannot be wondered upon because Seibel was responsible for a number of Gilley cocktail sets with ceramic "glasses."

Technically, these martini cups must be considered a separate *Impromptu* item.

In 1965—the next dated brochure in my possession—the availability list read as follows. Those items appearing in **bold** type did not appear on the earlier list.

Dinner plate, 10"	(510)
Salad/dessert plate, 8"	(508)
Bread & butter plate, 6.50"	(507)
Cup/tall	(580)
Saucer	(581)
Cup/low	(575)
Saucer	(576)
Coffee mug	(583)
Fruit compote	(502)
Lug soup	(503)
Cream	(540)
Sugar w/cover	(541)
Open vegetable, 32 oz.	(560)
Indiv. Platter/relish tray	(506)
Small platter, 11"	(592)
Large platter, 13"	(593)
Casserole w/cover, 2 qt.	(587)
Divided vegetable	(582)
Gravy faststand	(590)
Butter dish w/cover	(530)
Coffee pot w/cover, 7 cup	(550)
Salt	(594S)
Pepper	(594P)

A summary might be useful.

Available 1956,	New Items 1965	Items Not Appearing 1956 but Gone by1965
Salad bowl	Cup/low	Ashtray/coaster/butter pat
Cruet/stopper	Saucer [low]	Round cheese/butter dish
Mustard/cover	Butter dish	
Condiment dish	Coffee mug	
Centerpiece dish	Fast Stand Gravy	
Centerpiece insert		
Water pitcher		
Gravy		
Underliner		

When the collector becomes interested in the *Impromptu* line, he/she is suddenly dealing with thirty-four pieces: some easily located, some scarce. The items considered the most difficult to add to a collection are: mustard, coffee mug[4], condiment dish, centerpiece dish, and centerpiece insert. Those items that are somewhat less difficult to find are: cruet, water pitcher, ashtray, butter dish, and the round cheese/butter dish. The collector must note that the quarter-pound butter dish is not marked *Impromptu* (the only piece not so marked); it simply marked Iroquois.

Note the consumer is given a choice of cup and saucer! Yet this "choice" is probably only an illusion. The taller, more elegant cup with its own saucer was the original 1956 offering. The early brochures prove this fact. Why Seibel added a second cup—appearing more like the *Informal* cup—is not known[5]. At one time it was believed the various treatments were available with the customer choice of either one or the other of the cup/saucer sets. Then collectors realized this was not commercially feasible, and only a few treatments came with the low cup—ONLY the low cup. If this is true, the belief in a "customer choice" is nonsense. In my own experience, only *Impromptu's* Beige Rose appears with the low cup/saucer set. Yet with the very popular Bridal White treatment the first cups/saucers were tall. A brochure photograph shows this treatment with the tall cup. Still I own a small set of this pure unadorned treatment that includes 6 low cups and saucers. The wide popularity of Bridal White may have led Iroquois to manufacture it with both cup/saucer versions. Again, this reason is pure supposition, but it is the only treatment known (at this time) to possess both cups and saucers. The low cup is much more scarce than the tall version because, except for the Bridal White, it has been seen accompanying only two patterns: Beige Rose and, by way of an advertising photograph, Grapes. An interesting research problem would be to try to verify if BOTH low and tall cups/saucers appear wearing the same treatment.[6]

I have seen what seems to be an advertising item utilizing the low cups and saucers. The word "KINGAVARIE" appears in gold on both the cup and its saucer. Since the only "Kingavarie" I know has to do with Thoroughbred race horses, the reason behind the use of this term cannot be explained. Again, perhaps a reader can help?

Incidentally, the saucers of the low and the tall cups are NOT interchangeable: the two versions must stand separately as two distinct sets.

The *Impromptu* line was, in 1965, enhanced by the presence of a mug. Seibel loved to include a mug in many of his dinnerware designs. At times, the name changed, but it was still a "mug."

A rather intriguing question—having little to do with our discussion here—concerns the virtual disappearance of the ceramic tumbler as a normal piece in tableware lines. In the 1930s and 1940s, the tumbler was a standard piece in many tableware lines, but it went the way of the Dodo bird in the 1950s. A sad occurrence in my personal opinion!

Impromptu back stamps are quite uniform, although they do vary in color. They have been seen in gray, tan, and these two examples.

The pieces that are available in any tableware line are important to know—actually absolutely necessary to know for any serious collector, but the actual SHAPE of these pieces is—if anything—more vital. The shape defines the line! Since *Impromptu* was the first line Ben Seibel created after his involvement with Raymor, it bears some resemblance to *Contempora*, *Universal Raymor*, and Roseville Raymor.[7] The observant person can certainly see a relationship between all four gravy boats—this is the most evident. Too, the use of metal stands and warmers overlapped from the Raymor designs to those for Iroquois: it seems Seibel was committed to the metal (or ceramic) warmer. However, Iroquois wanted a much more conservatively oriented shape, and while Seibel complied the addition of very unusual items proclaimed his continued striving for some measure of independence.

The gravy boat, mentioned above, provides some unusual collector speculation. It does seem that Seibel worried and then worried some more about this piece within the *Impromptu* framework. There exist a number of varieties. The original 1956 gravy was accompanied by a separate underliner. This original underliner had a prominent well with a raised frame: the gravy fitted securely into this frame. By 1965, the paired gravy and underliner had been replaced by a "faststand:" noticeably smaller, narrower, shorter, and when compared with the broadness of the first gravy, more delicate.

We must now turn to the pattern known as Beige Rose. None of the brochures studied shows or lists Beige Rose as an *Impromptu* treatment. This delicate and pale naturalistic rose decoration also appears on *Inheritance*, using the same name. Since *Inheritance* did not appear until 1959, IT COULD BE that Beige Rose first appeared on the later shape and was placed upon *Impromptu* after 1959. Whatever the time sequence, there appears an *Impromptu* Beige Rose gravy with a separate underliner, and this underliner has no well in the center. Could it be the presence of this underliner—seen divorced from its gravy—gave rise to the 11.25" relish tray? The absence of the well allows the gravy to "swim" about on the small tray and really is not preferable to the welled tray. There was never any mention of a "pickle dish" in any brochure, but we wonder if this could have been the reason for this small plate. All of these items appear in my personal collection and have been closely studied. The separate gravy boat in Beige Rose is exactly the same shape, wider, longer, as the original piece, and yet the underliner is an entirely different shape from the original liner. Quite a mystery dish to set before the king!

There are few pieces more creatively unique than the union of a large shallow centerpiece bowl with a circular insert topped with five branched brass candleholders. It seems Seibel, ever since his Jenfred days, has been intrigued by brass and other malleable metals. The two pieces placed together become what is popularly known as the "candelabra." This name was not official. Each of the two pieces possessed its own individuality. The "Centerpiece dish" could be used as a float bowl—that popular table decoration of the 1950s. Or it could be used for a display of fruit, or even perfectly as a spaghetti bowl. This dish was, no doubt, often purchased for other uses than as the candelabra base. The candleholder unit is more rare than the dish: a fact that tends to prove more consumers were interested in the dish than in the brass holders. But placed together, as Seibel so wished, this combined piece was a "surprise" addition to *Impromptu* and "surprise" is one of the main characteristics of Mid-Century-Modern. Ben Seibel did not attempt another candleholder for any tableware line until his late work for Mikasa.

Even though some *Impromptu* pieces physically were quite low, all have sides that curve upward and project outward. The shape, generally, is vertical: it stretches upward from a smaller base, and this "fountain effect" gives the impression that the individual pieces are not bound to the tabletop. There is a lightness, an airiness, and these characteristics seemed to catch the customers' fancy—it was a very popular shape. Those pieces that do have a heavier base, i.e. the coffee pot, the jug, the pitcher, the cruet, extend upward enough to balance and relieve the solidity, and, besides, in a tall and relatively thin shape, the base must be stable enough to establish a firm footing.

Another sign of *Impromptu's* popularity was the number of treatments given to the customer: the choice was wide in both number and diversity. A few were planned to be the unifying treatments, Bridal White for one example—it went with any of the others. However, if the customer was careful and dedicated, within the varied delicate treatments some could be chosen to mingle and match perfectly. Aztec, Fjord, and Pyramids being color variants of the same design would prove a dramatic and exciting combination. The gold of Aztec would also match rather neatly with Tiara, and the calm pale blue stylization of Blue Doves could tone down some of the boldness of Wild Violets. A few patterns offered were rather insipid, but even here Ben Seibel (or the Iroquois marketing department—perhaps by suggesting) was wise—there are often among potential purchasers some that require the insipid and banal. It makes sense to appeal to all tastes.

Eight patterns arrived at the departments stores in 1956: Bridal White, Stellar, Pins and Beads, House of Flowers, Frolic, Jardinieres, Vision, and the rather mysterious Chrysanthemums.[8] The first three continued as highly popular, which means they are quite easy to collect today.

It is amazing how, when no "new" treatments are thought to be possible, another rides on down the road in merry abandonment—as if it were known by all collectors for a great long time. As this book neared completion, one of these "new" decorations made itself available, and, unlike "Blue Delft" (remember this is not the official name), it was not limited to a plate, but graced a wide number of *Impromptu* pieces. This appearance sent me to my files and folders, but no information arose: it was unknown to me and seems to come out of the Northeast! I christened it "Autumn Fruit" for it depicted—in a hand painted style—grapes, oranges, and apples in the fall colors of brown, orange, and muted chartreuse. Bold in execution, this treatment was nevertheless quite softly hued: the leaves were also a tan/brown. It certainly looks as if "Autumn Fruit" was geared to breakfast use. The quarter pound oblong butter dish was one of the available items, so it must have been quite popular.

Twenty-nine separate treatments graced *Impromptu's* "sculptural curves and linear contrasts"[9] ranging from the very easy to collect to patterns bordering on the rare. Seibel had exchanged the exciting experimentations—if indeed those earlier shapes truly could be called experiments—of his Raymor days for the solid commercial success of his first shape for Iroquois.

Impromptu was either the first or the second line Seibel created for Iroquois. The ranking depends upon each reader's opinion regarding *Interplay*. It really does not matter. These two lines—one a true Ben Seibel creation, the first, a Ben Seibel possibility—are powerful, dramatic, with shiny white glimmering glaze, and both are well worth a collector's time and effort.

The *Impromptu* 15" celery is an elegant creation. Elongated as an ancient Egyptian barge, it floats with practiced grace over the table. With such an unusual shape there is a potential problem: how to place the treatments correctly? Here are three examples: a naturalistic rose, some geometric pyramids, and a shield of the Southwest. All are placed perfectly. The genius of Ben Seibel at work. Price $18-22.

Although not dated, this is an early advertisement (1956-1957?): it shows the original seven treatments plus Bridal White. Unfortunately, the treatments are not named so we cannot be sure of Pompon (upper right hand corner). Notice Impromptu was "a lustrous translucent china molded in softly sculptured curves"—and it certainly was that!

This is a 1960 advertisement and shows later treatments. At the bottom an interesting group of three treatments using solid colors. It mentions the brass warmers, and, not surprisingly, the prices have risen slightly.

The small (5.25") footed compote is a delightful substitution for the fruit dish. These are not very hard to procure, but their never-ending popularity keeps them rather expensive. Price: $18-20.

This treatment is a minor mystery. It is the central portion of the El Camino design but without the black Southwest accompaniment. This accompaniment appears separately—upon pieces that would not accommodate the circle—and so we might expect some pieces to just have the rust-brown circle. However this sounds unreasonable. Is it a different treatment? A second question! Turn to Cosmos in the Library Section (page 100), and you will see the small platter. It certainly does have a different, more rounded outline than this "platter." This is probably the relish tray/individual platter. Price: $10-12.

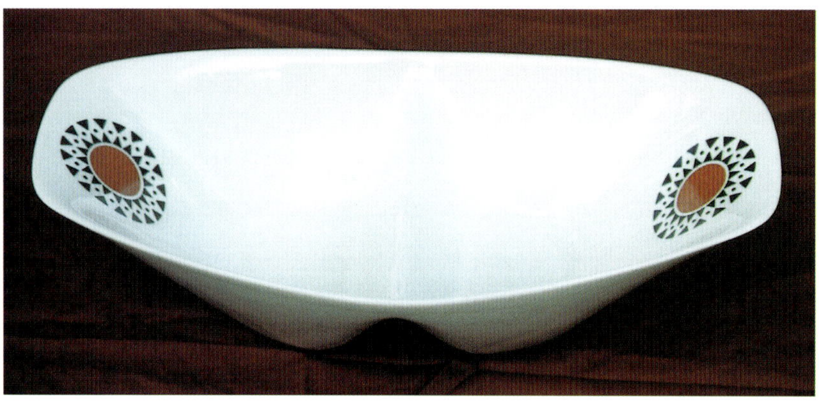

Here is the full El Camino on the divided vegetable bowl. Price: $15-18.

With the bases (or bottoms) of his divided vegetable bowls, Seibel creates quite a sculptural look.

A real beauty that was not produced long. The water jug follows the general outline of the coffee pot, yet is very different. These are very desirable items. The treatment is Jardinieres. Price: $45-55.

Close-up of a hanging "jardinière"—looks more like an ornate Victorian lampshade to me.

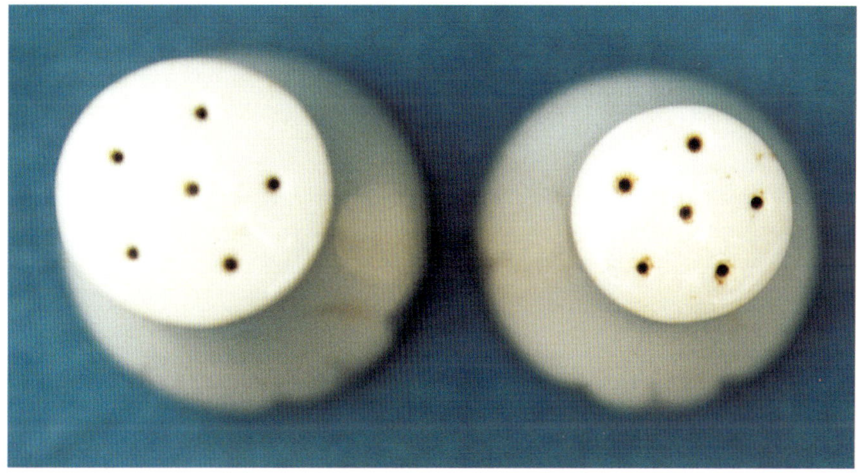

Above and below:
There is a minor mystery about the shakers also! For years it has been thought the tall shaker was the salt—this is quite a common occurrence in tableware designs. However, if the collector looks at the holes, those on the tall shaker are smaller. Does this mean Ben was joking again and reversed the order? Is the smaller shaker the salt? Not a shattering question, but interesting. Price (set): $12-15.

Like the water jug, the mustard jar disappeared within a few years. Due to their smallness, they are often overlooked by the blustery Seibel collector. Those collectors who are careful and walk their own careful path are well aware of the value of a mustard—or three—appearing in an *Impromptu* collection. Price: $22-25.

The condiment holder (along with two cruets) in Frolic—that friendly little treatment known among "inner-circle" collectors as "Eggs and Sperm." The condiment set included two cruets, the mustard, the shakers, and in this condition was a "Gift Set"—to be given to lovely hostesses after a frightfully fun-filled weekend in the country. It was sold separately, however, and had many uses. Price: $35-40.

The base of the condiment dish.

Above and left:
The cruet in Bridal White. Cruets are often seen and sold without their stopper—and this reduced their value over 50%. They sometimes are sold as "rare vases" when the stopper is missing. Beware of this hoax! Price: $30-35.

The three *Impromptu* plates: the bread & butter was added after the two larger examples. It is always nice to see the plates together to get a sense of comparative sizes. Beige Rose is the treatment. Prices: Dinner plate, $10-12; Salad plate, $6-8; Bread and butter plate, $3-4.

Two parings of the lug soup and the open vegetable bowl. Autumn Harmony within El Camino and Grapes within Garland. An interesting contrast of size: Prices: Open vegetable bowl, $15-18; Lug soup, $8-12.

BEAUTIFUL, DURABLE...and you can cook in it!

Look for the sculptured look in translucent true china

GROUP I: Pompon, Vision

GROUP II: Frolic, Stellar, Jardinieres, House of Flowers, Pins & Beads

IMPROMPTU RETAIL PRICE LIST

Stock No.	Item	Bridal White	Group I	Group II	Qty.
505	5-pc. Place Setting	$ 4.95	$ 5.95	$ 6.95	
516	16-pc. Starter Set	14.95	16.95	18.95	
545	45-pc. Service for 8	48.95	54.95	59.95	
520	Coffee Warmer Set	9.50	9.95	10.95	
527	Casserole Warmer Set	9.95	10.95	11.95	
522	Condiment Set	14.95	15.95	16.95	
523	Centerpiece Set	14.95	15.95	16.95	
510	Dinner Plate	1.90	2.20	2.40	
508	Salad Plate	1.20	1.50	1.80	
507	Bread & Butter Plate	.90	1.10	1.30	
580	Cup	1.30	1.50	1.70	
581	Saucer	.90	1.10	1.20	
502	Fruit Compote	1.30	1.50	1.70	
503	Soup	1.30	1.50	1.70	
540	Cream	2.25	2.40	2.60	
541	Sugar with Cover	2.75	3.00	3.30	
560	Open Vegetable	3.00	3.20	3.50	
592	Small Platter	3.00	3.20	3.50	
593	Large Platter	4.40	4.60	4.90	
595	Salad Bowl	4.50	4.70	5.00	
550	Coffee Pot with Cover	7.50	8.00	8.50	
582	Divided Vegetable	5.00	5.50	6.00	
551	Water Pitcher	7.00	7.50	8.00	
590	Gravy Bowl	3.30	3.50	3.80	
591	Gravy Stand	1.50	1.70	2.00	
587	Casserole with Cover	7.00	7.70	8.50	
506	Relish Tray	3.00	3.20	3.50	
594	Salt and Peppr (pr.)	2.50	2.70	3.00	
570	Cruet with Stopper	2.50	2.70	3.00	
571	Mustard with Cover	2.50	2.70	3.00	
572	Condiment Dish (with brass)	6.50	7.00	7.50	
573	Centerpiece Dish	7.50	8.50	9.50	
574	Centerpiece Insert	2.50	2.50	2.50	

Name____________________

Address____________________

City__________ Zone_____ State__________

☐ Charge ☐ C.O.D. ☐ Check Enclosed ☐ Money Order Enclosed

NEW

Impromptu

MARTINI SET

Now to the Impromptu collection Iroquois has added a unique martini set, styled by Ben Seibel in the inimitable Impromptu manner.

Excitingly shaped china martini pitcher with glass stirrer and 6 china martini cups comprise the set which stands by itself as a gift item . . . or does duty as an elegant supplement to an Impromptu dinnerware set. Inspired service for hot soup, hot chocolate, egg nogs, Bloody Mary . . . as well as cocktails.
Bridal White only.
$14.95 the set, retail.

There is quite a difference between the "tall" saucer (left) and the "low" saucer (right.)

Two pieces that appear in both *Impromptu* and *Informal*: the cheese dish and the ashtray/coaster/butter pat (4.25"). Both are scarce. The cheese dish does change its finial however. Price: Cheese dish, $25-30; ashtray, $10-12.

The butter in Bridal White. This photograph was taken in a Florida mall some seven years ago. Notice the asking price: $38! This I believed to be too high, so it stayed where it was. If I saw it today, I would be tempted because these pieces are not easy to find. Remember, they are all marked simply Iroquois China Co. Price: $18-20.

The low cup and saucer. Why did Seibel design a lower cup with its own saucer? The answer is not yet known. These are much scarcer than the taller version, but the price is the same.

Two examples of the *Impromptu* tall cup and its own saucer. In some cases, the saucer is a solid glaze. Price for set: $6-10.

The Kingarvie low cup and saucer. The only Kingarvie I know deals with Thoroughbred race horses, so perhaps this is a rather rare *Impromptu* advertising piece—or perhaps not!

The El Camino gravy with its solid glazed underplate. Set: $15-18.

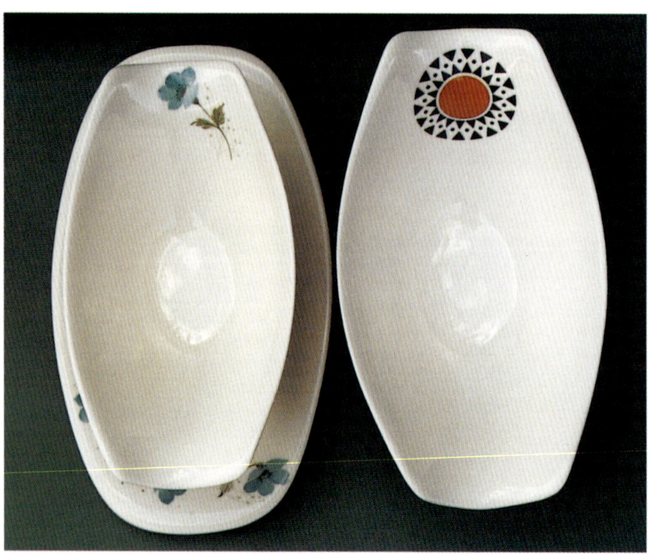

Compare the sizes of the gravy bowl.

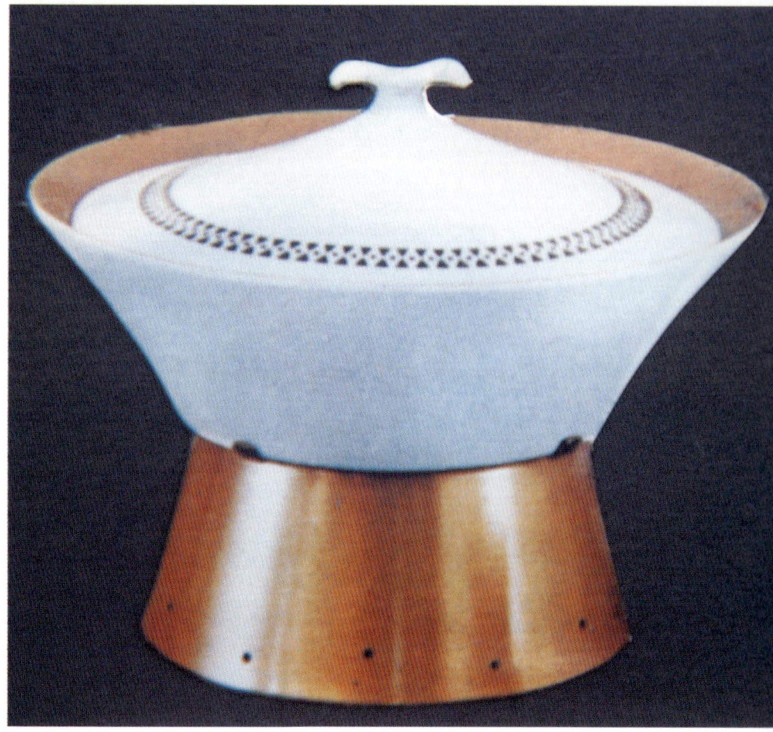

The El Camino casserole on its metal stand—or as it is better known, warmer. These metal stands are quite rare and vary in finish. There must be quite a few hiding around, but with no one to identify them as belonging to *Impromptu*. Price: Casserole: $25-30. Add 100% for warmer.

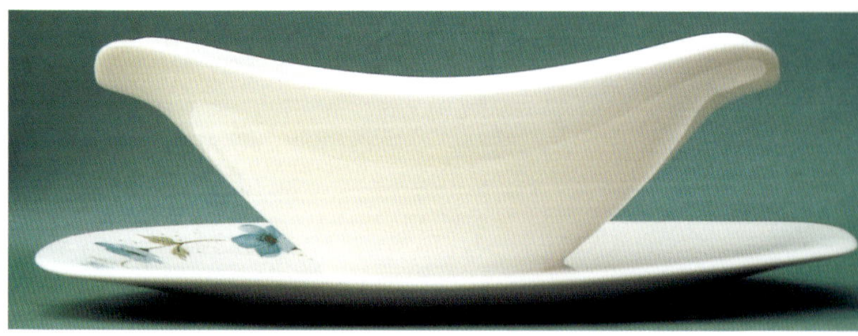

The Cosmos faststand gravy. Notice one tip is more elongated than the other, but hardly could be used to pour. $12-15.

The Beige Rose gravy with underplate.

The Pyramids gravy with underplate.

Ben Seibel must have been experimenting with his gravy boats. The Beige Rose underplate has no inner rim: the Pyramids does—and this allows for firmer use.

Seibel resisted the impulse to make the spout of the coffee server too extended. It is perfect as is. Here is grace without frailty. Price: $50-55.

The centerpiece bowl (14.50") is quite scarce, but not as rare as the candelabra that fits inside it. This bowl has many other wonderful uses, and perhaps, more were produced.
Price: $50+.

The casserole in its sweeping perfection. There is surely an oriental touch to this design: the cover reminds me of Mt. Fuji: an imaginative stretch I admit.

The candelabra unit in place.

The candelabra alone. These originally were sold separately. Price: $65+

The hollow base of the candelabra.

A Bridal White server perched upon its brassy warmer. Price (as a unit): $80-100.

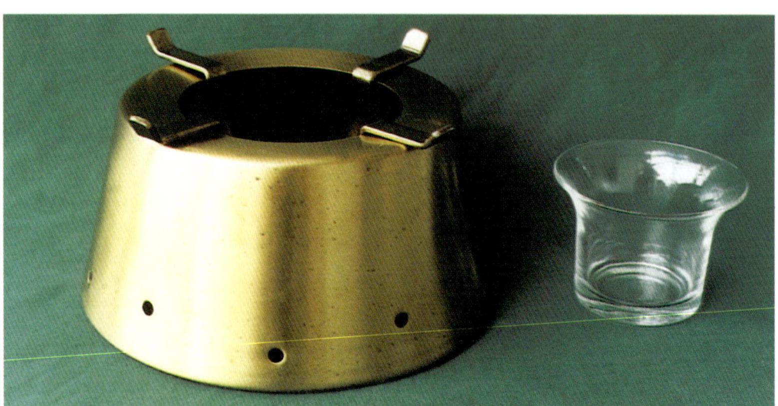

The brass warmer and its glass candle insert.

Gravy faststand in Autumn Fruit. **Price: $10-12.**

Above and below:
Two sugar bowls between two casseroles. The design theme is the same. Note the casserole (#27): this was purchased as an example of Frolic; but, when it arrived, the base turned out to be Parasols. When I complained to the eBay dealer, she simply washed her hands of the problem. Price (for the sugar bowl): $10-12.

A coffee server in Autumn Fruit: A rather scarce treatment, but not popular with many collectors. Price: $30-35.

Impromptu is also unusual in that it claims THREE types of cup/saucer sets, the tall and the low versions ... and here we see the third. When "Autumn Fruit" was discovered so was the third type of cup and saucer. To the left is the tall cup ("Knollwood") and its saucer (Pompon). To the right is the larger "Autumn Fruit" cup with its own saucer—note the larger well. My personal thought is that the "Autumn Fruit" treatment was very late in the production life of *Impromptu*: no other example of this type of cup/saucer has been located.

Impromptu: Library of Treatments

Up till now the only listing of *Impromptu* decorative treatments has appeared in Harvey Duke's *Official Identification and Price Guide to Pottery and Porcelain*. The 7th edition (1989) states:

> *Some of the decorations are: Beige Rose, Blue Vineyard, Colonial Blue, Colonial Pink, Grapes,* ***Harvest Time****, and* ***Old Orchard****.*

In the more extensive 8th edition, Mr. Duke expands the list to include:

> *Known decorations are Aztec, Beige Rose, Blue Doves, Blue Vineyard, Bridal White (all white), Colonial Blue/Pink, Country Garden, El Camino, Fjord, Frolic, Garland,* ***Georgetown****, Grapes,* ***Harvest Time****, House of Flowers, Jardinieres,* ***Lazy Daisy****. Luau,* ***Old Orchard****, Parasols, Pins and Beads, Pompom, Pyramids,* ***Sleepy Hollow****, Spring Flowers, Stellar, Tiara, Vision, and Wild Rose.*

The rise in listed decorations hints at a rise in both knowledge about and interest in Seibel's work for Iroquois. Naturally, Mr. Duke counted heavily on the advice of a number of "consultants," and while the 7th edition mentions no consultant for Iroquois China, the 8th edition does: a well-known Floridian, researcher, and commentator on subjects ceramic. However, I respectfully wonder at the inclusion of the decorations listed above in **bold type.** I have been interested casually in the Seibel Iroquois lines since the early 1990s, and in 1995, my interest grew like Topsy to become a near all-consuming passion. Still, never once in all these years has Georgetown, Harvest Times, Lazy Daisy, Old Orchard or Sleepy Hollow been seen on *Impromptu*. These decorations are, so I strongly believe, confined to the 1958 Seibel/Iroquois collaboration *Informal*. This information is presented for what it is—personal conjecture based on observation. My opinion will be immediately altered by the reception of a photograph showing any of these five (bolded) treatments on *Impromptu*!

There has been an attempt to present each treatment in two forms: a verbal description and the photograph of a plate. This has not been possible in every case. First, in the list above is a decoration called Country Garden. Mr. Duke describes this as:

> *A raised enamel border treatment. Meadow flowers in a muted gray and gray-green highlighted by pink and deep orange.*

Unfortunately, such a treatment answering to the above description has yet been found. The term "raised enamel" speaks for a type of embossment—extremely unusual for *Impromptu*. Another problem is a cup/saucer set bearing the treatment found on *Inheritance* and there termed Knollwood. Without official authority, this cup and saucer has been listed here simply as "Knollwood"—the parentheses indicating it might not be the correct designation. Another potential question in this list of treatments is Chrysanthemums. This decoration was one of the original seven listed as sold in 1956, yet the Duke list mentions it not, it has never been personally seen, and the description given in an original brochure SEEMS to match up with the treatment Pompon. The reader must choose the answer.[10] Finally, due to the inability to get a plate in two treatments—Cosmos and Pompon —these are shown in a platter (former) and an advertising brochure (latter). Bridal White is also illustrated with a platter. I apologize for this and would appreciate the generosity of any reader who might wish to share a plate photograph of these decorations.

Also included are three treatments never listed before—at least to my knowledge. One, Autumn Harmony was discovered in a brochure and that name is official. Two others—"Autumn Fruit" and "Blue Delft"—have NOT been discovered on any list and these two names are unofficial: to be changed when the true name is found. A goodly number of "Autumn Fruit" pieces have been seen, but no dinner plate, and thus a platter photograph was substituted.

The Library of Treatments starts with the seven original patterns offered in 1956. Then it continues with the other treatments listed alphabetically.

BRIDAL WHITE. All dinnerware designers like to offer an unadorned version of their shapes. Ben Seibel and Eva Zeisel were very fond of the undecorated examples of their work.

STELLAR. The original brochure states: "delicate stars in gray, green, and rust." Mr. Duke comments: "Star-like shapes in dove green, golden apricot, soft gray." I have heard these shapes referred to as amoebas with the dove green (or blue) spots as the nucleus, but they are rather too sharp and spiny. Perhaps sand spurs or burrs waiting to attach themselves to the unwary? The execution is very delicate, but the possibilities are pointed with potential danger. This treatment is one of the most common and popular.

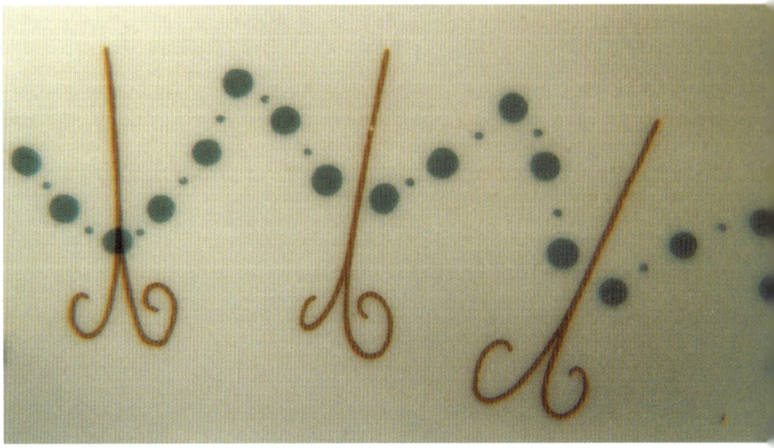

HOUSE OF FLOWERS. Informally known for years as "Confetti." Tiny stylized flowers and leaves dance near the verge of the plates, and these are slightly raised—one can feel each with the finger. The colors are a very pale pink—so pale that it nearly blends in with the white glaze, more flowers in dove green (or blue), pale lavender, yellow ochre, and rust. The greens are represented by a soft chartreuse (only three examples in intervals) and gray-green for three leaves—also in intervals. The same yellow ochre is used for six wheat spikes. The entire treatment does remind one of a light scattering of palely tinted confetti.

PINS AND BEADS. This is one of the most available treatments. The very thin "pins" are pale umber; the "beads" are turquoise and are linked in triangular motion around the plate. The careful viewer notes the arrangement is irregular and this subtlety keeps the design from becoming staid and boring. Looked at quickly, the "pins" bear some resemblance to long sewing shears.

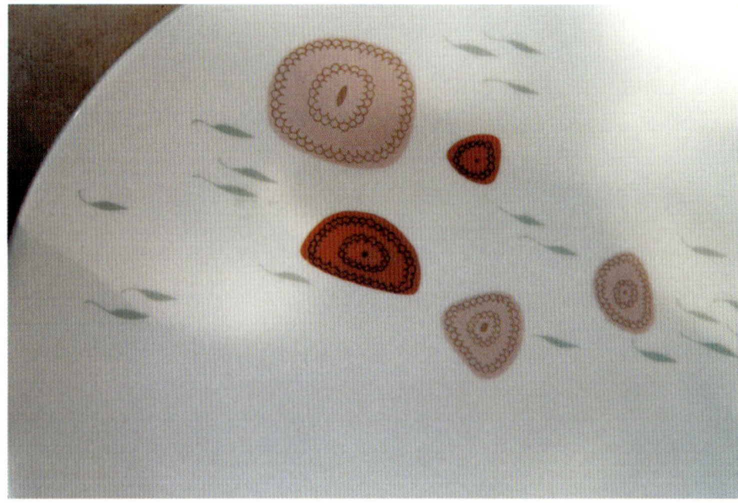

FROLIC. Here is one of my personal favorites. It is uncommon and back in the days when *Impromptu* decorative patterns were not well known, Frolic was known among some waggish collectors as "Eggs and Sperm." Here is drollery at its most whimsical. The "eggs" (or amoebas—here the word fits) are shown in deep pink and a dark and brownish orange. The spirals surrounding the inside edges of each are slightly raised. The aspen-leaf-like dove blue "sperm" swim with whipping tails in one direction among the much larger "eggs." Could this decoration have been Ben Seibel's innocent little joke on the public?

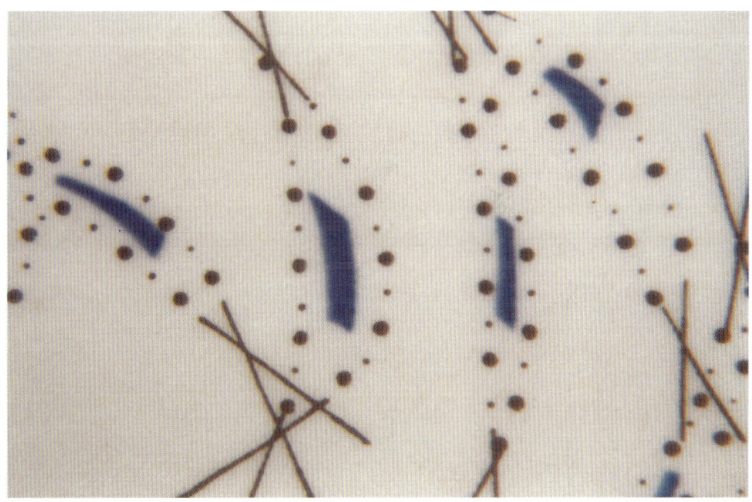

VISION. The first brochure states: "gray points with blue accents." Not a very adequate description for a striking treatment. Vision was confused with Garland for quite some time—and visa versa. Now that has been corrected. Vision caterpillars its way up one side of the plate: indeed it does have a "head" and a "tail." The small irregular segments are a clear sapphire blue, the connecting "points" and the many "legs" are gun-metal gray.

CHRYSANTHEMUMS. The original description of this decoration was: "delicate blossoms with orange centers and brown petals." It is known this name was changed before actual production. Please see Pompon below.

The following treatments were added after the January 1956 introduction.

"***AUTUMN FRUIT***": Examples of this treatment came as a personal surprise shortly before this book was completed. It simply showed up! When a dozen individual pieces of an "unknown" treatment are recorded, it must be assumed the design was legitimate and official. For example, when a collector finds a saucer bearing a "new" decoration he must assume there is a matching teacup somewhere. And if there is a salad plate (as happens here), there must be a dinner plate not yet discovered. This is a bold design with a hand-painted texture using autumnal colors. Again, I apologize (not wanting to disturb conservative collectors) for attaching my own name to this treatment. However, taking an author's privilege, I boldly do so.

AUTUMN HARMONY. A very scarce treatment, but one that has been seen advertised on a brochure. Probably not very popular due to the unusual green "sprayed" edge, it disappeared quickly. Today it is unusual enough to demand a place in an *Impromptu* collection.

AZTEC. This is one of three variants of the same decoration. Aztec is relatively difficult to find. Here are burnished gold and burnt orange: the former with an extended point to the tip of the triangle. This needle tip is barely noticed when viewing the entire plate, but its presence lightens the design and psychologically draws attention into the well of the plate.

BEIGE ROSE. Not one of the original treatments, but nevertheless quite easy to find: both on *Impromtpu* and on *Inheritance*—where it retains the same name. If a collector desires to acquire a full set of Iroquois *Impromptu*, this is one of the few decorations that might fulfill the need. Smaller roses and a bud or two accompanies a large, realistic, full-blown pale pink rose, and the atonal quality is maintained by using leaves and stems of the softest tan. Pleasant, conservative, Beige Rose nonetheless lacks the vitality of the more geometric modern patterns.

"BLUE DELFT." The name of this pattern is not official and it is so named because it is similar to Dutch tiles in a blue and white pattern. Unlike any other *Impromptu* treatment, "Blue Delft's" wide border decoration of stylized cobalt flowers on the stark white background seems to disguise the shape of the plate. The cobalt is highlighted by a bright emerald green: accents at the center of flowers and leaves. The scalloped rim design further disguises the plate. This is an effective decorative scheme. Hopefully some reader will recognize it and announce the true name.

BLUE DOVES. One of the scarcer patterns, the stylized Wedgwood blue birds nestling among greenery brings an Amish or Pennsylvania Dutch aspect to the table. While not easy to find, six or eight dinner plates could be acquired and would mix beautifully with Bridal White. On the smaller hollowware—sugar, creamer, cup—the two doves dwindle to one.

COLONIAL BLUE/PINK. The same pattern in two colors, and it would be hard to choose between them. The blue tends to be richer, the red/pink more vibrant. Neither are very common, and yet both appear on *Intaglio* under the names Old English Blue and Old English Pink.

COSMOS. Delicate and very feminine, this treatment was overlooked on the Duke list. And it does not appear very regularly. I have seen it on only three pieces: this platter, the gravy, and a creamer.

GARLAND. Once confusedly spoken of as Vision, Garland, like El Camino, makes use of solid glazes on some of the hollowware. It also presents a large dove blue circle in the center of the dinner plate—which is missing on the smaller plates. Dark blue cornflowers stand tall outside the blue circle on think black stems. There is a scattering of pink flowers that, to my mind, reduces the vitality of the treatment. Notice that the *Impromptu* decorations have either a design in the plate's well, or one encircling the rim, not both. Garland can be found with ease.

EL CAMINO. Well, this plate is almost El Camino. This decorative approach is bold, striking, difficult to find, and is one of the few *Impromptu* decorative approaches that uses solid glazes on some pieces. This plate is missing the black and white diamond band surrounding the dark rust circle. No, here we do not seem to have a "mistake" for I have seen about a dozen pieces (platters, smaller plates, a gravy) without the black/white band. However, without the trim this El Camino version lacks spirit and looks vacuous and unfinished. Was this an actual version? More examples will have to be found before an answer can be given. El Camino is a wonderful example of the way individual treatments can be altered on the various pieces. The bowls portray only the black and white diamonds on their extended lips, and the creamer bears a simple diamond band at its base: no solid rust to be seen. (Please see page 78.)

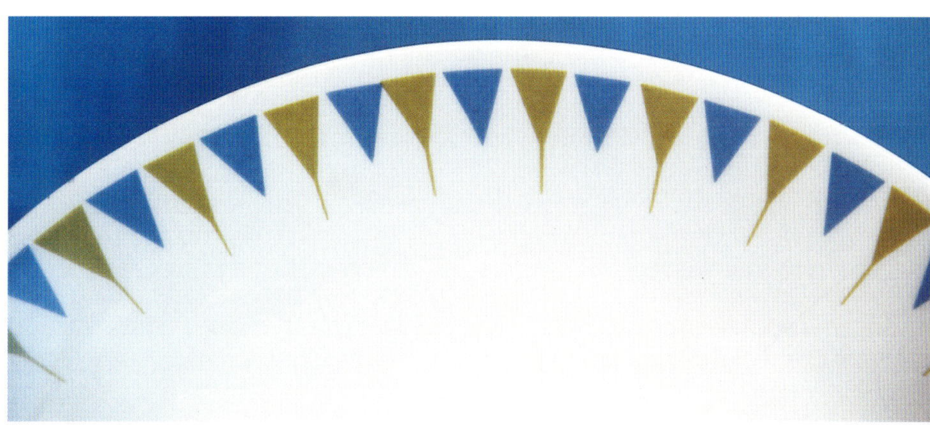

FJORD. The second variant of a stylish rim design. Instead of the warm colors of Aztec, Fjord is cool and refreshing. The contrast of the two saturated colors—yellow-green and delft blue—is exciting and adventurous. Not common, this treatment is unusual and worth a long search. Fjord is also important because, to date, it is the only decorated *Impromptu* to be found on both tall and low cup/saucer sets.

GRAPES. Rather overpowering on the plate: a little less so on the other pieces where the decals are divided. The leaves and grapes are naturalistically conceived, and while the color of the leaves is true, the grapes seem a little lavender.

JARDINIERES. Here is a popular pattern with collectors, and yet somewhat elusive. The varied hanging lamps are intricately drawn with very fine lines and decorated with tiny oval orange rounds: like fizzy champagne. One will find the unit decals appear separately on the various pieces, but all three are shown on the dinner plate. It is one of the more unique and fancifully imaginative treatments. Jardinieres was added soon after 1956 to become the eighth treatment available.

"KNOLLWOOD." Please note this name is also in italics and enclosed with parentheses. It might not be the real name here in *Impromptu*: the same pattern does appear on the *Inheritance* shape where the name is official. It also appears on a few *Informal* cups and saucers. Available on an *Impromptu* cup/saucer set, we can only guess how it would appear on the dinner plate. Look under the *Inheritance/Intaglio* Library of Treatments for a possible idea.

LUAU. Very striking and colorful, Luau, like Garland, makes use of solid colors: in this case deep mustard green. There are some collectors who dislike the solid green but dote on the pieces—bowls, etc.—that are decorated by the flame red flowers alone. While not especially easy to acquire, with devoted hunting a nice set can be gathered.

PARASOLS. One of the scarce patterns, Parasols is quite beautiful. The exact reason for the name is difficult to understand: it reminds the viewer of blue thistles floating among yellow grasses. Again there is an oriental delicacy of touch and execution that contrasts with the more blatant treatments—Grapes for example. A personal favorite, even though only a very few pieces have been seen.

POMPON. Unfortunately no dinner plate was available for photographing. A brochure cover had to be used. This is quite a rare treatment. It has been described as: "A Far Eastern motif of chrysanthemum blossoms. A bright orange center accents the sandstone petals." If the reader returns to the description of Chrysanthemums given in the first brochure a definite similarity will be noted. They are surely the same decorative design! Did Chrysanthemums change its name before or soon after *Impromptu* was first publicly offered? There is an assumption it did, but the question remains unanswered. I remembering reading when the great American writer Gertrude Stein lay dying in her Paris apartment, her long time companion Alice B. Tolkas whispered "Gertrude, what is the answer?" Gertrude, amused as ever replied: "The answer is not important, what was the question?" Gertrude died a few minutes later. A question/answer game is always stimulating!

PYRAMIDS. The third and last of the Aztec, Fjord, Pyramids tango, and one of the most common of the patterns. Gray and blue triangles with the gray one displaying the thin "spike." The contrast between the two colors is not as vibrant as Fjord. I have seen three full sets comprised of Pyramids and it appears regularly on eBay. Remember, however, easy to acquire does not necessarily mean cheaper in price. Availability can simply mean more people might want to gather full sets and the more people willing to purchase translates into higher prices.

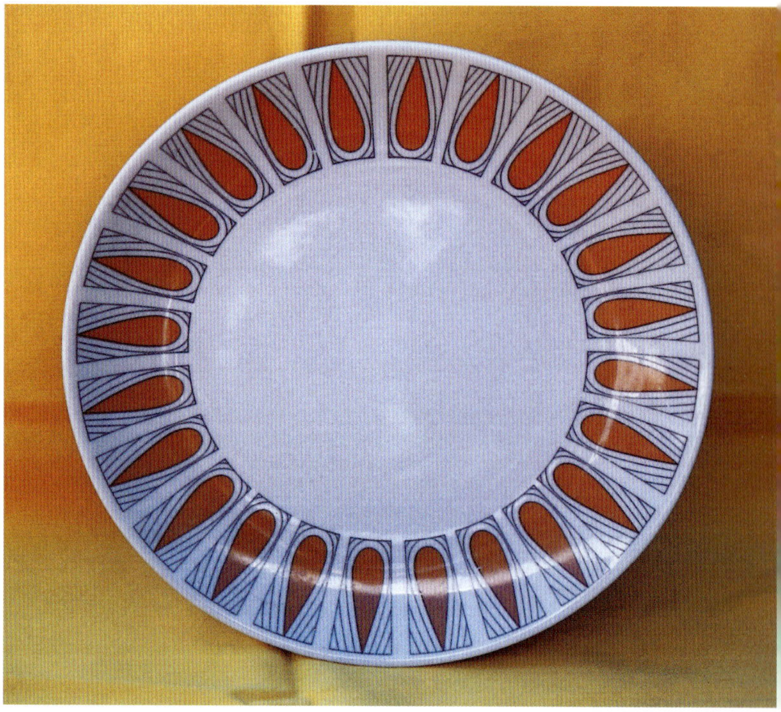

TIARA. Sometimes described as a Spanish design, Tiara is very bold. The pattern encircles the plate from verge to rim. It does resemble the "points" of an oriental crown or tiara—hence the name. The viewer must concentrate to see that the pattern is made up of a series of independent "plaques" with no connection. Burnt orange "teardrop" and thin black lines mingle prominently. Not easy to locate.

SPRING FLOWERS. Spring Flowers is another somewhat scarce pattern, but worth any extended hunt in order that the collector may enjoy its delicate execution. It has a bright and airy quality. Ben Seibel, if he indeed was responsible for the treatments, showed a predilection for oriental design. Bright yellow, grass green, and tan are contrasted with touches of deep apricot. The oriental technique is enhanced by allowing the color to flow casually outside the lines.

WILD ROSE. Unlike Beige Rose, these flowers are bright pink and twirl in the center of the dinner plate amid dancing pale green leaves. There is nothing too imaginative about Wild Rose, and it was probably offered for the most conservative of consumers.

WILD VIOLET. A bright wide band of blue flowers—in two hues—but they are not violets. Both the flowers and the buds look suspiciously like *Anemone hepatica*. The pattern is rich, full, conspicuous, and typically English. It also recurs on *Intaglio* but renamed Woodale.

Beyond the official treatments listed above, occasionally others appear. There is an unusual *Impromptu* advertising plate floating around. I tried unsuccessfully to obtain a photograph of this piece. It was sold on eBay for over $100. Hand painted examples also exist and are quite beautiful. These make lovely little additions to an extensive collection of *Impromptu* pieces.

Note

There appeared a notification in the trade journal *China, Glass & Tableware* (c. 1959) of three unusual treatments decorating the *Impromptu* shape. These have never been sighted, and while it can be assumed they were produced, this cannot be proven. If any reader has examples of these three designs, please contact me. All three are very similar and bear resemblance to those floral Hex Signs that decorated Amish barns and later became popular for the interiors of "country look" homes.

Country Garden: Stylized flowers, vines, and leaves rising up from a single spot near the rim of the plate. Colors are orange, blue, gold, and brown.

Lexington: Stylized thistles and roses encircle the plate. There are two inner rings of curving lines and small flowers. Colors are turquoise, blue, and platinum.

Dutch Treat: A balanced and uniform swirl and leaf design fills the entire plate. Color is dark blue.

All three retailed at $24.95 for a 16-piece starter set. The teacup shown was the low variety. In the same publication were also listed three further treatments, but with no photographs: Blue Petals, Brown Petals, and Tiara. We all know the last named was actually in production. Were the other two?

Informal Cookware

Informal back stamp.

This second shape, appearing only two years after *Impromptu*, was loudly touted by Iroquois as COOKWARE. This claim, whatever it was worth, set the *Informal* line apart. In 1956, *Impromptu* was advertised as being "flameproof," but this 1958 shape could move rapidly from cooking to serving. The hostess, worried, harried, and determined to be the "hostess with the mostest," could cook and then serve in the same pieces – or so it was supposed. So much for advertising hype.[1]

Impromptu was popular with consumers from the very moment it was introduced. Seibel, very cautious about not reproducing anything like his first shape, bent sideways and backwards attempting to give the public a new choice, a new, an entirely new, shape. And he succeeded.

There is no delicacy, not a hint of ethereality, no curving verticality designed into *Informal*: it was absolutely different from its immediate predecessor. The shape tends to be broad and weighty, settling on the tabletop with a secure solidity. While not lacking some modicum of grace, *Informal* is not graceful. Unfortunately, its burst of popularity could not be sustained and the public interest waned.

Still, *Informal* has some surprises, some cleverness, and since "informality" is the name of the game, this shape has always been considered more venturous than *Impromptu*. Whereas the latter shape follows the general rule of dinnerware philosophy and leads the eye upward, *Informal* flaunted this rule and draws the eye down. This simple one design whimsy sets the *Informal* shape apart from the other Iroquois/Seibel creations. This is not just luck, but a predetermined plan on the part of Ben Seibel. He wanted this line to be different—and it certainly was!

In general terms, *Informal* is horizontally inclined: it is rounder, lower. Even the finials lie very low, hugging the lids like two hollow triangles or a modernistic ceramic hourglass with no sand to run! Interestingly, in a quest for unity, Seibel turned this finial shape up on end to become the shakers: again, as in *Impromptu*, identifying the salt from the pepper by a size difference.[2]

Even if Seibel had nothing or little to do with the earlier Iroquois shape *Interplay*, he was aware of its existence and was impressed by use made of solid colors—just as they did in *Interplay*. The *Informal* salad and bread & butter plate always appear in plain colors, and this allows them to compliment more than one decoration. These colors received special names: Bristol blue, gray-green, burnt orange, citron yellow. The exteriors of a number of bowls and the backs of the dinner plates and the platters are also solid colors. It was an unusual and playful approach that stressed the line's informality.

Again comparing one with the other, *Informal* had a much more modest introduction than did *Impromptu*. Only four treatments were made at the beginning: Harvest Time, Lazy Daisy, Rosemary, and Blue Diamonds. The first named, Harvest Time, has become the ubiquitous treatment amongst Iroquois china. It does seem that seventy percent or more of all Informal offered for sale today is Harvest Time—*ad nauseum* as it were. Because it is so common, the wonderful color and detail of the oak leaves are overlooked, passed over by many collectors. If this treatment was as scarce as, say, Teuton, collectors would be exclaiming about its earthy charm, its naturalistic and rustic coloring. Sadly, this one treatment suffers from overexposure. It is everywhere!

Place settings of the other three introductory treatments also can be readily found, and in some parts of the country, full sets can be acquired with alacritous abandon. Some of the serving pieces will take some time in finding, and certain items—the lazy susan set, for example—will be hard to find in any treatment[3], but in general a very workable, usable set can be completed by those collectors who also regularly want to use vintage 1950s tableware.

Those patterns added after the first four seem drastically to drop in availability. And in some of these later treatments, the dinner plate becomes a problem to find. Thane and Teuton bowls, platters, and even divided vegetables are seen more frequently than the large plate. But the word "frequently" does not mean "abundantly:" these two color variants are still scarce—only the plate is scarcer still![4]

The *Informal* treatments possess more "pizzazz" than do the softer, more delicate treatments seen on *Impromptu*: they are bolder, use a stronger, brighter color palette, and have considerable shimmer. A few of them seem raised and enameled. This statement is not one hundred percent correct (what statement is?), but in general, the decorations on *Informal* are bright and youthful, ringing the rim with sparkle and color. Bombay Green and Bombay Blue are two of the most sharply defined and beautifully articulated rim designs to be seen on any dinnerware of the fifties. The Bombay pair is similar to Teuton/Thane—merely color variations of the same pattern. Just as Bombay is constructed mathematically, so another decoration—Sleepy Hollow—depends upon sinuous femininity. Entwining gracefully, petalled flowers in peachy-pink, cerulean, and powder blue, and leaves in tints and shades of olive, the colors are a narcotic of pastel charm. The name, I believe, refers to the soft, dreamy, and peaceful aspect of the design, not the short tale by Washington Irving.

The complete treatment list includes:

The original four:
- Harvest Time
- Lazy Daisy
- Rosemary
- Blue Diamonds

Plus those added later:
- Blue Vineyard
- Georgetown
- Old Orchard
- Sleepy Hollow
- Bombay Blue
- Bombay Green
- Teuton
- Thane
- Madrid
- Hearts of Gold

Fourteen patterns, all bold and well-suited to this heavy utilitarian shape cannot compete with the twenty-nine plus offerings of *Impromptu*, and yet afforded the public a generous choice. I have also seen white, plain white, listed as a pattern, and have seen a number of pieces with no decoration at all. However, all these have been backed with burnt ochre, so the impression is given that "something is missing" rather than a choice of a white treatment.

The true spirit of *Informal's* venturous style comes not from its treatments, but from its pieces and its shapes. The generalities of shape have been discussed above. Now is the time to discuss the individual items. The numbers and types of pieces fluctuated: to be seen briefly and then to disappear. The prime example of this is the huge "trivided" server. This piece is so rare that many collectors do not know of its existence. The name, "Trivided server," was listed in the original 1958 brochure, but was not mentioned in the next brochure published several months later.

The 1958 list:

Dinner plate	(710)
Salad/breakfast plate	(708)
Teacup	(780)
Tea saucer	(781)
Lug soup	(703)
Creamer	(740)
Covered sugar	(741)
Gumbo soup with cover	(723)
Open vegetable	(760)
Small platter, 12"	(792)
Large platter, 15"	(793)
Covered casserole, 2 qt.	(787)
Trivided server	(782)
Salt	(794)
Pepper	(794)
Ashtray/coaster/butter pat	(707)
Coffee pot/cover	(751)
Buffet server insert	(770)
Revolving base (metal)	(770B)

The cooking items included:

Covered fry pan, 10"	(706)
Dutch oven, 4 qt.	(722)
Covered sauce pan, 1 qt.	(771)
Samovar/stand, 23 cup[5]	(774)

These cooking items were the first of their kind to accompany a dinnerware line, and they created, at first, great explosive excitement. They are beautiful pieces: sculptural and yet, as befits the line, heavy and duty worthy. To use on the kitchen stove, a fry pan that matches the setting on the dining room table was an exciting experience for the housewife devoted to "matching." The public loved the idea, and yet, since rarely do used *Informal* cooking items show up in today's collectors' market, it is wondered if these handsome cooking items were purchased in relatively small numbers for display, not use.

A second price list appeared in a very short time: perhaps only a few months later. The trivided server is gone, but five "new" pieces appeared: (1) bread & butter plate (707), (2) fruit dish (702), (3) divided vegetable (783), (4) gravy boat (790), and (5) milk pitcher, 40 oz. (751). Counting the trivided server, Informal could boast twenty-eight items, and since some were very unusual, it was a very well appointed line.

There was also an attempt to be frugal: the cover of the huge samovar was interchangeable with the sugar bowl, ditto with the gumbo and the sauce pan, and the fry pan and the casserole.

The next brochure is dated June 1965: still no mention of the trivided server—it was gone forever. Also missing (and this is only within seven years) were four items:

Ashtray/coaster/butter pat
Buffet server and its revolving metal stand
Cheese dish
Milk jug

To counteract this loss, two new items were listed:

Coffee mug, 11 oz.	(783)
Covered butter dish	(730)

Thirty pieces to tempt the collector: some easy to find, others rare. Not only the three-part server belongs in the rare category, but also the revolving metal stand and the coffee mug. Others can be considered difficult: the ashtray, the oblong butter dish[6], the cheese dish, the sections of the buffet server, and the coffee pot with its lid intact. Almost ironically, the samovar (usually minus its stand) turns up with regularity, but usually overpriced.

The coffee server is the item most representative of the shape—insofar that it is the only coffee or teapot I have seen that deliberately draws the eye of the viewer down to the tabletop. In this, it is unique. The viewer's eye slides down from the top of the handle, rolls down the slanting cover, and continues to move downward over the most miniscule and insignificant spout ever placed on a coffee server. The eyes are entrapped downward. The shape of the coffee server is supplicated in the jug, and then graduated down to the creamer. We seem to have a Tweedledum, a Tweedledee plus one! The server, minus its lid, is often mistaken for the jug, and occasionally *visa versa*. This coffee server just does not look like it was meant to dispense hot liquid: thus the mistake is understandable. Despite the smallness, the creamer stands alertly upright over the rounded sugar bowl. All three—server, jug, and creamer—are identical in shape. This is quite a unique, and relatively unknown, situation in American dinnerware.

Alas, there is a structural problem with this server—its weight! When filled with iced tea or, even more dangerous, hot coffee, this server becomes nearly impossible to lift and pour. It cannot be imagined that any gracefully inclined lady who was given the duty of hostess could undertake the role. From a sitting position, the filled *Informal* beverage server is impossible to lift. One jokester remarked that Ben should have put a spigot at the bottom and turned it into an urn. Quite simply, all three of these similar pieces are not only heavy, but awkward to pour. Each of the three handles look wonderfully shapely, but to grasp with any sense of security is a lost cause. Unfortunately the ergonomist (and the user/collector?) has to fault Seibel: his pleasant form does not always adequately function.

There are a few design problems also—but these are minor. The cover of the gumbo soup is much too heavy and unwieldy for the shallowness of the bowl, and I have never seen a cover that properly fit. The casserole is itself much too shallow, and the faststand gravy is "stubby" and awkward. Indeed, whatever happened to the gravy boat that could be poured?[7]

However, the dinner plate is exceptionally well constructed: it is a magnificent foil for whatever food is placed upon it. Stretching a full 10-inches, the plate looks larger due to the absence of any verge or noticeable rim. There is no interruption in the surface (except the decoration near the edge) and this makes the Informal dinner plate practically and satisfyingly designed. An admirably functional piece—and designed with artistry.

These shapes became the base for a stool (left pepper) and a glass-topped table (right salt) in 1966. Seibel always tried to design distinctive shakers, and he usually succeeded. He liked the user to immediately distinguish between the salt and the pepper. Some designers relied only upon the size of the shaker holes. $8-10 a set.

The sexpartite buffet server has always been an object of collector desire. Remember, this piece was no longer made by 1965, and thus is scarce and will not be found in all the treatments. Indeed, while separate pieces are occasionally located, the only complete units seen have been in Harvest Time and Lazy Daisy—both original 1958 treatments. Collectors assumed or believed this buffet unit was to use as a relish server, i.e. tiny pickles, plump black olives, and acerbic green olives, tart pearl onions, chutney, florets of cauliflower and broccoli—whatever the hostess wishes to provide as an appetizer. But in the once popular glossy magazine *Bride & Home*, the summer 1958 issue, can be seen a very elaborate and grand buffet table showing the buffet server in an entirely new light: the six sections are filled with individual portions of salad. Indeed one is already placed on the dinner plates. Is it possible Seibel conceived of the buffet server not mainly as a relish dish, but as an unusual, venturous way to present individual portions of salad or vegetables?

Of further interest, the samovar in this idealized buffet setting is shown as a soup dispenser. Naturally, the soup was not a gumbo but a clear bouillon. Ingenious uses for two ingeniously designed pieces of *Informal*.

So what is the final count, the collector's judgment on *Informal*? Accepted for exactly what it is—a fun, informal, unsophisticated, sometimes awkward tableware line—it meets the mark and functions within reason. It accomplished its stated goal: destined to become the second dinnerware line in many homes. Not in the same class with *Impromptu*, and most certainly it never could substitute for *Inheritance*, the next—and third—shape Seibel developed for Iroquois.

This back stamp is used on most—but not all—of the *Informal* cookware.

Harvest Time solid accompaniment is burnt orange: it is also quite a delightful treatment. Only its appearance everywhere, everywhere, and still everywhere, makes it seem tiresome.

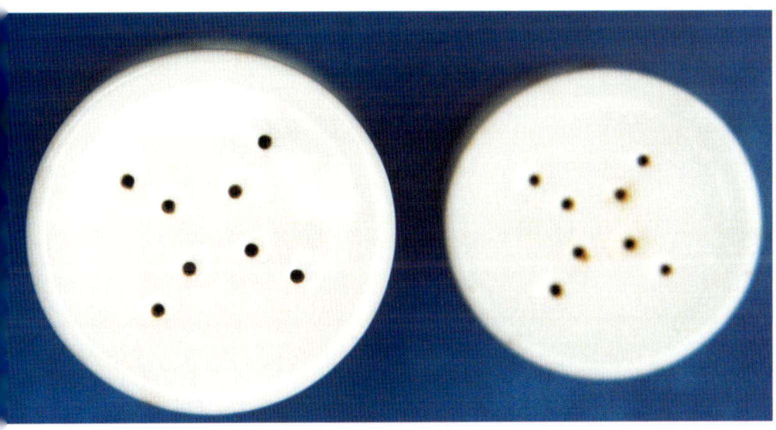
The shakers seen from the top.

The bread & butter (here in citron yellow) appeared a little later than the dinner and salad plate. The *Informal* smaller plates are always in solid colors. Note here that BOTH citron yellow and Bristol blue can mix with the Lazy Daisy decoration; but, because the back of this dinner plate is the blue, this is the "official" color of use. B&B plate, $2; salad plate, $4-6; dinner plate, $10-12.

Stiff heraldic decorations are difficult to place on smaller pieces. Note the cleverness whereby Thane (and Teuton) solved this problem. Since these treatments are scarce, this sugar bowl should be priced slightly higher: $10-12.

Teuton is even harder to locate than Thane: it is a beautiful combination of sand and bright russet. Note the one larger emblem on the creamer. Prices: platter, 15", $18-20; creamer, $8-10.

The soup bowl.

The two Bombay treatments are hard-edged and rather inflexible, but see how sparse, crispy, and well-suited Bombay Green looks on this 15" platter. Price: $15-18.

Sleepy Hollow with its entwined beauty. This is a flowing treatment and thus the two parts of the divided oval vegetable bowl (10.50") have been conceived as different. In Thane or Teuton they would be the same. Price: $12-14.

The Hearts of Gold pattern graces this smaller 12" platter.

The large and fabulous trivided server. Here is the Lazy Daisy pattern, this piece is quite rare. It might have been made for only one year. Price: $80-90.

Two little, unpretentious bowls. The fruit dish (left) was not one of the original pieces, and the ashtray/coaster/butter pat disappeared by 1965. Incidentally, its use as a coaster was very limited: it was too concave. A better use would be for a dipping saucer. Prices: Fruit dish, $3-4; ashtray, $10-12.

Even the base of the trivided server is beautiful.

The fry pan was low, large, and a clear and sparkling white. Seibel even had some of the lazy daisies scattered within the pan. Price: $40-50.

The gumbo soup and its cover in Bombay Green. By 1965, this soup bowl was no longer advertised with a cover; but, since the saucepan cover was the same size, the housewife could still obtain some type of lid—if this were desired. Price: $12-14.

The Dutch oven held four quarts of liquid, and while heavy is perfectly balanced. Price: $40-50.

However, there are no decorations scattered inside.

Notice the gracefully curved handle of this saucepan. When one looks at these pieces, a sense of delicate grace pervades, yet they are very heavy and solid: beautifully practical. The cook might not even want to mar this perfection by use. Price: $30-35.

Like the fry pan, the treatment is allowed to appear inside the saucepan. Here it is Old Orchard.

This scarce cheese dish also appeared in the *Impromptu* line—with its own finial. These pieces are in demand. They ceased production before 1965. Price: $20-25.

The base of the cheese dish has an indentation the exact size of a quarter pound of butter. Perhaps this led some collectors to assume it was a butter dish?

The hard-to-find mug. These are exactly the same in *Impromptu*—only the mark can identify them. This treatment is Blue Vineyards. Price: $25-30.

All butter dishes seen have this back stamp, which gives credence to the idea this piece was used in other Iroquois lines.

Just as the cheese dish, this butter dish has a place for the butter.

The stately samovar. The stand is quite difficult to find. This example is Blue Diamonds and the set is priced at $100+.

The oblong butter dish in Blue Vineyards. The top of the cover slopes slightly from ends to middle, and note the convenient little insert handle. Price: $20-25.

Note the unified and sculptural perfection of these shapes. They certainly are brilliant designs, but, unfortunately, they do not function well. They are awkward to hold and heavy to use. Coffee server (left): $70-80. Creamer in Blue Diamonds (center): $5-7. Milk jug (right): $35-40.

Note the small opening that qualifies as the spout.

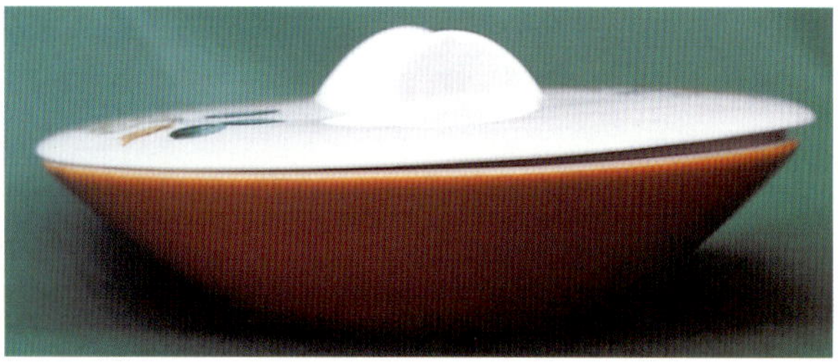

Try as I may, this saucepan cover will not fit this soup bowl. It should if the gumbo soup cover and the saucepan cover are interchangeable—at least according to the experts.

The complete buffet server minus the metal revolving stand. Usually the collectors build this item section by section. Price per unit: $10-12. If the collector finds the complete server on the stand he should be prepared to pay $75-85.

The faststand in citron yellow. One cannot pour from this gravy—the spout is useless—so a ladle is needed. It is wondered why Seibel did not include a ladle among the pieces. Price: $15-18.

A pleasant grouping of Sleepy Hollow. The 2-quart casserole (9.50" round) would be priced between $25-30.

Informal: Library of Treatments

As was done under the *Impromptu* Library, we will start with the four original treatments and then proceed with the other ten alphabetically. Regarding a pure white treatment such as *Impromptu's* Bridal White, it is now wondered if such a pure pattern did exist in *Informal*. If such a plain white treatment does exist, remember the reverse of the dinnerware is a solid color: thus the "whiteness" will be lessened. This shape was so tied to the solid glaze it is believed if the interior of a bowl, or the top surface of a plate or platter was pure white, the reverse must have been a solid glaze. I have seen plates, platters, and soup bowls with pure white surfaces and interiors, but the reverse is always glazed in some solid color: burnt orange, or teal, or citron, or gray-green. I do not believe this type of decorative approach can qualify as a pure white treatment.*

BLUE DIAMONDS. Based upon pure geometrics, this pattern is not really three elongated diamonds. If the collector looks closely there are really three triangles shadowed exactly by three reflecting triangles at their bases. Also, the color "blue" is misleading: slate gray and pale yellow are the most prominent shades and tints here. It is an exact, precise, rather inflexible pattern, yet pleasing because it stands forth so clearly on the pure white background. All *Informal* patterns have a reverse color—in this case a really very pleasant Bristol blue.

HARVEST TIME. This is the most available pattern of all the *Informal* treatments. As said before, its constant availability has reduced its value and leaves it an underestimated design. It is, if it were not so common, a striking approach: a large silver-gray oak leaf, medium burnt orange leaf, and a small leaf in rust. To unify the three, there are a few splashed dots of burnt orange scattered about the largest leaf. It could be ventured that well over seventy percent of all *Informal* treatments offered for sale are Harvest Time. I have heard the name Autumn Leaf also—and this makes absolute sense. The reverse color is burnt orange.

LAZY DAISY. Here is another fairly common pattern, but not reaching the ubiquitousness of Harvest Time. I have seen the trivided server in both Lazy Daisy and Rosemary—two of the four introductory designs. This server should also be found in Harvest Time and Blue Diamonds, but there I believe it will stop. Five "breeze-touched" daisies are arranged to the right of the plate, and on the other pieces these flowers are discreetly scattered. There is a great deal of white showing on the *Informal* plate. One tiny daisy is in citron yellow, and this is the reverse color.

ROSEMARY. This is another floral and the first of the two rose designs on this shape. Stylized roses—looking ever so much like pink cotton balls—appear in varying poses. It is a popular treatment and, like Lazy Daisy, charming. Its reverse is gray-green. While I have examples of all the *Informal* treatments, not all are on the dinner plate. In these cases, the treatment will be described from actual observation. The piece will be shown on another item.

BLUE VINEYARD. One must wonder what kind of vineyard is depicted. On what seems to be one winding stem (from right to left) are two strawberry blossoms in pale blue, strawberry leaves in olive green, four cobalt blackberries, a pale blue double marigold, one blueberry in the same color, and three dangling olives. Quite a mélange. Yet, when accepted as a possible entity, and viewed without criticism, this treatment is realistically portrayed in unified colors. However, it does seem rather scarce. The reverse is Bristol blue.

BOMBAY BLUE. Seibel liked to present two (or sometimes three) color variations of the same design—in the Bombay twosome the blue variety is the hardest to locate and the most stunning. This effect is caused by the contrast of the pale Bristol blue with the burnt orange boxes containing a black petalled stylized flower on a blue lozenge. The style is crisp and warm. The large *Informal* dinner plate presents a wonderful foil for many of the treatments and no treatment appears as perfectly as both Bombays. The reverse color is Bristol blue.

BOMBAY GREEN. Much easier to find, this treatment is just as clear and squarely placed, but the contrast between the lime green and Bristol blue is not as crisp. The reverse is gray-green.

GEORGETOWN. Although not many examples have been studied, this pattern appears to be raised slightly. It consists of two symmetrically executed groups of stylized flowers placed so closely they seem to run in a band about the individual item. The predominant color is green: a Kelly green, an olive green, and gray-green. There are also faint touches of beige in leaves and small flowers. There is a complexity about the treatment that defies a brief view. Not particularly handsome, it is serviceable. The reverse color is olive green.

HEARTS OF GOLD. This design does not appear in other dinnerware collector books, and I am sure this was a simple oversight. Rarely on the open marketplace: Replacements, Inc was the source of the dinner plate shown here. Again, like Georgetown, the plate is ringed with six separate but identical decals of heart-shaped ivy leaves in tan and gold. Each decal has eight leaves and the arrangements give the impression of a continuous rim pattern. The reverse could pass for citron yellow, but it actually mustard. The difference is easily seen if the two are compared. The color here is of the French's yellow variety.

"KNOLLWOOD." Please notice the parentheses. This pattern has not appeared on any official *Informal* treatment list: Knollwood officially appears on *Inheritance*. But, this light, delicate blue and green floral and leaf design has been seen on *Informal* and *Impromptu*. So far, only cups and saucers have been noted. The four Informal cups in my possession have the gray-green interior. The interiors of the tall *Impromptu* cup is white. The combination is very soft and winsome—hopefully other pieces will be located in the future.

MADRID. Another treatment passed over by a number of collector books. Like Georgetown, the three groups of brown, gold, and yellow stylized flowers seem slightly raised—especially when viewed under a slanted light. The encircling design is quite wide and prominent. It gives the impression of a quilted tapestry or bears a resemblance to an Amish decoration. The reverse is burnt orange.

OLD ORCHARD. Bunches of white grapes, three little blue plums (the hard variety?), and two brown/gold peaches cavort among grape leaves, six small blue florets, and what looks like some stray blueberries. The technique is fresh as a watercolor: the colors are pale and translucent. This pattern is quite a departure from the more formalized encircling border trims. Quite refreshing! The reverse is burnt orange.

SLEEPY HOLLOW. Even more delicately constructed, Sleepy Hollow portrays three arching clematis on a single vine. The blues are cornflower and turquoise; the central flower is peach and pale lemon. There is spidery delicacy and a sense of pure motion. These flowers seem to be going somewhere, as if caught in a moment of growth. Seibel's sense of pattern diversity is clearly seen by comparing the various *Informal* treatments. The reserve is citron yellow.

TEUTON/THANE. Another blue and brown variation of the same pattern, both are quite scarce, but Teuton is rather more difficult to find. Both appear on the more formally inspired *Inheritance*. Confusion reigned about how these heraldic motifs were arranged on the items. Please see the discussion under endnote 4. What does make both these *decoratifs* exciting is the manner in which they are "cut apart," or divided to fit the individual pieces: the lid of the sugar bowl is a very good example. The cups, for instance, only show the small *fleur de lys* sprinkled about the outside rim. The device is quite rigid and to be shown in a variety of spaces, had to be cut, not shaped. Teuton uses russet and sand with burnt orange as the reverse color. Thane is in sky blue and pale lettuce with Bristol blue as the reverse.

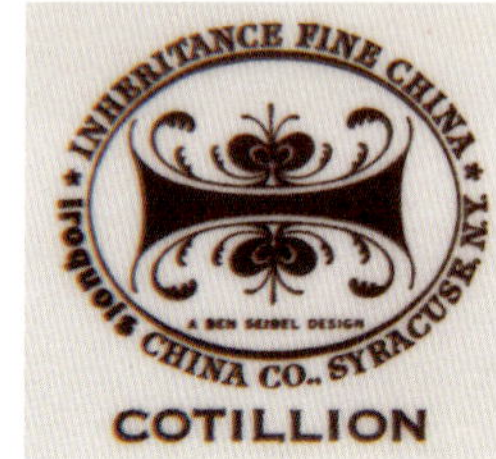

The back stamp. *Inheritance back stamps* always included the name of the treatment.

Inheritance: A Dinnerware Line Set Apart

Some readers must remember the television situation comedy staring the dusky-voiced and indomitable Bea Arthur. The program was a spin from *All In The Family*, but *Maude* was securely middle-class and outrageously liberal. The opening music followed a progression from the sooty streets of Brooklyn to tree-lined suburban streets. And finally the gracious Queen Anne house of MAUDE! At this moment, as Bea Arthur opened the front door and smiled a welcome, the chorus pealed out—"And then there's Maude!" She was different, unusual, a person to be set apart!

Here I proclaim—"And then there's *Inheritance*!"

Whenever Ben Seibel contracted to do more than one line of tableware for a particular company, he seemed to design each line to fulfill a different philosophy of eating. There would be overlapping of using potentialities. *Inheritance* filled the requirements for formal, refined, leisurely dining: it would be at home in Buckingham Palace, or on a "working breakfast" table in the Oval Office when the members of his "team" watched George W. Bush tear up another international treaty. *Inheritance* could go anywhere—as long as that "anywhere" was perfectly polished and conservatively purified.

Inheritance exudes elegance; it registers refinement; it is quintessentially conservative. It is a very special line of dinnerware and is perfectly compatible with the finest of dining experiences. The shape is conservatively simple, delicately graceful, and splendidly sculptural. Yes, seen individually and devoid of any decorations, the pieces have the quality of sculpture. *Inheritance* is Ben Seibel's most resplendent dinnerware shape. The year was 1959, when middle-class ladies wore white gloves in the afternoon, diamonds were reserved for special events after dark, and fine dining was an occasion to relish and enjoy. This line of Seibel dinnerware is—or was—the epitome of sophistication. One can only wonder if the management at Iroquois, obviously in a conservative mode, suggested to Seibel that the third dinnerware shape be modeled amid an aura of glamour and graciousness.

And it most certainly was!

The ceramic material from which *Inheritance* is composed approaches the thinness, the brittle delicate quality, of pure porcelain. There is a pure shimmering luster that comes from within the material, not merely a glazed surface veneer. With both the shape and the material reaching near perfection, no wonder *Inheritance* is a marvel to behold!

The shape is comparatively rare and relatively unknown. Notice the use of two qualitative words here: "comparatively" and "relatively." *Inheritance* is "rare" compared with *Informal* and *Impromptu*, but can be located by concerted and planned effort. The collector can go into most large collectibles malls and find examples of Seibel's first two acknowledged lines for Iroquois: not so with *Inheritance*. If the collector is fond of this Seibel shape, it should be purchased when seen. It does appear, but who can say how often? And it is unknown insofar as the general American dinnerware collector is concerned. Of course, Seibel enthusiasts know it well—its name at least is on every list devoted to the works of Ben Seibel. Some Seibelists have a rather affected approach to *Inheritance*: its design is not "funky" or "extreme" or even terribly unusual. One might even wonder if the shape could be called Mid-Century-Modern. Yet the handles of the teacup, creamer, and teapot arch a little higher than needed for normalcy, but also are supremely functional. And those finials! They are certainly examples of floating delicacy in motion.

Best to state: *Inheritance* is a conservatively designed, classically sculptural dinnerware line with a few Mid-Century-Modern tendencies especially in the handles and the finials. That certainly will do.

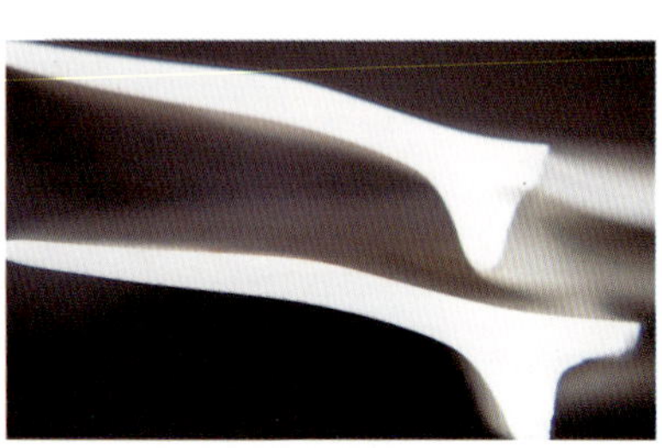

Notice the delicate curve of the thin porcelain-like china. This is a broken rim of a dinner plate.

The careful observant reader will remember I stated in the section on *Impromptu* it was the "first and the best" of Ben Seibel's Iroquois work. Do not, please, be confused by all the adulation given to *Inheritance*! My adoration of *Inheritance*—and it does border on adoration—does not mean it is the best and the first. One can adore a woman for her supreme beauty (say Rita Hayworth or Greta Garbo) or adulate a woman for her supreme intelligence (say Eleanor Roosevelt or Catherine the Great) but one would hardly feel at home and at ease in the presence of any of these awesome ladies! *Inheritance* is a fantastically beautiful dinnerware shape, but does it inspire warmth and congeniality? Near physical perfection can border on chilliness. What *Impromptu* lacks in pristine beauty it garners in friendliness and warmth and usability. This is what I meant by *Impromptu* being the first and the best!

In the number of individual pieces, *Inheritance* is a short line. A reminder: *Impromptu* consisted of thirty-four items; *Informal* boasts of thirty pieces. But not all were available at one time. Only nineteen pieces were produced for *Inheritance*. Short indeed when compared with the first two Iroquois shapes.

Dinner plate	(910)
Salad plate	(908)
Bread & butter plate	(907)
Teacup	(980)
Saucer	(981)
Rim soup	(990)
Cereal	(903)
Fruit	(902)
Cream	(940)
Sugar w/cover	(941)
Open vegetable	(960)
Medium platter	(992)
Large platter/S	(993)
Salad bowl/S	(995)
Casserole w/cover/S	(987)
Div. veg. w/cover	(982)
Gravy boat F/S	(991)
Teapot/S	

Eighteen pieces in china and the nineteenth, a large serving tray (901-W), fashioned out of black lacquered wood. Again, as with *Impromptu*, Seibel offered the customer auxiliary items but with a different twist. Instead of belonging to a special "gift ware" category[1], and instead of being made of brass, the extra *Inheritance* items were made of an oriental styled black lacquered wood and were offered free with the items they accompanied. Those marked with the /S above had such a stand: the serving tray was a separate piece priced $6.95.

Not only do these elegant stands—all hugging the basal shape of their piece—raise the piece slightly, they acted also as a display stand and thus placed the teapot, casserole, salad bowl and large platter into the category of usable sculpture. These stands were Seibel's most successful attempt at integrating wood or metal bases into a dinnerware line and strongly enhanced the oriental overtones. Unfortunately for today's collector, the stands—like the *Impromptu* brass warmers—are rare indeed. Lucky is the Seibel enthusiast who numbers some black lacquer stands among his/her *Inheritance* collection. They are cherished items.

"Choose your own INHERITANCE" was the advertising catch phrase. My Grandmother was the organist in a high Episcopal Church in Northern New Jersey and she would often describe her performance whenever the Bishop would make a visitation as "pulling all the stops out!" Similarly Iroquois pulled out all the advertising stops for *Inheritance*. A few of the press releases proclaimed:

Inheritance Fine China, significant new milestone in fine china elegance, crowns its design achievements with a price story never before told in fine china history—making it possible for every woman to own the very best.

The universal pleasure of enduring good design...the unmistakable quality of beautifully translucent china...prices that forever banish pocketbook pinch from fine china ownership—this is Inheritance, every WOMAN'S Inheritance Fine China.[2]

Fine china is the right of every women, the hallmark of an elegant home and a gracious way of life. Too often, however, the modern homemaker must forfeit this right...because today's budgets cannot always afford elegance. Inheritance fine china, designed by Ben Seibel and produced by the Iroquois China Company, makes American china history by giving classic fine china elegance contemporary form and function...and by recognizing that if it is the right of every woman to want fine china, it is also the right of every woman to be able to own fine china.[3]

Not only advertising hyperbole but Ben Seibel gave an interview where he discussed "*Inheritance* Fine China as seen by the Designer."

The creation of a new look is only one of many considerations when a designer takes on an assignment. He must think through a project in terms of the material he is to use, the effect he seeks to achieve, how well the finished product will work and how well it will look.

Above all, a designer cannot ignore what has gone before nor become so totally objective in his desire to create something different that his designs lose touch with the familiar, the emotional and with his own personality.

Throughout this interview, Seibel stresses "Classic design may be thoroughly contemporary and new, as *Inheritance* Fine China certainly is, yet have the appearance of belonging;" "[*Inheritance*] is never jarring to the sensibilities;" and that "fine china demands formal design of a certain serenity." The same words appear again and again: serenity, fine china, belonging, classic, sculptural, elegant, traditional, delicate, exquisitely tasteful—words pertaining particularly to *Inheritance* and certainly not to *Informal* and even barely to *Impromptu*.

Indeed all the stops were pulled out to prepare the public for this new Iroquois/Seibel dinnerware line.[4]

On the lists, the little fruit dish is not mentioned as having a foot: not a high one, but certainly it qualifies as a "footed fruit dish." Barely 4.75" round, this charming bowl stands up from the table and makes a nice presentation for shrimp cocktail. Pure white outside, the decoration is limited to the inside of the bowl.

Gravy boats are known by another earlier name—sauce dishes—and I really think they should "pour." Some of Seibel's designs allow for this pouring, some do not. The *Inheritance* gravy—4.36" round and twin spouted—was copied almost, but not quite exactly, as the Mikasa *Pivotal* gravy some twenty years later. Seibel must have liked the shape. This example has more flowing grace than the *Pivotal* gravy, and is quite a lovely form even if it can function only with a ladle. The base is a substantial 7.50" round.

The salad bowl is a spectacular item, especially when placed upon the accompanying black lacquer stand. It is 10.50" round, but because of the slight undulation in the rim, it looks off-center. The salad bowl is rare also: rarer than the teapot over which every Seibel collector fusses and fumes. Filled with flowers and fruit, this graceful footed bowl easily becomes a centerpiece. This piece certainly belongs in every Seibel collection.

The casserole, again footed and lidded with that fey arching finial—so easy to break—is very popular. However, one finds ten or twelve casseroles for every salad bowl. The casserole cover is exceptionally flat, probably to emphasize the finial, and the handles are gracefully arched and expertly molded to the base. The size is a tad under 9", and it owns it own stand. There is absolutely nothing "slap-dash" or "make-do" when dealing with *Inheritance*. As Gloria nasaled in *Auntie Mame*: "It's really top drawer!"

The covered, divided vegetable: here is a surprising, unexpected piece. It follows the rounded oblong shape of the smaller open vegetable bowl: 11.50" long, 8.75" wide. The rim is flat and unusually wide (1.25") and my example, Beige Rose, has a tiny rosebud on the rim. This rim can be seen when the cover is in place, and unlike the casserole, this cover is noticeably convex. Sophisticated elegance is the exact term to use. Perhaps strangely, this covered vegetable has no stand.

The teapot! Oh those furiously sought after teapots! I waited a long time to obtain mine, and I was not disappointed. But now that an *Inheritance* teapot sits on my shelf, I wonder, just a little, at all the fuss. This teapot is lovely, completely rounded, easy to pour, but—and I dread at speaking thus—I wonder about that handle. Too obviously flamboyant? Too aggressively vertical? Too uprightly arrogant? For myself, just for myself, I would wish for a more flowing and subtle handle: one that perhaps matched the gentleness of the spout. Just my personal opinion.

When first offered in the fall of 1959, *Inheritance* was advertised in the following treatments:

- Sheer White
- Gold Band
- Platinum Band
- Baroque
- Cotillion
- Grecian Gold
- Knollwood
- Su-Shi

Very soon after its introduction other patterns were added:

- Beige Rose
- Dynasty
- Medallion
- Teuton
- Thane

One author has also added Pyramids to this list, but this has never, to my knowledge, been seen on the *Inheritance* shape. Nonetheless, thirteen choices are very generous when the collector remembers that the much more popular and extensive line *Informal* boasted of only fourteen treatments. Beige Rose is probably the easiest to find. The three all white treatments and Knollwood are not quite as available, and Dynasty is—in my opinion—the most difficult. I have yet to see examples of *Inheritance* Dynasty outside of advertising sheets. Teuton and Thane might have two versions. I have seen an advertising sheet touting Thane/Teuton and it is exactly like the *Informal* versions (please see *Informal*: The Library of Patterns.) Yet Harvey Duke does show an *Inheritance* dinner plate with a larger, single, centered heraldic emblem.[5] Are there two versions? This is a conundrum waiting to be solved by an *Inheritance* collector!

In mid-2002, I almost acquired a Thane *Interitance* rim soup—erroneouslybilled as a "chowder bowl"—but the modish dealer reneged on the deal. This might have helped to solve the questions!

It must be surmised both Iroquois and Ben Seibel viewed *Inheritance* as being special: to fill the fine dining conservative niche. Strangely, all the advertising hype could not have caused much consumer commotion. In August 1964 (when *Intaglio* appeared) arrangements could no longer be made to acquire examples of *Inheritance* for photography. In a form circulated by Jean Forbes (of Robert Whitehill Advertising) *Impromptu*, *Informal*, the new *Intaglio*, and Russel Wright's *Casual China* (1946) were the only lines offered for photographic sessions. Is it correct to assume *Inheritance* was no longer in production?

But in the late '50s and the early months of the 1960s *Inheritance* seemed a valuable commodity—well worth thirteen treatments. The destined elegance of the shape was proven in the three white choices: no other Seibel/Iroquois creation placed before the public a pure white set trimmed in both gold and platinum and a third completely unadorned. Fine china very eloquently polished!

However, several of the proposed decorative treatments were borrowings: Beige Rose and, probably, Knollwood, came via *Impromptu* and the Teuton/Thane duo were directly taken from *Informal*. This still leaves nine patterns exclusive to *Inheritance*—most of which were cast in the oriental mode.

The very existence of this shape came as a surprise to those critics who, in the late 1950s, were watching the trends in American dinnerware. Who would have envisioned such a step back into the restrained past. After *Informal*, these critics were waiting for further developments toward exaggerated extremes in casual dining. But Seibel outsmarted the critics, hedged his bets, gathered his chips, and presented such a subtle polished shape as to confound his critics and astound us even today!

The footed creamer in Sheer White. Notice the curve of the handle: this is the handle shape I would like to see on the teapot. Price: $6-8.

Looking into the fruit dish. This treatment is Cotillion.

The most elegant of rim soups! Low and 9" round, this bowl has a 1.25" rim. This example is in Platinum Band. Price: $12-14.

The Sheer White sugar bowl—also footed—and with the lid topped with the fabulous finial. This finial has elicited many descriptive terms from assorted collectors. Price: $8-10.

Beige Rose on the three sizes of *Inheritance* plates. This treatment is readily available on this shape—but not common. The sloping well—so easily seen in this photograph—lends a different aspect to the design. It appears on *Impromptu* and probably appeared there first. Iroquois decided to use Beige Rose on *Inheritance* because it is so subdued and elegant. Prices: Dinner plate, $12-14; Salad plate, $6-8; Bread & butter plate, $3-4.

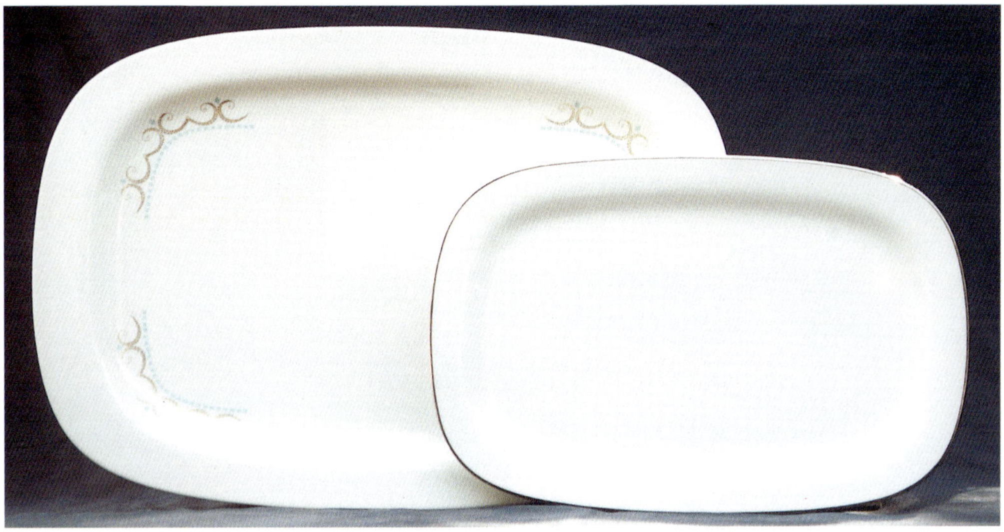

The two platters: The larger one (16") is seen in Cotillion and has its own lacquer stand. The smaller is 12.50" and is in Platinum Band. There is quite a difference in size. Platter (large), $18-20; Platter (small), $12-14.

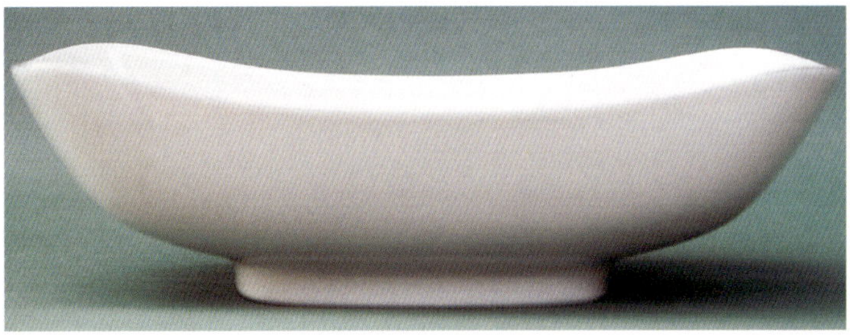

The side view of the Platinum Band open vegetable. It is footed and rises slightly at either end. At 9.75" it is relatively small. Price: $12-14.

Here is a pasted outline of the teapot resting on its small black lacquer stand.

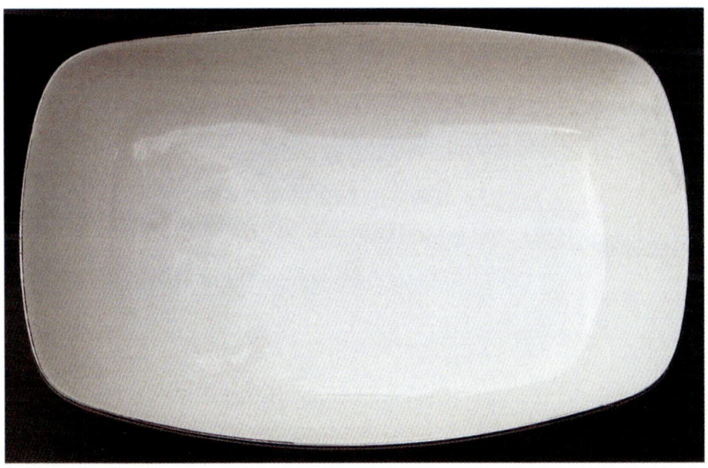

Looking down into the open vegetable.

Side view of the footed fruit dish. Not quite tall enough to be termed a "compote," it nevertheless bears resemblance to one. Seibel was adept at dealing with fruit dishes, and he often tried to make them special. Price: $4-6.

The lidded casserole in the Medallion treatment. Footed and with a flat cover, the piece throws a low profile, but this changes when it is seated on its lacquer stand. Take care of those finials, they snap quite easily. Price: $30-40.

Here is the rare covered divided vegetable: a very grand piece. Like the rim soup, the rim is wide—wide enough to hold a Beige Rose bud.
Truly a beautiful item. Price: $40-45.

Equally divided within, this dish makes an elegant presentation.

The round two-spouted gravy faststand. One needs a silver ladle: both for practical use and for sophisticated accompaniment. These gravies are rather difficult to locate. Price: $15-18.

The large Grecian Gold salad bowl: it has a black lacquer stand that is just the same size of its base. Probably the most dramatic piece in the *Inheritance* line (my opinion), they are not often seen in the marketplace. Note how the edges slope slightly up: it is, however, completely 10" round. Price: $30-40.

The teapot with it rigidly upright handle. Not completely comfortable to hold, this item is considered by many collectors a Ben Seibel masterpiece. Agreed, it is a sculpturally flamboyant piece, but perhaps overpriced? Price: $130+.

The teapot is a perfect round.

The casserole in Beige Rose seen from the top.

The Sheer White teacup and saucer. The handle, while still graceful, it not as extenuated as the creamer: it is easy to use. Price: $8-10 the set.

Intaglio

The Fourth and Last of Seibel/Iroquois Partnership

The *Intaglio* back stamp. Note, unlike *Inheritance*, the treatment is not named.

Not quite an afterthought, but quite close to it. *Intaglio*, the fourth and last of the generally accepted Iroquois shapes done by Ben Seibel, was offered to the public in 1964. It is definitely "the little sister." But before I get carried away on this "kid sister" routine, I wish to include some comments sent by a very perceptive Mid-Century-Modern collector—a fine author in his own right. Since I have not fully come to firm grips with all the aspects that make up MCM, Michael Pratt and I occasionally converse via e-mail. He kindly explains and re-explains his thoughts about Mid-Century-Modern characteristics. Here are two comments from a message dated March 31, 2001.

> *Much of what I like about MCM is that it is unexpectedly innovative. A lid may have a pinch finial and be on a severe slant, as it is in the California Seaside coffee pot by Laurel. A creamer may have a simplified flourish as an extension of its body as it does in Roseville Raymor. The Ben Seibel bun warmers in ceramic—surprise, surprise! Simple, sleek, mechanical innovations in ceramic.*

Mr. Pratt continues:

> Intaglio *is unexpectedly true to its name. The predominant decoration is a bold series of depressions in the surface that give the line dimensionality. The shapes are simple almost masculine with a durability that is obvious with handling. Yet, the line has presence and in the undecorated pattern, the genius of the in-mold decoration is seen. The obvious is actually unexpected. Whereas traditional decorations have been embossed, Ben Seibel uses the inverse to make a statement—bold debossment. This is surely unexpected. Look at all your traditional Homer Laughlin. Do you see any debossment or intaglio? How bold is the embossment?*

These are wise and perceptive words with which to start a section on *Intaglio*.

There are a few definitions in order. *Intaglio*, for example, is the perfect name for this '60s tableware shape: it is true to its name. The word means "a design or figure incised beneath the surface of hard metal or stone." The term "ceramic" must be added here. Mr. Pratt then coins a perfect word: a word not found in my dictionary, but it fits to perfection—"debossment." "Embossment" is a raised design; debossment a carved out design. One as the reverse of the other, or, as often stressed, the classic *ying* and *yang*! Please notice the other terms he uses to define *Intaglio*: "masculine" and "durability." The observations are true and they put *Intaglio* in a different category than *Inheritance*. We have concluded *Inheritance* gave the appearance of feminine fragility and brittleness. Not so *Intaglio*!

Even with the new concept of "rim-dimples," *Intaglio* was considerably more formal and graceful—solidly graceful—than *Informal*, and more rounded and less extended than *Impromptu*. While *Intaglio*'s weight was still as substantial as the first two lines, the general impression was much lighter. The "debossed" dimpled band produces a definite shadow and light effect—especially when seen by fluttering candlelight—and introduces an airiness and uplifting sparkle. This effect is similar to how the holes of a block of Swiss cheese visually enlighten it considerably over a similar block of white Cheddar. It is all in the effect! Candlelight heightens this condition: moving flame, both large and small, can cause the optical illusion of natural movement. This is why Byzantine mosaics (or any mosaics for that matter) must be viewed by flickering torch light. If not, they are heavy and lifeless. When a flickering torch is held before the mosaic depicting the portrait of Empress Theodora or the fabulous interior of the Mausoleum of Galla Placidia in Ravenna, the fluttering light causes entire images to "move." Under the same torch, the eyes of mosaic figures (if made of bits of glass) follow the viewers in illusionary eeriness.

On the table, to lighten and sparkle, to emphasize its different qualities, *Intaglio* also should be seen under candlelight.

Thus the researcher and the collector can believe that the "kid sister" grew up, left the parental household, and became a dinnerware force of her own.

Jean Forbes of Robert Whitehill Advertising stressed the same qualities in her press release of August 1964.

> *To watch a hostess bring off a dinner party beautifully and without help is enough to send her women guests home despairing of their own abilities and equipment and yearning for the secret of such efficiency. Iroquois' new* Intaglio *collection,*[1] *designed by Ben Seibel, introduces stunning sculptured design and a unique intaglio motif which rimes plates and circles hollowware pieces, capturing and reflecting natural light to create jewel-like brilliants again the shimmering white china body. Here is an altogether new look for table settings and appetizing presentation of food.*

Even though this new shape was different and heavily advertised, it was quite modest in the number of pieces offered to the public. As economic changes took place in the United States, businessmen, like Iroquois China Company executives, grew cautious and hesitated to offer similarly cautious consumers too much, too soon. As was noted in the preceding section, *Inheritance* did not elicit very much public interest and simply was not overwhelmingly popular. Perhaps the relationship between Ben Seibel and Iroquois China was stretching thin and the company's reins were becoming restrictive.

Like *Inheritance*, it seems that there was little change in the pieces: what was offered originally stayed. As stated, this could reflect hesitancy on the part of the manufacturer to undertake the expense of producing new items, or it can hint that by 1964 public demand for large dinnerware sets was waning, or it could simply mean the original number was so perfect for the times, no changes were needed. Whatever the reason, *Intaglio* was a very short line!

Dinner plate	(310)
Salad/dessert plate	(308)
Bread & butter plate	(307)
Cup	(380)
Saucer	(381)
Fruit	(302)
Soup/cereal	(303)
Creamer	(340)
Sugar w/cover	(341)
Large platter	(393)
Small platter	(392)
Open vegetable	(360)
Casserole w/cover	(387)
Trivet server	(388)
Beverage pitcher w/cover	(352)

Only fifteen pieces, but totally adequate for all manner of entertaining. There are a few interesting observations. For example, Seibel conjures a fairly deep fruit dish flaring upwards from a narrow base. This suspiciously reminds the viewer of the designer's dedicated dalliance with "compotes." The cup was envisioned having a pure and simple shape, heavy and utilitarian with none of the curving eccentricities (is that a good word?) of the *Impromptu* cup. The applied handle of this cup is just a bit too narrow for the average man's index finger, and the weight necessitates the middle finger give added support under the handle. There is an interesting fact about cup handles: the fingers work themselves automatically into a favorable position whatever cup is being lifted. There is absolutely no need to think about the best way to hold any cup; the fingers make this decision without consultation. The handle, also applied, of the rounded creamer is better constructed: it translates into near perfect balance, and, unlike the cup, there is no unconscious undercurrent of possible slippage.

The "teapot" was designated a "beverage pitcher" which, to my thought, is a jargonized term commensurable to labeling a garbage collector as a "waste management engineer." The reason is simple: to the average consumer, a "coffee server" is used only to serve coffee, and a teapot to make and dispense tea. Ben Seibel designed the *Intaglio* teapot to look like a teapot, and to act best like a teapot. The decision to rename this piece a "beverage pitcher" surely was not Seibel's. It must have risen within the "sales hype" department at Iroquois.

A major surprise does arrive with the fascinating trivet server. This is Ben at his best! Its center was raised like a tabletop and then gently indented to allow the casserole or open vegetable or even the smaller soup/cereal to be securely placed. A trough-like area surrounds this center, and the designer wisely left it un-dimpled to allow for a more efficient cleaning. This smooth area was obviously meant to house a variety of foods such as cheese, carrots or celery sticks, or even filled with flowers to become a modest but still effective centerpiece. Whatever its projected use, the 11" round trivet server seems thinner than the other pieces, and I have only seen it in pure white.[2]

The general impression given by the hollowware and platters is of an "oval." The outline curves in at top and base to present a very pleasing, unusual view. The teacup is more squared than the sugar and creamer, but has a very extended, graceful handle. The placement of the "debossed" dimples changes to add variety to the line—in the cups the dimples are at the base, the creamer has them at the top, the sugar, only on the lid. The slightly pedestaled fruit has the dimples around its narrow base; the open vegetable wears the incised decoration near the outside rim. This variation is subtle and intrigues the viewer without being obvious. The platters are a little unusual also: the large platter (15.50" by 11.25") is really large and the small platter (11.50" x 9") quite small. The dissimilarity is size is very plain.

The collector would not waste time making a study of all the Seibel finials. They fit perfectly with the shape and one finial would be severely out of place on another line. In *Intaglio* Seibel opts for a triangular, bended, "wet-noodle." Very simple and understated, but perfectly in tune with the soft oval view.[3] When working with Iroquois, Seibel greatly improved the functionalism of his finial/handles. Not only does the finger slip into the *Intaglio* finials with pure ease, the designer has improved this function by carving a gentle space that fits perfectly the back of the grasping finger. *Intaglio* could well possess the most perfectly functional finial coupled with graceful charm.

The number of available treatments had narrowed also. They are all botanically based. In the Whitehill press release quoted from above, the patterns were listed as: Wild Violet, Colonial Pink, Colonial Blue, Rosette, Dahlia, Painted Daisy, and pure white—here called Diamond White. The first three named were patterns taken directly from *Impromptu*, but very soon these were renamed (to prevent confusion?) Woodale, Old English Pink, and Old English Blue. Woodale has proven to be the most easily found *Intaglio* pattern.

The *Intaglio* treatments proclaimed a new, more hesitant approach by the Iroquois Company. While undecorated white was again repeated as it had been in *Impromptu* and *Inheritance*, the other treatments accorded this last Iroquois/Seibel line were done so with caution.

Three of the decorations were borrowed faithfully from *Impromptu*: Wild Violet translated to *Intaglio* became Woodale; Colonial Blue was renamed Old English Blue; and Colonial Pink became Old English Pink—same treatment, different name.

Moreover, three other designs—entirely *Intaglio-esque*—were doubled. Not really, as in the Wrigley's advertisement: double your pleasure, double your fun, but because one treatment in two color schemes seemingly gave a wider choice without actually doing so. Perhaps the double Old English choices gave the Iroquois art department the idea.

Thus Dahlia was divided into Dahlia Blue and Dahlia Golden, Rosette was sectioned into Rosette Jade (Blue) and Rosette Sun (Gold), and Painted Daisy also received two color schemes—without two official names—pink, yellow, ochre, and brown; blue, turquoise, and green. I choose to call these two Painted Daisy (Blue) and Painted Daisy (Pink).

It is interesting to note, only *Intaglio* Ivy (a rather unknown design in dark green) was pure and simply one treatment, not borrowed and undivided!

The patterns now can be listed.

Dahlia Blue
Dahlia Golden
Diamond White
Ivy
Old English Blue
Old English Pink
Painted Daisy (Blue)
Painted Daisy (Pink)
Rosette Jade
Rosette Sun
Woodale

Indeed here is a paucity of decorative approaches lovingly disguised by careful color use. With decals scattered sparsely upon a pure white glaze (the debossment representing a very strong decorative touch of its own), *Intaglio* projects informal durability, a provincial solidity, and a crisp purity. Never abundant, always elusive, this final Iroquois shape is, perhaps, the most satisfying, the most original.

As this shape is studied perceptively, it becomes apparent *Intaglio* is best appreciated in a rural setting. Perhaps bathed with softly curtained reflective sunlight in one of France's provincial kitchens. There rough-hewn tables are covered in blue or red checkered cloth with bunches of daisies or feathery dillweed in a terra cotta crock, and long loaves of crisp, fresh bread lie ready to be broken into bits. The brilliant white of the *Intaglio* ware catches the late afternoon light streaming through the open windows: the white turns to honey color in the slanting sun. It is a vintage setting, both honest and authentic: not sophisticated, but true. Deep red wine in a jug (certainly not in the so-called *Intaglio* beverage server) is poured into modest, thick glasses or into

Brochure front showing Woodale, a treatment called Wild Violet when it appears on *Impromptu*.

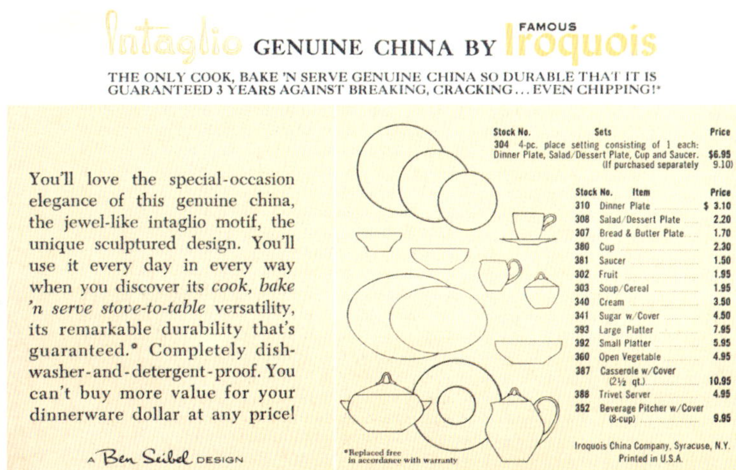

Reverse of brochure.

clear jelly jars—watered for the children, crisp and biting for the adults. Perhaps this is what Mr. Pratt meant by "durability," for nothing is as durable as French country folk!

Perhaps, dear readers, we have traveled a convoluted path during our discussion of *Intaglio*. I have led you on a circled route and have nearly contradicted myself at times. We—or at least I do—remain uncertain and unclear. Just what did Ben Seibel actually have in mind when he created *Intaglio*?

The small fruit bowl seen from the side. The debossment appears near the base and reinforces the idea of the piece being "footed." Treatments always appear inside. Price: $4-6.

The reverse of the trivet is lovely in itself and, if the back stamp were covered, could be used as a centerpiece.

The well-proportioned cup with its undecorated, un-dimpled saucer. However, the handle is awkward to hold. Prices: Cup, $5-6; Saucer, $2-3.

A teapot by any other name is still a teapot! However, officially this sculptured piece is named: Beverage server. The glaze is very reflective. This impressive item rises to 7.75", and at the expansive arc of the handle, the piece is nearly 8" wide. While heavy, the well-designed handle allows for perfect control. Price: $40-45.

The multi-use trivet. Price: $18-20.

The trivet and the fruit dish become a "chip 'n dip."

The trivet with the open vegetable: a canapé server?

The trivet used as a base for the covered casserole. Casserole price: $30-35.

The dimpling on the sugar bowl is confined to the cover.

The small platter is dwarfed by the larger one. Prices: Large, $18-20; Small, $12-14.

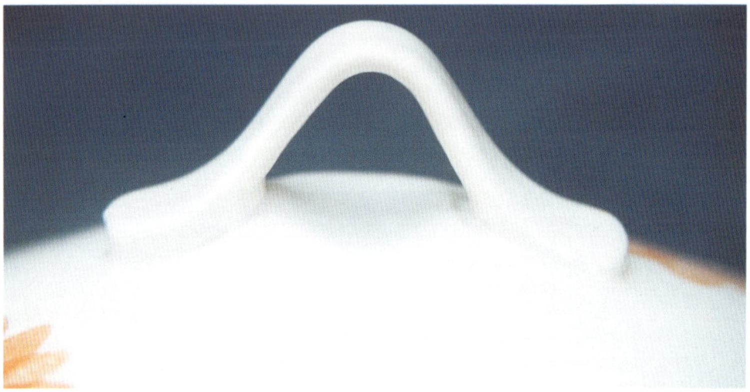

The very graceful applied finial appears on the teapot, sugar, and casserole.

The treatments appear inside the fruit dish. To the left is Rosette Sun, to the right Dahlia Orange.

A beautiful sugar and creamer set. This is Ivy—a treatment discovered only a few years ago. Prices: Sugar, $10-12; Creamer, $6-8.

Here are the two variations of the Rosette treatment. On larger pieces the Rosette Sun is very vibrant, almost startling in its brightness. Rosette Jade is much more modest.

A sampling of the Woodale treatment. This is the easiest treatment to find on *Intaglio*.

Inheritance/Intaglio: Library of Treatments

Since these two shapes are difficult to acquire, dinner plates cannot be used to illustrate all the treatments. If any reader does have a plate where I show none, and is willing to share a photograph of the same, the sharing would be deeply appreciated.

Photographs of all the treatments listed below have been seen and studied. These photographs were in black/white, but included color descriptions. Seeing a photograph, while helpful, does not compare with the actual touching and turning of a plate.

Beige Rose in the most abundantly located of the *Inheritance* treatments, and Woodale is preeminent on *Intaglio*. Other motifs are range from very scarce to rare: the collector must be willing to struggle to obtain representatives of each and every treatment.

INHERITANCE. This shape always identifies the treatment by listing it under the back stamp.

BEIGE ROSE. This is the same treatment appearing on *Impromptu*. It also seems reasonably available on this shape.

BAROQUE. A medieval scroll design that looks carved reaching from verge to the rim edge—quite dignified and stately in a restrained manner. The color has been described as taupe (a pale grayed beige.) Within each curve is a tiny pinpoint of soft gold—a very subtle addition counteracting any blandness. Baroque is a rare pattern. Although some advertising photographs have been seen, I had to wait a long time before procuring the plate shown.

COTILLION. "Dainty as a fairy queen's necklace" says an advertising blurb, and this description is quite accurate: it could be a gold and turquoise necklace. The design encircles the broad *Inheritance* rim—the tiny squares of turquoise near the verge, the golden crosshatched scrolls curving toward the edge with jewel-like turquoise diamond shapes interspersed. The smaller plates have the "necklace" moved to the central well. This is a very effective and subtle treatment.

DYNASTY. Extremely rare. This is composed of a narrow red and orange band inscribed with oriental characters in ochre. The teapot is primarily white with this encircling the opening. Very sophisticated and inspired by Japanese ceramic ware.

GOLD BAND. At one time it was believed Sheer White was divided into three categories: gold banded, platinum banded, and not banded. Research has brought forth that Iroquois considered these three separate treatments. The Gold Band is the most elusive of the three.

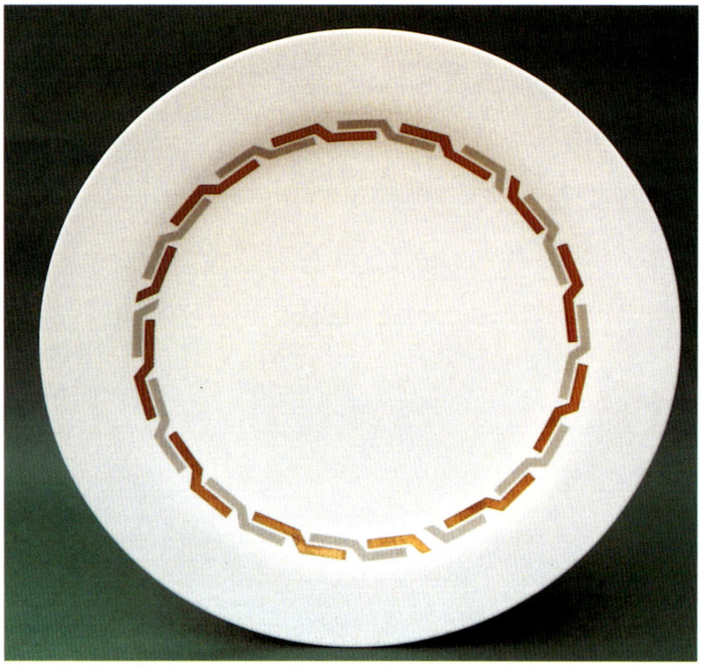

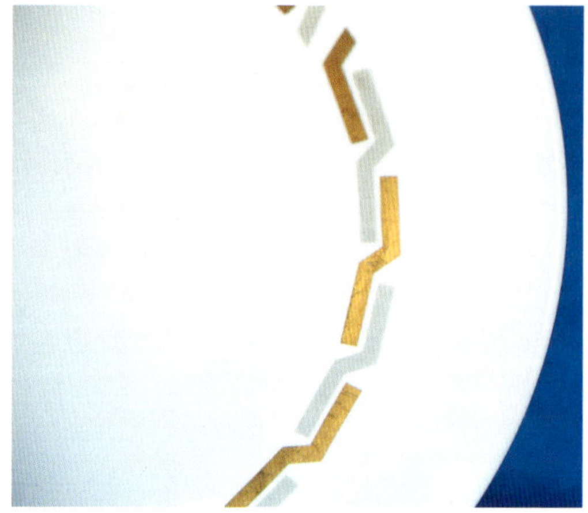

GRECIAN GOLD. This was one of the more expensive treatments—along with Cotillion. While the Sheer White covered divided vegetable was priced $10.95, Grecian Gold cost $14.95. This was 1959—the year the shape was first introduced. The design was touted as "regally distinctive." Since *Inheritance* plates had a verge (*Impromptu* and *Informal* plates were "vergeless") it was fair game to decorate them. Grecian Gold uses the verge to encircle the well with a modified Greek key decorative band in burnished gold and pale silver gray. It is surely the most sophisticated treatment on any Iroquois shape.

KNOLLWOOD. Until recently this treatment was thought to be exclusive to *Inheritance*, but the discovery of eight tall *Impromptu* cups and saucers wearing the same floral and leaf decals disrupt this conclusion. A further disruption was an August 2001 finding of five *Informal* cups (no saucers) bearing the Knollwood design. The researcher cannot be sure if the *Impromptu* pattern was known by the same name. But Knollwood—by any name—probably appeared first on the earlier shape. The pattern has an airy, extremely delicate, and widely spaced arrangement of olive green deeply indented leaves on spidery, trailing, vine-like stems. There are two small, stylized flowers in Bristol blue and one other in paler sky blue. Wandering between the verge and the rim, Knollwood has the look of a scattered salad. A mesclun mix favored by Martha Stewart—the salad she sprinkles with edible flowers.

MEDALLION. Defined as a pattern reminiscent of a royal seal, Medallion could also be described as a squared Maltese cross in pale gray-green with four ochre triangles linking the crossings. The gray-green is barely evident, but it is there, a hint. When quickly viewed or superficially seen, the cross and triangle unit becomes circular—thus a seal. This treatment falls into the category of a rim pattern: it skirts the plates and the cups at the edges and marches delicately at the top of the other pieces.

PLATINUM BAND. Silver trim rather than gold. A treatment that is easier to find and more popular.

SHEER WHITE. While none of the *Inheritance* treatments are overpowering, and the shimmer of clear white is always in evidence, Sheer White allows the viewer to appreciate the pure and simply sculptural beauty of the shape. Pedestaled on black lacquered wood, the Sheer White pieces become sculpture: Ben Seibel meant this to be.

TEUTON. Teuton and its color variety Thane are scarce treatments—scarce both on *Informal* where they originally appeared, and on *Inheritance*. The design consists of two devices: a large and rather stiff four-pointed figure usually termed "heraldic," and a smaller, curved, and easily placed *fleur de lys* that acts as an edge decorative motif. Both have never been seen on this shape, but the reader is asked to view the same treatments under *Informal*: they are exactly the same. Remember there seems to be two versions on the dinner plate: the single very large motif in the center, and a scattering of nine smaller motifs on the entire surface. The latter is almost disturbingly busy.

THANE. Teuton is a combination of red russet and warm sand. Thane is sky blue and lettuce leaf green.

INTAGLIO. This shape has built-in restrictions regarding treatments. The presence of the dimples severely limits the area where designs can be placed—on the plates, the verge and the well. Unlike *Inheritance* the name of the treatment does not appear in the back stamp.

DAHLIA BLUE. Two "dahlias" looking ever so much like spun sugar candy. The name reflects the color of the larger flower—a rich teal blue. The smaller is mauve and lavender, and the leaves are splashes of grass green. A photograph of a plate has been seen and the flowers—still only two—are quite large and float perfectly in the well.

SU-SHI. If this pattern were true to its name, it would portray tiny oriental fish ready to be devoured raw at one of those famous Japanese fish bars. Instead it portrays highly stylized chrysanthemums in amber and plum. The chrysanthemum is the symbol of Japan's Imperial Family, and has in the East the same status as does the rose in the West. This flower has been grown in oriental gardens for over 2,000 years. Su-Shi is supremely peaceful, calmly restful, and subtly understated: it is the epitome of the beauty of the orient.

DAHLIA GOLDEN. Exactly the same as the above treatment, but with the colors being buttery yellow and rose/pink: the leaves are warm brown and beige.

DIAMOND WHITE. Presenting the usual classic white with the debossment showing most effectively. These indentations are not round but tear shape. The pointed end of the inner row fits snugly between the tops of the outer. When light falls upon this rim, the edges of the dimples sparkle like jewels, and when the viewer moves the glimmer of the captured light shifts perceptibly. Quite remarkable.

IVY. Ivy was not widely known a few years ago. It has not been noted in original brochures or advertising sheets so it seems to have been a late introduction. Natural green leaves in three sizes tumble around the verge of the platter and plate, top of the cup and sugar bowl, and cavort on the center bulge of the creamer. The red/brown vine is rather prominent and looks hand painted.

OLD ENGLISH BLUE. Carried directly from *Impromptu*, but here the roses are framed by the edge dimples. The treatment tends to be a sprawling confusion of one old-fashion musk rose surrounded by leaves and smaller flowers. The *Intaglio* frame brings some order to a straggling treatment.

PAINTED DAISY. According to Harvey Duke, this treatment appears in two versions, but without any name differentiation: both are simply entitled Painted Daisy. It is not easily found. The blue version is slightly more available: the soft pink version has never been seen—except in a very small advertising slip. In each, three large daisies with five petals range about the well. In the blue version, the leaves are two shades of green. In the pink, the leaves are brown and ochre. Flowers and leaves are roughly, but not crudely, executed.

OLD ENGLISH PINK. The dark rose/pink version of the above. Less pronounced, more effectively defused.

ROSETTE JADE. One large, round, single sunflower combines with a second, smaller one to decorate the dinner plate. Both appear in turquoise with lime green centers. The large flower has no stem, but the smaller boasts of a dark avocado stem with two simplified chartreuse leaves.

ROSETTE SUN. Here is one of the most eye-riveting floral arrangements on any Iroquois plate. On the large platter it is spectacular! The center represents the burnt-orange dying sun putting forth rays in deep apricot. Rosette Sun is highly stylized but extremely effective—much more so than Rosette Jade. Again the large flowers stand majestically alone while the smaller one has a stem of brown and leaves of light ochre. No wonder the name is Rosette Sun. Both treatments are fairly easy to obtain.

WOODALE. Appeared first on *Impromptu* with the name Wild Violet—even though these purple and blue anemone-like flowers are hardly violets! As mentioned in the text, Wild Violet was the *Intaglio* name also when it first appeared, and only later was changed to Woodale. This is a common treatment and the collector can easily gather a complete set.

SPECIALTY. While some dinnerware manufacturers produced a multitude of specialty plates—tourist plates, personality plates, and historical plates—Iroquois rarely used its Seibel shapes in this manner. To date, only one has surfaced: a memorial plate for President John F. Kennedy. Where there is one, others may be found lurking.

The Mikasa/Seibel Connection: Including a Study of Five Mikasa Catalogs

Having been informed—several years ago—that Ben Seibel's widow was alive and still concerned with her husband's reputation, I had the temerity to write.I was, at the time, doing some preliminary research on Mikasa and, so it was believed, going to a prime source of information was the road best traveled. My letter was soon answered in a refreshingly open and earnest manner and soon several telephone conversations were exchanged. Lois Seibel was alert and ready to share information. She had, so she informed me, several Mikasa catalogs that showed some of Ben's designs. Did I want copies?

Did I!

Mrs. Seibel was at this time living with a younger woman, a companion, and it was this lady who would take the catalogs to a copier store for reproduction. During these months, Mrs. Seibel was in the process of transferring most of her valuable collection of Ben Seibel memorabilia to the Syracuse University Library: these papers and realia would be cataloged, classified, and housed permanently in the Special Collections Department and then made available to the general public. The Mikasa catalogs would be copied before they left for Syracuse.

No such luck! A day or so later, Mrs. Seibel telephoned again. The man who was advising her regarding her donation to Syracuse University—a noted Seibel scholar in his own right—wanted the catalogs sent immediately. In fact, he would pick them up at Mrs. Siebel's home and convey them to Syracuse personally.

My chance was gone! Or was it?

The events mentioned above took place, so I remember, in 1996, but just recently, copies of some Mikasa catalogs have entered my possession: the years 1971, 1972, 1977, 1978, and 1982, the last named being only a partial catalog. Even though in black and white—and naturally, being copies of copies—this material was one of the most important acquisitions in my attempt to learn about Seibel's connection with the Japanese manufacturer. The catalogs were special for another reason. Someone (Mrs. Seibel?) had written occasionally, in a thin and spidery handwriting, "Ben's"—on pages of photographs of dinnerware not previously known as Seibel designs! I like to believe Lois Seibel was determined to inform future researchers of the Mikasa shapes connected with her late husband.

What else could these handwritten notations signify? There are some discrepancies, and some Seibel shapes are overlooked. But in the latter case, it merely means the annotator realized that everyone already knew Ben Seibel designed *Duplex*™ or *Pivotal*™. The best approach is to go page by page through each of the five catalogs. This will flavor out appreciation of what Ben Seibel accomplished.

1971 Catalog:

Pages 2-5: *StoneKraft*™. A known clone of *Duplex*. No mention of Ben.

Pages 8-11: *StudioKraft*: A known clone of *Duplex*. No mention of Ben.

Pages 24-25: *Spectrum*™: On page 25 notation "Ben's"

Pages 28-31: *Duplex*: No mention of Ben.

Pages 56-61: *Pivotal*: No mention of Ben.

Page 72 (last page): A photograph of *Sophisticate* with "Ben" written over a large white platter.

This catalog informs us that, beside the known Mikasa shapes, Ben Seibel had some connection with *Spectrum* (a solid color clone of *Duplex*) and *Sophisticate*, an all white elegantly extended shape.

1972 Catalog:

Page 10-11: *Majorca*™: With handwritten notation "Ben's."

Pages 14-17: *Duplex*: No mention of Ben.

Pages 18-20: *Light n' Lively*™: Two handwritten notations, "Ben's"

Pages 24-25: *CeraStone*™: Handwritten notation, "Ben's."

Now we are into the section on Bone China. These are various shape designs. On page 28, the name "Ben's" appears with an arrow pointing to A5176 Trilogy™. On page 29, the added name "Ben" appears on A5162 Basonge™, and A5164 Angelica™.

Pages 36-37: *Pivotal*: With "Ben" handwritten over a Montina plate.

Page 40 (last page): The same photograph of *Sophisticate* that appeared in Catalog 1971 and here again the name "Ben's" appears over the large platter.

The 1972 Catalog links Ben Seibel with *Majorca, Light n'Lively, Cerestone*, and three lines of Bone China.

1977 Catalog:

Section 8: *TerraStone*™: Notation "Ben's."

Section 9: *Cordon Blue*™: Notation "Ben's."

Section 12: *Natural Beauty*™: Notation "Ben."[1]

Section 26 and 27: *Potter's Art*™: No mention of Ben.

The research picks up *TerraStone* (which appeared but was not noted as "Ben's" in the 1971 Catalog), *Cordon Blue*, and *Natural Beauty*.

1978 Catalog:

Pages 2-3: *Potter's Art*: No mention of Ben.

Pages 4-5: *LifeStyle*™: A known clone of *Potter's Art*. No mention of Ben.

Page 14: *The Flowers That Bloom in Spring*™: The notation "Ben's" appears both on a plate and an individual casserole.

Page 15. *Flower Arrangements*™: Notation "Ben" appears handwritten on the plate.

Page 17: *StyleKraft*™: Notation "Ben's is written on the plate C0901 Blue River.

Page 26: Fine Bone China™: The notation "Ben's cup" appears on A1102 Wheaton™.

Page 36 (last page): a new photograph for *Sophisticate*™ with the word "Ben" at the top of the page.

Duplex and *Pivotal* have disappeared and four new stoneware lines have been linked to Ben Seibel: two have lengthy floral names. *Sophisticate* continues to be mentioned as a Seibel design.

1982 Catalog (partial):

Page 8: Photographs of eight-sided plates and cups. There is no specific identification except that Fine China appears in the margin. The handwritten "Ben's" appears at the top left hand.

Page 15: Still under Fine China: There is a notation in the right hand margin pointing to a sugar bowl and stating "Ben's finial." Indeed it does resemble the finials on Iroquois' *Impromptu*.

The catalog ends at page 31.

A careful, page by page study of these catalogs adds considerably to the collectors' knowledge regarding Seibel's work for Mikasa. Now it must be acknowledged that some of my interpretations are purely assumptive and could be faulty, for I am depending upon the handwritten notations of a person assumed to be Mrs. Lois Seibel. Quite a plethora of assumptions! To be logical, the only information known to be true is (1) these are Mikasa catalogs and (2) some person annotated them—all the handwriting is the same. The rest is conjecture. But why would anyone—any "someone"—go to the trouble of annotating Mikasa catalogs only to confuse? This does not make logical sense. My thought—naturally very self-centered—is that these are the catalogs Mrs. Seibel originally agreed to copy for me, and that she made the notations to aid in my research. Well, I can hear the powerful pundits proclaim: WHO DOES HE THINK HE IS? Well, let me have my dreams. Let my statement simmer down for what it is: wishful thinking (but with a modicum of possible truth?)

To summarize the dinnerware shapes noted as Ben Seibel's within the five catalogs.

- StoneKraft
- StudioKraft
- Spectrum
- Sophisticate
- Majorca
- Light n'Lively
- Cera-Stone
- TerraStone
- Cordon Bleu
- LifeStyle
- The Flowers That Bloom in the Spring
- Flower Arrangements
- StyleKraft

Plus three we already know as Seibel's:

- Duplex
- Potter's Art
- Pivotal

The number of Mikasa shapes connected with the name of Ben Seibel has been advanced by thirteen. For a complete list of the Mikasa Connection see the end of this section.

There is no mention of the fourth "major" shape, *Mexicana*™, nor its clone, *Mexican Rainbow*™. It could be that these two colorful lines appeared and disappeared in the years between 1972 and 1977 or between 1978 and 1982.[2] *Mexicana* is not very common in today's collectible market and could have made a hurried entrance and exit. We know that Ben Seibel died in February 1985 so that *Mexicana* and the other Mikasa shapes were his last creative concerns.

Until now, the connection between Ben Seibel and the Mikasa Company has not been documented in its entirety. We do accept Seibel created four major shapes for this Japanese firm, we do know Seibel traveled to Japan and thus was intimately involved in certain productions. We have to acknowledge that, like Iroquois, Seibel created each one of the four shapes to fill a different consumer need or desire, and we do realize Mikasa, not very helpfully, confused research by producing various clones of the major four shapes, and by not placing the name "Ben Seibel" on a number of other shapes. All this we know. Surely more information will arise as researchers and collectors begin to find joy in the beauty, individuality, and unique qualities of the Seibel/Mikasa connection.

During the last decade of his life, Ben Seibel gained much of his income from Mikasa royalties, definitely proving the value of his designs. For three random years—1978-1980—it might be of interest to the reader to follow the month-by-month royalty income derived during these years from Mikasa.

1978	
January:	$2,223.23
February:	0
March:	$2,042.25
	$2,975.92
April:	$3,600.90
May	$2,416.62
June:	$2,029.54
July:	0
August:	$1,140.35
September:	$8,800.75
October:	$3,290.03
	$5,572.24
November:	$5,293.94
December:	$2,740.41
1979	
January:	$2,020.76
February:	0
March:	$2,987.45
April:	$4,672.10
May:	0
June:	$5,415.52
	$3,996.71
July:	0
August:	$3,262.29
September:	$5,606.83
October:	$5,255.50
November:	$6,423.61
December:	$4,424.48
1980	
January:	$4,349.54
	$2,347.34
February:	0
March:	0
April:	$7.446/00
May:	$3,221.96
June:	$4,295.05
July:	$4,248.58
August:	$4,238.00
September:	$2,087.22
October:	$17,167.73
	$8,965.62
November:	0
December:	$6,102.51
	$5,975.10[3]

On the following pages are illustrated some examples of the lines identified as "Ben's" in the catalogs. As our late president, Richard M. Nixon, was wont to expound: "I wish to make this perfectly clear," Or as our present Grammarian-in-Chief, George W. Bush, might say: There must be no misunderstanding here! NO claim is set forth that Ben Seibel designed these lines of tableware: only that someone believed that he did! The difference between "probability" and "possibility."

No Mikasa shape with any claim to the status of clone is pictured here: even those such as *Majorca* which uses only the *Duplex*-shaped sugar and creamer. A few of the possibilities, *Sophisticate* for example, bears in part some clear resemblance to a known Seibel line. When a person reviews the catalogs, page after page, various "bits and pieces" seem to have been interchanged. For example, the coffee pot handle that originally appears on *Duplex*, shows up with no major alteration on the *Epi-Q-Ure One* shape—as also does the handle for the creamer. The *Duplex* samovar stand returns over and over and over again, appearing and reappearing in the same four-arched design. The double-spouted round gravy boat is another concept that flits from shape to shape. Why? Or, better still, how did this work? What type of open business relationship existed between The Mikasa Company and Mr. Ben Seibel?[4] It does seem that this relationship was fluid enough for Mikasa to take design ideas created by Seibel and place them, scatter them, throughout their huge inventory of shapes! Since he traveled to Japan, Seibel must have been aware of this situation

Mikasa/Seibel Possibilities

Illustrated are a few of the shapes, not all, designated as "Ben's" in the four catalogs in my possession. The known Seibel/Mikasa clones are not included here: they have their own section. Absolutely NO claim is made that those listed are truly Seibel shapes. They are possibilities only. Yet they are quite lovely, and two are exceptionally beautiful. All are worth acquiring—especially for regular use.

CERA-STONE. A simple line whose flatware rises from the most non-existent of verges. Available in many variations of treatments, the plates are adaptable, serviceable, and range from the striking to the ordinary.

Dolly™: The chop plate.

Gem™: The chop plate, dinner plate, salad plate.

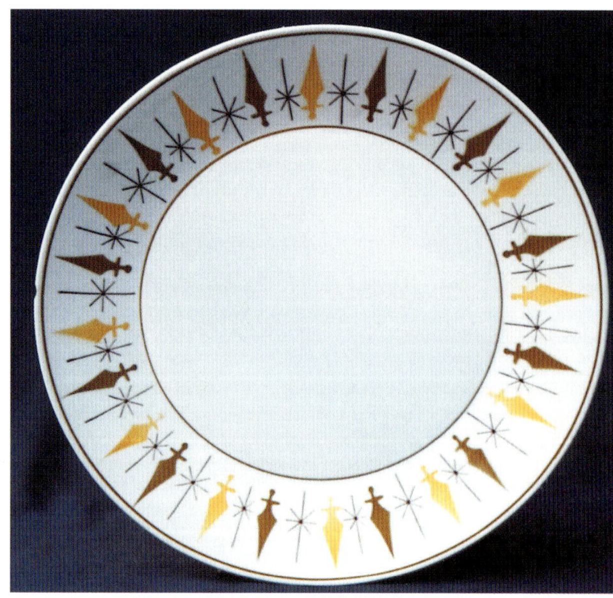

Norlic™: The dinner plate.

Provincial™: The dinner plate, coffee server.

Westwood™: The dinner plate.

CORDON BLEU. A speckled stoneware line reminiscent of *Discovery*™. The name SEEMS to refer both to the line and the treatment.

Above and below:
SOPHISTICATE: This is an exquisite shape and comes only in pure white. It bears strong resemblance to other Seibel designs: note how the *Sophisticate* teacup handle is a pure match for the *Impromptu* handle. The similarity is astounding.

LIGHT N' LIVELY: A heavy shape with an "up and over" rim, existing in a number of treatments. These are modern and clean. Here a salad plate in the treatment Flyte™ is shown.

STYLEKRAFT: A chunky stoneware line available in a number of treatments. Blue River™ (shown here) was the most popular and is a truly beautiful design. Shown here is the dinner plate, the salad plate, teacup and saucer.

TERRA STONE: Like *Cera-Stone*, this shape is available in many decorative designs, and it is unusually available in flea markets. Many of the treatments are very ordinary, however, I am fond of this one Sprite™ *Terra Stone* saucer acquired for a nickel. It reminds me, somehow, of *Impromptu*!

Mikasa *Duplex*: Considered the Most Available

Is *Duplex* the most important, the most desirable of the Mikasa/Seibel connection? Many collectors reply "NO." Some reply "YES," but there are a good number of Seibel enthusiasts who do not even recognize *Duplex* as a bona fide collectible. "After all," they murmur, "dinnerware is still being made by Mikasa today." This is an unfortunate situation, and quite a shame, because Seibel traveled to Japan to approve the shape, design the treatments, and give his general encouragement. The "problem" with *Duplex* is that it is a simple, straightforward shape with no quirks, no surprises, no extremely desirable "funky" qualities that Seibel used when he created some twenty years earlier when he worked for Iroquois.

Let us be honest! *Duplex* has an oriental slant—but that should not discourage Seibel collectors: it is oriental only in its purity of line. True, *Duplex* simplicity bores the sophisticates: it has no surprising pieces, no trivets, no perky mustard jar or shapely vinegar cruets, not one marmite or individual casserole, no cute ashtray or colorful coaster.[1] *Duplex* carries along only the most practical, the most utilitarian of items, but it does have some essential Seibel formulations. There are samovars perched on arched warmers, there are coffee servers with delicately arched spouts. There are—quite unexpectedly—a multitude of treatments.

Oh, Suannie Mae, honey, the Duplex treatments are as numerous as bees at the backyard barbeque!

Duplex plates—and the dinner plate is relatively easy to locate—can be picked up, snatched—if you will—for no more than twenty-five cents at many a local flea market. We wonder what Ben Seibel would have thought about that? A delightful collection can be made of just the dinner plates. At first, the collector finds the gathering easy, but after about fifteen separate treatments are added to the display case, or tacked up on the sunroom wall, or wherever these beauties are being kept—after the number fifteen or sixteen, the progress slows—sources wither and dry like a drought beleaguered marsh in Florida. If the Duplexist is definitely determined, he or she should resort to Replacements, Inc. This service located in Greensboro, North Carolina, is an outstanding source for the otherwise unobtainable: the nice ladies—and gentlemen too—who answer the telephone are helpful, courteous, and willing to submit to researching questions—but prices are high, unless the inquirer is willing to accept plates discounted because of minor imperfections. Even then, the effort to gather the over forty[2] treatments is daunting to all but the most devoted.

Surely the number of treatments alone makes *Duplex* an interesting and completely legitimate collectible, even if it does not fulfill the Mid-Century-Modern mode![3]

The number of items in the *Duplex* line stops at twenty. Not quite a short line—remember *Intaglio* boasted only fifteen—but certainly not within the so-called lavishly appointed category. There are no exotic surprises within this staid and practical shape—although the presence of a mug is intriguing, and the chimney-tall coffee urn perched on its arched warmer can be considered unique. Both of these are Seibel signature pieces.

A full set of *Duplex* includes:

- *Chop plate, 12.50"
- *Dinner plate, 10.50"
- *Salad plate, 7"
- **Bowl, fruit
- **Bowl, cereal
- *Bowl, vegetable, round
- Cup
- **Saucer
- Gravy
- Underplate
- Butter dish
- Casserole
- Shaker, salt
- Shaker, pepper
- Sugar w/lid
- Creamer
- Coffee server w/lid
- Coffee urn w/lid
- Warmer stand

Duplex back stamp used for decorated pieces. The name of the treatment and the number are always present.

Duplex back stamp for solidly glazed pieces.

The four pieces with the asterisk (*) always are decorated. The saucer, the two smaller bowls—fruit and cereal—with the double asterisk (**) occasionally have the decoration, much abbreviated, within the well. There is a notation on one of the information advertisements to the effect that the treatments officially meant to appear with Black hollowware have decorated saucers, fruit, and cereal bowls. All the other pieces—thirteen of them—bear no decorations. The only missing piece, to many collectors' beliefs, would be the 6" bread & butter plate. It can be assumed this small plate would also be decorated, but then to assume often makes an "ass of you and me." A careful examination of the Mikasa catalogs (1971 and 1972) can find NO example of the small *Duplex* plate, so Seibel simply did not want it, and it was never produced.

It must be realized that a *Duplex* table grouping will consist mainly of solidly glazed dishes. However, the patterns[4] are so colorful, so vibrant, so impressively different that they tend to dominate the entire shape. The plates and the vegetable bowl are the stars of the show accompanied by a chorus of pieces dressed in solid glazes.

Even though all the treatments are not going to be listed in this section, some of them will be discussed. Treatments "came and went," were added or deleted—no doubt to entice the public. They appeared and disappeared as they did in other dinnerware lines. As mentioned in the introduction to this Mikasa section, five catalogs of the pottery have come into my possession (1971, 1972, 1977, 1978, and 1982), making it possible to trace somewhat the Duplex line.

Catalog 1971 hints at a banner year for this shape. The salesmen could promise to deliver to retailers twenty-two Duplex treatments. On page 31, the collector can see the company officially assigned the various treatments to their solid pieces. This informational sheet does not appear in the 1972 catalog. We can also read the suggested retail prices, and immediately recognize the difference between the 1950s prices and those of the 1970s. For example: the covered coffee pot was $14.00, the covered casserole, $17.00, and the tall samovar with its stand, $25.00. Of the decorated pieces, the dinner plate's suggested cost was $3.50: a price much higher than its average cost today—some thirty+ years later. In 1971, *Duplex* could not have been thought a "bargain" line.

The following treatments were available in the 1971 catalog. The list includes the official Mikasa color accompaniment.

*Aspect™ (yellow)
Axiom™ (apricot)
Brunch™ (brown)
*Candy™ (pink)
Casablanca™ (black)
Concentric™ (black)
*Contempo™ (brown)
Dahlia™ (green)
*Dimension™ (pink)
Duet™ (yellow)
Eden™ (pink)
Extension™ (brown)
*Frolic™ (brown)
*Habitat™ (yellow)
*Hacienda™ (black)
Quadratic™ (green)
Segments™ (apricot)
*Sunflower™ (apricot)
Trellis™ (yellow)
*Vanity™ (apricot)
Village™ (green)
*Zuider Zee™ (blue)

A few of the official color choices seem arbitrary and seem not, to more modern tastes, the best choices. Those names (10) marked with an asterisk (*) were deleted from the next year's catalog, but three new treatments were added: Inspire, Largo, and Sunny Glow. The number of treatments for 1972 was fifteen.

Since there are forty-seven presently known *Duplex* treatments, and only twenty-five can be found in these two catalogs, there are still twenty-two uncounted and floating about somewhere in later salesmen's lists.[5] A very interesting fact is by 1977 (the date of the next catalog in my possession), *Duplex* has disappeared completely—not one mention. *Potter's Art* has replaced it as the much touted Mikasa/Seibel shape! Thus the other twenty-two patterns must have been part of the gradual ebb and flow within the catalogs of 1973, 1974, 1975-1976. Some remained for several years, others were soon dropped. On two undated brochure sheets (obviously meant for the much traveled salesmen), Alana, Eldora, Glen, and Plaza have the cruel word DROP darkly scrawled across them while Carnival, Herald, and Village are besmirched with the word POOR. The treatments simply climbed briefly upon the stage, and if they did not perform, they were gaggled off without ceremony.

It can, however, carefully be stated that the following were the most popular with the appreciative consumers: Brunch, Casablanca, Dahlia, and Duet. Their names are seen often and, thus, they must have been carried for a number of years.

Decorative treatments aside, this philosophy—accompanying a few decorated pieces with a grouping of solid colors—is a typical "Seibel-esque" (as often stated) technique. Naturally, other ceramic designers used this practical method, but it runs rampant throughout Seibel's work. If the collector accepts the unproved possibility that Seibel was connected with *Interplay* some twenty-odd years before *Duplex* was created, then the technique started with that shape. If this Seibel/*Interplay* connection is impossible to accept, then the pattern/solid color plan commenced with *Informal* in 1958. No matter, the idea of matching decoration with solid colors is a running tendency throughout Seibel's career—and is very practical indeed. The creamers, shakers, casseroles, and so on can be purchased in one solid glaze and thus form the background for several sets by the acquisition of plates in two or more patterns. Even though Mikasa assigned official solid colors, the consumer was not absolutely bound to them. Open stock was always available. Thus, for example: with glistening black, the user could get plates in modernistic Concentric, or interwoven Buffet, or best of all, the stunning Casablanca. Three sets for just slightly more than the price of one! A great idea!

Just what are the solid hues that spread themselves so graciously over forty-seven known treatments? There are Black and yellow, orange (apricot) and brown, bubblegum pink and grape purple, deep sky blue and a green halfway between olive and chartreuse. Seven richly saturated hues—dense and deep with very little touchings of gray—plus the neutral black, rich and stygian. Eight very intense colors to accompany decorated plates and bowls. I have found that orange, brown, and yellow tend to show up regularly. Stately black is rather unusual while grape purple should be considered scarce—in fact this purple really only fits with Plumberry. But except for the purple, no color is really difficult to locate.

The saucer is always glazed in a solid color (except, as mentioned above, when the treatment was officially planned to be mixed with solid Black.) But to brighten the effect, there are two versions: one completely solid, and the second with the rim and well in white. The term "well" is basically not correct in the case of *Duplex*. The center is actually raised and the cup bottom is indented slightly so the cup fits over the saucer center and "hooks" on it.

The underplate is merely a larger saucer with the same center design—the gravy then again easily hooks over. This is a very practical solution

And just how "simple" was the basic *Duplex* shape upon which all this color was so abundantly lavished? Very simple; outstandingly so. The wells of the plates and bowls were absolutely tabletop flat and the sides move sharply up at a 135-degree angle: no verge, no curves, and no little narrow rim to top the side: just simply an unadorned angled side. This angle was repeated, although not as starkly, in the cups, the creamer, the sugar, even the shakers, and both coffee servers: it became the hallmark of the line. And against this clear angle contrasted the arches—the magnificent elongated curve of the cup and creamer handle, the almost painfully beautiful stretched arch of the coffee server; the single McDonald's™ arch of the finials; and finally, the very singular repetition of the finial arch in the open work of the warmer. This warmer, by the way, always appears in white. These three arched shapes are emphasized dramatically by being always, like the warmer, glazed in icy white.

The tall and stately samovar with its stand: a votive candle will keep the beverage warm. Height is an impressive 15" to the top of the finial. The stands are always pure white. Note the arches in the stand match the arch of the finial—a very subtle touch. Price (complete): $30-35.

Hopefully, collectors will begin to find the simple lines and architectural qualities of the *Duplex* shape more intriguing after reading this account. The shape was very popular in the early 1970s. Mikasa cloned it with impunity. Perhaps too much of a good thing turned the pendulum in the opposite direction. Even though *Duplex* was consummately simple, crisp in outline, and sturdily constructed, Ben Seibel introduced touches of humor and whimsy. Small subtle touches, it is acknowledged, but they are there to be appreciated by the discerning Seibelist.

The 8.75" open vegetable is one of the decorated pieces in this line—always at the bottom of the bowl. The decoration is an abbreviated version of the plate's more extensive design. Rear: Quadric; Left front: Duet; Right front: Candy. This is the only example of Candy ever seen. In *Duplex*, the price often depends upon the design—how well it is liked by the potential buyer. Price: $12-18.

Some collectors find the small fruit dish (5.25") problematic. It usually presents a solid color, but occasionally a certain treatment will have it decorated—as does this Casablanca piece. These are simple no-nonsense bowls good for many uses. Prices: (decorated), $6-7; (undecorated), $3-4.

The brown *Duplex* butter dish contrasted with its heavier *StoneKraft* clone. Price (*Duplex*): $10-12.

The teacup versus the mug. These are always in solid colors. The latter is much harder to find. Prices: Teacup, $4-5; Mug, $10-12.

The sugar bowl. The base is 3" tall with an addition 1" to reach the top of the finial. Not flashy, but calm and sedate: it looks best in a dark glaze so the white interior seems to form a pure band around the top. Price: $8-10.

Here is the difference in size between the cereal/soup (right) and the fruit (left). The latter is harder to find.

So too are the cereal/soup bowls in two versions. The decorated example is Concentric—a fairly popular modern design. Prices: (decorated), $8-9; (undecorated), $5-6.

The three Concentric plates: chop, dinner, and salad. *Duplex* has no bread & butter plate. Prices: Chop plate, $14-16; Dinner plate, $9-11; Salad plate, $6-8.

A grouping of Casablanca with the brilliant black covered casserole and teacup. The treatment is very popular. Price (Casserole): $18-20.

The gravy boat and its round underplate. Since these pieces could be purchased as open stock, perhaps some purchasers mixed and matched *as la Fiesta*? The underplates are harder to find. Prices: Gravy, $8-10; Underplate, $10-12.

Examples of the eight solid colors. The black creamer matches the sugar bowl shown above. Brown and yellow are quite common, purple is scarce. Price (Creamer): $5-6.

Some saucers are completely one color; some have white raised wells and rims. Prices are the same: $1-2.

The shakers possess the same flair at the top as do many other pieces. These are very substantial—being 3.50" high. Both have five holes, but the holes of the pepper are much smaller. Price (set): $7-9.

Three coffee pots: (left to right): *Spectrum, StoneKraft*, and *Duplex*. Extremely well balanced for a piece measuring 10.50" high. Price (*Duplex*): $20-25.

Notice the difference between a real *Duplex* cup and saucer (left) and one of the many clones. Simply keep in mind the *Duplex* interiors are always pure white: the clone interiors can be pale colors.

Duplex: The Library of Treatments

There are very few, if any, American dinnerware shapes that offer such a wide range of treatments. It bears repeating this fantastic number was made possible by having only the three plates, the large open vegetable bowl, and, sometimes, the fruit and cereal bowls wearing the design. The rest of the line existed only in various solid colors that could be—and often were—interchanged with a number of treatments. Even the fruits and cereals appeared most often in the solid glazes. No matter the reason, forty-seven treatments is a mind-boggling number.

While all the treatments have been studied to varying degrees, some have been seen only in catalogs and advertising brochures, and, thus, there will be no photographs for these treatments. Commentary on these patterns will appear in *italics* in the list below.

The style of treatment varies greatly. Some are bubblegum sweet—charming but somewhat precious and girlish, rather in the style of the beach party movies. Some are stylized into twisting, convoluted, and highly original sculptural designs that remind the perceptive collector of Della Robbia wall plaques. A few are frankly very forgettable, while others are modern, stark, mathematically unembellished: almost brilliantly conceived. Not only are the numbers awesome, the variation is astonishing! These treatments can be divided logically into six categories:

- Naturalistic florals
- Stylized florals
- Overall patterns using florals
- Fruit
- Kaleidoscopic[6]
- Modern geometrical

The appropriate solid color glaze is noted at the end of the commentary of each treatment. The list gives the official names of the solid colors.

Yellow	(2557)
Brown	(2558)
Green: an olive green	(2559)
Apricot: orange	(2561)
Pink	(2562)
Black	(2560)
Blue	(unknown, but probably 2556 or 2563)
Grape	(3600)

ASPECT™ (2540). This treatment is quite difficult to find, but it does appear in the 1971 Mikasa catalog. It cannot be found in later issues. Extremely simple, this includes a small yellow and black petalled design in the center of the flatware. The only other decorations are two stripes where the verge would be: the inner and wider one being yellow, the outer black. Solid yellow hollowware would suffice, but Black is suggested.

ALANA™ (2521). Reminding the viewer of an overall quilt design, Alana is one of the harder treatments to locate. It also is not very exciting: forgettable almost except for the clear yellow and orange tones. Mikasa used the term Apricot to describe the burnt-orange solid glaze. In a double-sided salesmen's sheet showing twenty-four treatments, Alana (at the lower left) has bold term DROP scrawled across the well. From the early 1970s, this sheet proves Alana came and went with rather rapid fire! Apricot or Yellow is the solid glaze to accompany this treatment.

BUFFET™ (2516). Based on the quilt pattern "Cathedral Windows," Buffet uses the same style that later appeared in *Pivotal's* Tangents or Tangerine. If the viewer looks too closely or too intensely, this treatment becomes "ultra-busy," but one should fasten on the overall aspect, not the individual parts. The salad illustrates that some small plates are nearly mirror images of the dinner plate—unlike Brunch. Yellow is the official glaze, but Black would be more dramatic.

AXIOM™ (2532). A very striking and powerful treatment. The photograph will explain this simple treatment: not really beautiful, but one of the most compelling of the many *Duplex* patterns. Its solid glaze is Apricot.

BRUNCH™ (3804). A popular design and quite available. While the open vegetable bowl causes some difficulty, the plates are easy to find. This is a good thing (as Martha Stewart would say) because it is one of the best among the stylized floral plans. The salad plate is also illustrated to show the smaller plate is decaled differently. Brown.

CANDY™ (2530). One of the sugary designs, Candy is reminiscent of the more forcefully crisp Brunch. Since no plate was available, the open vegetable is illustrated. The solid color is Pink, and this treatment is one of the more acceptable of the "pinks." It possesses moderately modern design sense.

CARNIVAL™ (2512). The first treatment discussed belonging to the series/category known as "kaleidoscopic." Looking very much like an Amish hex sign, Carnival fills up the entire well with a busy double sunray. The *Duplex* Green—here it paints the slanting rim—is a mingling of olive and chartreuse—not my favorite color. And Green is its matching solid glaze.

CLEAR DAY™ (2515). A myriad of blue six petalled daisies cavort with some attempted grace over the entire well of this dinner plate. While not very stylistically arresting, the lovely cornflower blue does save this treatment. Blue is most often chosen as a favorite color in communities with higher incomes and levels of education: it has class. Blue can save a weak design—often when pink cannot. Blue is the solid glaze.

CASABLANCA™ (2517). I always have wondered about the name of this treatment. It is mainly grays—in various degrees—with a black border just before the rim rises. While an elusive pattern, it is popular, subtle, and extremely modern. Gray is always sophisticated. Completely stylized, the florals present a pleasant and peaceful design. This is, I must confess, one of my favorite *Duplex* treatments. The only solid glaze worthy of accompaniment is Black.

CONTEMPO™ (2525). Another of the "geometric" treatments: a simple flower placed within a brown triangle surrounded by a tan circle. Clean, very *avant-garde*, sharp, and modern. Brown would be the solid glaze to accompany this treatment although Black would be very dramatic.

CONCENTRIC™ **(2533)**. The cereal bowl is shown here. The three plates can be seen illustrating the preceding section. One of the modernistic patterns, it appears as a modified bull's eye. Even though the dominant color is yellow, Mikasa sold it with Black solid pieces. Remember, those treatments using Black as the solid color allowed the treatment to appear on the smaller bowls. This was a rather interesting company, or designer, quirk.

DAHLIA™ **(2511)**. A naturalistic floral design, this treatment fills the well with shaggy dahlias. Notice that the salad presents just a smaller version of the dinner plate. One of the pleasant, easy to find flower patterns, it could not be labeled outstanding. Green.

DAMSEL™ **(2513)**. This treatment could be either stylized or naturalistic, but the presence of white pushes into a stylistic flower arrangement. Damsel is one of the more appealing designs with a slightly sculptural effect. Because of the leaves, it could—in a stretch—be matched with Green, but, as seen by the fruit bowl, Blue is its natural bond.

DIMENSION™ **(2539)**. *A small, stylized, round flower device is placed in the center of the well, and is surrounded by a wide expanse of pure white. A narrow strip of pink appears at the verge point. Pink is the official solid glaze.*

DUET™ **(3301)**. Two yellow poppies bend and twist to contain themselves within the well. A great deal of white surrounds them—almost frames them. The rim is yellow. Duet is one of the most easily found treatments, and if desired, the collector could acquire, little by little, a complete set for six, eight, or even ten. Yellow.

EDEN™ **(2522)**. Four flowers in pink or yellow nestle on a bed of olive green leaves. The pink encircles the well. The size of the daisies and dahlias dominate this well and yet leaves a frame of white. The better *Duplex* treatments show an expanse of white. Pink.

ELDORA™ **(2508)**. More elaborate than Carnival, this does belong to the same category of treatment. It looks Moorish—Spanish-Moorish, and, if one has a persuasive imagination, could represent the inside of an Islamic dome: working down from the high arched ceiling to the fanciful buttresses supporting it. Architectural, perhaps? Incidentally, like Alana, on my copy of a salesmen's sheet, Eldora has the worrisome word DROP scrawled over it. Thus, it could not have been popular with the consumer. Yellow.

EXTENSION™ (3837). One of the pure and simple treatments, Extension presents a small central motif based loosely on the Maltese Cross. This "cross" in dark brown and olive is surrounded by four arches outlined in black and with half-moons of olive. Except for a narrow sandstone strip at the verge, the rest of the plate is pure white. The catalogs mention this treatment being sold with hollowware in solid brown.

FRUIT PUNCH™ (3404). Plums and huge plump figs constitute the "fruit punch." This treatment is one of the most popular of the "fruit" decals. The design is beautifully constructed and cleverly managed with plenty of surrounding white. Yellow is the solid glaze, but these plates would be wonderfully striking with the rare purple glaze.

GLEN™ (2507). Daisies and heraldic chrysanthemums cluster in the well surrounded by a narrow, but prominent band of white. Colorful, but ordinary. On my copy of the advertising sheet, the word "DROP" is scrawled darkly on this plate. This pattern is not mentioned in either the 1971 or the 1972 salesmen's catalog, so it came and went swiftly.

GRANADA™ (2515). This is a beautiful treatment—yellow and blue and looking like a huge dahlia, or, perhaps, a little like a "bloomin' onion" from an Outback Steak House.™ This allusion is, of course, quite stretched, but it is to be wondered how and why these titles were obtained. What is "Granada" about this pattern? There is no hint of the Moorish soul of Spain. This is a favored design of mine—one of the best; however, it seems not to have been a treatment popular with the public in the 1970s. The solid glaze could be either Yellow or Blue. The collector must take the choice.

GYPSY™ (2524). Pink and gray with a vacant stare: a checker board or quilt pattern. Pink is the solid glaze.

FROLIC™ (2510). This name is one that appears with some regularity. Frolic is one of the most fanciful treatments in the Impromptu line, and here again the name (not the same design) appears in *Duplex*. How Seibel seemed to appreciate dahlias—here are more naturalistically portrayed. The accompanying solid glaze has to be Brown—there is no evidence of any other choice.

HABITAT™ **(2502)**. One of the kaleidoscopic treatments and not very impressive but I have heard it described as "richly geometric." Thus some collectors must appreciate it more than I. The coloring is sunny and more uplifting than the greens and browns. Yellow is the solid glaze to accompany.

HACIENDA™ (2518). Luckily some years ago, Hacienda was offered for sale on eBay, and a color photograph was copied. The center of the well is plain, surrounded by a wide band of stylized overlapping "petals." Like all scroll designs, the collector can see lozenges, triangles, and hearts: the last named bring to mind the heraldic "eyed" shields of Viking raiders. The colors are green and black; either color would be perfect as the solid glaze.

HARVEST™ **(3202)**. The large, bold fruit designs are much more successful—and sought after—today than the rather fussy "all-over" designs. This pear is exceptionally well drawn, and the browned leaves hint at the harvest. Also, the inclusion of an inner border frames and completes the treatment. The problem with the bold, dramatic treatments is they sometimes overpower the food placed upon them. Brown would probably have been the best solid glaze for hollowware.

HERALD™ **(2509)**. This is one of the elusive treatments—discovered only when the Mikasa catalogs came into my possession. A kaleidoscopic example in the greens and browns described above as less than uplifting. Rather busy. Brown.

HIGH SUMMER™ **(3305)**. Fruit ripening in the heat of high summer: surely one fruit is a mango. The colors are more golden, and the encircling frame is yellow. Surely the solid glaze is Yellow.

INSPIRE™ **(3201)**. Another striking example of the dahlia motif: shades of Duet or Brunch. The designer was fond of the wide opened flower. Instead of a frame, the entire rim is orange. And, of course, Apricot is the solid color.

JULIETTE™ (3101). This was the first piece of Duplex in my possession. This was about ten years ago when I discovered this plate for ten cents in an outdoor flea market. Since I was just becoming aware of Seibel's Mikasa lines, I snatched it up. However, no other pieces with this treatment have ever been added—probably because I never liked Pink.

LA GRANGE™ (2529). It is amazing how "new" Duplex treatments keep being discovered. In January 2003, a 12.50" chop plate (platter) was offered on eBay. Laura Kane of California brought this discovery to my attention. The chartreuse and blue stylized flowers completely fill the well: it looks like a design for a paisley fabric. There is a thin blue line at the well. The best solid color would be Blue.

LARGO™ (3403). More flowers—here in blues with a lavender center. The stylized leaves are mustard. Solid glaze should be Blue.

PINK RIBBON™ (3102). Pink daisies and tan foliage undulate in separate strips across the plates: five in the dinner plate, four in the salad plate, and, I would suppose, six cross the chop plate (round platter.) There is a mild sense of delicate frothy movement. Far from a modern design, it could be serviceable for a breakfast set. Pink is the logical solid color, but Brown is more striking.

PENTHOUSE™ (2503). Not as exciting as the magazine of the same name, or the luxurious living accommodations on the top of a tall building. Emerald green and dull lemon yellow form a design, looking like part of a stained glass window, that forms a ring near the verge. This is one of the less attractive treatments—at least in my mind. Brown.

PINK SCROLLS™ (2523). A kaleidoscopic venture that could be another Amish hex sign. Among the scrolls and hearts, the viewer can discern six large, very stylized tulips with their petal tips just touching the verge point. As the name implies, the overall hue is pink and that must be the accompanying solid glaze.

PLAZA™ (2500). Another kaleidoscope: this time of vaguely rectangular shapes in emerald, bright blue, and chartreuse green. More useful as a wall decoration, one would have to be careful about the foods presented on this plate. Either the Blue or the Green would work as the solid color.

PLUMBERRY™ (3501). This is quite fascinating: a purple strawberry—although the leaves are not three-lobed. This is the only time the color purple appears. It has its own solid glaze: Grape.

QUADRATIC™ (3436). Very modern, almost stark, in the mode of a Japanese heraldic shield. One of the simpler designs. Black.

SEGMENTS™ (3231). Little simple orange sunflowers captured in an ochre teardrop: traditional with a modernistic touch. The variety of designs on *Duplex* is amazing. Apricot or Black—for a Hallowe'en dinner?

SUNFLOWER™ (2519). Contrast the staid, prim sunflowers of Segments with these twisting and energetic blooms filling the entire well. These plates are alive with action but still have the look of a carved Della Robbia plaque. Apricot.

SUNNY GLOW™ (3304). A naturalistic floral of wood yellow woodlilies. The yellow rim frames the well and leaves considerable spaces of white. Yellow.

TRELLIS™ (2526). More sunflowers but here they are stylized. They could also be stylized clematis and this would explain the name. This is a sunny and bright treatment. Yellow.

VANITY™ (2520). Vanity is one of the "vacant" treatments and is a rehashing of the "yellow floral" design, but with little excitement. Yellow is the official solid accompaniment, but Apricot would be more lively.

WHITE SURF™ (2500). *Rare and startling in its pristine purity. Black would be the only logical solid glaze to set a dramatically accomplished table. I was informed regarding White Surf about five years ago by Herb Fogliano, a New Jersey dealer, who saw it in a mall. While this gentleman is very reliable, the information never could be verified. Then too, the collector must remember that Mikasa LifeStyle—a clone of Potter's Art—presents a treatment called White Surf. Rather confusing! However, the official number (2500) has been recently verified by Replacements, Inc. and, since this number fits in perfectly with the Duplex sequence, it must be believed that THIS White Surf is an elusive all white Duplex treatment.*

VILLAGE™ (3405). More chrysanthemums—those ubiquitous Imperial flowers of Japan. This is the dinner plate; the salad has only two flowers. What the name signifies is impossible to discover. The solid color is also problematic: Yellow, Apricot, or Green?

ZENITH™ (3701). What a change from a folly of flowers, Zenith is sophisticatedly stark, and a dramatic contrast of shapes: circles with squares. Wisely, the outer areas are left pure white—causing the viewer to concentrate on the well's design. Black, of course!

ZUIDER ZEE™ (2541). Dare I speak of "stylized mums"? I would like to see this treatment also in brown or green. If only *Duplex* called upon the reds: crimson or maroon—what a gloriously exotic treatment this would make in red! This is a favorite, a favorite for more than one reason. Zuider Zee is the only *Duplex* treatment now known that has a decorated saucer and the white cup has an inside narrow band decoration. Zuider Zee seems to be the exception to the rule. Naturally, if it happens once, it might have happened again. Blue would be the solid glaze—unless there are more secrets residing within this treatment.

Pivotal: The Gracious One

The *Pivotal* back stamp on decorated pieces. The name is always present.

Until Earl Martin's fortuitous discovery that *Mexicana* was introduced in 1968 (and disappeared in 1971) (Please see the discussion in the *Mexicana* section), *Pivotal* was believed to be the second Mikasa shape designed by Ben Seibel. However, this gracefully rounded shape has now been demoted into third place. In the 1971 catalog, *Duplex* vastly outnumbers the *Pivotal* entries, and, thus, we say tentatively that the public could purchase *Duplex* before *Pivotal*.

We have discussed before Ben Seibel's ability to create a series of dinnerware shapes aimed at different target markets. This was successfully accomplished for Iroquois in the late 1950s and early '60s. Here the designer is achieving the same results. *Pivotal* stood in relationship to the other Mikasa shapes as did *Inheritance* among the Iroquois four. It was the most "gracious" of the group.

Pivotal was planned to be delicately rounded, very feminine, and small-scaled in size, weight, and number of pieces. It was "cute" and clever rather than elegant, and it made no strong claims to being sophisticated. *Pivotal* possessed charm rather than sophistication. It was piquant rather that prepossessing. Teas and luncheons—for "ladies who lunch" with no man in sight—are the correct events for this shape. If this is what Mikasa and Seibel decided, then *Pivotal* is successful.

According to one press blurb: Ben Seibel used "the timeless character of the sphere, the ovoid, and the circle"—and that tells the entire story. *Pivotal* is rounded—smooth fine porcelain cast is a series of "rounds." Seibel used this concept most admirably on some twenty-three pieces, and some were quite a surprise. Dear Ben, how he loved his surprises! There was humor in his design concept.

The pieces that composed the *Pivotal* line were:

Dinner plate
Salad plate
Bread & butter plate
Soup
Compote, individual
Teacup
Tea saucer
Platter, 12" round
Bowl, vegetable
Bowl, salad
Sugar bowl w/lid
Creamer
Coffee pot
Gravy boat
Shaker, salt
Shaker, pepper
Butter dish
Casserole w/lid
Soup tureen
Ball jar, large
Ball jar, medium
Ball jar, small

The back stamp of the solidly glazed pieces.

Back in the 1970s, suggested prices for *Pivotal* were substantially higher than for *Duplex*, and, since both lines were offered at the same time, this reflects upon the better quality of the former. For example: the suggested retail for a 20-piece *Pivotal* starter set was $30.00 as contrasted with $24.00 for *Duplex*; the 45-piece set was $70.00 versus $50.00. The *Pivotal* dinner plate in open stock was priced $4.50, and the *Duplex* was $3.50. Mikasa surely regarded *Pivotal* as the superior line.

One has the feeling that Homer Laughlin's Frederick Rhead was a very seriously minded man. He was British, reserved, and dourly expressive. Ben Siebel, New Jersey born and influenced by the vagaries of Manhattan, was a much more light-hearted, disengaged designer. Ann Kerr speaks of him as a delightful person! He laughed along with the customers! Why else would he have designed three rotund, plump, and seemingly specious ball jars for *Pivotal*? They have little or no use on the dinner table. They resemble the Homer Laughlin *KitchenKraft*™ jars—those that possessed the notoriously impossible finals—finals that no man could grasp with security. These three ball jars—the Manny, Moe, and Jack of the Mikasa line—served an unknown role. They certainly were not for salad, or soup; there was a huge and satisfying salad bowl for the greenery and a humungous plate-settled tureen for the soups, stews, and chowders. So what was Seibel thinking about when he offered three lidded ball jars? Could they reside on the sideboard and look exclusively pretty? The smallest of these jars was nearly the same size as the sugar bowl—so what was the purpose? An engaging surprise? An attempt to be different? An attempt to extend the Mid-Century-Modern concept well into the 1970s?

The one piece, among all these charming rounded shapes, of the greatest importance is the individual compote. Here, yes here, Seibel returned to his favored piece—the small, footed compote This piquant piece fulfilled the role of the fruit dish. Over and over—with some determined effort—this small and obviously beloved item appeared and reappeared. In *Interplay* (yes, Virginia, he's returning to that dumb idea again!), in *Impromptu*, in *Inheritance*—Ben Seibel introduced this small, slightly footed fruit dish into his shapes. I believe, against all the rearing gurus, that this constantly reappearing dish is a jolly Ben Seibel signature piece

Was Ben Seibel chuckling again when he designed the *Pivotal* sugar and creamer set? It has been repeated and repeated, Seibel's creamer was taller, straighter, and more masculine than the "flat," less prepossessing lidded sugar. However, he did catch us here in *Pivotal*: the creamer crouches low next to the larger sugar with its lid resembling a clown's tasseled cap. For once the feminine sugar bowl dominates the masculine (although not very masculine here) creamer. A merry sense of humor can keep the doldrums away!

Now it must be reinforced that *Pivotal* has no clones. There are no Mikasa lines that have the *Pivotal* shape without the Ben Seibel name. This is true, but whoever made the marketing and design decisions at Mikasa was determined to complicate a seemingly uncomplicated situation. Nothing worth anything is easy. Instead of clones, Mikasa decision makers offered FOUR varieties of the *Pivotal* dinnerware line. They were all referred to as *Pivotal* in advertising brochures and salesmen's sheets. To lessen the confusion, happily, there were two divisions: Formal and, what has come to be called, Regular. The differences lie mainly in the design and color of the teacup.

The *Pivotal* Line Divided by Type

1. Formal *Pivotal* (embossed edge, tapered teacup)
2. Formal *Pivotal* (ball teacup)
3. Regular *Pivotal* (straight-sided teacup)
4. Regular *Pivotal* (ball teacup)

All the treatments fit into one of the above categories. There are no overlaps. Now, please do not think we have completed the roller coaster ride—no, not quite yet! Do not blame me: Mikasa seems to have been playing a little identification game with this line. Nothing really complicated, but it did take me some months to draw these conclusions. Here they are, all done for you! Once learned, never forgotten, and you can return to enjoying and collecting this curvaceous shape.

The last "complication" is that Category 4: Regular *Pivotal* (ball teacup) is further divided into a) a decorated teacup and b) a solid colored teacup. Yes, here Seibel has returned to another one of his penchants—the solid glaze. Actually, the solid glaze graced more than the teacup (this was just a convenience of term), it washed over all the hollowware. Thus, the collector will find sets of *Pivotal* with decorated plates and platters accompanied by solidly glazed teacups, sugar bowl bases, creamers, bowls (outside only), coffee pots, and so on. The lids and interiors were always pure white. Conversely other regular *Pivotal* treatments will have the plates and platters accompanied with DECORATED teacups, sugar bowl bases, and so on. Easily remembered!

Wait, dear reader and potential *Pivotal* collector, there is one final twist! One final Mikasa-inspired hurdle to jump! Listen carefully, please. There are a few (only a few, not many) treatments that appear with BOTH decorated and solid glaze hollowware and when this happens there is a name change. WOW! Here are some examples of this name switch:

Tangents™ (5005) (decorated hollowware) become Tangerine™ (solid hollowware)

Counterpoint™ (5006) (decorated) becomes Flower Garden™ (solid)

Noir™ (5003) (decorated) become Onyx™ (solid)

Since ALL *Pivotal* has the name in the back stamp, it is easy to identify. If the collector finds a plate with the name Noir, he/she knows IMMEDIATELY this plate was accompanied originally by decorated hollowware, but since it is EXACTLY the same pattern as Onyx it can be substituted safely in an Onyx set—undetected unless, of course, one of your guests is the snoopy type and turns over the plates to check if the host/hostess is trying to "pull a fast one!"

As Jonathan Parry, late art director at the Homer Laughlin China Company, once explained to me: collectors tend to believe that manufacturers made (or make) decisions to complicate collecting—no, this is not true! China manufacturers make decisions based SOLELY upon business—what will sell! Mr. Parry was certainly to be believed. So all these convolutions touching upon *Pivotal* were the results of Mikasa management decisions taken to sell the product!

Here is a listing of *Pivotal* treatments according to category. To view some of these treatments, please turn to the Library of Treatments. Unfortunately, since this line is relatively scarce, not all examples could be photographed. When there is no illustration, the treatment will be described.

Pivotal treatments listed by type:

Formal *Pivotal* (embossed rim, tapered teacup)
Laurette™ (9383)
Melody™ (9371)
Tapestry™ (9370)
Vista™ (9384)
Formal *Pivotal* (ball teacup)
Antigua™ (5022)
Blake™ (5021)
Milano™ (5018)
Montina™ (5023)
Snowflake™ (5024)
Westbury™ (5019)
Regular *Pivotal* (straight-sided teacup)
Fantan™ (1864)
Fantasy™ (1361)
Focus™ (1763)
Morning Sun™ (1365)
Peppermint™ (unknown)
Tiara™ (1460)
Regular *Pivotal* (ball teacup) (solid glaze)
Bachelor Button™ (blue) (5031)
Bikini™ (tan) (5027)
BonAire™ (black) (5011)
Care Free™ (tan) (5029)
Flower Garden™ (blue) (5025)
Jade Garden™ (green) (5010)
La Ronde™ (green) (5032)
Onyx™ (black) (5016)
Orbit™ (orange) (5030)
Ovide™ (black) (5007)
Pivgreen™ (green) (5014)
Surrey™ (green) (5033)
Tangerine™ (orange) (5028)
Thistle™ (black) (5035)
Wildflower™ (tan) (5036)
Regular *Pivotal* (ball teacup (decorated hollowware)
Chartres™ (5001)
Counterpoint™ (same as Flower Garden) (5006)
Noir™ (same as Onyx) (5003)
Reflections™ (5004)
Tangents™ (same as Tangerine) (5005)
Tides™ (5002)

Thirty-four dainty dishes designed to set before the king! The solid glaze hollowware had the same consumer use with *Pivotal* as it did with *Duplex*. The housewife (there were still women practicing housewifery in the 1970?) could purchase black hollowware and then obtain some Onyx, Ovide, and Thistle plates and have three sets instead of one. There would be a slight problem with the saucer as these pieces were also decorated; but, since the teacup and the saucer could be purchased separately as open stock ($3.00 and $2.00), this problem was easily solved.

The Mikasa sales gimmickry as discussed above proves nothing in relation to the shape's public popularity. The reasons could pendulum from (1) the need to revive gloomy sales figures or (2) to capitalize on wild customer demands: either diametrically opposed reason could suffice. It is my personal feeling that *Pivotal* was not overwhelmingly popular. It posed, and was touted, as "fine china" while not really belonging to that class. It certainly was not stoneware or ironstone—the categories wherein the other three known Seibel shapes securely fit. Nor was it really fine china, porcelain! If premier class dinnerware was desired, why not purchase Mikasa Bone China in such patterns as Boulton (A1155), Lorenzo (A1128), or Bakaota (A5163)? As a matter of interest, the handwritten "Ben's" appears next to this last named shape. No, it might just have happened that Seibel's *Pivotal*—a lovely, although rather overtly feminine, shape—just did not conqueror any particular niche and waned away like the dying swan—beautiful but unwanted!

A few *Pivotal* back stamps replace Ben Seibel's name with the term "fine china." We know, however, from the catalogs that Seibel was the designer.

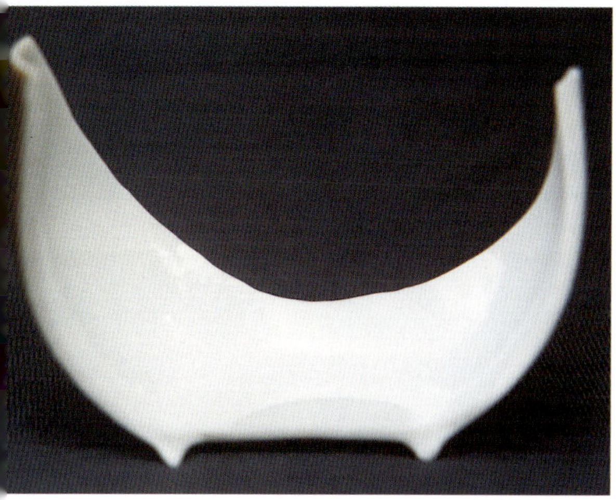

Pivotal is a very delicate and fragile line of tableware—as this shard shows.

Here are the four plates in the Tides treatment. Prices: Chop plate, $15-17; Dinner plate, $10-12; Salad plate, $7-9; Bread & butter plate, $3-5.

This shape is rarely found in sets, so this was a fortunate acquisition. The dealer took a photograph for me.

The butter dish in pure white. Price: $15-17.

The small coffee pot is quite hard to find. Here it is in Noir and flanked by a tan creamer and a black individual compote. Price (coffee pot): $25-30.

The large Tides ball jar compared with the sugar bowl. These jars are very difficult to find. Price for ball jars: Large, $40-45; Medium, 20-25; Small, $12-18. They are rare pieces and it is not known if they were available in all decorations or in solid glazes. To date (2003), they have only been seen in the Tides treatment.

The individual compote in solid olive. Price: $4-6.

The individual compote in a decorated treatment: Price: $10-12.

We know by catalogs and brochures that *Pivotal* came in variations—all designed by Seibel. Here is an example of Tapestry: a Formal *Pivotal* line with tapered cup. The ware has a raised oval emboss-ment—rather like Iroquois' *Intaglio*, but in reverse. These are very scarce pieces—however, they have not yet captured the collectors' imagination. Price (set): $8-10.

Close-up of the oval and cross embossment.

Back stamp of the Formal line—with a name but no mention of Ben Seibel.

An example of the regular *Pivotal* with the straight-sided cup. The catalogs list only four treatments: Focus, Tiara, Fantan, and Fantasy. This is Tiara. These also are quite scarce. Price: Cup/saucer set: $8-10.

Even the shakers for Formal *Pivotal* are different. I like to call this a "stove pipe" shaker because it reminds me of the Scandinavian wood burning porcelain stoves that stood in the corner of every room. Price (set): $6-8.

The cup and the creamer are in the Noir treatment. The dinner plate could be either and the collector will not know until it is turned over.

A few pieces of Surrey. The delicate pinks and greens of the treatment match well with the solid olive hollowware.

The salad (or soup) bowl—quite low and wide. The decoration appears within the bowl. Price: $8-10.

The regular shakers: solid and decorated. Price (set): $10-12.

Two examples of the decorated cup and saucer. These cups are very feminine and dainty—perhaps too dainty. They are the exact opposite from the rugged masculinity of the *Potter's Art* set. Price (set): $12-15.

Here is the solid salad/soup bowl. Price: $6-8.

The vegetable bowl—the decoration appears outside. These bowls are very hard to find. Price: $15-18.

Pivotal: Library of Treatments

Because this shape is scarce, not all the treatments can be shown. This is an unfortunate state of affairs, and again I hope those readers who do have treatments not illustrated in this Library will share and send a photograph. Twenty-nine treatments have been photographed: all but Antiqua and Chartes as plates. These will be shown on the item possessed. Eight have escaped the camera, but luckily they have been viewed on the pages of catalogs. Thus they can be verbally described. This is certainly not a perfect scenario; but, because of the shape's scarcity, it is acceptable.

After some thought, it has been decided to list the pictured treatments alphabetically. All *Pivotal* decorated pieces bear the name/number of the treatment in the back stamp. There is no mention of the four varieties in the mark; so listing in this manner is useless. The treatments for which there are NO photographs are placed at the end of the section.

There are only five colors used for the solid glaze. They are:

Black: Matte darkly saturated.

Green: Shiny olive with variations in the wash.[1]

Blue: Wedgwood blue with some noticeable differences in shade.

Mushroom: Very strongly grayed tan.

Burnt orange: Shiny, the most difficult to find.

To distinguish between the five Pivotal variations, the following abbreviations are used.

FP: *Pivotal* Formal (ball teacup)
FPR: *Pivotal* Formal (raised rim)
RPSG: *Pivotal* Regular (ball teacup, solid glaze hollowware)
RPD: *Pivotal* Regular (ball teacup, decorated hollowware)
RS: *Pivotal* Regular (straight-sided teacup)

ANTIGUA™: (FP) (5022). The plates are simply elegant: thin edge rims of gold, then a wider circle of olive green. The richness of the combination and the pure simplicity counteract my usual aversion to olive green. In the Formal variation of *Pivotal*, the hollowware is always decorated.

BACHELOR BUTTON™ (RPSG) (5031). Pale blue stylized flowers. Many thanks to Ron and Karen Legamans (Arizona) for sharing this photograph.

BLAKE™: (FP) (5021). Here is another gracefully sophisticated member of the Formal *Pivotal* group. A one-half inch border of subdued gold is set off by a very narrow band of matte black. There is understated scrollwork on the gold border—reminding the viewer of two curved "Cs" resting back to back.

CAREFREE™: (RPSG) (5029). Quite similar to Japanese paper cutouts. Intricate, yet the white surrounds make the design clear and fresh. Mushroom.

FANTAN™: (RS) (1864). Perpetual circular motion: four rows of circles, and some rows are circles within circles. The well is awash with circles. The dizziness is kept to a minimum by neutral coloration: blacks and tans with touches of white.

CHARTRES™: (RPD) (5001). This is one of those *Pivotal* treatments that appear only with decorated hollowware. One of the more difficult treatments to locate, the dinner plate has proved impossible to find. The comma-like multicolor figures seen on the gravy boat's sides encircle the plates and leave the wide well pure white. The name Chartres refers no doubt to the stained glass window effect.

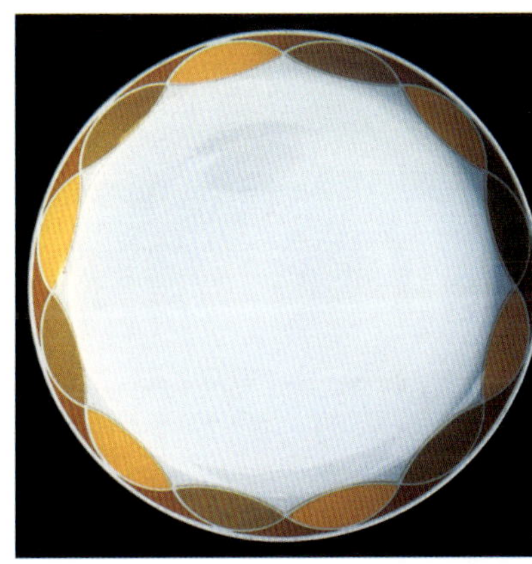

FANTASY™: (RS) (1361). All the regular *Pivotal* lines with the straight-sided teacups have decorated hollowware. Gold, olive, and ochre make a very fluid ring near the edge of the plate and encircle the hollowware where the ovals become plumper, less extended. Fantasy is marked *Pivotal*, but does not carry the Ben Seibel name.

FLOWER GARDEN™: (RPSG) (5025). Exactly the same as Counterpoint, but with the solid blue hollowware.

COUNTERPOINT™: (RPD) (5006). Three, four, and five petalled flowers in two tones of blue—interspersed with lime green leaves—ring the flatware and are strewn on the hollowware. Since a Counterpoint plate is exactly the same as a Flower Garden plate, both treatments can be found with little frustration—and interchanged!

FOCUS™: (RS) (1763). The same approach as Carefree—although coarser: The curls and convolutions of master paper cutting. If the viewer looks closely, the head of an owl—complete with beak—can be seen staring from the center. Notice the straight-sided cup.

LA RONDE™: (RPSG) (5032). A lacey, frothy central concoction reminding one of those doilies delicately crocheted by innumerable maiden aunts in the 1930s. To increase the gossamer qualities, there is a tiny double dot and stylized *fleur de lys* at the very edge of the rim. Green.

JADE GARDEN™: (RPSG) (5010). Quite scarce, no doubt because it was not popular in 1971, and quickly dropped. The rim design reminds the viewer of cotton paisley; a colorful swirled pattern of abstract curved shapes. Since the design is small, it takes considerable study to learn all its secrets—something few customers seemed to want to do! Mushroom.

MELODY™: (FPR) (9371). With the wide rim speckled with raised ovals and dots, Melody belongs to the Formal *Pivotal* family. This technique is exactly the opposite from the one Seibel used on Iroquois' *Intaglio.* The raised embossments add considerable roughened texture to the shape, but in no manner did it approach the shimmering quality of *Intaglio*'s incised debossment. The very delicate verge design is made up of jesters' caps, diamonds, dots, and arrows.

MONTINA™: (FP) (5023). Shows the same basic concept as Antigua, but in this case, the wider matte black rim border contracts with the narrower platinum inner band. Sophistication is the name of the game here.

NOIR™: (RPD) (5003). The narrow border uses a Scandinavian inspired design in black. Noir is easily available and quite popular. Except for the fact that it contains no metallic color (i.e. gold, platinum, bronze), it could be a variety of Formal *Pivotal*.

MORNING SUN™: (RS) (1365). Simple circles with a twist, the central one is white surrounded by gold, brown, and burnt orange rounds with off-center attitudes. Morning Sun reminds one somewhat of Mikasa's *Indian Feast* line: Arizona colors at their best. Unfortunately, since no plate is available, we have to illustrated with a soup bowl. Morning Sun is not marked with the Ben Seibel name.

ONYX™: (RPSG) (5016). Exactly the same border design as Noir, but uses the matte black hollowware.

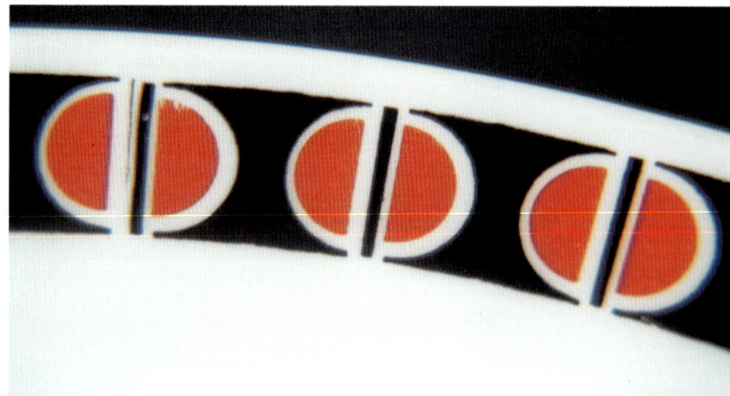

OVIDE™: (RPSG) (5007). Another understated rim design, but here there is a snazzy little "zip"—little facing half-moons of brilliant scarlet. The tiny size of these bits of color keeps them subdued although noticeable. This is a fairly scarce treatment. Black hollowware.

PIVGREEN™: (5014). As mentioned above, this treatment is a "puzzlement." Usually examples of the solid glazes are not named or numbered. Thus, is Pivgreen a legitimate treatment? Are the plates decorated or are they all green? This green is NOT the usual hollowware solid color. Can any reader assist?

REFLECTIONS™: (RPD) (5004). A scattering of dark blue and pale yellow poppies roughly "crayoned." The asymmetrical design (four flowers on the left, three on the right) enhances interest.

SNOWFLAKE™: (FP) (5024). All the formal designs—the ones with the ball teacup—have a welcome metallic touch. Snowflake has the gold rather lavishly spread: the figure is edged in matte gold, and the rim has the barest reflective line.

SURREY™ (RPSG) (5033). A favorite design: single roses of the softest beige pink, deeper pink strawberries amid dark olive leaves—again with a frame stripe. There is something "woodland" about this treatment: peaceful and hushed. Green is the solid glaze.

TANGENTS™: (RPD) (5005). In quilt making, the most difficult and painstaking design to construct is called Cathedral Window: it calls for much matching and careful folding back. Only the most experienced quilter should attempt it. Here it is transferred to a *Pivotal* treatment. The teacup has only one unit within the small circle.

TANGERINE™: (RPSG) (5028). The same treatment as Tangents, but with Orange hollowware. Tangerine is readily available.

TAPESTRY™: (FPR) (9370). Another Japanese-style paper cutout, but here, however, it is much more ornate than Carefree. Of the four embossed formal *Pivotal* treatments, Tapestry is the most common. There are nine pieces in my collection, and more could be added if so desired.

THISTLE™: (RPSG) (5035). Black and white—what could be cleaner, starker? It is quite the perfect design: it fills the plate without being obtrusive and will frame any food. Black.

TIDES™: **(RPR) (5002)**. Everyone is startled by this treatment, and some collectors are amazed at its psychedelic properties. Not only do the soft, curving shapes swirl like a Dali dream, the colors (chartreuse, teal, and orange) surprisingly work well together. I owned a rather large set of Tides (see photograph in preceding section) but it is getting smaller as collectors beg for an example.

VISTA™: **(FPR) (9384)**. With a black sunburst in the middle of the well and tiny triangles—each topped with a dot—at the verge, Vista repeats the formality of the embossed shape. The name was re-used for a much different *Mexicana* treatment. Please note how much smaller the well has become in this *Pivotal* variety.

WILDFLOWER™: **(RPSG) (5036)**. Another treatment bearing a slight resemblance to Surrey—at least in artistic approach. This is one of the seven early treatments and depicts poppies in two shades of softly grayed mushroom. There is absolutely no inflicted green. The affect is neutral and restful. The solid glaze is Mushroom.

The *Pivotal* treatments for which there are no illustrations are listed below.

Bikini™: **(RPSG) (5027)**. Tiny ovals of taupe, tan, and black form an edge band.

BonAire™: **(RPSG) (5011)**. Tiny gray and black florals in a narrow edge band; complete with a small, frothy central design.

Laurette™: **(FPR) (9383)**. A verge design of tiny, but intricate, scrolls.

Milano™: **(FP) (5018)**. A gold matte tapestry design banding the pieces.

Orbit™: **(RPSG) (5030)**. A central design in tan reminiscent of flying atoms.

Peppermint™: **(RS) (no number available)**. Symmetrical leaf design in the center of the well consisting of dark, medium, and light green. This is surrounded by a four-lobed cartouche and the rest of the well is bright green.

Tiara™: **(RS) (1460)**. Leaf green scrolled band around the edge: vertical on teacup. (Please see page 161.)

Westbury™: **(FP) (5019)**. Simple, thin, matte gold band around the edge.

This whole page:
The *Potter's Art* back stamps. A wide variety of back stamps provide interesting information. The only consistent fact is that ALL provide the official PF number. The "PF09—series" (five treatments from PF095 to PF099) are totally different—as is their cup and saucer: these are enclosed in a box. The back stamp of PF099, Natural Hues, is unusual because it states "Shape by Ben Seibel" not merely "Ben Seibel Design."

Potter's Art: The Subtle Mingling of Beauty and Simplicity

I must be as careful as Croesus and as wise as Solomon when commenting upon *Potter's Art*. This shape is by far my favorite—not only of Seibel's Mikasa work, but a favorite among all his ceramic designs. Thus my enthusiasm must not swamp the individual reader with highly colored, positively prejudicial, and obviously overstated conclusions.

I will try to be modestly eloquent!

From among all the Mikasa lines touched by the wand of Seibel's genius, *Potter's Art* stands out. It is stamped by a subtle uniqueness of expression and a masculine sturdiness of approach that, could it be said, makes it matchlessly supreme among the Mikasa/Seibel liaison. *Potter's Art*, when understood with care and assayed without prejudice, can stand equally among the most famous of all Seibel shapes: Roseville *Raymor* and Steubenville *Contempora*. I believe that *Potter's Art* is more sturdily constructed than *Contempora*. We are viewing Ben Seibel at his magnificent prime.

To restate: *Potter's Art* must be considered a major line. It is, quite frankly, the ranking Seibel shape among all the designer has accomplished for Mikasa and, dare I speak so, probably one of the most significant of all lines in the entire "Seibel-esque" tableware catalog.

I am trying not to be grandiloquent! Still my admiration bursts forth!

Such a statement, such an allegation, to flap and flaunt, like a red flag, before the bullish collectors of *Contempora* and Roseville regular line. But I do it! In its approach, i.e. shape being supreme over imposed decoration, *Potter's Art* is equal to these two important Mid-Century-Modern tableware lines. Think of it for a moment! These two earlier 1950s shapes were produced wearing the purest and simplest of hues: browns, grays, basically neutrals, except perhaps for a "froggy" green! There is no impressed or stamped decal to befuddle the outline of these shapes. So does *Potter's Art* subscribe to the same philosophy: its shape is certainly not as curvilinear, nor fluidly expressed, but the overall design is approached cleanly and purely without the added subterfuge decaled decorative devices. In *Potter's Art*, as in *Raymor Modern Stoneware*, whatever decorations appear are intrinsic parts of the shape itself: i.e. color and texture!

Shall we then putter, you and I, among the fields of *Potter's Art*?

Several years ago—in a forgettable but long article—it was suggested, strongly suggested, by me, in a moment of unjustifiable "wisdom," that the astute collector—those with good taste and limited finances—should begin to acquire *Potter's Art*. It was certainly one of the last shapes Seibel designed,[1] and was available in such fine stores as Fredericks & Nelson's in the late 1970s and early '80s. Unlike the Raymor lines and the Iroquois group, Seibel's work for Mikasa is probably still doing dinnerware duty in a good number of homes throughout the United States. As sadly, one by one, the no longer replaceable *Potter's Art* dishes are broken, the sets grow smaller and finally are relegated to summer cottages or the attic or the garage sales. The time to collect this tableware is now, before it becomes "collectible"!

The *Potter's Art* shape is ruggedly honest and sophisticatedly simple. It will appear so to both urbanites residing in spaciously gleaming city lofts overlooking glittering skylines, and country folk dwelling in charming cottages surrounded by tumbling gardens. *Potter's Art's* speaks, eventually, to everyone.

However, it is easy to be misled! Upon first view, the shapes tends to look "clunky" and eminently suitable only for the buffet table or use during a rough hewn backyard barbeque or for rural picnic ware to celebrate with suitable restraint a spinsterish aunt's latest birthday. Yet upon serious reflection and careful contemplation, the individual pieces of *Potter's Art* are seen as no longer "humble" but "cleverly sophisticated." While the shape will not appeal to all collectors, sooner or later it should be appreciated for its classic, although zoftig, beauty.

Potter's Art has another viable link to *Raymor Modern Stoneware*: its reliance on large pots and individual covered casseroles, and like Mikasa *Duplex*, it lacks the "essential" bread & butter plate. Due to the lucky acquisition of an official Mikasa advertising sheet, the correct terminology can be used in the following list of *Potter's Art* pieces.

Dinner plate	(201)
Salad plate	(202)
Teacup	(204)
Tea saucer	(205)
Fruit	(210)
Cappuccino cup	(216)
Cappuccino saucer	(217)
Soup/cereal	(220)
Onion soup (no lid)	(229)
Au gratin	(232)
Gravy and liner	(242)
Round vegetable	(250
Marmite/cover	(260)
Bean pot	(262)
Covered casserole	(264)
Covered sugar	(280)
Creamer	(290)
Round buffet platter	(313)
Oblong platter	(315)
Teapot	(323)
Warmer for teapot	(325)
Candle links	(340)
Salt/pepper stackable	(350)
Covered butter	(360)
Napkin ring	(366)
Snack set (Handled plate and Cappuccino cup)	(374)

Twenty-eight pieces, all of which are extremely well designed; solid, heavy, superbly useable, many have that "snap," that different touch which constitutes an element of surprise. We can start down the line.

A mug disguised as a Cappuccino cup and accompanied by its own saucer: now that is surprising! Seibel was on the cappuccino bandwagon before there was really a bandwagon at all. In the mid-to-late 1970s, cappuccino was an overt, sophisticated mark of "Yuppiedom"—securely confined to such centers as the Upper East Side of Manhattan, Seattle, San Francisco, and the hills surrounding Los Angeles. Perhaps New Orleans could join the short list. Cappuccino had not reached the hinterland of America—in fact, it has not reached there yet! Ask for cappuccino in Mobile, Alabama, even today, and probably you will receive a quizzical look and a plate of grits! So Seibel was either taking chances, or hedging his bets: without the saucer, the Cappuccino cup dwarfs into a mere mug.

Twenty years prior—when Seibel was involved with the Iroquois China Company, Eva Zeisel was presenting her outstanding shape *Tomorrow's Classic*. She designed for this illustrious line both covered onion soups and covered marmites. In 1975, Seibel repeated this combination but divested the onion soup of its lid. His design was more practical than Zeisel's because true onion soup must spend a short time under the broiler (to melt the cheese and slightly toast the bread topping), and to add a cover after this experience is a little *recherché*. A marmite is more specifically an individual casserole—such a piece was befriended by Seibel during his creation of *Raymor Modern Stoneware*.

The au gratin is certainly an unusual item of very specific use, yet this use can be extended in a number of ways. Just as the onion soup, the au gratin must spend time under the broiler. This is the first time that Seibel created such a specific piece for one of his tableware lines, and it hints at the growing informality of family/guest occasions.

The usual Seibel gravy needs a ladle, and since he never included a ceramic ladle–as did Eva Zeisel—one must be substituted. Even if a gravy boat has two spouts, such as the *Impromptu* version, these spouts cannot really be used for pouring. When he was considering Mikasa, Seibel chose to created round gravies in all four major shapes, and three of these have double spouts. But who could grasp such a bowl and pour from either spout? With *Potter's Art*, Seibel grows even wiser: he adds a sturdy handle.[2] The existence of this handle is a good reason for surmising *Mexicana* was designed BEFORE *Potter's Art*! For what perceptive designer would return to a non-handled round gravy after the exceptionally useful *Potter's Art* version worked so well on the tabletop? The separate liner is indented, but is sometimes mistaken for a plate, or it has been advertised as a "relish" dish. Because it is a separate piece, and often separated from the gravy itself, it must be counted individually.

The bean pot is a formidable item: a large and impressive giant adaptation of the covered marmite. Its height (5.50") and width (6.75") demand respect, but it is not as formidable as the Roseville Raymor bean pots, and the rounded and strong handles are much more convenient that the latter's rather awkwardly stretched holders. This pot is very compact and extremely useful. Once I rather cautiously used the bean pot in my favorite treatment—Fire Song—to bake (what else) homemade beans. Even though Bush's Best Baked Beans (remember the group of television advertisements with the Labrador named Duke?) produces an awesome dish of beans, mine were even better baked in the *Potter's Art* pot. There is not a hint of physical awkwardness in this pot either in the cooking or in the serving, not even potentially.

What of the casserole? If the bean pot is impressive, the casserole is a behemoth! Wider (9.25"), lower (3.50"), and heavier, the casserole needed a different type of handle: filled with *trípes à la modes de Caen*,[3] *cassoulet*,[4] or *sauté de lapin au vin blanc*[5] this becomes weighty indeed. The horizontal handles are adapted for this type of use. Surely, this casserole, with its high rounded lid, can compete with those pieces of similar use in the Roseville Raymor line, and is certainly more sturdily statuesque than the more fluid but also more thinly conceived Steubenville *Contempora*. These facts must be recognized as true!

Now, being in mid-stream of our analysis of the individual *Potter's Art* pieces, is the time to touch upon and call attention to the finials: or, more properly, the lack of finials. What about these gloriously fascinating lids? Recessed "finials" (what else can they be called?) are absolutely unique in American tableware. The *Potter's Art* lids—both casserole-weighty and sugar-bowl-light—are supremely simple to grasp. Smoothly indented, perfectly rounded "finger holes" provide ultimately secure use! What a one hundred percent reversal from the awkward and slippery flattened finials on *Contempora*.

Other items of note: The return to the Seibel basic of low, crouching sugar bowl and tall creamer with the wide flap-bottomed handle; the huge chop plate—here titled a round buffet platter;[6] the oblong platter prodigiously massy, yet exactly the same shape as the porcelaneous one in the *Pivotal* line; and the teapot with its warmer! The simple beauty of the Seibel warmer stand must be recognized as perhaps the supreme signature piece of the designer. He firmly believed these stands should be a standard item[7] in any tableware line where their presence is useful.

Stackable shakers? Smaller round-topped pepper seated securely on the flat salt? Snack plate, a.k.a. television or "party" plate? These abound among the work of the Mid-Century-Modernists!

The true design surprises have been saved for last! What touch of genius impelled Ben Seibel to include within the *Potter's Art* group, two, not one but TWO, pieces unique to his *oeuvre*: candle links and napkin rings!

One could argue the *Potter's Art* candle links had a predecessor in the *Impromptu* candelabra. Yet the candle links are much more practical: their size and shape allows them to be usefully employed on the tabletop. Several can be ringed in a charming oval, or placed in front of each individual guest. In one magazine advertisement, these links were stacked loosely like bricks and filled with all manner of candles along the back of a buffet presentation. Quick drama!

Still it is the napkin ring that captures the collectors' collective imagination. A ceramic napkin ring designed to accompany a set of tableware is a rare item indeed. Homer Laughlin offered one in their *Post86 Fiesta*™ line, but this was merely a "lopped-off" teapot handle and it was discontinued after a number of years. For a manufacturer and designer to give the consumer of the 1970s the choice to purchase coordinated ceramic napkin rings was unique. Not since the bakelite napkin holders of the thirties and forties have these rings made such a splash.

Napkin rings have always been the cultural bastion of the middle-classes. They were never used by the wealthy because those with money used fresh napkins at each meal. This fact informed guests that their hostess could afford a laundress to do the linens. The poor and underprivileged rarely used napkins. The middle-classes, practical, careful, and conservative, thrived on napkin holders or rings. In the kitchen these items were colorful, whimsical, and aimed to brighten the breakfast table and lighten a child's gloom at having soon to leave for school. In the dining room, holders were often silver: given to a child as a christening or baptismal gift by an aunt or favored friend of the family. These often competed as gifts with the curved baby spoon. On a shelf reserved for special mementos, I have placed four silver napkin rings important in my memories. One, heavy and ornate, was my grandfather's and is engraved "Frank, 05." This was so valued in my family that in 1955, my name was engraved on the opposite side. Such is the need for middle-class continuity. The second silver ring was more feminine: octagon-shaped and narrow. It has no date, but presents a classically scrolled "C" in an elaborate cartouche. It was my grandmother's. Mine from babyhood was long and oval with representations of Mother Goose rhymes upon it. So important (or so it seemed) was the need for individual napkin rings that my mother purchased her own—round and engraved in the dart and dash motif—in 1947. Ideally then, each member of the family had an easily identified ring of his or her own: this fact is really more than an "ideal," it is the napkin ring's *raison d'etrê*. Thus perhaps the *Potter's Art* napkin ring was merely a conceit—but what a charming conceit!

However, after all this conversation about the individual pieces and the uniqueness accrued to a good number of them, we must talk of the treatments. Rather than list all the decorative approaches here, the reader is requested to turn to the *Potter's Art:* Library of Treatments. There treatments will be listed alphabetically.

Some general comments are necessary. There are no decals or applied decorations, no embossments or embellishments—except for some artfully disposed glaze drippings to add a rough-hewn aspect to some of the hollowware. The colors of nearly all the treatments fit into either the "brown" or "neutral" category. There are a few exceptions. The browns are a severely misunderstood color category: many people dismiss them as drab and dull!

Yet these erroneous beliefs must be, will be, blown away by knowledge's cool breezes. While brown is technically a color produced by the combination of red, black, and yellow, its range is huge—monumentally huge and extended. The browns encompass such fascinating hues as mahogany, tobacco, coffee, chocolate, fawn, and seal. The United States textile standards further list beige, ecru, oakwood, sandalwood, cork, champagne, caramel, maple, cocoa, spice, and toast, and even a red-brown distinguished by the lovely name "autumn leaves." How can the "browns" be dull? Then further, there are such colors as alizarin brown, antique brown, biscuit brown, bone brown, brown madder, burnt umber, café au lait, coconut, dun, Dresden brown, Havana brown, olive brown, otter brown, taupe, and then two favorites, "French nude" (a beige flesh hue) and the cuddly color known as "bunny brown" (a soft dappled muted nutmeg.) And we have not even touched terra cotta, liver, cordovan and chestnut, roan and russet. Browns dull? Never!! *Potter's Art* wisely has elected to remain well rooted within the wide and expansive family of browns.

One of the true joys of this Mikasa line—if the collector will allow himself or herself to be so absorbed—is that the colors seem limited. If one of the *Potter's Art* treatments was red, another blue, and a third a shade of green, then the collector could simply say—in a rather imprecise manner—the red, the blue, and the green treatment of *Potter's Art*. However, if all *Potter's Art* patterns encompass mainly, almost completely, the hues of brown, then the collector and the researcher, musts learn the correct, and truly descriptive, names for all the browns existing in the color compendium. Rusticana (PF005) is the color of bittersweet chocolate; the cups and creamer of Butterball (PF802) possess the deeper but much warmer reddish quality of Dutch milk chocolate. The Sahara (PF026) cups are a speckled tan color with a medium glaze—both inside and out. Adobe (PF001), with its true matte finish, is dull sandalwood. Country Cabin (PF852) also possesses a matte glaze, but here the color becomes grayish oatmeal. Fire Song (PF003) washes the sides of its hollowware with the glossy color of oxblood. What *Potter's Art* demands is a precise color sense—one easily acquired if the collector so wishes. And this, for me, is one of the major pleasures of collecting *Potter's Art*!

The neutrals are represented by the black of Cummerbund (PF024) hollowware at one edge of the shaded scale to the near white—dotted with yolky yellow speckles—of Wild Rice (PF910). The color of Freestyle (PF506), besides being spectacularly different, sent me fumbling for a copy of the Gerard Manley Hopkins' (1844-1888) short lyric, "Pied Beauty."

> Glory be to God for dappled things;
> For skies of couple-colour as a brindle cow;
> For rose-moles all in stipple upon trout that swim:

Freestyle indeed is a unusual treatment!

Which treatments, among so many, could be termed popular among collectors and users. For one cannot forget *Potter's Art* is very usable today—if one is careful when cleaning up, and guests are reliable. Again it must be stated that popularity depends largely upon availability. A treatment cannot be highly sought if there is little to seek! Fusion is an example of this conundrum: it is a stunningly beautiful treatment—richly colored, almost perfectly glazed, and possesses a mirror-like shimmer. Yet Fusion is scarce, and the odd pieces coming into the general marketplace are quickly purchased by those few collectors attempting to gather a small set. Presently Fusion is widely admired, but weakly collected. Studio Kiln, Fire Song, Buckskin—three very different lines—are quite common, and this availability brings a rush of collector interest. Country Cabin (flatware only) is also easy to find and constantly coupled with the hollowware of "Regular" (PF850) also has many avid collectors.

With more collector interest—hopefully aroused by this book—sources for the now scarcer treatments will grow and such pale beauties like White Tie and Wild Rice, or honeyed Sonora, or the trout-speckled Free Style will become eagerly sought.

Before we can close on the *Potter's Art* shape, we must acknowledge a "problem," a confusion within the ranks of the shape. As in dealing with *Pivotal*, the collector must accept that Mikasa tread its own unique path! *Potter's Art* possesses clones: pieces that look exactly like the shape and yet have a different name. Clones are a proliferating problem with the Mikasa/Sieibel connection. Accept it you must! In the midst of this line there is a group of five treatments that (1) bear an entirely different *Potter's Art* mark and (2) possess a cup and saucer that belongs to a clone line—*Discovery*. At this time, there is no explanation regarding this anomaly. It is simply a fact. I have chosen (arbitrarily it is admitted) to label these five treatments the "PF09—series." There is no basis for this label, just my own convenient way to differentiate.

This series includes:

Coral Sea™	(PF095)
Dune™	(PF096)
Big Surf™	(PF097)
Studio Expressions™	(PF098)
Nature's Hues™	(PF099)

These are NOT clones: they bear the name *Potter's Art*, albeit in a different style of back stamp. They are, however, delicately glazed in confusing similarity: a mingling of the most luminous of soft hued bands—in the same manner as the much darker and more brash Studio Kiln. These are soft and natural colors: they reek of the seashore. These five are *Potter's Art* with a soft salt-scented twist!

(Left) Sand Dune teacup in front of a dark Rusticana salad plate. In front a Sahara teacup. (Center) Butterball cereal bowl. (Right) Blue Honey dinner plate stands behind an Adobe salad plate with a White Tie teacup saucer (left) and a Buckskin cappuccino saucer (right). In front is a Sonora teacup.

One final note: To create variety and an element of surprise, Mikasa wisely altered the color emphasis from flatware to hollowware. It is lucky the pieces are identified because some of the cups, sugar bowls, and creamers bear little glaze resemblance to the plates and platters.

Please turn to the *Potter's Art*: Library of Treatments to enjoy the many variations of the color brown.

The casserole with its absolutely unique indented lid. This is "Regular"—actually an unnamed treatment with the number PF850. Up to this time NO flatware has been discovered in this treatment. Price: $35-40.

The inside of the casserole cover: indented "finials" are distinctively "Seibel-esque." The heavy covers and lids of *Potter's Art* can be handled with aplomb.

Even the casserole bottom is decorative.

The bean pot in one of the most popular treatments—Studio Kiln. I have used this pot a number of times in the oven and it cleans perfectly. Taller and smaller than the casserole, it still is very heavy and supremely impressive. Price: $45-50.

The cups and saucers would make a nice collection in themselves. Remember, some cup/saucer sets are quite different from the flatware in their own treatment—certainly not difficult to distinguish, but present a potential challenge. Sand Dune is unusual for the stripe inside the cup; Fire Song's color is known as "ox-blood" and it is another favorite with collectors; Buckskin is also popular and has the added perk of being readily available. Price (set): $10-18.

The Rusticana soup/cereal (6.50"): a much more traditional shape. Price: $6-8.

Another cup/saucer set. An excellent example showing striking color differences within one treatment. This is Butterball: the hollowware is dark brown—picking up the dark brown stripe encircling the flatware.

What makes Studio Kiln popular is the continuation of the design inside the piece. The color spacing is reminiscent of the fainter hued PF09—series. These larger bowls (9") are styled like the fruit bowl—straight sides—not the cereal bowl. Price: $12-15.

This is the Rusticana fruit dish—indeed quite a scarce item. What makes it unusual is that Seibel often distinguished his cereal/soup and smaller fruit one from the other. Many designers just worked with size differences. Anyway, these are little beauties (4.75") that should be welcome in any collection. Price: $9-15.

The butter dish in Sunrise—a very pale cream-yellow. The base is 8" x 4.50" and has an inner ridge to contain the quarter pound of butter. The indented "pinch handles" make it easy to lift the relatively heavy cover. Price: $18-20.

An onion soup (4.75"). These are really fruit dishes with handles. The official listing mentions this piece is "without cover," and this is the way it should be. An onion soup bowl that cannot go directly under the broiler is really nonsense, and a cover is absolutely unnecessary. Price: $12-15.

Buckskin is another fairly popular treatment—very smooth and understated. Here is the cup/saucer and the cappuccino/saucer. Often termed a "mug," the cappuccino saucer is completely different from the regular saucer—and quite scarce. Price for cappuccino set: $15-18.

Shown are two cappuccino cups. The handle of the Buckskin cup (right) has been attached slightly lower, and, to my mind, seems better balanced. The lowered handle regularly appears, but cannot be considered a true variation. The cup to the left is Studio Kiln; the cappuccino saucer (read) is Country Cabin.

The covered marmite. In a photograph where size might be difficult to assess, the collector can always separate the bean pot from its smaller cousin, the marmite: the handles of the latter are horizontal. Four and one-quarter inches round and three inches high, this is a very nice substantial little pot. It is hard to notice, but the sides slope outward to the top: the base is only a little over 3.50". There is also a wide inner rim. Price: $18-20.

Here is the Studio Kiln au gratin shown above the *Discovery* au gratin in Coral Surf. *Discovery* is a pure clone of *Potter's Art*. These pieces give a larger impression in photographs: 7.75" long (not counting handles) x 5.75" wide. Price (for *Potter's Art*): $10-14.

Seibel must have been at his creative peak when he designed *Potter's Art*—or else he might have been drawing on all his cumulative experience. Here we have a double-spouted gravy that really can be poured. The existence of the handle makes it all so easy. The gravy has its own round underplate (7.50") sometimes sold as a salad plate. Price (gravy and underplate): $25-30.

A very small grouping of a scarce treatment: Wild Rice. This pale gray pattern is rarely seen. Notice the round gravy underplate in the center.

Notice the rich creamy well-saturated cover on this casserole! It looks like melted milk chocolate. The decorative approach with *Potter's Art* is likewise rich—simple, yet rich. Drips, spatters, oozes, and running wavers decorate the sides: each casserole is slightly different. This is a supreme example of Rusticana, and it must be admitted, not all Rusticana is so perfectly finished.

The very desirable Fire Song bean pot. Ox-blood red, deep cobalt, and pure white make a stunning combination. This piece is included because it sold for $110 on the eBay auction in mid-year 2000. Some bidder surely wanted it! It could almost be said that Fire Song commands a 50% premium.

The Sonora creamer and sugar. Again Seibel combines the short and the tall. Sonora reminds one of melted butterscotch. The creamer stands 4" tall; the sugar 2.25" but the arched cover brings it up to 3.25". Beware of "open sugars," these are simply sugar bowls without a cover and really should never be purchased. Prices: (creamer), $6-8; (sugar), $10-12.

White Tie creamer. Note the large, molded handle that still portrays elements of grace.

Close-up of the creamer handle: the oval underlip balances it perfectly.

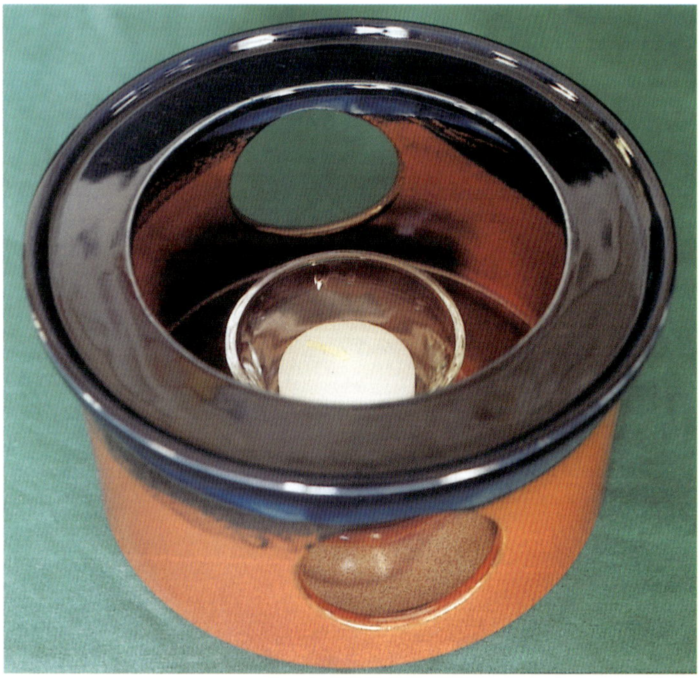

The Fire Song teapot warmer. These are quite rare. Price: $30-40.

The spectacular teapot in Fusion. This is an elusive treatment and was priced $110. Teapots usually bring from $70-80.

Since Fusion is a scarce treatment, I wanted to include a well-photographed example of the Fusion glaze. Here, on a cereal bowl, one can see the deep, startlingly deep, and rich color. More mahogany than Fire Song, Fusion has much more shimmer and is not "dulled" by being juxtaposed with dark cobalt. Except for its rarity, it would be much more popular (I believe) than the "much-in-demand" Fire Song.

The large oval platter. Cummerbund is the name of the treatment: black and sandstone gray. These platters are very expensive in such replacement services that carry them: $90-125. However, the careful collector should be able to find a platter for between $35-45. They are HEAVY!

Seibel liked to "stack" and here are two Buckskin stacking shakers being kept carefully apart. These are unique little items, but not as popular as they should be. Price (set): $12-15.

Sunrise shakers joyously stacked. The salt is below.

Snack plate in Country Cabin. This item is nearly as scarce as the fruit dish: not many are seen. Price: $25-30.

Occasionally, a Cappuccino cup will be found with a different handle. Obviously, some worker has fastened the regular Teacup's handle to the taller Cappuccino. While interesting, a Cappuccino cup with a Teacup handle does not demand a higher price.

The cappuccino cup (mug) in its role as "snack cup." The added lip-handle makes the unit much easier to carry.

Potter's Art has so much to offer the serious collector. Here is another unique item: the napkin ring (Studio Kiln). These are approximately 2.75" long and stand 2" high. Price: $8-15.

Another very unique *Potter's Art* piece: the candlelinks. Not since the 1956 *Impromptu* has Seibel dabbled in a candleholder. These are scarce and expensive, but the wise collector should wait and not overpay. Price: $30-35.

The candlelinks turned over.

Free Style is the most unusual of all the treatments, but not very popular. It makes use of blues and sand color. The reason for its lack of popularity might be because it is difficult to find. I have yet to see an open vegetable bowl or a cereal bowl.

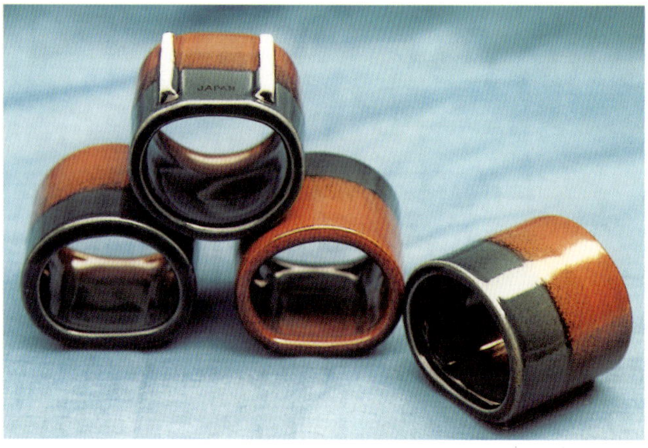

A lovely set of Fire Song napkin rings. Notice these pieces stand on a elongated dry foot.

More examples of the dramatic Fusion. The glaze seems to rise from within the pieces. Notice how smoothly the color lies on the large dinner plate. No skips here! A perfect example of the glazing art.

Cummerbund is another treatment that can fool the unwary. We have already seen the large oval platter, and here the dinner plate follows suite. But, the cup and the creamer are pure black matte with a deep dark gray band.

Comparing the two lightest of the *Potter's Art* treatments. Wild Rice (left) is lighter and brighter while White Tie is noticeably sandy colored. Together they are easy to distinguish, separated rather confusing.

An extreme—probably the most extreme—example of difference between hollowware and flatware. The treatment is the scarce Old Hickory. The cereal bowl is completely different from the shiny black and gray creamer.

A pleasant grouping of smaller *Potter's Art* pieces. (Left to right): The stacking shakers in Sunrise, the sugar bowl in Cummerbund, the covered marmite (rear) in Rusticana, the napkin ring in Studio Kiln, the onion soup in Rusticana, and the rather scarce fruit in yellow rimmed Sonora.

Potter's Art: Library of Treatments

These treatments can look quite similar—to the undiscerning eye. True, a few do stand out, such as the striking blue and white Free Style, or the blood brown Fusion, and all *Potter's Art* devotees know and appreciate Fire Song. When contemplating the treatments to grace this line, Ben Seibel and Mikasa approached it with an entirely new philosophy. There would be no myriads of pinks, blues, and yellows. There would be no frothy flowers and kaleidoscopic hex signs. There would be no shimmering frazzle or colorful dazzle. There would be no viewer exhaustion or jaded *ennui* due to overabundance. For a surfeit of color and lavish design, the collector embraces *Mexicana;* the general collector might even dabble with *Duplex* and perhaps *Pivotal,* but the staid and sophisticated among those who revere Seibel revert with relish to the subtle basics and the subdued approach inherent in *Potter's Art*. The *Potter's Art* treatments are highly appreciated by those collectors who dote upon the finer qualities of calm neutrality and basic earthy richness. The differences between the treatments are very finely drawn, but easily learned. However, there are some funny little tricks to master! Remember, Seibel often pulled some merry pranks, and the hollowware—cups, sugar bowls, creamers—is sometimes completely different from the plates. And still, sometimes not. Old Hickory is an excellent example of this philosophy of making the customer think!" (See three other examples in the preceding general commentary on this shape.)

The redeeming feature is that *Potter's Art* pieces are usually named or numbered, or both, and are quite simple to identify, but if the collector finds a piece without a name, a careful perusal of this Library of Treatments can usually solve the mystery.

Not all treatments are easily available. In fact, Laguna (PF507) has never been viewed outside a black and white photograph. Others can be located without too much problem, and these are also very popular. Buckskin (PF012), Country Cabin (PF852), Fire Song (PF003), and Rusticana (PF005) are readily acquired for those who delve and dote. A clever and practical use would be to get a place setting of eight, ten or twelve designs—perhaps doubling on those mentioned above—and use them together: they mix and match beautifully—the textures and colors meld into each other with rustic, honest grace.

Thus, in the case of *Potter's Art*, there will be no accompanying descriptive paragraph. The subtle differences are better seen than described. Whenever there is a marked difference between the flatware and hollowware, examples of both are given.

BLUE HONEY™: (PF016)

ADOBE™: (PF001)

BIG SURF™: (PF097)[8]

BLUE MOUNTAIN™: (PF025)

BUCKSKIN™: (PF012)

BUTTERBALL™: (PF802)

BUTTERSCOTCH™: (PF014)

CAFÉ NOIR™: (PF801)

CORAL SEA™: (PF095)[8]

COUNTRY CABIN™: (PF852)[9]

CUMMERBUND™: (PF024)

DUNE™: (PF096)[8]

FREE STYLE™: (PF506)

FIRESONG™: (PF003)

FUSION™: (PF004)

INDIAN YELLOW™: (PF827)

LAGUNA™: (PF507)

"REGULAR:"™ (PF850)[9]

NATURAL HUES™: (PF099)[8]

REFLECTIONS™: (PF002)

OLD HICKORY™: (PF022)

RUSTICANA™: (PF005)

SAND AND SEA™: (PF851)

SAND DUNE™: (PF009)

SEA GREEZE™: (PF017)

SHIBUI™: (PF018)

STUDIO KILN™: (PF008)

SONORA™: (PF015)

STUDIO EXPRESSIONS™: (PF098)[8]

SUNRISE™: (PF019)

WHITE TIE™: (PF023)

WILD RICE™: (PF910)

Mexícana: Banana Yellow, Mango Red: A Riot of Color

This shape was inspired by castanets, marimbas, ocarinas, huaraches, pineapple on tops of turbans, and bananas behind the ears! Or we could have said: the mambo, the rumba, the samba. So let us go "cha-cha-cha-ing" down Mexico way!

Mexícana has for quite some time be regarded as the LAST of the four major Mikasa/Seibel shapes, but this was a personal and an arbitrary placement. In the early Fall of 2002, Earl Martin, a resident of New York City, discovered that *Mexícana* was the FIRST of the four, and this is the reason it did not appear in the Mikasa catalog of 1971—by that time it had ceased production—colorfully arrived and summarily disappeared, as the saying goes.

Mr. Martin was researching in the New York Public Library and happened upon the following information in various issues of the trade publication, *China, Glass & Tableware*. This proves absolutely that *Mexícana* was the premier line.

> *December 1967, "The Accessories Scene," p.36.*
>
> MIKASA. *This bold new Mexicana ironstone will debut in Atlantic City; shown here are three tiered casseroles in an accessories group called 'The Pampered Pantry.' The line was designed by Ben Seibel. A 45-piece service retails for about $80.*
>
> February 1968, "New Directions in Dinnerware," p.16.
>
> MIKASA. *Functional and attractive* Mexicana *stoneware designed by Ben Seibel has opaque inside, semi-matte outside in deep blue. Six colors in accessories complement 19 patterns in a complete line. Shown is Sonora, priced at $69.95 for a 45-piece set.*
>
> February 1968, "The News in Pictures," p.31
>
> *Among the attention-drawing displays at the Atlantic City show in January was this one featured by Mikasa on the stage of the Convention Hall. Spotlighted in the presentation is the company's new Mexicana line designed by Ben Seibel.*
>
> November 1968, p.17.
>
> *La Flora, new in the Mexícana stoneware dinnerware line, highlight orange flowers and trim, bronze-yellow lines, rose red, yellow and green. The oven-to-table ware retails for $69.95 [for] a 45-piece set. Mikasa.*

What is learned from this valued discovery? (1) That there was actually a division in the line: dinnerware and accessories, and that the latter had a special name: "Pampered Pantry; (2) Mikasa viewed *Mexícana* as stoneware with oven-to-table possibilities; and (3) the line possessed nineteen treatments, originally introduced in 1968.

The shape does have an aura of celerity—as if it were designed and produced with great haste. It is not a finely wrought and meticulously executed work: it, like *Contempora* could be considered flawed. The ceramic material is not fine, it does not seem solidly constructed, and there is a general slapdash weakness clinging to it. Yet, despite its lack of physical strength, or the finish and polish of *Duplex*, or the rough-hewn solidity of *Potter's Art*, *Mexícana* sings with riotous color: hot pink, warm rose, cerulean blue, royal blue, lime green, dark olive, pure orange, lemon yellow, cinnamon, and nutmeg brown. The cynical collector might mumble the color was used to take attention away from the poor workmanship—and this might be true! However, the color combinations are spicy: the effects are as brilliant as blue and yellow macaws clambering up flaming lianas growing thickly and lushly on monkey-filled mountainsides. The shape bodes no hint of refinement, no touch of class, no breath of elegance. *Mexícana* is earthy, bold, brassy, saucy as a lady-of-the-night, and unabashedly delightful.

Drinkin' rum and coca-cola
Go down point to Mana,
Both mothah and daughtah
Workin' for the yankey dollah.

So did Patti, Maxine, and LeVerne sing about *cuba libras* and the joyous work of the native ladies! But *cuba libras* go well anywhere—not just Cuba or Hawaii, and the "latin-beat" works well for Mexico. Ditto margaritas, but we will stop at the true Mexican libation *pulque*. This truly Mexican drink roughly distilled from the sap of the mature *maguey* (aloe) plant it bears a taste of sour milk laced with gunpowder and Limburger cheese. Mexicana on the run!

Whatever the menu, or the beverage list, the near psychedelic colors of *Mexícana* make dining a hot event!

Since no official list of *Mexícana* items has yet been discovered, the collector is now reduced to educated guesses about the number and type of pieces. Through the illustrations on a two-sided small single brochure we can conjure up what was offered in the line. Even though the brochure is a copy of a copy and very dark and in black and white, it has become an important source of information. Here we can see the two divisions mentioned in the December 1967 *China, Glass, & Tableware Journal*: regular items and "accessories," or to give the last named their correct designation, "The Pampered Pantry" items.

Only the regular items displayed the gorgeous exotic treatments, and they consisted of:

- Dinner plate, 10.25"
- Salad plate, 8.25"
- Saucer, 6.125"
- Platter, 15.25 x 10.75"
- Cereal bowl, 6.625"
- Vegetable bowl, open, 8.50"

The last two named had the decoration in the bottom of the bowl.

As was done in the Iroquois *Informal* dinnerware, each of the decorated pieces had a solid color on the underside or the outside (in the case of the bowls), coming up over the rim to show at the edge. Thus in *Mexícana*, unlike *Duplex*—the shape that was the next Mikasa shape design by Seibel—the choice of matching hollowware (accessories) was predetermined.

Again, the collectors are faced with the mixing of decorated flatware (regular pieces) with solidly glazed hollowware (accessories)—an design idea now firmly established as a Ben Seibel approach. These solid colors were named and numbered separately from the decorated pieces. They were:

(691)	Blueberry Blue™
(692)	Goldfinch™
(693)	Sunflower™
(694)	Nutmeg™
(695)	Parrot Green™

Goldfinch (yellow), Sunflower (orange), and Parrot Green (yellow-lime) are vivid, vibrant, sizzling, while the other three are dark, heavily saturated, wonderful foils for the popping, splashing decorations.

The Pampered Pantry items were dressed in one of the above six glazes, and included: (Those marked with the asterisk (*) have only been seen in the small dark black-white photograph mentioned above.)

- Gravy boat
- Underliner
- Salt shaker, 4.50"
- Pepper shaker, 4.50"
- Butter dish
- Relish tray, three compartments, 12.25" x 5.50"
- Vegetable, rectangular, two compartments
- Sugar
- Creamer
- Fruit bowl, 5"
- Compote w/lid, 8" round
- Casserole w/lid, 10" round
- Coffee pot (beverage server), 11"
- Three tiered serving casserole unit
- Stand, low with flared base *
- Unidentified square accessory item *

(696)	Tawny Olive™

A total of twenty-four pieces including a stand and the magnificent architectural folly, the three tiered casserole unit. This stacking set is composed of three complete "casserole" units that, when combined becomes the behemoth of the table.

A true anecdote regarding the tiered unit is in order. In 1998, a friend mailed me a photograph of his casserole in Tawny Olive. As I am always anxious to add interesting photographs to my file, I considered this a precious gift as *Mexicana* casseroles are rarely seen. This was my first introduction to this rather scarce piece, however, by luck or by pluck, a Goldfinch casserole did appear on eBay, and with more luck and more pluck, I won it. Immediately upon its arrival, it was photographed. I now had research access to two lidded casseroles.

Or did I?

When the film was developed, I placed the photograph of the yellow piece in my album next to the Tawny Olive example. The two items seemed different: the finials were the same, yet the proportions seemed different. If I had access to the actual Tawny Olive casserole the problem would have been immediately solved—as it was the feeling of "different-ness" was not pursued.

Then when the small *Mexicana* brochure was made available to me, all fell delightfully into place. My Goldfinch piece and my friend's Tawny Olive items were not casseroles at all! They were the two lower levels of the three tiered piece mentioned above. The Tawny Olive photograph showed the lowest of the three and had a flat bottom and low finial, my Goldfinch piece had the same low finial, but had a concave bottom allowing it to fit over the lid and finial of the lower piece. The top unit had the tall regular *Mexicana* finial and the concave base. All was understood. Here was a specturlarly tall, architecturally complex, explosive *Mecixana* surprise. Ben Seibel at his best! A version of Montezuma's revenge with a happy twist.

Just as with the three bell jars in *Pivotal*, Ben Seibel had included a merry little, totally unexpected surprise in the line called *Mexicana*! Since this shape was the first Seibel produced for Mikasa, he tried an experiment and it worked!

Even with all the complaints that *Mexicana* is not "well made," or even excitingly conceived, it does not possess the ever present crazing of *Kasuga Vitrestone*, nor does it have the structural "airiness" of *Universal Raymor*. The real excitement is whipped up not by the shape, but by the glazes. These glazes are deep, richly uniform, solidly saturated and present no fluctuations in color depth—such as one might see in the vintage HLC *Fiesta*. Granted, we are talking about the late 1960s, not the late 1930s and the skills of color glazing must have improved greatly. Still the color saturation of *Mexicana* is as rich and internal as the glazing upon Roseville Raymor. Even though some collectors might not approve wholeheartedly of the actual colors, the use of these colors is spectacular.

Physically, *Mexicana* is naturally rounded, but not "orange or tennis ball round" as is *Pivotal*, but it is a "soft-edged" shape. There is no sharpness or shininess such as can be found in *Duplex*, and for all its circular design, *Pivotal* possesses a brittleness not seen in *Mexicana*. The handles too are natural: half of a Valentine heart cut from construction paper by a child. Everything about *Mexicana* is restrained and natural: no pulled extensions, no extraneous additions, yet it is the color that dazzles and razzles, capturing and holding hostage the eye of its beholder!

Mexicana back stamps always identify the treatment.

The riotous La Flora saucer shows the raised well over which the recessed cup base hangs. If found alone, such a saucer should cost between $3-5.

A small set of *Mexicana* La Flora. This treatment is rather easy to locate: the solid glaze is Sunflower. The gravy and its liner (center front) are interesting. The liner turns up with regularity, but the gravy is scarce—in any color. Price for gravy: $12-15.

The soup/cereal with the Vista treatment. These bowls are readily available, and could be called the most common of all the *Mexícana* pieces. They are worth collecting, by all means, but remember, the same treatment can change radically on a large plate or a platter. Price: $5-8.

The solid color glazes. The glazes on the two sugars (Tawny Olive and Sunflower) are quite common. The small dark fruit bowl (back left) is Nutmeg: hard to find.

The bottom portion of the three "stepped" casserole combination. This is known due to the flat finial over which the mid-section easily fits. This, naturally, has been called a casserole and certainly could be used as one. Glaze is Tawny Olive. Price: $20-25.

With the permission of Lee Russell, here are shown a selection of hollowware pieces in Sunflower (orange) and Goldfinch (yellow.) The large true casserole is placed in the center with the gravy (*sans* underplate) directly in front. To the left: the three-part relish and the middle and top section of the stack unit. The coffer pot appears in Goldfinch. To the right: a rather rare piece: the two part (or divided) server. This is the first time this piece has been seen by the author. Since the divided server is found less often than the three-part relish, be prepared to pay $22-25.

Above and left:
The middle section of the casserole combination. The color is Goldfinch. This mid-section seems to be slightly smaller and taller. Price: $20-25. Incidentally, the top section has a finial exactly like the large compote.

The Conchas saucer with its matching olive cup. Since Conchas seems to be quite scarce, I had to use in same saucer in the Library section. Price for the set: $8-12.

The tall (4.50") "stove pipe" shakers in sunflower. The shakers belong in the scarce category and are quite elegant. Price (set): $12-15.

Above and below:
How Seibel enjoyed designing divided relish trays! The *Mexicana* example is slightly over 12" long and divided into three equal parts. As often happens, the base reflects these divisions. Price: $18-20.

Shakers seen from the top. The shaker with the smaller holes is the pepper.

The large compote. Really quite unusual and adds to the *Mexicana* "casserole mix." It is 4" high at the rim and the cover and finial add another 2.25". When first seen, some collectors assume this piece IS the casserole. The foot is completely hollow. Price: $30-35.

Notice the deep smooth glaze on these two bowls. The one on the left (Goldfinch) is the large open vegetable. The one on the right (Parrot Green) is the more common soup/cereal. Remember, both are always decorated within. Price for vegetable bowl: $10-12; the soup/cereal: $4-5.

The scarcest of the bowls: the fruit bowl. It is never decorated. It is pretty, well proportioned, and useful. Price: $6-7.

The *Mexicana* butter dish is elusive, and unusual due to possessing no ridge on the base. This does allow the cover to slide precariously when there is no stick of butter. The reason? Perhaps to allow for a separate use for the bottom. A pickle dish? Price: $25-30.

The Tawny Olive coffee pot (beverage server?). I admit that the more I study this line, the more I appreciate its understated charm. For example, this coffee pot is much more gracefully conceived than the *Duplex* pot. It is tall (nearly 11") and flows outward from top to base—and note that perfect handle! Price: $35-40.

Even the handle on this cup, while more "ear-like," still portrays the essence of "half-a-heart." The cup also has a well-defined rim.

The sugar is not as available as the creamer, and many are found minus their cover. Complete, the price should be $10-12.

The creamer is Goldfinch. These pieces are relatively easy to find. Price: $6-8.

The platter—here in La Flora—is quite dramatic. Over 15" long and nearly 11" wide, it is an impressive piece. Price: $18-20.

This exceptional photograph is courtesy of Kathy Cullen. It shows the regular casserole to the left with a taller finial. This piece is 9.75" at the base, 3.25" to the rim, and 5.50" to the top of the finial. The stacking set to the right is missing the bottom piece. The middle piece (here at the bottom) is nearly 8" round and the rim is 4.25" tall. The lid and the flat finial fit inside the concave base of the top piece. This top is 7" round, 4" to the rim, and 5.50" to the top of the finial. The problem with evaluation of these pieces is many collectors view these as single casseroles, not part of a triple unit. If complete, this unit would sell for $100-125, or even more.

Mexicana: Library of Treatments

Even though *Mexicana* has garnered some strong negative attributes (less easy to find, less sophisticated and elegant, less well made, and so on) there are a good number of Seibel collectors and vintage Mikasa collectors that dote upon it. It attracts those who are fond of the underdog. Even though it is not as graceful and well constructed as *Pivotal*, *Mexicana* seems much more popular—at least popular with the youthfully oriented who enjoy colors that tease the sensibilities or who enjoy the backyard patio/picnic ambience of informal festive gatherings. *Mexicana* teases and it swings; it calls out and catches both the collector and the user in a vibrant trap. If one overlooks its less than positive qualities, it becomes a great little dinnerware line.

Unfortunately, there is a paucity of plates to be photographed. The cereal bowl is the most easily found *Mexicana* piece. But then, fortunately, I have access to black and white photographs of a number of plates, and can use these to describe how the treatment translates from cereal to dinner plate. If the reader will bear with me, he/she can develop a fine sense of the *Mexicana* Library.

There are a few treatments which have never been seen: these treatments will appear in *italics*. However, the series of black/white pages do have verbal color descriptions, and these descriptions will be quoted in full. The name given for the rim color will be confusing unless the reader remembers these are "advertising usages" and really will be one of the six solid glazes illustrated in the preceding section. For example: Goldfinch becomes lemon yellow.

CASTANET™: (601) "Design in cinnamon, sky blue, white, and royal blue. Rim is royal blue." A rich and deeply satisfying treatment, but to visualize the plate, it is edged with the halved circle design: the complete circles and red stretched diamond design do not appear on the plate.

CERO-GORDE™: (611) This treatment has never been "in hand," but a black and white photograph of the plate has been studied. The official description reads: "Arabesque design in black with white outline on cinnamon brown. Rim in brown." The arabesque design is contained within a wide band around the plate and other flatware and is composed of curved, short, vine-like figures occasionally sprouting tiny leaves. Everything is severely contained within the band.

After this book went to "press," Lee Russell sent me four photographs of *Mexicana* pieces in his collection. These photographs will add considerably to the readers' understanding of the *Mexicana* treatments. Here we have an open vegetable with the Cero-Gorde (or Cerro Gordo) treatment. It looks very Moorish or possibly Aztec in origin.

CHICO-CHICO™: (610) "Arabesque design in flander's blue on white. Rim is soft brown." Chico-Chico might be described as one of the "paper-cutout" treatments—the technique used in several of the *Pivotal* patterms. The flowing curves of the arabesques appear crisply on the pristine chalk white background. Instead of the more obvious Blueberry Blue rim, here Nutmeg is used.

CONCHAS™: **(619)** "Design in moss green, lines in dark green with a touch of orange. Rim in olive green." The "moss green" has touches of mustard, but this relatively dull treatment is enlivened with the diamonds (in the centers) and the triangles of red-orange. While the saucer (note raised well) is shown, the plate is similarly decorated.

DEL RIO™: **(606)** This treatment frequently is offered for sale. After La Flora, it is most available. It is bright, pretty, and sunny. "Stylized fruits in orange, empire rose red, and yellow. Outlines in light tan. Rim in lemon yellow." So says the advertising blurb. The fruits are bananas, oranges, lemons, one pear and one apple: appropriate fare for topping the turban of Carmen Miranda.

GUADALUPE™: **(605)** At the bottom of the cereal bowl is a triangle of nine smaller triangles. The small units are naturalistic cosmos—except for the unusual shape. Like Del Rio, this is a sunny treatment. The blurb announces: "Flowers in dark and light Chinese yellow, center in dark and light orange. Rim in lemon yellow." The plate has two bands of this cosmos design: the one at the rim is halved, the inner band consists of twelve triangular florals.

IGUANA™: (607) See endnote 3.

LA FLORA™: (608) La Flora is the *Mexícana* treatment most easily found. Small sets occasionally appear at auction and in malls. Personally, I find it a little florid and fussy. The daisies and cosmos are roughly drawn and painted with rough broad strokes of bright colors. "Flowers in orange, empire rose red, and lemon yellow with a touch of green. Rim in orange."

LA MANCHA™: (614) Another Mexicana treatment that is rarely seen. Luckily a dinner plate was recently acquired; it does bear some resemblance to Sonora. Like *Potter's Art*, Mexicana treatments do mix and match very well, but NOT because they are similar but because each and every one is so distinctive that one never dominates. La Mancha has the two flowers are double-petalled dahlias in blue and yellow. "Flowers in colors of blue, green, mustard yellow, and beige. Leaves in mustard yellow outlined in moss green. Rim in veronese green."[1]

Here is the treatment Guadalupe as it appears on the *Mexícana* platter. We thank Mr. Russell again for sending it. While the reader can view this treatment on the bottom of the cereal bowl, here it is noted the large yellow and orange florals ring the edge of the flatware.

NUEVO™: *(615)* Thanks the third time to Mr. Russell—for here we can see Nuevo in color on the *Mexícana* platter. From the advertising description, the colors were known, but now it can be appreciated that the "purple dots" punctuate the green stripes. A very simple, but extremely effective treatment.

RIO GRANDE™: (609) Double alas, no personal experience with Rio Grande either. It is based on the same "radiating" concept as Nuevo. "Design in pastel shades of orange, blue, and lemon yellow. Rim is orange." Three stripes flow uninterruptedly toward the well, but the next three are broken to allow a small maltese cross to be formed halfway down. Small blue squares ring the top of these spokes; very tiny blue squares ring the bottom. A complex treatment.

SAN CARLOS™: (613) For this treatment we do have several cereal bowls. "Stylized flowers in empire rose red, leaves in moss green. Rim in veronese green." Parrot green is the official name of this color. The design in formed on the plate exactly as it appears on the bowl: a double ring of these "pinkish" flowers march about the edge.

Here the reader gets a mild surprise: unlike some other treatments, the San Carlos treatment rings the edges of both the bowls and the plates. The "moss green" leaves flicking delicately between the empire rose red daisies seem more gray than green. This is the fourth example send by Mr. Russell.

SONORA™: (602) A simpler floral design than La Mancha. The flowers seem hand painted in bold, rough strokes. "Flowers in three shades of blue, center in orange with a touch of green. Leaves in light and dark olive green. Rim in royal blue." An apt description, but when one looks at the orange center of these flowers a sunburst is discerned—a nice touch not mentioned in the blurb.

TAXCALA™: (618) "Design in colors of seacrest green, burnt orange, blue and royal blue on white. Rim is olive green." A very ornate but disciplined treatment in which the overall impression is the art of the ancient Mexican Indian—it would be exciting to know if this design were really influenced by Taxcala carving.

TOLTEC™: (603) The final treatment for which there is no color photograph. The description reads: "Design in two shades of blue with a touch of yellow and red. Rim in royal blue." What these words do not tell is the mysterious quality of Toltec. About the rim edge swirl two rows of floating teardrop "eyes" very reminiscent of the ancient Egyptian representation of the eye: the eye of the Heavens, or the eye of the fear of guilt. They seem to be watching.

For purposes of understanding and research, the above treatments must now be listed according to their production number, and we will also include their exterior color. [2]

601	Castanet	Blueberry
602	Sonora	Blueberry
603	Toltec	Blueberry
604	Vista	Goldfinch
605	Guadalupe	Goldfinch
606	Del Rio	Goldfinch
607	Iguana[3]	Sunflower
608	La Flora	Sunflower
609	Rio Grande	Sunflower
610	Chico Chico	Nutmeg
611	Cerro Gordo [4]	Nutmeg
612	**Unique** (?) [5]	**Nutmeg** (?)
613	San Carlos	Parrot Green
614	La Mancha	Parrot Green
615	Nuevo	Parrot Green
616	**unknown**	**unknown**
617	**unknown**	**Tawny Olive** (?)
618	Taxcala	Tawny Olive
619	Conchas	Tawny Olive

The reader can see why this list is important. It places the exterior colors in groups of three, and allows us to carefully assume the exterior colors of the unknown treatments: 607 and 617. Treatment 612 has been rumored to be called Unique and would (if the units of three solid glazes continues) have Nutmeg exterior color. Treatment 616 is a complete mystery, but we know it must exist because the notation of nineteen treatments in the December 1967 issue of *China, Glass & Tableware*.

Extremely interesting to note is that the exterior colors mentioned above—Blueberry, etc—stand as additional treatments on their own, with their own numberings, and refer to the hollowware. The interior color of all is pure white.

691	Blueberry™
692	Goldfinch™
693	Sunflower™
694	Nutmeg™
695	Parrot Green™
696	Tawny Olive™

Treatments 620 through 625 refer to the clone *Mexican Rainbow*.

VISTA™: (604) With the last treatment we are brought back to the "stripe." The blurb: "Design in bright orange and lemon on white. Lines in light tan. Rim is lemon yellow." In the cereal bowl, these stripes cover the entire well. Expand this design and imagine it covering the entire plate—from center to rim. This concept makes the Vista stripe design different.

Mikasa/Seibel Clones: Many Questions, Few Answers

Or Beneath the Blankets, Under the Trees, In the Bushes, "Clonal" Activities Abound

Firstly, the collector must differentiate between Mikasa/Seibel possibilities (note: "possibilities" not "probabilities") and the Mikasa/Seibel clones. Research for both is done within the pages of the obtainable Mikasa catalogs. A great deal is learned about these two groups by a careful reading of the catalogs. Some conclusions are absolute and true; other conclusions are logical likelihood's, and others are merely wishful thinking. But there is no frivolity. My approach might be light-hearted, but never frivolous!

In this section, I will NOT discuss those marked "Ben's" in the important catalogs—those Mikasa shapes identified as the work of Ben Seibel by an unknown annotator.[1] These are Mikasa shapes that have not been officially recognized as the products of Seibel's genius—and, really, might never be accepted as such. What we are discussing in this section are the known clones! Those Mikasa tableware lines that duplicate—in varying degrees—the accepted Seibel work.

And very important to remember, some of these clones bear the name of Ben Seibel.

Repetition is next to Godliness, so here I repeat. The four known major Seibel shapes are *Mexicana, Duplex, Pivotal,* and *Potter's Art.* These four are accepted as Seibel's work and acknowledged as major contributions: all are signed by the designer. Of this group, *Pivotal* can be placed swiftly aside: it has no clones, although, as has been noted, there is considerable variety within the basic shape.

Now to forestall my entrapment and dismemberment for the above statement—my popularity among collectors is not secure—the following codicil is necessary. I am not one hundred percent sure that the four Mikasa lines listed above came first in time and then generated clones unto themselves. For example, my assumption is—because *Potter's Art* appeared on my Seibel list FIRST—that *Potter's Art* is the "parent" line and *LifeStyle* and *Studio Glaze* are the clones. But in all truth, *Studio Glaze* might be the "parent" and *Potter's Art* one of the clones: although the Mikasa catalogs do not bear this premise out. The indulgence of the readers is requested when I repeat the four MAJOR Mikasa lines designed by Ben Seibel are *Mexicana, Duplex, Pivotal,* and *Potter's Art*—in that order!

Mexicana's Clone

Working up the scale from bottom to top, the collector notes that *Mexicana* has only one clone : a line that parrots exactly in number of pieces and uses the same—albeit solid—startling colors. Actually, the spectrum of colors could be said to be nearly the same. Notice the two creamers shown. The one on the left is *Mexican Rainbow's* Cena (624); the example to the right, *Mexicana's* Blueberry Blue (691), and they are not quite exactly the same shade of blue. The *Mexican Rainbow* creamer is just a bit brighter. Also, its interior is washed with pale color.[2] The reason for having a clone so closely duplicating the parent is not understood now and probably never will be fully comprehended. Perhaps the reason was just to give the customers a wider choice, but this reasoning seems stretched. While my collection of *Mexican Rainbow* includes plates, platters, fruit bowls, and sugar and creamer set, the larger, more desirable solidly glazed "accessories" are not represented. There is a good likelihood they were never produced. And—a most important point—*Mexican Rainbow* is, as is *Mexicana*, signed "by Ben Seibel."

Five of the six (assumed) treatments belonging to *Mexican Rainbow* have been discovered: the sixth (625) rounds out the required number. The actual number sequence follows directly after the *Mexicana* numbers. The second color refers to the interior.

620	Tacos™	Sunflower™	Yellow
621	Tequila™	Goldfinch™	White
622	Pinata™	Parrot Green™	Lime
623	Tortilla™	Nutmeg™	Cream
624	Cena™	Blueberry™	Sky Blue
625	**unknown**	**Tawny Olive™ (?)**	**unknown**

A *Mexican Rainbow* large platter is the Tacos (620) treatment: yellow and orange.

The interiors of the *Duplex* and *Mexicana* hollowware are usually pure white while those of the clones are washed with pale color. Here is an example: *Mexican Rainbow* (a clone) (left) creamer is called Cena and has a pale blue interior; *Mexicana's* Blueberry Blue (right) has a white interior. Prices for the clone cannot yet be determined. Once collectors recognize them as works of Ben Seibel, pricing will probably level at 50% of the parent line—but this is pure speculation. In the meanwhile, a collector, if interested in a Mikasa clone, must pay what is thought appropriate.

The collector can see this clone is signed by Ben Seibel.

The back stamp.

A 9" dinner plate in Pinata (622)—yellow and parrot green. These clones all wear solid colors.

Potter's Arts Clones

Reaching *Potter's Art*, the collector will find three clones: two are major lines in themselves: *Discovery* and *LifeStyle*, and the third, relatively unknown: *Studio Glaze* stoneware. The first mentioned duplicates all the *Potter's Art* pieces except the cup and saucer,[3] and also uses the same approach with the treatments. However, the second line, while reproducing all the *Potter's Art* exactly (including the cup and saucer), does widen the variety of treatments to include applied designs on the plates. This would allow mixing and matching, but again, this is a very thin reason for manufacturing an entire clone line.

Both are identified as the work of Ben Seibel, but his name appears only on the larger pieces.

Discovery appears in the following treatments:

Aruba™	(P3004)
Blue Reef™	(P3003)
Blue Thunder™	(P3005)
Brownstone™	(P3002)
Coral Surf™	(P3001)
Salmon River™	(P3006)
Sand Drift™	(P3009)

If I were a person addicted to betting, money would be placed on the fact that two *Discovery* treatments are yet to be located: (P3007) and (P3008). Lee Russell has made me wary of missing sequential numbers. Naturally, we dare not assume Sand Drift was the last: for there might be lurking somewhere a (P3010) and upwards, also just yearning to be pulled into the Ben Seibel spotlight.

The design of these treatments also duplicates *Potter's Art*: a rim band contrasting sharply with an inner band of color. The well is off white, and the hollowware is a solid color—in some cases the same shade as the inner band of color. There is no impressed decoration. *Discovery* can only be labeled as a pure extension of *Potter's Art*.

The same scenario works admirably for *LifeStyle*: the shape absolutely duplicates *Potter's Art*—even the cup and saucer are exact images—and the pieces are marked "Ben Seibel." There is one great difference between *LifeStyle* and *Potter's Art*: the plates of the former wear, rather proudly, additional decorations of stylized flowers and vegetation, or brisk geometric concoctions that either completely fill the well or peek from a side or march in curved grandeur up and across. This stoneware was intimately connected with *Potter's Art*, and in one Mikasa catalog two treatments were shown within the *Potter's Art* pages *sans* their own name.[4] *LifeStyle* should be considered rather difficult to find: much more difficult than *Discovery*. It is, nevertheless, worth the hunt.

Here is a listing of the known *LifeStyle* treatments. Those not illustrated are described.

Birch Lane	(not known)
Blue Ridge	(PG904
Bouquet of Four	(PG012)
Desert Gold	(PG002)
Garden Path	(PG011) (Five petalled flowers in chartreuse curve through the well)
Indian Song	(PG010) (Four light blue geometric "stars" are centered in the well)
Mandarin	(PG905) (Three medium-sized blue blossoms surrounded by twigs and scattered tiny florets cluster at the bottom left of the well)
Mother of Pearl	(PG006)
Temple Tile	(PG001)
Vineyard	(PG003) One dark brown grape leaf and an outlined bunch of grapes are placed at the exact center of the well: a thin band encloses them.
White Surf	(PG009)
Wind Blown	(PG007)

Again as in *Discovery*, the researcher must deal with a number lapse: (PG008) (see endnote 4), White Surf, and Mother of Pearl have no well decoration and, except for the back stamp, could be mistaken for *Potter's Art*. Note: Do not confuse *Lifestyle* White Surf (PG009) with *Duplex* White Surf (2500).

The third clone, *Studio Glaze* stoneware, should not be considered a major line, and yet it still uses the *Potter's Art* shape. There are four known treatments—all signed with the Seibel name: Charcoal (PH701), Earth Treasure (PH801), Fruitwood (PH851), and Sea Shell (PH901). This last named treatment seems to have been one of Ben Seibel's personal favorites. In early 1979, he ordered quite a few pieces of this line to be sent directly to his lower Broadway Manhattan address.

The Mikasa Company presented *Potter's Art*, *LifeStyle*, and *Studio Glaze* one after the other—in that order—at the beginning of the 1978 salesmen's catalog. It might be of interest to read the blurbs that headed each line.

> *Potter's Art*: *"The glaze-on-glaze look of today in today's soft terrazzo colors. Designed by famous N.Y. designer Ben Seibel, only for Mikasa. Hand-detailed, hand-dipped 4 times and custom contoured to the human hand."* We can only speculate what type of *"non-human"* hand would want to hold *Potter's Art*!

> *LifeStyle* : *"Mikasa blows it! The windblown look on a light, airy background. Each design hand-painted by a painstaking hand. Each piece double-glazed and hand banded. The style? Nature stylized, yet never unnatural or stiff."* Glazed only twice as compared with four times for *Potter's Art*.

> *Studio Glaze*: *"The pure little rich plate. The artful art-less plate. The plain plate with the elegant planes. Set off by a shimmery background and a fired-in band. Even Mikasa salt and pepper shakers are beautifully stacked!"*

Would the "poor little rich girl" Gloria Vanderbilt have wanted to eat from *Studio Glaze*?

How can advertising agents write such outrageous prose—almost purple? Nevertheless, they do and make well-stacked salaries doing so!

Discovery should be considered a major Seibel line. While not having the fascinating surface treatment of *Potter's Art*, it is beautiful in a more delicate manner. Here is a lovely gray Aruba chop plate with a pale blue border.

The Aruba back stamp surely proclaims it as a Ben Seibel piece.

Discovery Blue Reef uses a combination of two richer blues than does Aruba.

Since some pieces of *Discovery* hollowware do NOT mention Seibel's name, a few collectors might be misled.

The Blue Reef cup (right) is exactly the same shape as those mysterious *Potter's Art* PF09—series. To the left is *Potter's Art* Nature's Hues (PF099)—admittedly more interesting with its blue and blue-gray stripes.

A Blue Thunder dinner plate. While some of these treatments might look similar, there are intriguing, subtle differences.

The rim of the dinner plate.

The Blue Thunder stacking shakers.

The Blue Thunder cup. Compare how differently the hollowware is glazed than the flatware of the same treatment. Remember this same anomaly occurs in *Potter's Art*.

The Brownstone dinner plate.

A Brownstone covered marmite in pale tan stands before a salad and a dinner plate. Again, the hollowware is different.

Rim of the Brownstone plate.

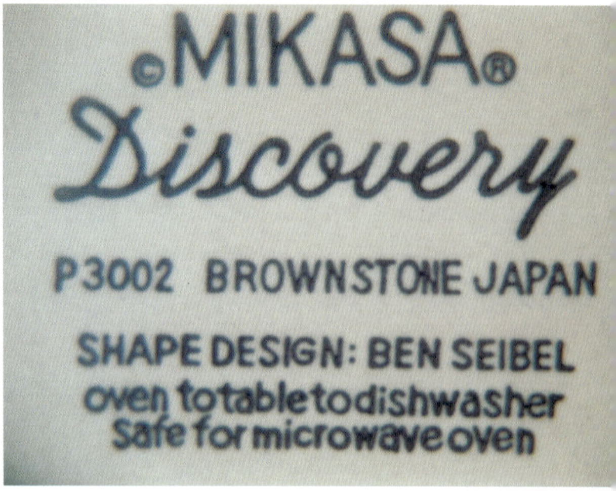

Brownstone back stamp—Ben Seibel again!

A selection of *Discovery* Coral Surf (many collector want to automatically say Coral Reef). The au gratin stands in the rear with (left to right) the gravy, the butter dish, and the elusive small fruit bowl.

The Coral Surf creamer and sugar—exactly the same as *Potter's Art* and a most attractive coral pink. This treatment should be a favorite because it is relatively easy to find.

Discovery Salmon River. Notice how many of the treatments bear names reminiscent of the sea.

Sand Drift. Another very beautiful treatment.

The rim of Sand Drift: pale blue and the softest pink.

Of all the *LifeStyle* treatments, only Temple Tiles can be located with ease. I have seen small sets offered occasionally, and I have about 20 pieces in my personal collection. Here is the dinner plate.

Even though his last name is obliterated, one can surely see this is Ben Seibel signed.

While Temple Tiles is more easily found, Windblown is a favorite. I hunted down without too much trouble some 12 pieces of this treatment. The flatware looks hand painted.

Again notice how differently the hollowware can appear. Confusing perhaps, but certainly intriguing and practical. Windblown shaker set.

The Windblown back stamp.

Not all *LifeStyle* treatments are subtle or beautiful: this is Blue Ridge (PG904) and quite a "hodgepodge" design.

Desert Gold and Bouquet of Four use the same hollowware—another potentially confusing curiosity.

Bouquet of Four is a more acceptable design, but I find most of *LifeStyle's* treatments do not meet the high standards of *Potter's Art* simplicity.

Studio Glaze is a one hundred percent Ben Seibel design, but cannot be considered a major line. This design, Sea Shell, seemed to be one of the designer's favorites.

One cannot argue that *Studio Glaze* belongs in the Seibel lexicon.

The Clones of Duplex

Now that the reader has digested the idea of clones even though their existence has yet to be explained, the most complex clonal area is now broached. *Duplex*, perhaps because it is the simplest of shapes, albeit with a superfluity of treatments, presents a nightmare of clones. Some are full clones, some are partial, and a few "borrow" just a few miscellaneous *Duplex* pieces. But when one of these "few" pieces is seen or purchased standing alone and lost, confusion can reign. As an example of the last situation: since 1995, I have owned a sugar and creamer labeled *Majorca* and the twosome was a dark brown duplication of my *Duplex* sugar/creamer sets. Mistakenly, I believed *Majorca* was a full-fledged clone. It was not! After purchasing some other pieces of this shape, quickly, so very quickly the clonal connection burst! Some decision-making official at Mikasa liked the *Duplex* sugar/creamer set, and, we hope, got Seibel's permission to incorporate it into the *Majorca* line.

Categorizing *Majorca* is problematic. If the collector had only the cream and the sugar bowl in—say—seven or eight treatments, he or she would swear *Majorca* was a *Duplex* clone. However, only those two *Duplex* pieces were used—all the rest are different. We will NOT go into the fact here that the word "Ben's" appears handwritten in the *Majorca* page of the Mikasa catalog. What do you think? Do the other pieces look like a Seibel design?

Only the sugar and creamer were based on *Duplex*, the other pieces played their own tune. Completely understandable because, as stated in the section about the Mikasa catalogs, we know that on pages 10-11 of the 1972 salesmen's issue, the word "Ben's" is scrawled at the top of the page. The shape shown is *Majorca*.[5] The *Duplex* sugar/creamer set was transferred hardy and whole to this new shape.

Majorca stoneware appears in a round of Italianate treatments such as: Intaglio (7501), Lodi (7514), Murano (7506), San Marino (7510), and Terrazo (7502)—all looking so much like medieval tiles impressed in rich and dark backgrounds. It is a Romanesque inspired bevy of designs—all dark and murky and shrouded in mysterious, ancient shadows.

Spectrum, light and preeminently "eatable," inhabits the second classification. All the pieces in this brightly colored tableware are *Duplex* shapes, including the samovar and stand, the coffee pot, and the flat casserole. The only piece not borrowed is the butter dish. It is round and the lid fits securely within a deep base. However, the finial belongs to *Duplex*. Prime *Spectrum* treatments are well-saturated solid shades such as Berry Blue (7705), Café au Lait (7703), Caviar (7704), Papaya (7700), Pineapple (7702), and a Pistachio (7701). The last named is a mixture of lime green and chartreuse and sports a yellow interior. Collectors will remember *Mexicana* when viewing some of *Spectrum*'s glazes.

StoneKraft and *StudioKraft* are one hundred percent clones, and these two are rather common—at least in some of their treatments. *StoneKraft* consists of a matte stoneware finish upon which is imposed semi-glazed decorations. The quality is rich but muted. Avitra (7810) was in my possession long before I owned all the true *Duplex* pieces, and through this *StoneKraft* set, information about *Duplex* was easily learned. This tableware line can be acquired in full sets, and until the name of Ben Seibel become generally attached, *StoneKraft* will be, generally, quite inexpensive, usably practical, and subtly attractive. In some respects—subtly is one—this line is more artistically refined than the parental *Duplex*! Naturally, this is my personal opinion.

StoneKraft has a number of strongly conceived treatments:

Avitra™ (7810)
Colorado™ (7809)
Fanal™ (5052)
Gobi™ (7816)[6]
Indian Summer™ (7819)[7]
Jadestone™ (7806)
Limestone™ (7808)
Mesabi™ (7814)[6]
Sahara™ (7815)[6]
Sistine™ (7818)[7]
Stoneflower™ (7820)[7]
Tahoe™ (5051)
Woodstock™ (7821)[7]

StudioKraft differs from *StoneKraft* only by having a wider assortment of intricate floral and geometric treatments and it lacks the matte finish. The advertising blurbs are quite expressive regarding this line: "Dramatic Mexican, Mediterranean or Spanish flavor in warm tones of Brown or Black in durable stoneware." It was further noted that the decorations were applied in a brush stroke technique and were permanently sealed under a cream color opaque glaze. All this verbal consideration does impress that this line was not in the minor leagues. *StudioKraft* also gives the choice of two solid colors for the hollowware: Susepia (7910) a deep dark brown and Stublack (7911) the velvety black of outer space. In the list below those marked (*) were accompanied by Susepia, those marked (**) with Stublack.

Andes™ (7904) (*)
Bahia™ (7908) (*)
Capreol™ (7913) (**)
Cortez™ (7912) (**)
Escadrille™ (7920) (*)[8]
Esperanza™ (7919) (*)[8]
Fayette™ (7909) (*)
Gavan™ (7916) (*)
Perspective™ (7918) (**)[8]
Strata™ (7921) (*)[8]

Before we reach an amusing trio mentioned below, there is the mysterious line called *Casual Sophistication*. Not only does it match *Duplex* piece by piece, but it bears Ben Seibel's signature in the back stamp. The presence of this signature caused some collectors to believe it was a completely separate line, and it appeared in some early lists—those valuable and compelling lists drawn up and freely shared by Michael Pratt. These were the days when the connection between Mikasa and Seibel was just being broached and any information was vital. *Casual Sophistication* not only bears an interesting name, it reinforces or enhances the belief that Mikasa used and reused the Seibel shapes with a variety of material. Even though scarce, enough examples of *Casual Sophistication* have been seen to make the statement it consisted of a ceramic material almost oatmeal in color with an abundant scattering of flecks. The surface was reflective, but not shiny, nor was it completely matte: it was a dulled surface. I have seen several treatments (but only have recorded the name of three). The four pieces in my collection are: a sugar bowl in Shannon (FA401), a salad plate in Rambling Rose (FA102), and two plates in a delightful treatment named Flights of Fancy (FA302). This line is worth concentrated study because it is an officially recognized Ben Seibel shape, carries his signature, and fits into the same category as do the *Potter's Art* clones *Discovery* and *LifeStyle*. Its name also appeared on the original Pratt list.

While the final three *Duplex* clones are not well known, they probably abound in malls and flea markets. Mikasa (or Ben Seibel) must have been amusing themselves (or himself) because these three are popularly known as "The Mates." They are the Checkmates, the Colormates, and, most intriguingly, the Playmates (shades of the Playboy Club®). Labeled under these names, these treatments are flavorful treats such as Spearmint, Kailuha, Azure, Citrus and Patio. Fresh, bright, inexpensive, yet using a Seibel shape, these friendly little "mates" make delightful cottage or picnic companions. Most of the pieces personally purchased have cost between ten and fifty cents and can fill a number of casual uses about the kitchen or garage. If a reader spots some wide plates in pastel blues, deep yellows, lemons and limes, pink with fluffy florals, or shaded plaids these should be turned over and checked. In your hand is probably one of the "Mates." They are not very serious, but they are fun to own, and a pleasure to use.

We have certainly had a delightful romp among the clones or near clones. Even if the collector does not know "why" they existed, at least these look-alikes have been identified, pulled out into the open, and frontally faced. Now these lists cannot and do not pretend to be complete. Other clones might surely exist (read on) and surely other treatments will be located to add to the names included in this section. Remember, it is all fun. Those collectors and researchers who take themselves too seriously become pompous, deadly dull, and rather sententious. So lighten up, do not be a bender, be a lender, smile, enjoy, and share!

To review: here is a list of the known Seibel clones produced by Mikasa.

Mexicana:	*Mexican Rainbow* (signed)
Potter's Art:	*Discovery* (signed)
	LifeStyle (signed)
	Studio Glaze (signed)
Duplex:	*Majorca* (partial) (unsigned)
	Spectrum (except for the butterdish) (unsigned)
	StoneKraft (unsigned)
	StudioKraft (unsigned)
	Casual Sophistication (signed)
	Checkmates (unsigned)
	Colormates (unsigned)
	Playmates (unsigned)

Thus, the avid Seibel collector gets twelve separate lines instead of merely three!

The small and pretty *Majorca* Lodi beverage server. This handles beautifully and I use it daily. Some of these Mikasa pieces almost demand use, they are so attractive.

The *Majorca* cream and sugar—the treatment is Vivenda.

A *Spectrum* salad plate in the Pineapple treatment.

Majorca Lodi (E2854). All of this line is dark with rich Spanish designs. Remember Spain is more conservative and austere than the brilliantly slanted Mexico. These are very lovely pieces of dinnerware, but are they Seibel?

The salad plate with a saucer (note the raised "well") and the creamer.

The *Spectrum* back stamp with no credit given to Seibel.

The *Spectrum* coffee pot in Pistachio with an egg yolk yellow interior.

A rather large set of *StoneKraft* Avita was purchased long before I knew the existence of all the *Duplex* pieces. Thus Avita gave me considerable knowledge regarding the *Duplex* shape. *StoneKraft* is pure stoneware: heavy with a matte finish, but with a raised shiny design—again, as in *Duplex*—only on a few pieces. The shape itself is pure *Duplex*.

The Pineapple creamer accompanied by a sister shape—this time in Papaya. The orangey color matches the papaya fruit exactly.

Through this Avita covered casserole I knew there must be a similar piece in *Duplex*, but the latter took me almost two years to find it!

The general StoneKraft back stamp.

StoneKraft Gobi cup and saucer. Very simple and stark.

The Gobi back stamp.

An attractive little salad plate in *StoneKraft* Mesabi.

Limestone (7807), while still physically heavy, the general aspect is delicate—not unlike a stained glass window.

StoneKraft Woodstock. I wonder if these treatments were at all popular—they do not seem to be very attractive when viewed today. Again, the design is raised. If you like Woodstock, it is not hard to find.

Stoneflower has always been touted as a rare treatment, yet it appears prominently in the 1971 and 1972 Mikasa catalogs.

A very ornate black and gold *StudioKraft* Cortez chop plate—a very impressive piece.

The Cortez back stamp.

Finally, a *Duplex* clone signed by Ben Seibel. This simple *Casual Sophistication* covered sugar bowl has been in my possession for nearly ten years. Once thought as a separate shape, it is now recognized as another clone.

The Capreol back stamp.

Another *StudioKraft* treatment: a salad plate in Capreol. Again, quite ornate in design.

The back stamp of the sugar bowl.

This is probably the most gentle and delicate of all the *Casual Sophistication* treatments, called Flights of Fancy.

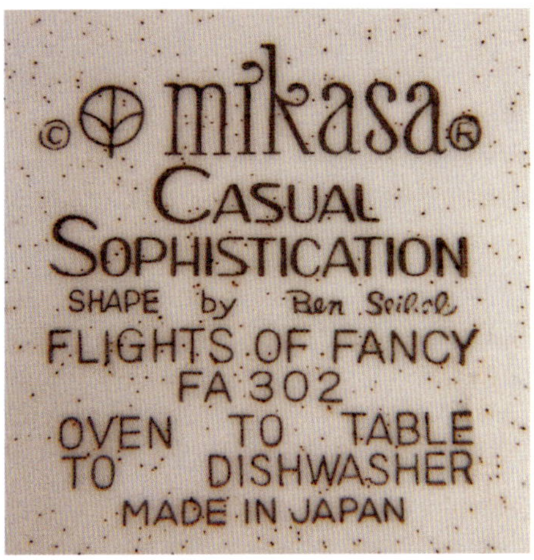

The back stamp of Flights of Fancy.

Casual Sophistication salad plate in Rambling Rose. This shape is quite rare, but still a Ben Seibel collection should have a few pieces.

The back stamp.

All *Casual Sophistication* has a textured surface—slightly peppered.

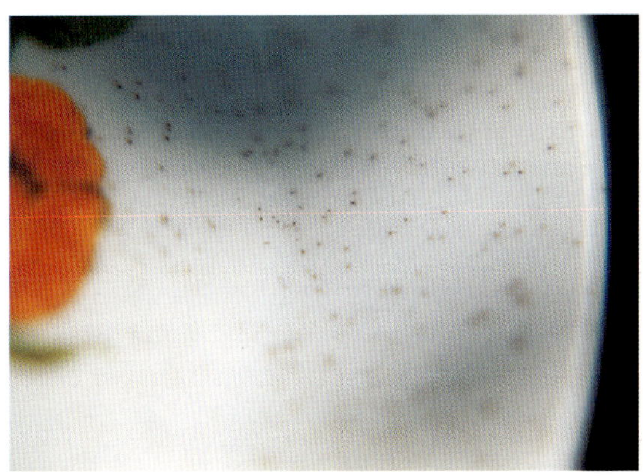

Dinner plate, salad plate, cup and saucer of *Checkmates* Spearmint. I wonder why the horse and buggy appears in the back stamp?

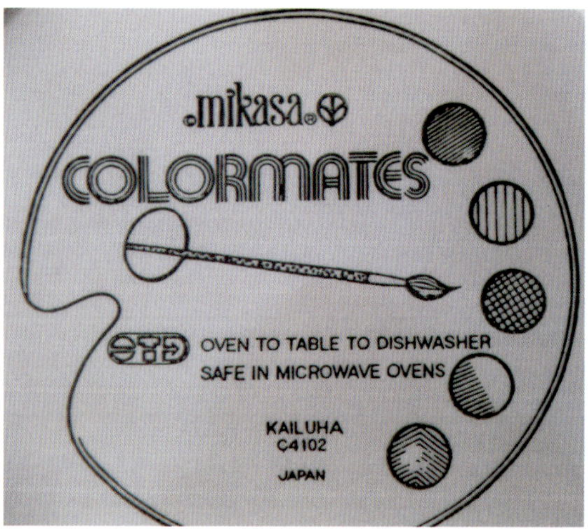

"Think pink" when you think about *Colormates* Kailuha. A small set of these was among my mother's dishes when she died. I never remember seeing them used, so perhaps she disfavored them. One thing to be said: the back stamp is very original.

The most provocatively named "Mates" has the most austere treatment. This is Azure of the *Playmates* line.

The Citrus back stamp.

Playmates Citrus—dinner and salad plate. This line had a number of simple treatments based on color.

A rather luscious treatment—Sweet Chocolate—on *Playmates*. Each of these many treatments is different: some boring, some exciting, they were meant to please all tastes.

The Sweet Chocolate back stamp. (I keep wanting to say Sweet Charlotte.)

Kasuga/*Vitrastone*

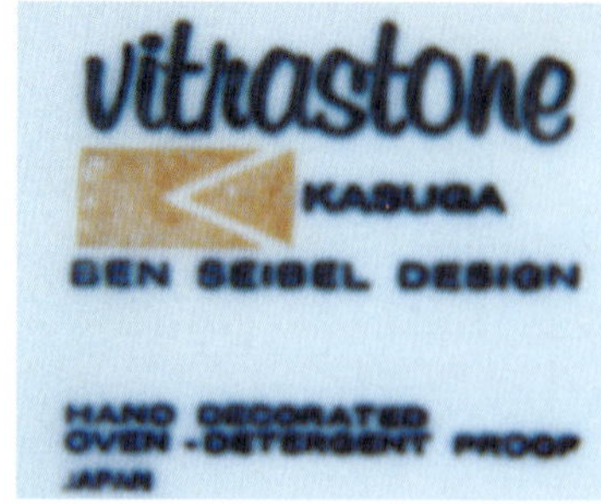

Humility Can Be A Good Thing

What's in a name? A rose by any other name would smell as sweet? Poor Juliet Capulet trying to justify her passion for Romeo Montague! Sad!

But with this line of ceramic dinnerware, *Kasuga Vitrastone*™, we must admit the above quotation from Shakespeare's *Romeo and Juliet* might not be exactly true. Kasuga is a strikingly important name in Japanese ceramics. As an experiment, type in the name as an eBay search and the reader will be looking at some of the most elegant oriental porcelain ever seen. Purely Japanese at its most simple and sophisticated, authentic Kasuga ware is a series of collectible masterpieces.

Yet, the reader occasionally might see an entry for this Ben Seibel design: *Kasuga Vitrastone* sandwiched like a tasty slice of common salami between layers of raw blowfish served up as an expensive and dangerous sushi.[1] It has to be admitted, these auctions are rarely seen, and in general, *Kasuga Vitrastone* is considered difficult to acquire.

But, thinking about that last statement carefully, I realize also that *Vitrastone* is so removed from general collector knowledge, sometimes one can come upon a small treasure trove in the most unexpected places.

An advertising brochure recommends: "Kasuga: a Ben Seibel design. Graceful, dramatically elegant, so very practical ... this is Vitrastone ... dinnerware for today—by Kasuga." A hyperbolic statement to be sure! *Kasuga Vitrastone* is practical, admittedly practical—in a slightly fragile way. It is an informal set, charming, childlike in its exuberance, but hardly elegant or dramatic. It is, in my opinion, just the opposite. Both the shape and the treatments present a country look, perhaps even a "French country breakfast look." Now, the careful reader will remember I used this ploy of the "French country kitchen" once before—when describing the ideal use for Iroquois *Intaglio*. My mind has not changed, and I am not at all suggesting there is a stylistic connection between *Intaglio* and *Vitrastone*! But, be aware, there is more than one type of Country Kitchen! *Intaglio* would appear in that model country kitchen created by a Bloomingdale's designer in the fifth floor gourmet kitchen shop: all panache, all clean-crisp, all cleverly *outré*, with Martha Stewart dressed in a simple, well-cut designer frock (with a coordinated apron?) and carrying a large wicker garden basket piled temptingly with fresh vegetables: baseball round cabbages, feathery celeriac, yellow beets with perfect greens, exquisitely orange baby carrots, and bunches of dill, tarragon, summer savory, and opal basil. She smiles at the wandering (and wondering) Bloomie customers and murmurs: "Do be sure to go out to your garden every day and choose the freshest vegetables for a delightful summer supper."

No, *Vitrastone* surely was meant to have more humble surroundings. Martha would not like the inevitable crazing. I have a friend who had a grandmother, sadly now deceased, who was a strong, reliant, determined, self-sufficient woman born outside Norway's Lillihammer village on a mountain farm run by her even more resilient mother.

This grandmother, then a sixteen-year-old girl, fled the farm in 1904, and came to America. She immediately removed from her mind anything European. Years later, after World War II, she and her husband (a reasonably affluent electrician—as electricians often are) took a trip back to Norway to visit the aging mother and the one brother who remained on the farm, to see what changes had been made. My friend's grandmother was horrified: her mother was still cooking for the pigs at the back of the kitchen's wood stove. Back to America the middle-aged couple rapidly returned and ensconced in Seattle's Ballard, both of them quickly forgot about farms, and Europe, and allowed the Old World to sink into moral decay!

This is no implication that *Vitrastone* belongs in a country kitchen that provides meals for pigs! This is not meant to demean the line. Not all rural culinary settings can be arranged to suit the picture perfect Martha Stewart. *Vitrastone* is humble; a very humble tableware line. Tableware—if the designer is wise—can be created for a particular dining situation. Buttered toast, scrambled eggs, rich, dark, and aromatic coffee consumed at leisure in a cheery breakfast nook while the wind outside the window whirls the icy snows (keeping the pigs cozy in their sties) is a situation just as "legitimate" (and perhaps more delightful) as a formal candlelit dinner served on *Inheritance* china, or chatting, among flagstone floors and pewter plates, with Ms. Stewart regarding the charms of cold cream of celeriac soup.

Vitrastone plays well its part as an unpretentious breakfast set.

Not only are these modest *Vitrastone* pieces scarce in today's marketplace, information about the shape is also difficult to find. Since sharing information has become as rare as a happy hooker (indeed an oxymoron), I have seen only one brochure for *Vitrastone*. The prices mentioned in this brochure are also listed.

Chop plate, 12"	($2.70)
Dinner plate, 10.50"	($1.60)
Salad plate	($.90)

Soup plate	($.80)[2]
Fruit dish	($.60)
Teacup	($.80)
Tea saucer	($.60)
Salad bowl	($2.40)
Sugar pot with cover	($1.60)
Creamer	($1.20)
Coffee pot	($5.00)
Salt	($.90)[3]
Pepper	($.90)[3]
Milk pitcher	($3.00)
Covered butter	($2.00)
Gravy boat with tray	($3.00)
Casserole with cover	($8.00)

A short line—sixteen pieces. There are a few practical observations about the above list. The well of the tea saucer seems too large for the teacup: large enough for the cup to slip about within the well, but the fruit dish fits within that well perfectly. This fact has led some dealers to sell the fruit dish and tea saucer together as a bouillon set: a very honest and understandable mistake. This marriage of fruit dish and saucer works very well, but was probably not what Seibel had in mind.[4]

Again the easily understood anomaly: the plates, teacups, and saucers are much scarcer than the coffee pot, sugar bowl, and, certainly, the creamer.

This 5" creamer is the easiest piece for the collector to acquire—as situation similar to *Universal Raymor.* Many Seibel collectors, even advanced ones, tend to get their first glimpse of *Vitrastone* by seeing a cute but stalwart creamer on a flea market shelf, and discovering delightfully (once it is turned over) that is was designed by the same man who was responsible for their large and expensive collection of Roseville tableware! The reason for this ready appearance is not hard to discover: creamers are charming items, small, easy to store, and have many extracurricular activities, such as small boudoir vase, or a holder for color coordinated, well-sharpened designer pencils (remembrances of Ms. Stewart!). Many more uses than a plate or a sugar bowl.

In its original role, the creamer squired a shorter covered sugar bowl (4.25" to the top of the donut finial): another Seibel characteristic of matching the tall with the short. This creamer is the one of three *Kasuga Vitrastone* hollowware pieces[5] with a broad base: all the other hollowware curves inward toward the bottom.

All the handles consist of a rustically solid yet consummate curve, and this could be the reason for the advertising use of the term "dramatically elegant."

Note too the presence of the pitcher designated for milk— for the children at the breakfast table? Even in creating a simple line of dinnerware, Seibel felt the need of a jug.

And then there is the presence of handled shakers—rather a rare design option for Seibel. This is the first and only time, I believe, that Ben Seibel attached handles to his shakers. Throughout his career, the shakers never devolved into "little round bulbs" and each salt and pepper design was matched, as far as possible, with the rest of the set. His shaker sets were never an afterthought, but a carefully considered and fully-fledged member of the group.

However, while all these observations make for interesting contemplation, there are few real surprises. *Kasuga Vitrastone* must remain quite securely outside the borders of Mid-Century-Modern.

The background glaze is a warm white—white with a tiny drop of yellow, and scattered upon this are various decorations of ripe, sweet strawberries, fall-colored asters, chrysanthemums, plump Bartlet pears, and grapes. These shapes are small but not delicate as are the miniscule decorations on *Universal Raymor*. In keeping with the general informality of the shape, the cozy hominess of plump, red strawberries, juicy pears, dark purple grapes, fall leaves, and blue and violet asters reinforce a sense of unaffected unpretentiousness. Unfortunately, the glaze of *Kasuga Vitrastone* is extremely susceptible to crazing: some pieces are spider-webbed with lines, crossed with tiny tracks.

If a collector wishes to compile a modestly unassuming luncheon set of this *Vitrastone*, it would be best to start with Golden Pear: this treatment dominates today's market.

Among the treatments available on *Kasuga Vitrastone* are:

- Antique Gold™
- Dancing Leaves™
- Delphinium
- Golden Pear™
- Mace™
- Mint™
- Sage™
- Strawberry™
- Sunflower™

Nine spicy and summery decorations on sixteen individual pieces keep this shape within modest means.

Even those Seibel connoisseurs who dote on Roseville Raymor, exult over *Contempora* by Steubenville, or are charmed by Pfaltzgraff's *Country-Time* have little interest in *Kasuga Vitrastone*—it is not IMPORTANT enough! While never disputing the rights of these collectors, I do believe this shape deserves more popularity and certainly more study. It is, after all, one of the signed, true-blue Ben Seibel creations, and we all know how important it is to many collectors to have the name incised before it can be believed to be Seibel's work! Of course, *Vitratone* is not major, we all must agree with that statement, but it does have charm, a certain pleasant countrified grace, and while probably not up to the standards of a Martha Stewart, it can never be called "fodder for pigs!"

And it is the design of Mr. Ben Seibel!

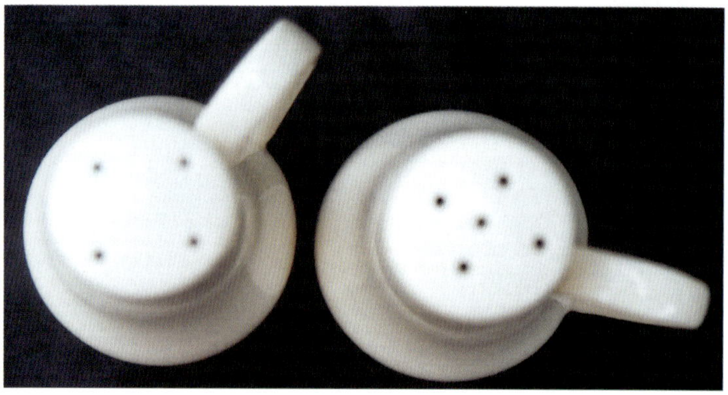

The Forum International Family

Rugged Beauty Can Be A Problem

Without "hedging the bets" or "obfuscating the obvious," it must be announced immediately: The four *Forum International* lines are problematic! No doubt about it! Beshrouding mysteries hang like a pall over this family of informal ware. All four appear on Michael Pratt's 1997 listing of Seibel's work, but two of them are so rare as to be non-existent.

FORUM INTERNATIONAL *Stoneware*™ (1962)
FORUM INTERNATIONAL *Buffetware*™ (1966)
FORUM INTERNATIONAL *Ironware*™ (1962)
FORUM INTERNATIONAL *Wood Filigree*™ (1962)

The last two named—Ironware and Wood Filigree—are the rare—no, ultra-rare—lines. In fact, these lines are so absolutely rare that, for a number of years, a few Seibel collectors questioned their actual existence. The word was circulating that perhaps these two were only names on a drawing board or existed only as a few fanciful prototypes. Then on sultry summer morning, a gentleman (a man whose influence over the Seibel archives and over Seibel information in general is monumental) answered a query on the Russel Wright Discussion Group. He spoke of seeing one piece of the Wood Filigree line, and knowing about a number of the metal cookware (Ironware?) items housed in the collection of Mrs. Lois Seibel. Suddenly the realization: the Ironware line was cookware. Any snippet of information to dispel the fog of confusion is welcome.

And it was announced that advertising sheets also exist.

It must be admitted that I posted the original query regarding the existence of the *Ironware* and *Wood Filigree* lines. When this person announced he owned a copy of a brochure on these two lines, I wrote him personally. His exact words to the Discussion Group were:

> *I did see one piece of the Forum Wood Filigree in the collection of the late Sandy Cohen. It was quite stunning. And pieces of the metal cookware were included in Mrs. Seibel's collection of Ben's designs. I have an ad[vertisement] for Forum showing these pieces, and stating "available in stores everywhere."* ...

Here is my message written privately to the noted authority and his reply.

> [RGR] ...*About four Seibel collectors have assured me these two Forum lines exist only on the drawing boards. I wonder if you would share a copy of the brochure you mentioned* [in your message to the RW group]???
>
> [Noted Authority] *Unfortunately, I can't do that at this time. The ad[vertisement] itself is a proof copy not of my ownership, and I have no evidence it was actually published. It doesn't contain any information or images on the Forum line not already known. For all I know, the pieces I saw may have been prototypes, but at least some quantity of the metalware/filigree was indeed produced. Sandy Cohen is no longer alive, so he can't be asked, but my impression was that these lines were all produced and marketed.*

Clever obfuscation, indeed! What do these words mean? Surely the above reply—from a collector ostensibly committed to the dissemination of information about Ben Seibel—does nothing to dispel any foggy misconceptions. In fact, his reply, in part, directly counteracted his original Group comment; begging the question, I would certainly say. Surely the clear "NO I WILL NOT SHARE" proves my theory that the sharing of information between legitimate researchers is, due to a few isolated persons, lessening.

The Forum International pieces that have been seen have two types of identification: a stamped one like this and a paper label pasted onto the base.

Another frequent commentator on the RW List also mentioned he owned an "original brochure" on the two "mystery" lines, but knowing his answer would be an even firmer and more hostile NO, I did not wish to demean myself by requesting for a copy.

The answer could be that these two gentlemen do not regard me as a legitimate researcher. Oh, well, all the honest and earnest Seibel collectors will have to wait for these two gurus to open their windows and let the desired information fly from their facile fingertips! Or perhaps until one or both publish a book and disseminate the information in that manner. Whatever the medium, ordinary Seibel collectors await! What the readers and I have learned—from this little tussle with the great and the powerful—is that *Forum International Wood Filigree* and *Forum International Ironware* do exist and were actually marketed in small quantities, and proof is given by an advertising sheet and an original brochure.

Enough said on the two rare lines!

However, there can be more said due to the kindness of a more equitable researcher and my own persistence. *Wood Filigree* and *Ironware* remain extremely hard to find—nearly impossible—but do exist. The most obvious statement regarding these two lines is that they are technically NOT tableware. Yet the pieces must be listed because all those interested in the work of Ben Seibel possess curiosity now about to be assuaged.

Forum International Wood Filigree almost fits into the category of furniture accessories, and consists of the following items:

Hanging screen (670), 3' x 8'
Folding table (640)
Trivet, rectangular (632), 10" x 24"
Trivet, round (631), 17"
Trivet, round (630), 7"
Serving tray (610), 24" x 11"
Serving tray (611), 20" x 11"
Waste basket (620), 14" high, 9 1/2" diameter
Waste basket (621), 10 1/2" high, 8" diameter
Planter, large, w/liner (652), 8 1/2" high, 12" diameter
Planter, medium, w/liner (651), 7" high, 9 1/4" diameter
Planter, small (650), 6" high, 7 1/4" diameter

Only the three trivets and the two serving tray could be termed "tableware," and perhaps the folding table—this piece resembles what used to be called a "drinks" or "butler's" table: a small, easily moveable table with a tray as a top.

All the pieces are composed of latticed, openwork wood. The effect is airy, comfortable, very British, and delicately charming.

Forum International Ironware is pure cookware, although some of the larger pieces could find an appropriate place on the buffet table. They are darkly and metallically elegant with bright and shiny lids. The line consists of the following:

Fry pan (831), 10" w/cover
Fry pan (830), 8" w/cover
Dutch oven (822), 10" (4 quarts) w/cover
Dutch oven (821), 8" (2 quarts) w/cover
Dutch oven (820, 6" (24 ounces) w/cover
Casserole, (860), 10" (3 quarts) w/cover
Saucepan (811), 8" (2 quarts) w/cover
Saucepan (810), 6" (24 ounces) w/cover

The use of this cookware is expanded by having the 10" fry pan, Dutch oven, and casserole each available with a alcohol warmer and a charcoal cook stove combination—with these additions the pieces could form grand and impressive units on any buffet table.

Under no circumstances, by reading the mildly confrontational account above, must anyone believe the two remaining Forum International lines, *Stoneware* and *Buffetware*, are easy to locate and easy to purchase. They are not! However, they are offered occasionally on the Internet auctions and in prestigious malls. The prices are high, competition active but not frenzied. With care, discernment, good luck, and persistence, a quite respectable collection of both shapes can be gathered. Of the two, *Buffetware* is a little more difficult to acquire. A former friend had some perceptive words to say:

> *...the Buffetware seems ...a simple serving line only. I think of it in terms of the "casual living" philosophy Russel Wright espoused, as a colorful but elegant line meant for get-togethers of young couples in the 1960s—not for a party at a fraternity house, but for entertaining friends from work or business partners (it strikes me as an eminently middle class, suburban line). Personally, I'd use it, were I to use my set, for a small party of people who had an artistic sense and could appreciate good design.*

Buffetware came onto the scene some four years after the stoneware line, and is very different in style and material. It has a porcelain look—clean, delicately crisp, and more formal, but no doubt this sense of formality arises from the ceramic material. The basic glaze is a stark, highly reflective white containing no softening yellow. The pieces are ringed with an alternating lozenge and rectangle decoration in either burnt orange (the more common) or lime green.

Many of the pieces are accompanied by trays and holders with raffia wrapped handles. These trays and holders are quite light and when this was discussed with another collector, he replied:

> *I do have a damaged tray, and you can clearly see what it is made of. The core is a thick portion of some type of brown cardboard. Over this is that outer, plastic, orange surface material. So while it does have plastic in it, the bulk [of the tray] is cardboard!*

Cardboard is another material the collector can add to those used by Mr. Seibel. I wonder if the use of cardboard generates enough surprise to push the *Buffetware* line into the category Mid-Century-Modern?

Here is a descriptive list of the known pieces.

Jam or condiment covered jars (two) on an oval handled tray
Handled crudités tray (triangular) with dip dish
Condiment set (four) on a small square handled tray
Cream
Covered sugar
Beverage server
Demitasse mug
Ashtray set (three) on small handled tray
Footed salad bowl, large

A conservatively minded researcher should never try to project items into any line of tableware, dinnerware, buffetware—any ware. This is a dangerous undertaking and leaves one open to instant decapitation by any hovering enemy. The above are the only pieces I have personally viewed. But, using some logic, it seems possible there might be smaller salad bowls or plates for use in combination with the large—super large—salad bowl. And the beverage server, sugar and creamer bespeak of another cup (perhaps with saucer) larger than the miniscule demitasse mug. Salt and pepper set? Seibel seemed almost obsessed with the shaker sets: always determined to integrate them with the overall design of the line. Other designers often viewed the shakers as a worrisome event, but Seibel exulted in the challenge of presenting to the public a well-constructed, useable salt and pepper set. Not mere adjuncts of the more dramatic items, but as distinguished little gems with their own significant personality—but this idea has been stated before.

The *Buffetware* might also have included other serving trays with ceramic inserts. This is highly possible, but I will not be rash enough to predict any specific items. Again, we will simply have to wait for elucidation from those persons lucky enough to have ensnared unto themselves—and themselves alone—brochures or advertising sheets. Praying to the gods of ceramics will really not help at this point. We must clearly be patient and wait!

A major source of confusion about *Buffetware*—or, as a matter of fact, any set composed of individual parts—is that these part can be separated and often are. Then these lost orphans are sold individually. For years, I owned a lidless single condiment that was sold to me—quite honestly, I believe—as a sugar bowl. It was not until I purchased the two condiment jars, replete with their own arching handled tray, that the mistake was discovered. Remove one of the ashtrays from its siblings and an honest but unknowing dealer might have a problem deciding just what it was. This happens in some of the most important tableware lines. Recently, a single Iroquois *Informal* triangular relish insert (one of six on the lazy susan) was offered as a "quiche dish." Highly inventive that![1]

Contrasted with Forum International *Stoneware*, *Buffetware* is less exciting, perhaps just a smidgeon over-refined, studied, and slightly affected. Perhaps! Some of the trays with inserts are a tad *recherché* to say the least. Who really has the time and inclination to live like this anymore? To chat with intellectual friends while nibbling on stuffed olives, pickled onions, and the crispest of toast points is not very popular anymore. But this is what collecting is all about—reaching back and absorbing a little of the past. Nonetheless, whatever the reader's opinions—or lack of them—some pieces of *Buffetware* really should be included in a serious Ben Seibel collection.

Now, please accept this opinionated insertion: suddenly I feel it is necessary, and I do hope no offense is taken—for I mean none. Let's be practical! How much time is spent during an evening of good talk and friendly camaraderie—when good friends feel safe and secure among each other—how often during these pleasant times, does the conversation turn to the bowls and pots and trays upon which the food is served? Intense interest in ceramics, dinnerware, tableware, glassware, and fondue pots is a rarified interest, indeed. During early magazine advertisements, or those fifteen minute "stories" that filled the radio waves in the years before television, conversations occurred which were built completely upon false premises—to sell a product. Did housewives in the 1950s really spend so much time discussing the merits of laundry soap: was *Duz* really that different from *Rinso*?

Vestiges of the same philosophy are still seen occasionally during television advertisements—as when Mr. Wimple squeezes the *Charmin*. But today, viewers and readers and listeners are getting more discriminating, and TV has progressed (or reverted) to flashy and catchy sophistication to sell products viewers might want, but do not need!

> SCENARIO: *A well-appointed, modernistic living room in (what seems) a high-rise building in a large city. White walls, polished tile floors. A white lacquered low table is casually set with a series of Forum International Buffetware. The doorbell chimes. A handsome youngish man in evening clothes and a tailored apron crosses the room. Smiling gently, he opens the door, and greets the shimmering couple standing there.*
>
> HOST: Hello there, Freddie. *(looking at the stunning young woman in clinging blue chiffon)* And this must be Birgit.

BIRGIT: *(holding out a gloved hand)* Hi, and you must be Frankie?

HOST: *(ushering them into the room)* I certainly am. Say, Freddie, she is certainly a fantastic creature.

FREDDIE: *(embarrassed) I know.*

(The three enter the room. Freddie and Frankie exchange a brief smile. Suddenly Birgit stops, her eyes riveted on the low table in the center of the room. She presses her hands together. Turning to the men, she warbles)

BIRGIT: *(ecstatic)* What a gorgeous set of buffetware! It is fantastic. *(turns to Frankie)* Oh, tell me where did you get it?

HOST: *(putting his arm around the shoulder of Freddie, he draws him over to the table. Removing his arm, he bends over and picks up a* Buffetware *tray containing pickled oysters, smiling and looking at the other man)* Oh, this, this is Forum International *Buffetware* designed by Ben Seibel. *(He holds the piece up for inspection.)*. I use it when I entertain friends who have an artistic sense, and appreciate good design.

BIRGIT: *(crooning)* It is gorgeous. And those sweet decorations! They are stunning. *(She reaching down and removes an ashtray from its rattan holder)* And this? So lovely, so perfect, and so charming. So wonderful for some many uses.

FREDDIE: *(proudly)* It does catch the eye!

BIRGIT: *(sitting down carefully on the edge of the low table—her dress flows becomingly upon the polished floor)* Oh! *(she reaches over and caresses the delicate coffee pot, reminding the standing men of Salome caressing the head of John the Baptist, then she turns her radiant face up towards Frankie)* Oh, Frankie, do you think if I really try that I too someday might have a set of Forum International *Buffetware* just like this?

HOST: With your obvious good taste and artistic discernment, I jolly well would think so.

BIRGIT: *(eyes swelling with glistening tears)* Oh, Frankie, I do hope I will persevere. It is so lovely.

HOST: *(standing close to Freddie)* I knew you would like it. *(He turns to Freddie, he then waves his hand over the table)* All these pieces—the trays, the large salad bowl with its geometric design, the delicate demitasse pot with its lovely little cups—everything was the gift of a very close friend.

BIRGIT: *(awed)* And you are willing to share all this with us?

HOST: *(holding out his hands towards the couple)* Oh yes, it is the least I can do!

FREDDIE: *(reaching down and picking up a handled triangular tray with some vegetable bits, he holds the tray towards Birgit)* Have a pickle?

(SLOW DISSOLVE ON THIS SCENE OF JOYOUSNESS)

I doubt if this advertisement was ever aired anywhere. But some of its intensity of thought and purpose permeates a great deal of "collector conversation."

This has been called a "shrimp tray," but it certainly could be used for a multitude of purposes. This "interchangeability" was Seibel's aim for this useful line. Price: $25-30.

The ashtray set. Price: $20-25.

Buffetware: the serving tray made of a type of *papier-mâché* with rattan wrapped handles. The ceramic inserts may be moved about on the tray. Price (if complete): $40-50.

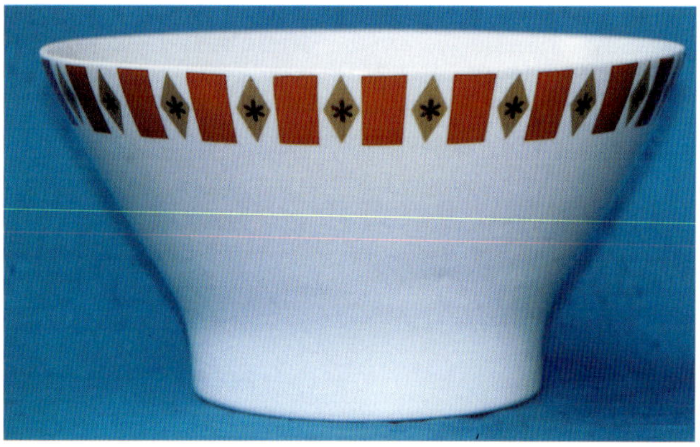

The mammoth salad bowl: huge, yet designed with considerable grace. The "foot" stabilizes it securely. It measures 6" high and 11.75" round, and was meant to hold a well-tossed green salad, or a copious supply of freshly popped corn. Price: $45-50.

The creamer with the true sugar. These are small and delicate pieces—probably meant for a demitasse set. The creamer is barely 4.50" high, and the sugar just 2.50" plus the cover and finial. Price (set): $25-30.

My first purchase of a Buffetware piece was the base of one of these jam/relish sets. It was sold to me (some ten years ago) as a sugar without a cover. This is completely understandable as then (and now) knowledge about this line is thinly stretched. Again, the *papier-mâché* holder with the rattan wrapped arching handle. Price: $18-22.

The coffee pot—probably a demitasse pot, but this is not absolutely known. Fully 11.25" to the top of the finial, this piece looks attractive, but the handle is somewhat awkward, and the lid has a tendency to tumble. The whiteness of the glaze is amazingly pure—almost with a blue overcast like skim milk. Price: $30-35.

Stoneware

Forum International *Stoneware* is four years older than *Buffetware* and projects a heavy, monumental stance. It is incised with triangular patterns resembling the carving on Egyptian tombs or Mayan temples. While the *Buffetware* projects an aura of delicate femininity, the stoneware projects carved monumentality! Some of the larger pieces rear like mountains over any surface whereon they sit. The very hugeness demands attention.

Again, the same general rule falls into place when the collector attempts to acquire Forum International *Stoneware*. Perhaps this ever-present tendency should be formulated into some type of "rule of collecting"? The simpler, more common pieces of yesterday have become the scarcer pieces of today. When plates, cups, mugs, saucers, and small bowls appear for sale or auction it is an unusual occurrence. Over and over, it must be repeated (and I do repeat), these smaller items were used, chipped, broken, and thrown away while the casseroles and samovars—in all their grandeur—were carefully preserved. The persevering collector can own a lovely selection of coffee pots on warmers, huge oval covered bakers, and trayed bean pots, but still lack the simple plate, or mug, or coffee saucer.

Stoneware, like *Buffetware*, can be found in only two treatments.[2] In this line these two are bone white with a yellow ochre triangular motif, and chestnut with a brunt orange ochre triangular motif. The former is the scarcer of the two, but lacks, somehow, the solid richness of the latter.

Because Seibel reveled in designing a piece with multiple parts there arises a very persistant problem—not only with the Forum International lines, but also with *Country-Time* or any other shape that included inserts, stands, and warmers—and that problem is the natural separation of the individual pieces. Some collectors who considered themselves strict connoisseurs disdain with some vehemence any piece that is not pristinely complete. This is not to be questioned—it is their prerogative. Yet, when these men of exquisite taste shower their disdain on collectors who do purchase a cheese tray without the wooden insert, then I rankle. The demand for "perfection" in this case becomes a petty prissiness!

When listing the pieces in the *Forum Internation Stoneware* line, those that consist of stands or pedestals were referred to—by Seibel himself—as a service or a set. Here are the items.

5-qt. Casserole service (280S)
3-qt. Casserole service (281S)
2-qt. Covered bean pot with wood tray (261)
Covered ramekin (19 oz.) (223)
Gravy (16 oz.) with wood tray (291)
Coffee warmer set (74 oz.) (253S)
Steak platter (17") with wood cutting wood service (293)
Tall mug (14 oz.) (283)
2 1/2-qt. Oval covered baker (260)
Relish tray with wood cheese board insert (282)
Salt shaker (11" tall) (294S)
Pepper grinder (11" tall) (294P)
Creamer (16 oz.) (240)
Covered sugar (16 oz.) (241)
Wood service tray (210W)
Dinner plate (11") (210)
Salad/buffet plate (8.50") (208)
Coffee cup (10 oz.) (275)
Coffee saucer (276)
Square egg skillet (6.25") (271)
Samovar set (24 cup) (254S)
Salad bowl (96 oz.) (295)
Wood serving spoon/fork[3] (420)
Soup (18 oz.) (6.25") (203)
Open vegetable (34 oz.) (262)

Twenty-six items, and with such a plethora of wood! Three items—service tray, spoon, and fork—are constructed completely in wood. This should remind the collector of the Iroquois *Inheritance* black lacquer serving tray—again all wood. Additionally, eight other items are accompanied by a wood tray, stand, insert, and some of these items—the samovar set, for example—are very elaborately constructed pieces of ceramic architecture.

The samovar is a magnificent structure, and when critically studied, has to be accounted the most successful of all the Seibel samovars. It is not tall like a stovepipe hat, nor does it teeter (metaphorically) on its stand like the round Humpty-Dumpty. It projects a graceful bulbous shape not unlike a symmetrical pear. The wide and open handles not only make this samovar easy to carry, but also lighten the profile while still keeping a certain monumental uniformity.

The Master of America's samovars created a masterpiece here. The wooden base plays an important role: it widens the contact with the table surface and solidly settles the entire ensemble. This samovar does not threaten to totter (the Mikasa *Duplex* samovar?) or foreshadow a roll (the Iroquois *Informal?*)—nor does it swing.

If the collector accepts the widely publicized definition whereby any shape with a plate, a cup, and a saucer is deemed a legitimate dinnerware line—then *Stoneware* is dinnerware. But when the overwhelming number of serving pieces is considered, this definition can hardly be true! Take away the cup, the saucer, the two plates, and even the mug, and Forum International *Stoneware* still exists as an extraordinary line of buffet ware. In fact, the wise hostess with a flair for the dramatic would match the architectural magnificence of *Stoneware* with the most delicate of bone china and the most refined of glassware. The shock of this abutment might send the guests reeling!

Actually, *Stoneware* is even more suitable for today's entertaining. While expensive to purchase as a collectible, one does not really need a great number of pieces. If the collector dares to use them, a buffet using the samovar, the large casserole ensemble, the tall salt shaker and pepper grinder, and the huge salad bowl would suffice to set an astounding service. Really *Stoneware* is much more impressive (if to impress is the object) than the flirtatious flippancies of home entertainment, the modern day *Fiesta*. Let us stick to solid and true basics here.

Admittedly, this section lacks a solid base. Nothing is really known of *Wood Filigree* and *Ironware*. Knowledge about *Buffetware* is scanty. Only the *Stoneware* emerges as a known and really viable line of tableware. There is still so much to be learned, so much to be ferreted out, information to be spread forth like clean bed linen in the sun, so many exciting bits to tickle the interest of the Seibel collector. Perhaps this section will stand as a skeleton—fragmented as Lucy's—upon which to drape new knowledge bit-by-bit, layer-by-layer. If the reader will accept this section as a "beginning" not as "finality" then my aims have been justified.

The 8" *Stoneware* salad plate. Price: $8-12.

The dark lustrous brown of this relish tray reminds me of a few of the dark brown glazes Seibel used in *Potter's Art*. The size is impressive (17" x 7.50") and it is also weighty. The wood cheese insert fits in either of the end triangles. Only the fastidious require that this insert be present, but its presence or absence does affect the price. Price (without insert): $20-25. Add 25% or more with insert.

The bottom of the relish tray. This is a paper label: easily lost through washing.

The *Stoneware* sugar and creamer in bone white with yellow triangles. This color is seen much less frequently than the chestnut brown. The creamer (6" high) especially is quite substantial: to hold milk or cream for a group. Very easy to use: the thumb fits perfectly in the indentation at the top of the handle. Prices: Creamer, $12-14; Sugar, $15-17.

The majestic 5-quart casserole service complete. It hovers over the table like a star-trekking space saucer. The impressive beauty of some of the *Stoneware* pieces is awesome! Price (if complete), $100.

The coffee, tea, or cocoa server—and obviously meant for a small crowd. Over 13" to the top of the finial (the stand adds an additional two inches), and the excellently designed handle allows for simplified pouring. The lid has double "hinges," it stays securely in place. A really thrilling piece of work. Price (complete), $75-80.

The tall mug—and these are quite rare. They are eagerly sought for all *Stoneware* collections. Price: $30.

The steak platter without the wood insert. These inserts are almost impossible to find. My belief is that many were stained with repeated use and were simply discarded. Still, this makes a very welcome platter for all types of use. Price (without insert), $20-25.

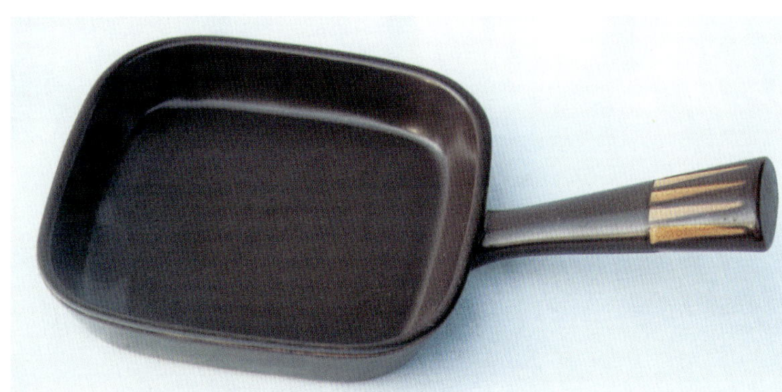

Called the "square egg skillet," it is doubted if many eggs were "skilleted" within it. Just as the Roseville Raymor shirred egg dish, it was probably meant more for serving than cooking. This 6.25" square skillet was my introduction to Forum International *Stoneware*—and quite an introduction it was! Price: $18-22.

This whole page:
Surely one of the most impressive of all Seibel pieces: the samovar complete with base.
A samovar among all samovars—designed to perfection. Price (if complete) $125+.

Oneida Melmac

Putting More "Sell" in Dinnerware Sales

The Oneida *Premier* mark. Often I have heard this line called Oneida *Premium*. I fall into this habit myself.

There are a number of my friends—well, not good friends, simply those who seem to keep track of my endeavors, and one of these erstwhile advisors constantly descries: "who wants to read your collector books? What you write about should be in a novel, not in a collectors' book. They are not about collectibles at all. You ought to write about sex, murder, and mayhem!" Well, I simply disagree. Mayhem does not interest me at all. Collectibles do! Collectibles are about remembrances, a personal history, a history of your family, "what comes about, goes about!" How can you divorce memories? How can one write about collectibles—any collectible—without bringing in past memories? Some writers do, naturally. Those with intellects like ice and minds like brutal steel traps: these people never make mistakes (supposedly), but they continually laugh at those writers human enough to make mistakes.

When I was a boy, my aunt—not much older than I—used to sing a song to me.

Be you is buggy? Sure I are! Everybody dooz!

Well, in the world of dinnerware design, everybody "dooz." Which simply means all the important designers of the mid-twentieth century turned to creating dinnerware lines in smooth and silky molded plastic. Russel Wright was notoriously prolific in this area, as was Ben Seibel. And he "dooz" it so beautifully.

In her book *Consultant Design* (Pembridge, London, c. 1981), Penny Sparke spoke incisively upon the various national concepts of "design."

> *While Germany sells design in the name of science, Italy in the name of art, Scandinavia in the name of craft, and the U.S.A. in the name of business, all these national images of design were necessary strategies in the highly competitive markets of the immediate post war years. The role of the designer was to help develop a marketing strategy that would give his product a special place in that market.*

As one of a new breed of independent freelance designers, Ben Seibel was ready and able to offer new thrilling creative concepts to a number of manufacturers. He was not alone in conceiving dinnerware in both new forms and new materials. As mentioned above, Russel Wright excelled in various materials—and Eva Zeisel also. These two were his collaborative competitors, and as freelancers they would influence all design areas—furniture, glassware, tableware, metalware, and lighting. Perhaps at no other time of human history since the fall of Christian Constantinople (1453) presaged the Italian Renaissance was the world of the creative arts so fully and absolutely devoted to the conception of the NEW and the EXCITING.

Melamine was one of these new and exciting concepts. It was the name given to a plastic made from a resin derived from a white crystalline compound $C^3H^6N^6$ and this technical name was applied to the dinnerware itself. Melmac was the popular rendition, and it was purchased and enjoyed by many consumers in the postwar years. The new name and the new concept created a great deal of business in America.

This new material was first used during World War II in a purely military capacity, but after the war ended The Watertown Company (Watertown, Connecticut) is credited with the first introduction of a line of plastic dinnerware for civilian use. The year was 1946, and the name of the Watertown line was *Lifetime*. Plastic dinnerware became very popular, and within a few years, many enterprising companies were literally flooding the market with plastic products.

Oneida was only one of many companies producing this tableware touted as sophisticated, colorful, unbreakable, dishwasher safe, and sanitary! Not quite one hundred percent correct! Melmac can break, and can scratch and become unsanitary, but it was colorful, slick, cheap, and a very excellent civilian use for one of the many plastics developed by scientists during the frightful years of World War II.

Also, the Oneida Company made excellent use of the American business savvy commented upon by Penny Sparke. Their salesmen traveled the roads and byways of the United States carrying special sets made up of their various lines of plastic tableware. A few of these Salesmen's Sets have been discovered in perfect condition—the one in my possession consists of an oval platter, dinner plate, salad plate, and a saucer with a very luxurious design of three pears in caramel and salmon surrounded by small fruits and florals. The other pieces are in a deeply saturated solid salmon color: coupe soup, fruit, large vegetable bowl, sugar, creamer, and teacup. Only the last four mentioned are Oneida *Premier*.

This salmon color has not been seen on any other Oneida Melmac, but it would be presumptuous to state it was never in full production.

There were three major lines of Oneida Melmac: Oneida *Premier*, Oneida *Delux*, and Oneida *Budget*. Only the first named, *Premier*, was designed by Ben Seibel.

Quite often when a designer discovers a new, successful merchandising ploy he (or she) carries the idea from manufacturer to manufacturer. Seibel convinced the Oneida administrators to follow the successful scheme of Iroquois *Impromptu* and offer to the consumers a group called Serving and Gift Pieces—seven very elegantly created items using brass and wood as accents. This mixing of materials and offering of gift sets was an approved and sustained bit of Seibel strategy. Collectors cannot be sure Seibel suggested this distributive plan to Oneida, but such a belief sounds logical.

The sets were sold separately and advertised as hostess gifts and house warming gifts. They were available only in white or turquoise.[1] These sets were introduced in 1960, and, considering the value of a dollar "back then," were substantially priced. These seven items were:

Hostess dish with wood block insert
Serving tray, 12" with removable handle
Serving tray, 15" with removable handle
Serving dish (double) with solid brass cover
Serving dish (single) with solid brass cover
Sauce bowl and tray

Sauce or jam set with solid brass cover and stainless steel ladle

An annoying and recurring problem arises for the collector *vis-à-vis* the gift items: rarely are they found intact. The sauce tray (underplate) and the wood block rarely accompany the bowl or the hostess dish—and the "removable" handle is often removed. This is unfortunate, but should never discourage the serious collector from acquiring a piece. Alas, the block and the handle really never find their way back again, but there are lone sauce trays floating about.

What of the *Premier* shape? Seibel designed the individual pieces with considerable care, and this care is reflected in Oneida's advertising statements. By the 1960s, Seibel seems to have been more concerned with ergonomics—or perhaps this was stressed by the powers at Oneida! Three distinct goals were stressed.

1. Each piece, of itself, must be beautiful—and complement its companion pieces.
2. Each piece must be functional—convenient and easy to use.
3. Each piece must be durable. No piece will be approved unless it represents a perfect balance of these vital qualities.

Oneida continued by stating:

—*Top of the cup rolls in slightly to increase durability and minimize cooling. Full 8 oz. capacity. Saucer rim is reinforced from below to eliminate chipping without sacrificing delicate look.*

—*Sculptural handle [of cup] is equally comfortable in finger-through or pinch grip. Slightly peaked top for thumb keeps entire cup from slipping in fingers.*

—*Plates have reinforced rims to prevent chipping...provide "sure-edge" grip for easy handling...lets plate be picked up gracefully and with ease.*

Beauty AND convenience, unlike *Contempora*, where convenience (Function) was sacrificed to the goddess Beauty (Form)!

There are faint shadows of other lines in Oneida *Premier*. Seibel was possibly working on *Inheritance* during this time and the arching *Premier* creamer handle reflects the self-same arch in the Iroquois shape. The sugar bowl lid finial is very similar to the Roseville Raymor finials—except it is "closed"—and marches very closely the long, low *Interplay* casserole lid handle.[2] The last shadow exists between the *Premier* soup/cereal bowls and the *Impromptu* bowls; however, I admit, one prominent Seibel collector strongly disagrees with this last point. Similarity, like Beauty, can lie in the eye of the beholder.

Both the finish and the feel of the surface is satiny smooth, with a faint and attractive luster, or, perhaps, a diffused and understated shimmer. There is nothing brittle, thin, or sharp about *Premier*: although these negative characteristics do appear in many other plastic dinnerware lines. Cost, naturally, had much to do with the quality of this Oneida shape—it was not the "budget" line, as consumers were willing to pay for a superior plastic dinnerware.

Following his predilections, so apparent in the ceramic tableware, Seibel divided the regular *Premier* items into decorated (flatware) and solid colors (hollowware). The decorated pieces are:

Dinner plate, 10.50"
Salad plate, 7.625"
Bread & butter plate, 6"
Saucer, 6"[3]
Serving platter, 12"
Serving platter, 15"

Not all the decorations have been identified: one, for example, includes realistic orange and yellow cosmos scattered on a soft white background. This treatment is rather non-Seibel-esque. There is another treatment without a known name: a series of plums, oranges, and small pears cavorting in a wide rim band about the plates.

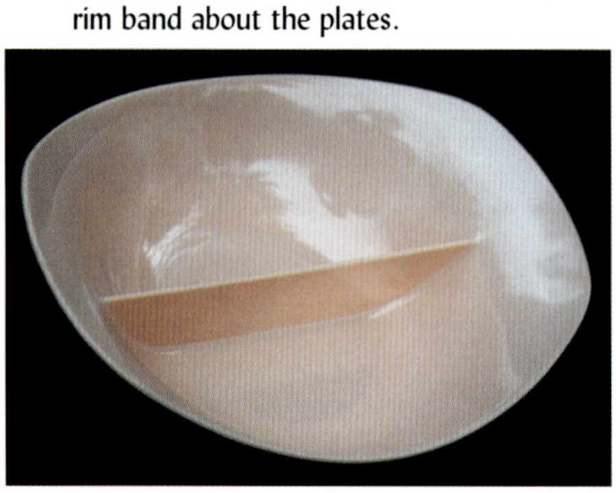

If this piece were white or turquoise, the viewer might believe it was a Gift Set item without its metal cover. Yet, in pink, it is merely a divided vegetable. This piece, however, is hard to find—Gift Set or not! Price: $10-12.

The stark and evocative Autumn Melody dinner plate; modern to the extreme and still having all the qualities of a chill autumn morning.

AUTUMN MEMORY: Five beech leaves clinging tenaciously to a branching twig. "A dramatic design in rich contrasting colors, fresh, sparkling, smart."

BRIGHT MORNING: An inner band of spring-like small leaves and flowers. "A luxurious yet delicate design with great style and charm."

CORONATION: Rich, golden scrolls encircling the plates and platters.

The Enchanted Garden dinner plate possesses the crumbling urn. This is a very popular *Premier* treatment, and not too easy to find. Thus, the dinner plate might command a slightly higher price. $8-10.

ENCHANTED GARDEN: An oriental inspiration in various blues. "Reminiscent of ancient gardens and scenes of grandeur."

This treatment is known as Engagement. Not too popular, but interesting because of the wide, pale blue border which, unfortunately, visually reduces the plates size.

ENGAGEMENT: Wide rim band in pale blue with verge decorated in small blue and gold leaves. A series of gold dots ring the leaves.

Seibel reveled in roses. Simply called Rose, this treatment is singularly lovely.

ROSE: A long stemmed pink tea rose.

WINTER SONG: Pure satin white. "Always in good taste, always lovely, this go-with-everything pattern accents colorful table appointments with great success."

Much is to be learned about the available treatments gracing Oneida *Premier*. Surely as interest develops and collectors begin to catalog what is located, the above short list will be expanded. In fact, a naturalistic bunch of pale purple grapes complete with leaves and tendrils accompanied by avocado green hollowware, and a "Pennsylvania Dutch" combination of frying pan, metal coffee pot, and a rooster weathervane—in grays and reds—have both been brought to my attention. There is little in the way of modern expressionism in *Premier* decorations, nothing new and stylishly chic, but old-fashioned honest and conservative values were very appealing to the many consumers of Melmac dinnerware.

The solid pieces are:

- Teacup, 8 oz.
- Soup/cereal bowl
- Fruit/dessert dish
- Sugar/lid
- Creamer
- Serving dish (single), 10"
- Serving dish (double), 10"

Also on this list belong the sauce bowl and tray, the 10" serving dish, and the 10" double serving dish. Were these open stock items produced to accompany the regular treatments FIRST and then appropriated, given brass covers, and then used as gift sets, or was the sequence in reverse order? Quite a conundrum. But, in reality, the problem arises only with the colors white and turquoise. If the collector finds, as I did, a divided serving dish in pink, it can immediately be classified as belonging to a regular set. However, if this piece is in white or turquoise, it might be a gift set item without the brass cover. Take your pick!

The solid colors were: white, avocado green, cocoa brown, butterscotch, pale pink, pale blue (turquoise), and the deep salmon found in the Salesmen's Set which might, or might not, have been in general production.

With only thirteen individual items, *Premier* must be accepted as an extremely short line. Some "shapes" were used more than once. The base of the gift jam set was merely the sugar bowl with a new brass lid. The two serving trays in the gift line were simply the regular platters with an added (and removable) arching metal handle. Thus there were really only thirteen items—barely enough to allow *Premier* to claim the status of a dinnerware line of some distinction. Is it a major Seibel creation? No, not really, and it cannot be listed among the Mid-Century-Modern crowd, but there is a freshness, a softly molded beauty, a quality of gentle softness, a shape with a sense of history, a modest modicum of reflected interest: it was, after all, designed by Ben Seibel!

Elegant as fine silver ... carefree as stainless.

Here is the delicate line, the graceful shape and satiny texture that has always meant the finest in dinnerware. Here, too, is the remarkable resistance to breaking, chipping and cracking that has established melamine as dinnerware's "miracle material." In shapes that represent a perfect balance of beauty, convenience and durability ... in patterns American women selected themselves as their favorites ... here is Oneida Premier, the finest melamine dinnerware.[4]

One of the finest, anyway!

The Salesmen's Set: a beautifully coordinated group made up of four *Premier* pieces and six pieces of Oneida *Deluxe*. The decorated plates, saucer, and platter exude a rich golden Baroque feeling. Price for set: $30-40.

The four *Premier* pieces.

The Oneida *Deluxe* mark.

Two examples of what was known as Gift Sets: the Hostess Dish—minus the center wooden insert, and the Jam or Sauce Set—minus the spoon. The color (turquoise) tells the collector these are original sets. Prices: Hostess Dish, $8-10; Jam Set, $12-15.

Here is a Hostess Dish not belonging to the original Gift Set ensemble. Gift Sets were produced in turquoise and white only. The wooden inserts usually are missing.

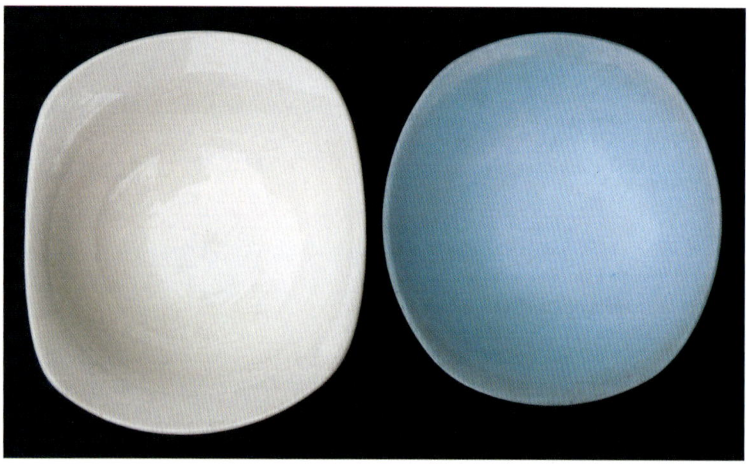

Personally, I see a resemblance between the Iroquois *Impromptu* bowl and the Oneida *Premier* bowl. Other collectors often do not.

Enchanted Garden bread & butter plate, cup, and saucer. There is no "urn" on the smaller plate. Prices: bread & butter plate, $2-3; cup and saucer set, $6-8.

Serving platter in the Coronation treatment. The platter is the same shape and size of the Hostess Dish—minus the divisions. Price: $9-12.

Some of the *Premier* treatments are stunning! Due to the lack of an official name, I have dubbed this treatment "Golden Cosmos." Hopefully some reader will let us know the official name. Prices: dinner plate, $7-8; salad plate, $4-6.

The satiny quality of the *Premier* finish is easily seen on this lovely fruit ringed dinner plate. The close-up photograph of the edge shows pears, quinces, crab apples, cherries—a naturalistic assortment.

This is not a Gift Set gravy set—the color tells the collector that. The gravy and its underplate are both quite scarce. Price: $18-20.

Notice, as in some of his other lines, Seibel makes use of the "raised well" on this plate. The boat hooks securely over the "well."

The seven known solid colors seen on Oneida *Premier*. The gold is the most common. Rumors have been floating about the existance of a dark blue, a bright cherry red, and a pale lemon yellow. Since all *Premier* pieces are marked, identification should be easy. Can any Melmac collector help?

1/3 OFF *liquidation* SALE!

SERVING and GIFT PIECES

IN FINE MELAMINE DINNERWARE

SAUCE OR JAM SET
with solid brass cover
and stainless ladle

ONEIDA PREMIER*

DOUBLE SERVING DISH WITH BRASS COVER . . .
ideal for many foods

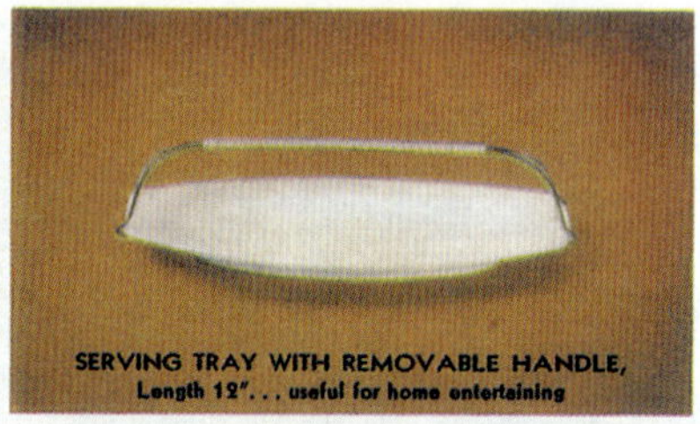

SERVING TRAY WITH REMOVABLE HANDLE,
Length 12". . . useful for home entertaining

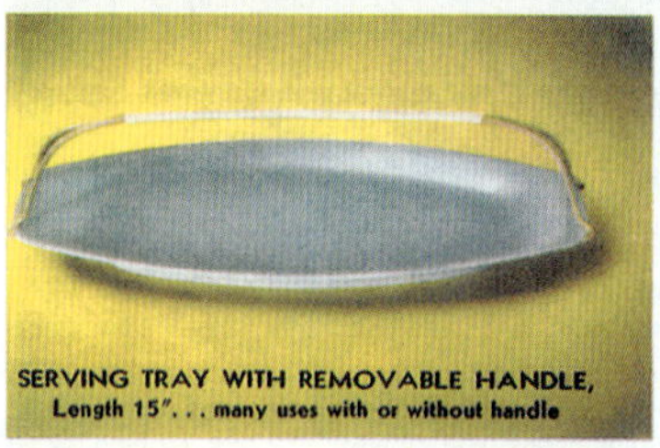

SERVING TRAY WITH REMOVABLE HANDLE,
Length 15". . . many uses with or without handle

SERVING DISH WITH BRASS COVER . . .
for fruits, vegetables, snacks

SAUCE BOWL AND TRAY . . .
bowl nests securely on tray

HOSTESS DISH WITH WOOD BLOCK . . .
for serving cheese, crackers, cold cuts

LIMITED TIME SELLING OPPORTUNITY ON THESE ATTRACTIVE GIFT AND SERVING PIECES . . .

Take advantage of this close-out. You can offer these pieces at 33⅓% less than present prices and still make your regular profit.

These are regular ONEIDA PREMIER quality gift and serving pieces . . . functional, durable, beautiful. Dramatic shapes, graceful contours with the addition of metal and wood to make them exciting and practical.

All pieces shown on this page are available in white or turquoise. All are gift boxed except the Sauce or Jam Set which are packed six in carton.

LIQUIDATION SALE PRICES FOR SPECIAL GIFT PIECES

White	Turquoise	ITEM	Standard Pack	Reg. Price Each	⅓ Off Sale Price
032915	082915	Hostess Dish with Wood Block	4	$6.95	$4.63
032960	082960	Serving Dish with Solid Brass Cover	4	5.75	3.83
032980	082980	Double Serving Dish with Solid Brass Cover	4	6.45	4.30
032902	082902	Serving Tray with removable handle, 12 inches	4	5.95	3.97
032905	082905	Serving Tray with removable handle, 15 inches	4	6.95	4.63
032950	082950	Sauce Bowl and Tray	4	4.85	3.23
033912	083912	Sauce or Jam Set, solid brass cover and stainless ladle . .	6	4.95	3.30

Sale Prices shown are subject to regular trade discounts. Always specify by number to get color desired.

*Trade-mark of Oneida Ltd.

Raymor Modern Glassware

Ben Seibel designed some simply shaped glassware to accompany his 1952 line, *Raymor Modern Stoneware*. This glass was manufactured by the Morgantown Glassware Guild and was offered in four colors: gray, green, honey, and crystal. The shape was gracefully conceived with a quilted pattern providing a subtle decoration.

Five items were produced. All are scarce.

Ice tea, 10 oz.
Tumbler, 6 oz.
Juice
Old fashioned
Dessert bowl

I sincerely wish to thank Michael Pratt for allowing his photographs to appear in this book.

This whole page:
The glasses possess a "quatted" texture, and are in great demand. Prices range from $50-75 up.

Fostoria Glassware

All of the major Mid-Century-Modern designers stretched their wings and fluttered into the difficult realm of glassware design. They expertly dabbled like so many ducks in these clear, fresh ponds, or like so many swans in watery sylvan surroundings. Ben Siebel was no exception. When he created the beautiful new conceptual ceramic designs for Roseville Raymor, a series of glassware soon followed. These early glasses are avidly collected today. But Seibel's main and most lasting glassware collaboration was with the Fostoria Glass Company of Moundsville, West Virginia. Commencing in the early 1960s and continuing until his death in 1985, Ben Seibel was continually, although certainly not exclusively, involved in the creation of glassware. Over the years, he submitted literally hundreds of drawings. These, having been given Fostoria "in-house" numbers, i.e. B-28, B-39, E-4, are no longer easily identifiable. They do, however, besprinkle his correspondence with the Fostoria Company. Thus it is known the Seibel versatility of conception produced a wide spectrum of glass patterns and shapes—from the most avant-garde to the most predictable stemmed conservatism.

It is interesting to note—and this is not a negative criticism, merely an observation—that researchers do not seem to care who designed the many varieties of glassware produced by such manufacturers as Imperial, Duncan Miller, Fenton, and Fostoria. They are content to describe the patterns, discuss—as far as possible—the history of each line, but, unlike tableware or ceramics, the man or woman responsible for the glassware shape is often overlooked. Granted, in many cases it would be virtually impossible to discover the name or names of the persons responsible for such great classic glassware as *Candlewick, Cape Cod, American*, much less the myriads of individual candleholders, vases, bowls, and boxes that swamped the gift shops, department stores, and jewelry shops stretching from Manhattan to the hills of San Francisco. And who designed those hundreds of etchings worked into the many glassware blanks? To put a designer's name to each any every glassware pattern is not feasible. Companies involved in the manufacture of ceramics, dinnerware, and glassware are notoriously remiss where record keeping is concerned. If records are kept, the resultant muddle makes research unrewardingly difficult.

In the case of Fostoria glassware, collectors generally are interested in facts about Fostoria, or even more concisely, Fostoria *American* or *Century* or *Coin Glass*. They, the collectors, generally seem to be uninterested in the designer behind their favorite glassware pattern. There are exceptions, of course: some collectors are vitally interested in "who" designed "what" glassware. The glass itself seems preeminent, not the designer.

Occasionally, the designer is of such stature—a Russel Wright, an Eva Zeisel, a Ben Seibel—that the collectors are determined to expand their knowledge of these favored few into all areas. Then the researchers must probe and hunt to fulfill these collector wishes. While I am not knowledgeable regarding all books on glassware, the only one seen wherein the designers are listed is Ann Kerr's book *Fostoria*. On page 11, she lists the In-House Designers, and the Contract Designers with their patterns, albeit these lists seem to be incomplete. Here appear Raymond Loewy, Helen Tynell, George Sakier, James Carpenter, and Ben Seibel.

Raymond Loewy is a fascinating example of how designers of world stature still try to translate their monumental abilities to the world of glassware. Raymond Loewy, designer of ColdSpot refrigerator for Sears Roebuck and Company and the Greyhound Scenicrusiser, among other prestigious commissions, in 1956, took his talent to Fostoria and created the shape named *Radiance* (2700). It was a full dinner service of pressed glass and was admirably popular. The world of glass enticed all manner of famous designers.

Moundsville, West Virginia, was located in the spur of the state and nestled on the dark and winding Ohio River that separates Ohio from West Virginia. Here was the home of the Fostoria Glass Company. Even though he was living and working in Manhattan, Ben Seibel visited regularly to supervise the work, check on molds and models, present new ideas, and confer the company designers and administrators. The record of the visits:

January 31 - February 2, 1972
April 19 - 21, 1972
July 10 - 11, 1972
October 2 - 3, 1972
January 22 - 23, 1973
February 13 - 14, 1974
April 1 - 2, 1974
December 4 - 5, 1974
May 6 - 7, 1975
July 24 - 25, 1975
September 9 - 10, 1975
December 21, 1975
April 5, 1976
July 27-28, 1976
September 8 - 9, 1976
March 9, 1977
July 27 - 28, 1977
July 19, 1979

Luckily, some correspondence between Ben Seibel and Fostoria has come into my possession. These are copies of originals in the Seibel archives at Syracuse University Library, and fall into two major categories: statements of account (bills) sent from Fostoria to Seibel, and regular letters received or sent by Seibel. The former category consists of sixteen statements dated 1976 and 1979. Purchases by Seibel included *Monarch* (2903) double old-fashions, *Wimbledon* (6126) crystal goblets, sherbets and wines, and *Festive* (6127) goblets and clarets. The glassware was sent both to the Seibel home and the studio.

The second correspondence category is, by far, the largest and most important. They run for eleven years: 1972 until 1983. While probably only a partial correspondence, these letters reflect strongly on the relationship between the executives at Fostoria and Ben Seibel. The breakdown of the years is interesting:

1972: 12
1973: 3
1974: 9
1975: 11
1976: 5
1977: 5
1978: 7
1979: 3
1980: 3
1983: 4

There were no available letters dated 1981 or 1982. There are, in total, sixty-two letters: fifty-two from Seibel, ten from Fostoria.

Correspondents included: Mr. David B. Danzell, President; Mr. Edward Kennedy, Executive Vice-President; Mr. David B. Danzell, Jr., Advertising Manager; Jon Saffell,[1] Designer; Judith N. Olert[2] (first as Table Top Consultant, 1977, later as Product Development Manager, 1983). Business subjects, i.e. royalties and sales, were discussed with Mr. Danzell and Mr. Kennedy. Correspondence regarding designs and modeling were with Mr. Danzell, Jr. and Mr. Saffell. In 1983, tension seemed to be developing between Ms. Olert and Mr. Seibel regarding new product designs.

It seems that Seibel spent a considerable time during his last years designing for Fostoria. It should not be assumed that all the designs he offered were ultimately produced. There are a number of sketches that cannot be identified, and comments about glassware shapes that evade verification. For example: On February 10, 1972, Seibel writes to Fostoria Executive Vice-President Edward Kennedy discussing drawings for a "zigzag" creamer and sugar. The shape that immediately comes to mind is *Facets*, but by 1972 that line had been out of production for seven years—and it does not have a cream and sugar. Was Seibel likely to have been designing a *Facets* set in 1972? *Gourmet* does have a cream and sugar, but the set had already been designed. As we look at the list below, only the last three could have still been on the drawing board, i.e. *Corsage Plum*, *Monarch*, and *York*. None of these are "zigzagging," nor do any have a cream and sugar. So, either this set was never produced, or has been lost among the many giftware sets manufactured by Fostoria after 1972. The mystery of the "zigzag" line was solved through. A chance remark by Mr. Jon Saffell solved the mystery of the "zigzag" line.

> *"Zig-zag" line was a pattern Ben designed which was approved for mould work on 8-25-70. He was probably referring [in his letter] to the mould joint line, which looked better following the "zig-zag" pattern as opposed to a straight line.*

Further, Mr. Saffell identified this pattern as the #2828 ash tray and vase first pictured in a price list on January 1, 1974. A photograph of these two pieces appears on page 296 of *Fostoria Tableware, 1944-1986* by Milbra Long and Emily Seate (Collector Books, 1999) Thus a perusal of the letters can be both intriguing and frustrating.

The following Fostoria shapes are attributed to Ben Seibel:

Facets	(2762)[3]	(1961-1965)	Pressed
Vase, 5.37"	(2758)	(1963)	Pressed
Vase, 7.37"	(2759)	(1963)	Pressed
Gourmet	(2785)	(1964-1974)	Pressed
Precedence	(6108)	(1967-1974)	Blown
Pebble Beach	(2806)	(1968-1973)	Pressed
Goblet	(2822)	(1970)	Pressed
Contrast	(6120)	(1970-1972)	Blown
Eloquence	(6120)	(1970-1974)	Blown
Venise[4]		(6120)	(1970-1974) Etching on Blown glass

The Venise etching (#688) that decorated the *Eloquence* stemware from 1970-1974.

Module	(2824)	(1970-1972)	Pressed
Corsage Plum	(6126)	(1973-1974)	Blown
Ashtray (ZigZag)	(2828)	(1974)	Pressed
Vase (ZigZag)	(2828)	(1974)	Pressed
Centerpiece, 6"	(2827)	(1974)	Pressed
Candy jar	(2829)	(1974)	Pressed
Candy box	(2830)	(1974)	Pressed
Coaster	(2833)	(1974)	Pressed
Wimbledon	(6126)	(1974-1982)	Blown
Tara[4]	(6126)	(1974-1982)	Etching on Blown glass

The Tara etching (#34) that decorated crystal *Wimbledon*, 1974-1982.

Festive[5]	(6127)	(1975-1982)	Blown
Serenity[4]	(6127)	(1975-1982)	Etching on Blown glass
Candle/bud vase	(2937)	(1976)	Pressed
Monarch	(2903)	(1979-1986)	Pressed
York	(2932)	(1979-1982)	Pressed
Gazebo	(2162)	(1980-1982)	Blown
Gazebo Rust	(2162)	(1981-1982)	Blown

A very respectable list. Although some of the above creations are simply variations of the same design. See the discussions of the individual lines for explanations.

Yes, Ben Seibel was indeed deeply involved in the world of Fostoria glass. For over twenty years, he strived continually in this field, and although the results were prodigious and the connection prestigious, his financial gain was not outstanding. Compared to Mikasa, for example, Seibel's royalties from Fostoria were meager. Picking three consecutive years—1978 to 1980—the researcher can follow the monthly royalties paid by Fostoria to the firm of Ben Seibel Associates.

1978	
January:	$1,000
February:	0
March:	0
April:	0
May:	$595.76
June:	$536.89
July:	$586.98
August:	$137.41
September:	$297.62
October:	$429.65
November:	$353.83
December:	$553.55
	$211.09
total:	$4,702.98
1979	
January:	0
February:	$220.79
March:	$405.79
April:	$404.45
May:	$670.76
June:	$621.74
July:	$607.08
August:	$165.25
September:	0
October:	$394.81
November:	$713.69
December:	$515.37
total:	$4,719.73
1980	
January:	$339.36
February:	$217.87
March:	$565.92
April:	$442.17
May:	$300.47
June:	$296.66
July:	0
August:	$539.58
	$566.18

September:	$498.72
October:	$500.15
November:	$451.02
December:	$423.18
total:	$5,141.28

These figures were hardly impressive—even for the late 1970s and early '80s—when they are juxtaposed beside the income from Mikasa. During the same years, Mikasa royalties averaged about $4,000 per month. Still, Seibel expended much energy and thought on his work for Fostoria: he was meticulously concerned that his designs be accepted, and once accepted, molded perfectly. The letters prove how he was concentrating during these years to perfect his submissions to Fostoria.

In general, glassware can be divided into five main groups: Tableware, Dinnerware, Stemware, Casual Ware, and Giftware. There are some collectors who believe the first two groups are the same; but, as I stated at the beginning of this book, I believe tableware includes "non-eating" items such as candleholders, epergnes, ashtrays, centerpiece bowls, and vases. Dinnerware is made up of pieces actually used in the consumption of food. If a line of glassware has a cup, a saucer, and a dinner plate, the expert collectors consider it dinnerware.

Stemware is the major category in glass: it is made up of pieces that are used in the consumption of liquid, and, technically, these do not need a "stem." Tumblers and juice glasses belong to the stemware category. Quite often a stemware pattern might have a plate or bowl included, but the line is still simply "stemware."

Casual Ware is a motley grouping. Sometimes the individual pattern includes pieces of stemware, sometimes is consists of just ashtrays, or relish trays, or covered candy dishes. The easiest way to identify this meandering category is to determine what it is NOT. If a design is NOT tableware or dinnerware, and if it is composed of more than just stemware, then it is Casual Ware.

Giftware is primarily purchased as one item to be given as a gift. A Giftware line can include only one piece, i.e. a glass fondue bowl, a lovely bud vase, or a candlestick. A small set of four ashtrays graduated in size and sold in a decorated box is also Giftware. A glass bell is Giftware—so are glass animal figures and cigarette boxes. This does not mean that a bowl or covered candy dish belonging to a small casual line cannot be given as a gift! The difference between Casual and Giftware is hazy, and probably depends mainly on the intent of the Fostoria Company. Ben Seibel did not design Tableware or Dinnerware for Fostoria—although *Pebble Beach* comes close.

Ann Kerr, one of the revered commentators on designers such as Ben Seibel, and glassware lines such as Fostoria, has this to say about giftware:

> *Fostoria's extensive gift lines are rooted in the dinnerware and casual dinnerware lines. Many items in those lines were lifted and became part of the general gift selections. Decanter Sets, Smoking Sets, Candy Jar Assortments, Cheese Sets, Salad Sets, Bowl Collections, Vase Assortments, and more, made for a rich and varied gift offering.*

As the reader proceeds through the following Seibel/Fostoria commentary, a number of colors will be mentioned. The actual name of each color must be considered particular to the individual line being discussed. Some like "pink" are immediately self-explanatory while others, such as "Dusk," can be confusing. There will be an attempt to translate these subjective Fostoria color names into more understandable terms. There are two points worth remembering: (1) in the world of Fostoria glass, the same color often changes names when it relates to different lines, and (2) retailers and distributors (such as Replacements, Inc) sometimes use their own names for official color descriptions. An example of the first point is *Pebble Beach*'s Black Pearl, which is exactly the same color as *Module*'s Dusk. An example of a retailer's whimsy is Replacements calling the slightly greenish yellow Lemon Twist simply yellow, or Dusk becomes merely black.

Facets (2725)

Consisting of ten pieces, the *Facets* casual ware[6] was made in crystal and pink (lavender overtones) plus a few items appearing in gold—actually a warm honey amber. The crystal is the most impressive of the three color variations. The sides of the pieces (and the top of the cigarette box) are thick and deeply incised by slightly curving triangles—like arches in a gothic cathedral. These facets in crystal collect the light and throw it back to the viewer in a series of flashing rainbow colors. The pink lacks this multicolor "flash," while the amber-gold, pretty but tame, appears on only two pieces (bon-bon and candlestick), and is usually priced lower.

Facets includes:

Ashtray, 8" (120): made in crystal (1961-1967) and pink (1962-2965). It also was used as a lead crystal gift item.

Ashtray, 11", oblong (124): made in crystal (1962-1967) and pink (1962-1965)

Bowl, 9", oval (189): crystal (1962-1965) and pink (1962-1965).

Bowl, 10" (211): crystal and pink (1962-1965).

Bowl, footed and covered (347): crystal and pink (1962-1965).

Bon Bon, covered (350): crystal, pink, and gold (1962-1965).

Candlestick (314): crystal, pink, and gold (1962-1965).

Candy box (flat), covered (354): crystal and pink (1962-1965).

Cigarette box, oblong, covered (374): crystal (1961-1965) and pink (1962-1965).

Shaker, chrome top (635): crystal and pink (1962-1965).

Only the three smoking items (two ashtrays and a cigarette box) break the four year production period. *Facets* is difficult to find, yet worth the extended search. A piece or two belong in all serious Ben Seibel collections.

The oval ashtray seen from above.

The candlesticks in gold. Only three pieces of *Facets* were presented in gold: the 9" oval bowl, the bon-bon and cover, and these candlesticks. For some reason this color is not very popular with collectors today. Price (per pair): $20-25.

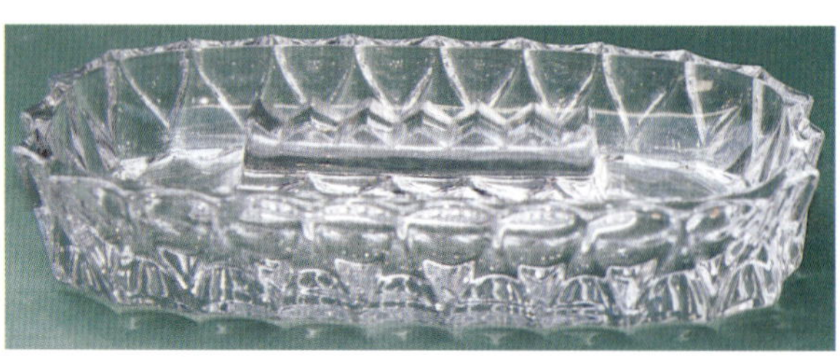

The large oval lead crystal *Facets* (2752) (1962-1967) ashtray. It is 10.75" x 5.50" wide, and HEAVY—weighing in at 4.50 pounds! This ashtray will not slip across the top of the coffee table. Notice how the pressing creates a triangular affect. The suggested price on such a magnificent and relatively scarce piece is, today, quite low. Price: $15-18.

The *Facets* candlestick in pink. Only a little over 3.50", it is still a grand piece. Price (per pair): $38-42.

Gourmet (2785)

Another Casual ware line,[7] *Gourmet* is more fluid, lighter, and is based on incised rounds or arches rather than triangles as was the case in *Facets*. It was produced from 1964 until 1970, but not until 1966 did Fostoria make it available decorated with either platinum or gold trim. It appears only in crystal and includes a bowl, a plate, three relish dishes, shakers, and a cream and sugar: eight pieces in all.

Bowl, 10", footed (224).
Plate, 14", known as a torte plate (567): never decorated.
Relish dish, 2-parts (620).
Relish dish, 4-parts (643).
Relish dish, 5 parts (644).
Shaker, chrome top, (653): never decorated.
Cream, footed (681).
Sugar, footed (no cover) (679).

Gourmet is a very abbreviated and elegantly simple shape. Not easy to find, but the sugar/creamer set is a "standout" addition to any Ben Seibel collection.

The *Gourmet* creamer and sugar. The base is hollow and this reduced the weight of these pressed pieces. The sugar stands 3.25" and the creamer is 4" at the spout. This is not a pair—the sugar has platinum trim (decoration 699) available from 1966-1970. There was also a gold trim (decoration 668). Price (set): $38-42.

Precedence (6108)

This line belongs in the blown glass stemware category: tall, elegant, sophisticated, and conservative—and, better still, not at all difficult to locate. A collector enthralled by the Fostoria designs of Ben Seibel easily can acquire an entire set—to display with pride or use with care. All the six pieces are beautifully proportioned stems designed to rise dramatically from the tabletop. Precedence was widely publicized and is seen frequently in old Fostoria magazine advertisements: these attest to enthusiastic acceptance by the public. The bowls are clear glass, rounded and swelling, with no optics[8] to compete with the gracefulness.

Precedence can be acquired in the following pieces:

Goblet, 12 oz., 7.50"
Claret, 8 oz., 6.25"
Champagne, 9 oz., 5.75"
Tulip wine, 7 oz., 5.75"
Footed ice tea, 14 oz., 6.50"
Liqueur, 2 oz., 3.75"

These six items appear with bowls in three different colors: crystal, gray mist (both produced from 1967-1973), and onyx (black) (1967-1974). The clear crystal is the most glamorous: the clarity enhances the color of whatever drink is being served. As often happens with stemware lines, Fostoria offered two sizes of plates to accompany the group: 7" in crystal and gray mist, and 8" in crystal only.

In these glamorous and elegant Fostoria lines, the most impressive stems are the easiest to find: the tall goblet and the champagne. The collector will have to hunt a little for the beautifully proportioned liqueur—and pay quite a bit more for it. No matter, a set of Fostoria *Precedence* is well worth acquiring, and well worth using on those very special occasions.

A *Precedence* ensemble. From left to right: the liqueur (3.87") with the onyx bowl; the goblet (7.50") with gray mist bowl; the champagne (5.75"); and the claret (6.12"), also in gray mist. Not only is the small liqueur the scarcest, it is the most expensive. Prices (crystal at the lower end): Goblet, $28-35; Champagne, $28-35; Claret, $28-35; Liqueur, $32-40.

Pebble Beach (2806)

This Fostoria pattern is the most easily available of all Ben Seibel glassware designs: in fact, a few of the pieces—sherbet for example—can be called quite "common." Yet, the Ben Seibel collectors are quite divided over the merits of this glassware. One either finds the heavy solidity attractive or distasteful: there seems to be no middle ground, and this fact is compelling. The name is brilliant: the design reminds one of the rocky, pebbly free of soft sand beaches of New England and Canada, no refinement here!

One of the most descriptive words to describe *Pebble Beach* is "chunky," but some detractors—delighting in their own wit—have called it "clunky." Whatever its nickname, I find this pattern earthy and refreshing: like icy beer, grilled hot dogs, corn, and clams steamed over a driftwood fire, and consumed with gusto on a moon-drenched sandy (or pebbly) beach with the cool, salty smell of iodized seaweed, the sound of a gently rolling surf, and enough wind to keep the midges away. Add a group of close friends, pleasant yet serious conversation, and we certainly have the setting to use Seibel's *Pebble Beach*. Both its sturdiness and well-designed informality are perfect.

Pebble Beach evokes good memories of good times, and it is completely practical. The longest of the Seibel Fostoria lines—seventeen items—it could nearly be classified as dinnerware. It possesses a small plate and a small cup.

- Torte plate, 14"
- Cake plate, 11"
- Plate, 8"
- Dessert bowl, 4.75"
- Punch bowl, 11.50" (9 quarts)
- Punch cup (6.50 oz.)
- Relish, 3-part, 10"
- Salad bowl, 10"
- Pitcher, 7.125" (1 quart)
- Cream, 3.25"
- Sugar, covered, 4"
- Shaker set, chrome top, 2.75"

Then the stems:

- Goblet, footed, 6" (10 oz.)
- Ice tea, 5.75" (14 oz.)
- On-the-rocks, footed, 4.125" (8 oz.)
- Sherbet, footed, 2.75" (7 oz.)
- Juice, 4" (7 oz.)

There are two very noteworthy design elements in *Pebble Beach*. The relatively small pitcher has a clear, heavy, solid glass foot that anchors it perfectly to the picnic table or into a comfortable sand dune. But most surprising is that Seibel conceived the "pebbles" as concave rather than convex. This intensifies the sparkle, and can be seen best by firelight. One friend of mind decided to use a number of footed goblets as votive lights to decorate her patio tables. The effect was spectacular!

Finally, this glassware line has been produced in a number of delightful colors: Flaming Orange (1968-1973), with amberina qualities; Black Pearl (1968-1973), light and smoky with purple tones; and Lemon Twist (1968-1973), green overtones. These three are really easy to locate. Crystal Ice (1968-1970) and Mocha (1969-1970) are harder to find, while Pink Lady (1968-1970) is quite scarce. All the names were carefully chosen for "drinkable" qualities.

"Clunky?" Never! In any of the six colors, *Pebble Beach* would be the perfect, absolutely perfect, matching glassware when using Mikasa's *Potter's Art*!

Three sherbets in (left to right) Lemon Twist, Black Pearl, Flaming Orange. This piece could be called "common" because it is the item that is offered for sale the most often. Price: $7-10.

Samples of *Pebble Beach* stemware: the juice (4.75") in Mocha; the ice tea (5.75") and "on the rocks"/wine (4.25") in Lemon Twist; and the goblet (6") in Flaming Orange. Notice the goblet is narrower than the other pieces. "On the rocks"/wine is the official name of that piece. I wonder, was the term "on the rocks" used by Ben Seibel in a wry manner? After all, when you sit on a pebbled beach you are "on the rocks." Prices: Goblet, $10-12; On the rocks/wine, $12-15; Ice tea, $12-15; Juice, $10-12.

The rugged and stalwart *Pebble Beach* (pressed glass). As I stated, some people love it, many dislike it—there seems to be no middle ground. I believe it is fascinating. Here is the quart pitcher in Lemon Twist, the 8" plate, and the desert bowl in Flaming Orange. For all of its startling beauty, Flaming Orange is easy to find. This color appeared on the plate and dessert bowl for only two years, 1969-1970. Prices: Pitcher, $75-80; Plate, $15-18; Dessert bowl, $14-17.

A pair of shakers in Mocha. The tops are chrome and tend to discolor: these are perfect. Price (set): $26-30.

Crystal *Pebble Beach* is one color not easy to find and is quite beautiful. The new piece here is the punch cup that comes only in crystal. It is a very welcome item in any collection: Price: $15-18.

It is my opinion that Pink Lady is the hardest color to locate in *Pebble Beach*. It rarely is offered for sale, and this plate is the only one in my possession. Of course, in other parts of the county Pink Lady might be readily available. I would pay twenty-five percent more for this color, but that is a personal pecularity. Price: $10-12.

Contrast (6120)

Contrast is a very unusual and striking line: its name gives a hint as to the coloring. It was made only for two years (1970-1972) and the excitement it arouses is due to the mingling of a soft white bowl on top of an onyx stem and base. Suddenly we are confronted with the classic "black and white" syndrome so ably expressed in all manner of design. Again we are called to witness the famous Black and White Ascot sequence in the film *My Fair Lady*. Black coupled with white—*ying* matched with *yang*—and the excitement is always explosive.[9] Yet, some film buffs were not fond of this combination. I have always appreciated Sir Cecil Beaton's approach to life in general, and thus, *Contrast*, with the ying and the *yang*, is a favored Seibel/Fostoria pattern.

Since *Contrast* is simply a color variation of *Eloquence*, please read the next section for the number of pieces available.

It is not difficult to understand why manufacturers name certain items the way they do! Here is an *Eloquence* goblet with a white bowl and Fostoria chose to name it *Contrast*. Made only during 1970-1972, it is not easy to find. Price for goblet: $50-55.

Eloquence (6120)

Introduced in 1970 (the same year as *Contrast*), *Eloquence* has exactly the identical shape. Five stems were available in two versions (NOT counting *Contrast* which is considered totally separate) and three decorative additions. It is a "no optic" design. I like to think of *Eloquence* possessing a rounded "balloon" shape: the bowls are generous and act as a foil to the flattened stem disk just below them.

The pieces are:

Goblet, 7", 14 oz.
Footed ice tea, 6.75", 15 oz.
Sherbet, 5.50", 10 oz.
Claret, 6", 9 oz.
Liqueur, 3.50", 2 oz.

From 1970 until 1974, these pieces could be purchased in crystal and with a crystal bowl and a black stem. During the same years, the two varieties came with three decorations: *Eloquence Gold*—with a simple gold rim on the bowl;

Eloquence Platinum—with a platinum rim on the bowl;
Eloquence Venise—etched with decoration #688.

The platinum decoration was seemingly the most popular because it was offered for three additional years: 1970-1977.

I believe, with the mention of the etching *Venise*, this is the time to discuss another rather arbitrary factor in Fostoria glass nomenclature. Many readers will know this, but there might be some who have not mulled it about long enough to draw conclusions. Those expert Fostoria collectors will have realized a mistake was made when *Venise* was identified above as *Eloquence Venise*. The word "*Eloquence*" has no place here: it was added merely for clarification.

Let me try to explain logically. There are three manners in which a Fostoria glass shape is named. Let me use a goblet as an example. The first possible name is simply the number of the blank, say #5099. The blank #5099 can appear with various colored bowls, but the goblet itself only appears in rose and topaz (a pale yellow). When the goblet blank #5099 is etched, the etching becomes the name. For example: blank #5099 when etched in the Versailles (etching #278), the Trojan (etching #280), or the Kashmir (etching #283) design, the goblet is immediately known by one of those names: blank #5099 disappears as a name. The paper labels bear the names *Versailles, Trojan, Kashmir.*

Here is the true *Eloquence* with crystal bowl and onyx base. Shown is the tall sherbet (5.75"). The bowl is "non-optic." Price: $30-35.

These are the first two ways of naming a Fostoria line of glassware.

The third can be a combination. Take blank #6127. Fostoria (or the designer) gave this blank a specific name: *Festive*—and the line is known by this name. Take blank #6126. Fostoria (or Ben Seibel, the designer) named this blank *Wimbledon*—and the line is known by this name.

However, when *Festive* receives the etching (#35) called *Serenity*, the name of the line changes from *Festive* to *Serenity* and *Serenity* appears on the label.

And when *Wimbledon* is etched with *Tara* (#34) the name changes to *Tara*. To describe *Tara*, the collector usually states: *Tara* appears on blank #6126: notice terminology bypasses the name *Wimbledon*. Ditto for *Serenity*.

Thus if a glassware line is etched, the line's name is the name of the etching. Lines without etching are known by the blank number, or if the blank has been given a specific name, the line is known by this name.

The *Eloquence* footed ice tea (6.75") in crystal. It also bears decoration 687—the platinum rim band. Price: $30-35. This suggested price is approximately the same as undecorated; but, if it bore the etching *Venise*, the price would be $40-45.

Module (2824)

This pressed stemware pattern fits most comfortably in the mood of Mid-Century-Modern, but it is virtually unknown by those collectors who avidly acquire this style of ware. *Module* is also scarce, and this is very understandable seeing it was produced for only a few years (1970-1972). The possibility also exists that its very modern shape was not then popular.

If the reader will look carefully at the photograph, he/she will see an example of regular optic—a band running top to bottom. These optics are subtly decorative in themselves and pleasantly break up the surface of the glass into interesting planes. Regular, and narrow, this optic (because it runs vertically) lends a sense of needed height to some shapes. This occurs with *Module*.

A very short line, *Module* consists of only three stems: a large tumbler called the ice tea (13 oz.), the goblet (9 oz.), and the wine/juice (5 oz.). The latter two have the heavy flared stem that is the trademark of the pattern. Some critics place a nappy and a dessert plate with the three, but others do not.

The consumer had the choice of three colors: Dusk, Sunshine, and crystal. Dusk is shown in the photograph: it has definite amethyst undertones and is, by the way, the same color as *Pebble Beach*'s Black Pearl. I have never caught a glimpse of the color Sunshine, but I would venture a bet it is the same as Lemon Twist.

I like *Module*. I appreciate its daring difference and bold modern charm. It certainly stands out broadly from the general run of tall, elegant, conservative stems. With daring, I place *Module* in the same category as Roseville Raymor: they both present a strikingly new way to look at tableware—and, I also believe, they would match perfectly on the dining room table.

Module is the one line of Seibel Fostoria that might, just might, fit into the Mid-Century-Modern category—although it was produced from 1970-1972. Note the regular optics. It is quite scarce and appears in crystal, Dusk (shown here), and Sunrise. I have never seen the last named color, but I assume (if Dusk is dark) it is a yellowish tint. The larger piece is the goblet: the other is the wine juice. The only other piece is the 13 oz. ice tea. Prices for both range from $14-16.

Corsage Plum (6126)

With *Corsage Plum* the reader must follow through some rather convoluted discussion. It simply has a rather complicated story behind it! This pattern certainly fits into the category of elegant, conservative stemware, but, interestingly, *Corsage Plum* has a family and, as often happens within families, problems arise.

Let us put things in order. First, this pattern dates from 1973-1974, and this is the shortest span of any of Seibel's work for Fostoria. The base and the straight ribbed stem are topped with a nine petalled blossom that can be only fully appreciated by looking down at it from the bowl. The color of these sections is officially "plum," but the color changes with the light. Against the light of my computer screen (as I type this) it loses its pink tones and becomes pure lavender; on a brown wood tabletop it looks tan. *Corsage Plum* is a highly changeable lady!

There are no optics.

Left at the above situation, this stemware line would be very similar in standing to *Precedence*—one of the many fitting the category of graceful, formal, Fostoria glassware. But, there is, as you remember, a family.

In 1974—one year after the introduction of *Corsage Plum*—*Wimbledon* was introduced and ran until 1982. This was a reasonably long run for Fostoria stemware. *Wimbledon* is only found in crystal and has a bowl with regular optics. Except for the crystal stem and the optics, *Wimbledon's* shape is exactly the same as *Corsage Plum*.

In 1980, another variation appeared and continued until 1982. This pattern was titled *Gazebo*, and was exactly the same except that the base, stem, and "blossom" were black. In fact, so dark as to make unnoticeable the beauty of the "blossom."

Finally, in 1981 and running also until 1982, the third variation occurred: *Gazebo Rust*. This line again was the same except the bottom half of the glass was a honey amber now called "rust."

All three of the named variations had regular optic bowls: only *Corsage Plum* was plain.

During all my research, only *Corsage Plum* was ever attributed to Ben Seibel. It was the first, so perhaps it can be assumed Seibel designed the pattern with a plain bowl, and seven, eight years later Fostoria adapted the original design into three new ones with completely new names. The most interesting item in this story is that *Corsage Plum* never stands alone but always appears as a variation of *Wimbledon*. Except for a careful reading of the dates, the collector would believe *Wimbledon* was premier in this strange little family. So, the collector really has four lines (actually five) for the price of one! Or something like that!

What pieces belong to the family? Only four.

- Goblet, 7" (12 oz.)
- Wine, 5.75" (7 oz.)
- Champagne, saucer, 5.75" (9 oz.)
- Ice tea, footed, 6" (13 oz.)

Quite a great deal of maneuvering for such a small number of items.

Looking directly down into the bowl, only the plum "petaling" presents such a lovely sight.

The beautiful *Corsage Plum*—a part of the *Wimbledon* line—was made only through 1973-1974. It has no optics, unlike the others making up this "family." The color is terms "plum" but it is really amethyst—a most lovely soft tint. There are only four items: shown here (left to right) saucer champagne (also termed tall sherbet), goblet, wine, and footed ice tea. There were also some matching 7" plates. Prices: All prices run about the same: $25-30.

Centennial II Collection

Here is a large and varied collection of lead crystal gift items. It must certainly contain a number of Seibel creations since it was introduced in 1970 and some items continued until the year of his death (1985). Unfortunately, the only two pieces that can be identified are 2828/111 and 2828/157. The former being a round 6" ashtray, and the latter a 6.50" bud vase. Both ran from 1974 to 1978. These have been also identified as the "zigzag" pieces mentioned in Seibel's letter to Edward Kennedy dated February 10, 1972.

When I turned to Emily Seate for advice, she replied:

> *You are running into the same difficulty we did* [Ms. Seate and her mother Milbra Long during their research for their Fostoria books] *when dealing with lead crystal and late production items. When the numbering system changed, it became a real challenge to follow a piece. Most likely, the numbers for which you search were included in catalogs and price guides as LE-??? Or some other two-letter configuration followed by numbers. Wouldn't it be wonderful to be able to find pictures of all these?!*

Until some research can translate all the many new numberings into the older four-digit identification we can only wonder and surmise. At least, the researcher has a list of the Seibel items.

Wimbledon (6126)

Wimbledon (1974-1982) is simply *Corsage Plum* in crystal with regular optics. During these eight years, *Wimbledon* was also available with etching #34 *Tara*. Jon Saffell acknowledges this line as a Ben Seibel design. An interesting point: *Wimbledon* is the name under which the others appear. There does not seem to be any logical reason for this except, perhaps, this version had the longest production run, and, no doubt, sold well. For a general review, please see the discussion under *Corsage Plum*.

When this line appears in crystal it is called *Wimbledon*—and here is a footed ice tea. Note it bears the regular optics. Prices for *Wimbledon* tend to be slightly less. The suggested price for this footed ice tea would be $18-20.

Serenity champagne in crystal. Price: $20-22.

Serenity (etching #35)

Jon Saffell lists *Serenity* as both a blank and an etching and states it was designed by Ben Seibel. However, I believe he is referring to blank #6127, a line that has received the name *Festive*. Thus, I strongly suggest that *Festive* must be a Seibel design.

Serenity appears in three versions:

- Crystal (1975-1982)
- Yellow bowl (1975-1980)
- Blue bowl (1976-1982)

Here is *Serenity* and it is so marked on the paper label. The shape is *Festive* with the *Serenity* etching. Shown is the goblet with the yellow bowl, and the claret (blue bowl). Actually, *Festive* is much harder to find than *Serenity*. Prices: Goblet, $22-24; Claret, $24-26.

The *Serenity* etching (#35).

Festive (6127)

Festive is placed here on my assumption it is a Seibel design. It was used as the base for the *Serenity* etching. The only possibility for *Festive* to NOT be a Seibel design is if he designed ONLY the etching: this seems unreasonable. Also, Seibel ordered quite a few examples of *Festive* for gifts and for his own personal use. He ordered *Wimbledon, Monarch*, and *York* in the same manner. *Ergo!*

While I have not been able to procure examples of this line, the reader can look at the illustrations of *Serenity* and in the mind's eye strip away the etching and see *Festive*. This line is the only example of a Seibel pattern in looped optic, and *Festive* has the same three versions, as does *Serenity*.

Monarch (2903)

Monarch has an story attached to it. There are five items in this stemware line, all commencing in 1979, but two of these pieces did double duty and were made until 1986—four years after the other three ceased production. The highball and double old-fashioned were labeled as "barware" and accompanied the *Kimberly* pattern (2990). The oval cuttings at the top and bottom of *Monarch* match the cuttings of *Kimberly*. Both lines were produced in pressed lead crystal. Barware seems to be the designation given to a highball and double old-fashioned meant to coordinate with a larger more extensive line.

To satisfy a whim, I took my one *Kimberly* stems—a 6" tall sherbet—and the *Monarch* highball and without comment showed both to a friend. After looking closely at both and commenting the design was the same, he stated whoever designed one, designed the other. Interesting thought. *Kimberly*, like *Monarch*, is heavy pressed lead crystal, and the pressed design is the same—except on the rounded *Kimberly* bowls where the "arrowhead" indentation is wider to fill the space.

Monarch (#2903) is pressed lead crystal and is known as "barware." The double old-fashioned is on the left, the tall highball to the right. In the center is the *Kimberly* (#2990) tall sherbet. The former was expressly designed to accompany the latter. Both lines are very heavy, but quite inexpensive. Prices: Old-fashioned, $8-10; Highball, $10-12; *Kimberly* sherbet, $15-18. All are eminently usable.

There are five pieces of *Kimberly*: goblet, 7.50"; wine, 6.50"; sherbet, 6"; champagne flute, 7.50"; and magnum, 7.50". Like *Gourmet*, this line had two decorations: a platinum band and a gold band encircling the rim. The time of production—1979-1986—coincides perfectly with the years of *Monarch*. Is it logical that Fostoria would commission Seibel to create the latter line and someone else to adapt the same design for *Kimberly*—or visa versa?

Monarch is very heavy with deep facets that catch the light, and, in certain circumstances reflects a pale rainbow of colors. It is flared at the top and bottom, making the grasping and holding of such a heavy piece quite easy. Easy to grasp and easy to hold! It is easy, very easy, to use. The usability of this pattern can cause some minor mistakes. My barware set was being continually used until two highballs were broken and I realized even though this was modern glassware, it was no longer available for replacements—except, of course—at very high prices through special service companies. So I took the remaining glasses out of the kitchen cupboard: they are still used, but only for special occasions. This decision comes to all collectors: to use or not to use, and Ben Seibel's later glassware is so comfortable and beautiful—albeit practical—the collector desires to use it daily.

A complete set of *Monarch* consists of:

- Goblet, 6.50" (11 oz.)
- Ice tea, footed, 6.50" (14 oz.)
- Wine, 5.50" (6 oz.)

And the barware:

- Highball, 5.50" (12 oz.)
- Double old-fashioned, 3.50" (10 oz.)

Typically, Fostoria added an additional service piece: a small dessert or salad bowl. These were sold in sets of four and match the stemware exactly.

Monarch also offered small bowls as part of the line. Here the reader can see the elegant decorative pressings. Price: $8-10.

Close-up of the *Kimberly* decoration. Because of the shape of the sherbet, the "spear-like" indentations are wider than appear on *Monarch*.

York (2934)

York, the last of the official Fostoria lines created by Ben Seibel, is truly barware. It was produced from 1979 until 1982, and was advertised as pressed lead crystal—the same category as *Monarch*. It is, however, considerably heavier than *Monarch*: taller, straighter, with no gentling curves at top and base. The design is quartered indented diamonds that catch and return the light with even more sparkle than does *Monarch*. Place the two barware lines together—two highballs, two double old-fashioneds—and, in my opinion, *York* will win the contest. It is most impressive.

Being a true barware line, *York* contains just two pieces: the traditional highball (13 oz.) and double old-fashioned (10 oz.). Nothing else! And nothing else was needed because this barware shape was created to go along with the huge Fostoria *American* line. Actually, if a new collector looks at *York* briefly and without concentration, it could pass for *American*.

Why in 1979, did the Fostoria executives decide that *American* needed two new glasses? Although, if the reader will look at a page of *American* tumblers, none are as sturdy and tall as the *York* highball, and there is no double old-fashioned. Perhaps there was a market niche for these two pieces. Fostoria had good expectations regarding *York*, for in a letter written by David B. Danzell, Jr. (Vice President for Marketing) on August 21, 1980, he comments to Seibel: "The *York* pattern being offered with our *American* promotion has sold 6006 highballs and 3384 double old fashioned. This shows a good start of selling."

It should be noted that if Fostoria planned *Monarch* and *York* as complements to *Kimberly* and *American*, Seibel was certainly restricted in his design. There is, however, no evidence of this "restriction" in the correspondence.

The second barware line was *York*—even heavier than *Monarch*. Made as late as 1979-1982, it is relatively cheap and can be used (carefully) for everyday. The interesting note regarding this line is that it was specifically made to accompany the most famous of all the Fostoria lines, *American*. Prices: Old-fashioned, $8-10; Highball, $10-12.

When viewed casually, *York* seems to be the same as *American*. Notice how the double old-fashioned and the highball fit in with *American*'s regular tumbler, whiskey, and single old-fashioned (left to right).

Gazebo (2126)

Gazebo, with its clear regular optic bowl and onyx base, is simply a version of the earlier and more popular *Corsage Plum*. Thus it cannot be considered a new Seibel design. *Gazebo* was available from 1980-1982, and it must be assumed Ben Seibel approved of the change. Unfortunately, *Gazebo* was never mentioned in the correspondence.

Here is *Gazebo*: *Wimbledon* with a black stem. The pieces are exactly the same as those for *Corsage Plum*. Prices: all $18-20.

Gazebo Rust (2126)

The fourth of the "*Corsage Plum*" family had a limited run (1981-1982)—as limited as *Corsage Plum* itself (1973-1974). "Rust" is actually an amber color, and this hue has never been overly popular.

Thus the relationship between Fostoria and Ben Seibel existed from about 1960 until just before he died. For some twenty-five years, Seibel submitted drawings to the Fostoria design department: probably running into the hundreds.

There are some personal, unsubstantiated, and actually unfounded suspicions about a few other Fostoria patterns running about in my mind. We know that Seibel was definitely the designer of two barware lines, *Monarch* and *York*: the former to accompany the *Kimberly* stemware; the latter *American* stemware. There is other barware in similar production circumstances: for example *Heritage* (2887) was made to accompany *Radiance* (3113).[10] Might researchers in the near future discover more Ben Seibel Fostoria designs? This might be very possible!

Gazebo Rust: *Wimbledon* with an amber stem. Pieces and prices are the same as *Gazebo*.

Miscellaneous Ben Seibel Not To Be Missed

Introductory Note Concerning Gilley, Inc.

The discovery of new information involving Gilley, Inc. necessitates the insertion of some explanatory information. The following section of Gilley will stand as first written for it is, in general, correct.

While under the controlling aegis of the Raymor distribution organization, it is now understood that the role of Gilley is slightly more complex than once believed. Gilley, Inc., with headquarters in New York City, is really a production company and one should refer to its various designs as *Town House China* by Gilley or *Tempron Taste Tempters* by Gilley, and so on. The term "Gilley" standing alone refers to a number of lines just as the name Steubenville includes a number of individual dinnerware shapes.

Thus Ben Seibel designed separate lines for Gilley—and not all Gilley pieces can be attributed to him. In the past some collectors viewed Gilley/Seibel as synonymous. This can no longer be considered correct: Gilley, Inc. has become a blanket term covering at least four (and perhaps more) individual lines. These lines include:

Town House China: ceramic ware, most in soft white with brass, wood, and/or raffia.

Tempron: glassware with black metal with sea grass-wrapped handles or brass with black cord wrapped handles.

Copper and Milk Glass serving pieces.

Brass and Crystal serving accessories.

Chrome and Crystal serving accessories including the Chillit mixers.

More Gilley, Inc. lines by Seibel surely might be discovered in the future and the reader is encouraged to add them here if and when this material is identified. Seibel research is a growing proposition and researchers must be flexible enough to absorb new ideas and information.

The typical Gilley tag with Raymor taking pride of place.

Gilley, Royal Haeger, DeMaray, Tempron, Tea Kettles

These five categories do not fit together very well: the reader must be patient and accept this roughshod grouping. There is certainly no intended implication that "these are minor lines." If there was any hint of this, the committed Gilley collectors would march me briskly to the guillotine, and in recognition of this *faux pas*, I would stride along with them without complaint. Gilley can certainly demand pride of place, and there are many people who rightly find it a stunning and sophisticated line of tableware. Thus, with an apologetic mien this hodgepodge of subjects in linked together in one section.

Gilley Casual Serving Accessories

Of these four, Gilley is the best known—and considered by many collectors very important! The official designation is Casual Serving Accessories by Gilley. Serving accessories they certainly are, but not at all physically casual. The term "casual" seems to refer to the use of this most elegant line. Composed of glass, ceramics, metal, rattan, and wood created for the modern contemporary scene, the extensive list of serving pieces is sophisticated and sleek, urbanely cultured, absolutely *soigné*—elegant, precisely designed, modishly modern, and deco adaptable.

This is one of the many Raymor full-page advertisements that appeared in home and design magazines during the 1950s. Covering a wide assortment of products for the home, this advertisement appeared in *Living for Young Homemakers*, May 1955. Raymor represented such companies as Howard Miller Clock, Ravenware, Woodline-Hall, and a variety of industrial designers. The Gilley "Juice or Cocktail" designed by Ben Seibel appears at the upper left.

Gilley was another line under the indirect aegis of Raymor and it was strongly marketed in the 1950s—in fact, it was often seen advertised by Raymor along with *Contempora*, Jenfred, Ravenware, and bar furniture by Woodlin-Hall. As the Raymor tag states:

> *The Raymor tag is the hallmark of design achievement in home furnishings. It identifies authoritative contemporary pieces created by the world's foremost designers.*

This is known as the "Chillit." Ice is placed within the metal tube to cool the liquid without dilution—a clever idea practiced by many designer, but rarely in such a sophisticated manner. Price: $20-25.

The owner of the above "Chillit" was clever enough to keep the tag safe within the piece.

There are two intriguing quarter-page advertisements in the August 1957 issue of *The Gift and Art Buyer* listing some Gilley products. Gilley, Inc. was located at 240 East 152nd Street, Bronx 51, New York. The upper advertisement listed the following:

Bucket (FC-104) 2-quart, Pyrex lines, brass base, handle and knob, china cover.

China cup (FC-364) with polished brass base.

Celery dish (FC-80), 14" x 5". Cane-wrapped handle.

Martini/coffee server (FC-69), 42-oz., brass collar and cane-wrapped handle, chrome brass-tipped spoon.

Coffee pot (FCE-60), 16 cups, with electric warmer, brass collar and cover, brass base.

All the above pieces are illustrated. Other pieces are listed as being casseroles, trays, condiment sets, decanter sets, pitchers, punch and salad bowls. These pieces are labeled Town House China, distributed by Richards-Morgenthau & Company, New York and Chicago. The "Richards" is Irving Richards of Raymor.

The lower advertisement showed the following:

Triple susan server (3333-W), 10", walnut base with brass trim, three 12" shaped glass removable platters.

Martini mixer (609-W), 42 oz. with stirrer.

Casserole (684-W), 2-quart, brass with cover, with candle warmer.

The major distributor was William H. Fenton, Inc., New York City, but also Monogram Glass Company of Chicago, Peter Goff in Los Angeles, and Joe Silverman in Miami. It seems that Gilley produced its own items and Raymor was only the distributor—sharing this honor with William H. Fenton, Inc. also of New York City.

One example of the many Gilley Chillit cocktail servers. A very practical idea. Price: $30-35.

If the Gilley pieces have a problem, it is that they are NOT marked in any manner considered permanent. They came with tags—tags most often torn off and lost years ago except when removed and placed inside the piece and thus preserved. Gilley pieces are often sold as Russel Wright, some as Ben Seibel, but without the tag who could really know? As I write these words there sits before me a lovely single 7" candleholder of simple but exquisite charm. It has a tag—yet without this identification, I could only say "this looks likes Gilley." With such popular product appeal, other manufacturers climbed aboard the "look-alike" bandwagon and produced items obviously based upon some Seibel/Gilley designs. So, without the tag, who could be absolutely sure? Here the role of the researcher becomes difficult. While I am not well versed in Gilley-iana (this is boldly admitted), I understand just enough to know some advertisements blatantly announcing this and that are examples of Russel Wright are really touting a Ben Seibel design. Everyone knows that advertisements do not always tell the truth! One must learn true examples of Gilley ware one by one, slowly, surely. This is the point that separates the casual Seibel collectors from those "who know!" A strange occurrence when so many of the experts insist that the piece must be labeled "Ben Seibel" before it can be attributed to him. This belief simply does not work!

Even though the Gilley Casual accessories were rooted in the 1950s, it does have the air of the sophisticated 1930s. The pieces are pure tableware, used alone or in conjunction with other lines. There are no plates but mostly service pieces revolving about alcoholic beverages: the dry martini was pre-eminent. In my mind's eye, I catch glimpses of Nick Charles swizzling up a round of those extra dry martinis before lunch and before tackling Nora or solving a mystery. If Jenfred conjures leather armchairs, smoking jackets, and book-lined libraries, Gilley snaps with sleek sophistication: men in tuxedoes and ladies in clinging backless gowns. Gilley drink ware, barware, and serving ware is brittle and heady: I enjoy it, but only from a distance.

The engraved mark at the bottom of the martini shaker.

The Town House martini set by Gilley: smoothly elegant and very chic. It appealed to the so-called sophisticates of its day. Price: $35-40.

Another pitcher in the same lovely ivory ceramics. Plumper than the first pitcher, this one seems more likely made for lemonade or ice tea. Price: $35-40.

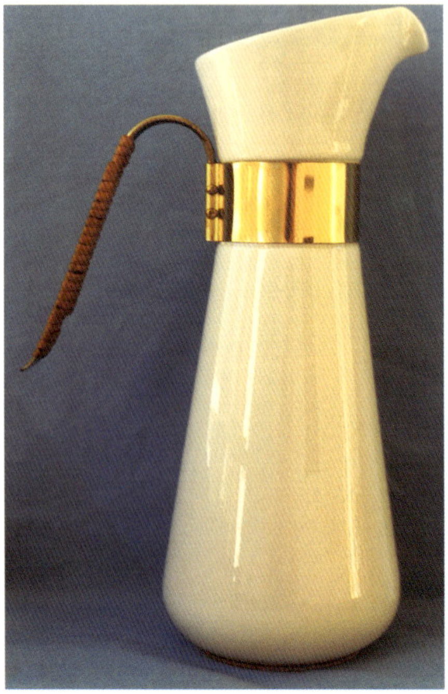

Known as a pitcher but seen described as a martini mixer in an advertisement, this is long, thin, and "Nick Charles" elegant. With a brass collar and a rattan-wrapped handle, this piece was important on the "cocktail circuit." Price: $40-45.

Notice the smooth porcelain cup fit into the copper base. The cups are not supposed to be removable. This cup just happened to come loose.

The elegant Town House samovar in place: seated securely on its electric warmer and accompanied by the sugar and creamer. Quite an exciting set.

Seibel designed samovars for Gilley also. This statuesque piece bears a little resemblance to the *Forum International Stoneware* samovar in that the two handles at the top counteract the wideness of the bottom. This is, however, more than just a samovar: it is part of a coffee set. The samovar resides on an electric warmer positioned on one side of a low metal frame with wooden handles. To the other side, in their own little holding spaces, are the sugar and creamer. The sugar has the same type of lid as does the samovar. An example of how, sadly, these items get separated. Price (just the samovar): $25-30.

The electric warmer tray with space for the samovar and two holders for the cream and sugar.

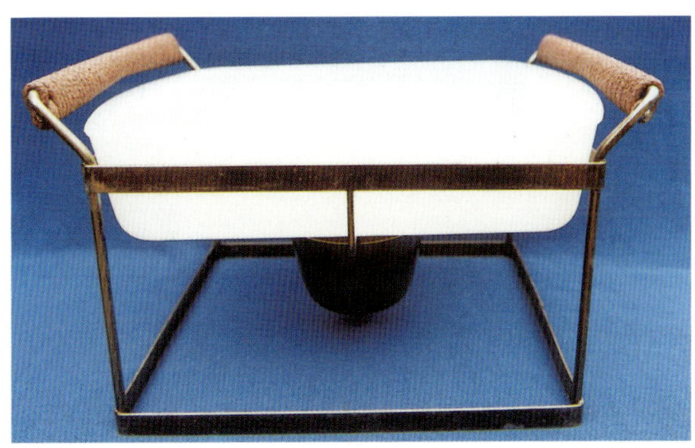

A stunning and simple example of Gilley's Copper and Milk Glass line. It is a 2-quart milk glass casserole (MK-6) with a single candle warmer, copper cover, and stand. The cover has disappeared. The handles are wrapped in brown cord. Price (if complete): $20-25. A double unit also was offered. Other pieces in this line included three sizes of round butter/sauce warmers (MK-1, 2, and 3), a round 2-quart casserole with stand and warmer, a 3-quart soup tureen with stand and warmer, and a startlingly sized (23" x 4.50") casserole server with warmers and stand. There were four individual round casseroles in this serving piece—all with copper covers. These items are very desired by advanced collectors and, if complete, can be priced very high.

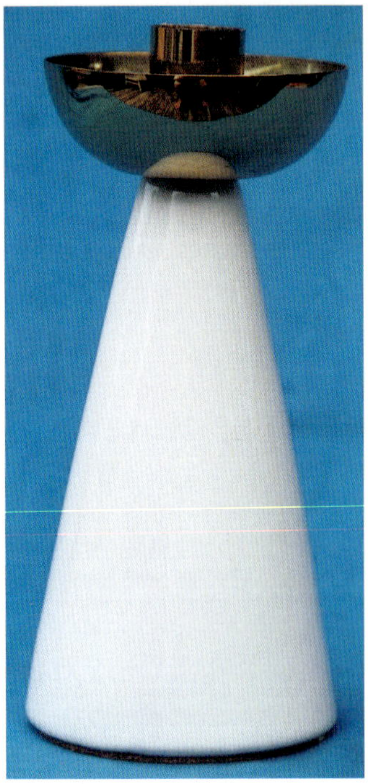

The small Gilley candleholder—barely 7" tall, it has a simple yet commanding presence. Price: $20-25.

The candleholder adorned. One of the most attractive pieces in my Seibel collection. Perhaps the candle and flowers should be white?

The Gilley coffee set: the glass is Pyrex. Smart, sophisticated, and clever, I predict collecting Gilley items will grow as more people become aware of their pure elegance. Price (for set): $50-60.

Tempron by Gilley

Originally the pieces produced under the name *Tempron* were quite unknown. This is not to say these pieces have suddenly "swam brightly into our ken" but due to the help of a Canadian acquaintance, Mr. Iain Baird, we suddenly know much more than was first reported.

There now is proven connection between the Richards Morganthau Company, Gilley, Inc, and *Tempron*—all three are bound with cords of unified interest. In fact, my information states that Tempron was a subsidiary of Gilley, or, if that term is too strong, at least, closely connected—one with the other. This accounts for a series of advertisements wherein the reader cannot tell where the Gilley pieces stop and *Tempron* begins. I dare not submit that glass pieces of Gilley are *Tempron* (if that makes sense) but it might be suitable at this time to state that Gilley produced ceramic serving pieces, and *Tempron* included glass and ironware serving pieces. The two lines are closely linked—almost intertwined.

An advertising statement proudly declares: "The manufacturer [Gilley?], proud of the designs and craftsmanship of Tempron...offers Taste Tempters of people of good taste." And Ben Seibel is accredited in writing!

It is definitely recognized that not all Gilley pieces were designed by Ben Seibel. Dare I use the expression of the Seibel-esque masters-at-large and state: "Some Gilley items simply do not LOOK like the work of Ben Seibel?" There are a few photographs in this section that are incised with Gilley identification, but certainly do not have the flowing aspect of Seibel's designs. Could we just agree that Ben Seibel worked on the ceramic *Town House* line and the glass/ironware[1] line *Tempron*? These two are closely allied, mingle well, and could compliment each other on the same buffet table.

There is a wide diversity of pieces in the *Tempron* accessories line—many more than originally believed—but all are glassware[2] "clasped in wrought iron"—so say the advertisers. Most of the handles are wrapped in sea grass. The general aspect is light, low, and rectangular, although some shapes are rounded: with the smaller ones ball-shaped. The clarity of the material allows for excellent food presentation—the hostess must pay attention to the colors of relishes, salads, or soups. The only color visible on the *Tempron* pieces seem to be the lids of the jam and marmalade set, the shaker set, and the sugar bowl: these have been seen in orange, yellow, and black. Other colors probably exist.

What follows is a list of known *Tempron* items. All pieces are fitted with metal frames: those asterisked (*) have polished brass frames.

Pyrex™ platter, rectangular (BW1233)
Pyrex platter, square (BW1222)
Pyrex pie plate, round (BW1210)
Jam & marmalade (or relish) w/spoons (BW365-22)
Torte tray, round 14" (BW3514)
Torte tray w/center cheese board, round, 17" (BW3527)
Torte tray/lazy susan, round, 14" (3544-BR) *
Torte tray/lazy susan, round 16" (3546-BR) *
Flat tray, round, 14" (BW3114)
Tid-bit, 2 small round trays (BW48)
Relish & cheese board tray, rectangular (BW1220)
Relish (triple) carrier, 24" x 4" (123-BR) *
Relish (double) carrier, 17" x 4" (122-BR) *
Jam & marmalade or relish combination (two small glass bowls w/covers, two small square and four larger rectangular receptacles) (BW1265)
Casserole w/cover, 1 quart (BW1682)
Casserole w/cover and burner, 1 quart (BW1684)[3]
Casserole w/cover, 2 quarts (BW1684)
Casserole w/cover and burner, 2 quarts (BW2684)[3]
Double casseroles w/covers, 1 quart each (BW2682)
Double casseroles w/covers and two burners, 1 quart each (BW2684)
Salt & pepper (BW363-11)
Sugar & creamer set (BW365-33)
Sugar w/spoon & creamer set, brass tray (65-BR) *
Bowl, salad or punch, round 13" (BW3513)
Bowl, party punch (removable rack to hold twelve tapered 4 oz. glasses) (3563-BR) *

Bowl, salad, round 10" w/ brass base, removable (3511-BR) *
Bowl, divided salad, round 10" (BW3510)
Cruet set (oil, vinegar, salt, pepper in narrow rectangular frame) (BW7553)
Oil & vinegar set (BW755)
Double vegetable, two rectangular Pyrex receptacles (BW2212)
Vegetable & platter combination, three rectangular Pyrex receptacles (BW3312)
Bowl, divided mayonnaise w/ spoon, 5" (BW3508)
Bowl, divided mayonnaise w/ two spoons, 6" (58-BR) *
Buffet set, four rectangular receptacles w/ covers (BW1251)
Bar tray server w/ ten highball glasses (BW4310)
Beverage carafe w/ warmer, 16 cups, Pyrex (BWS61)
Beverage carafe, 8 cups, Pyrex, w/ sugar & creamer (BW59)
Beverage carafe, 8 cups, Pyrex w/ burner, brass stopper, and base (72-BR) *
Martini set, (mixer, stirrer, eight ball glasses) (BW6078)
Martini set (mixer with handle 42 oz., stirrer) (67-BR) *
Martini set (mixer 30 oz., brass handled tray, six roly-poly glasses) (578-BR) *
Martini set (mixer with handle 22 oz., stirrer) (66-BR) *
Roly-poly glass, 5 oz. w/ brass ring (34-BR) *
Cordial set (decanter 28 oz., brass tray, eight 2 oz. cordial glasses) (529-BR) *
Decanter set (three decanters, brass carrier) (549-BR) *
Ice bowl w/ handle, 2 quarts, brass base (59-BR) *

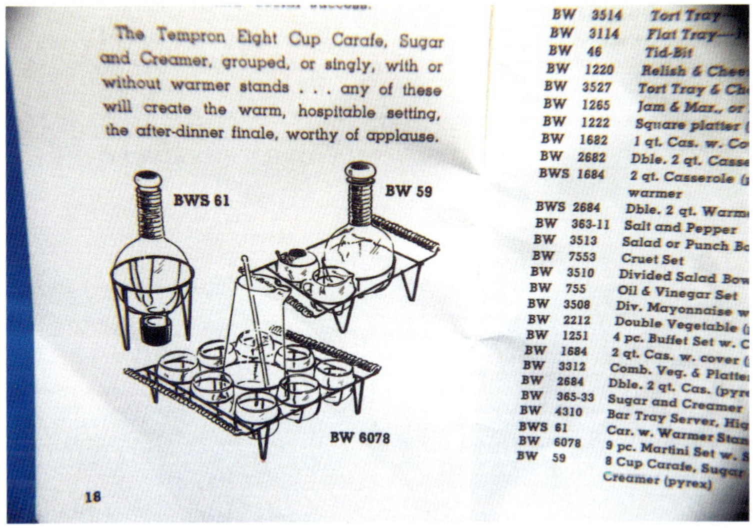

The collector can perceive *Tempron* exists in a wide variety of individual pieces and, except for its elusiveness, should be considered a major accomplishment. Certainly, *Tempron* is more graceful and delicate than the *Forum International* foursome. The problem is, like Gilley, the pieces are tagged, not marked. Perhaps the above list will provide an identification list for those who enjoy a glass/metal combination. Surely, *Tempron* deserves much wider exposure among less specialized collectors: it is an stimulating challenge, to collect, and an exciting change from the more accessible work of this master designer.

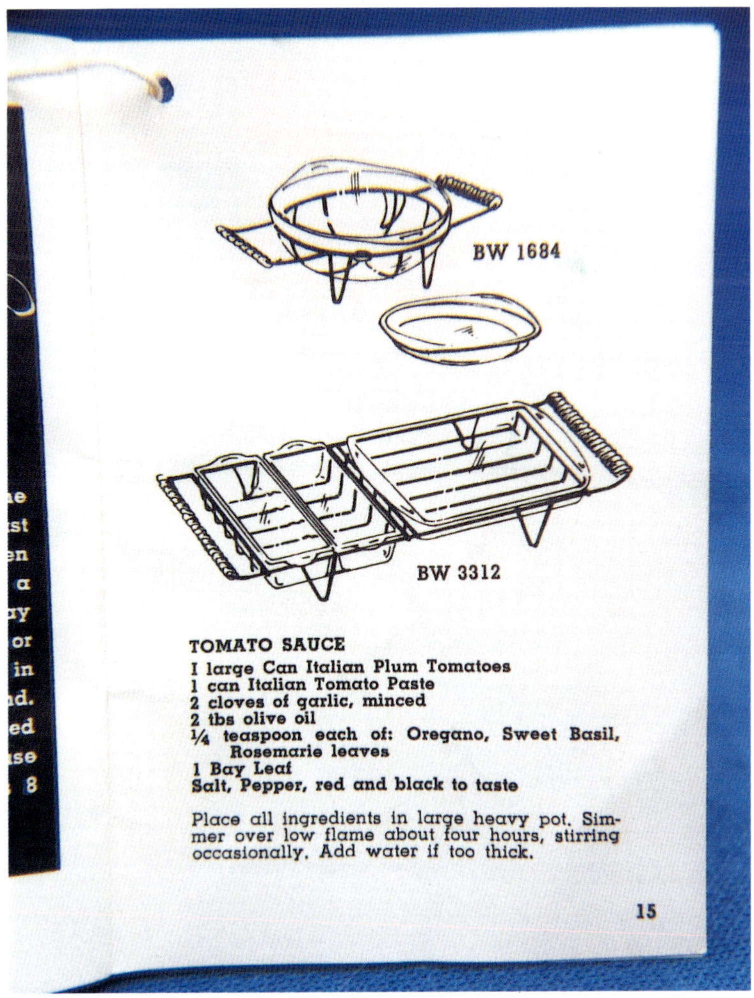

This whole page:
Excerpts from a *Tempron* brochure that includes simple recipes to serve in the various pieces.

Royal Haegar Potteries

The Royal Haegar pottery line (c. 1971) is the antithesis of the Gilley line of casual serving pieces. Whereas the latter is martini sophisticated and has drawing room ambience, the Haegar stoneware is totally rustic, sturdy, and peasant cottage orientated. It reminds one of ice tea or snappy lemonade! There is great honesty about the orange and sandstone picnic-patio line. It is a buffetware with which one can feel totally at ease. No underlying current of striving to be better: Royal Haegar Potteries Stoneware is simply what it is, and no hedging about the need to be lofty. I am very fond of this line, but have seen very little. Very scarce might be the phrase to use.

The pieces are ovenproof, and while there are no actual plates there is a square—with rounded corners—snack tray that is a very solid, practical substitution. A tall mug can be placed on this 10" x 7" tray. There are baking dishes, casseroles, individual covered ramekins, and again one of the designer's favorite pieces—a warmer. All are marked "Royal Haeger," but none seen bear the name Seibel.

The actual pieces are:

Piece	Number
Snack tray, 10" x 7"	(3207)
Rectangular baking dish, 6.50" x 10"	(3209)
Rectangular baking dish, 8.50" x 13"	(3208)
Casserole, covered, handled, round, 10"	(3205)
Casserole, covered, round, 7"	(3210)
Warmer for the above	(3206)
Ramekin, covered, round, 5"	(3211)
Bowl, salad, round, 10"	(3212)
Bowl, salad, round, 7"	(3213)
Salt	(3214)
Pepper	(3215)
Mug	(4240)
Pitcher, 6.50"	(4241)

Completely adequate for what it was designed to do—rough and tumble cooking, serving, and heavy enough to be childproof. My collection of this stoneware is miniscule, but I have seen an advertisement sheet. Here is another case where I ask readers to share a photograph or two.

A pale gray Gilley cook pot—it still works. The trim is teak and aluminum. The name "Gilley, New York" is incised in the base of the ceramic pot and might be an example of a non-Seibel design. Price: $15-20.

The Royal Haegar back stamp. No mention of Ben Seibel, but he has been given full credit is advertisements.

DeMaray

Notice we are getting progressively more mysterious. DeMaray is really rare. I have owned only four small, squat covered individual casseroles—one without its lid. This one and another covered example were given away. With two left, I decided to see if anyone wanted to trade one of these small, yet heavy, pieces for another DeMaray item, and thus placed a notice on the Russel Wright board. No one was interested.

Including the two short, stout handles, these ramekins are 7.75" round, but only 2" high. Mine are glazed cocoa brown inside and pale yellow outside. The base in dry—unglazed. Each piece seems to have been individually signed—all four had similar, but differently executed, signatures as if hurriedly written with a permanent marker:

DeMaray
5101
Ben Seibel
Design

There are other known pieces: a small bowl, 6.25" round with a pale lime green interior glaze and a wood-grained finish outside. This piece is numbered 5102. There is also a water pitcher with a set of mugs; but, unfortunately, this group is owned by a collector who will not share even a mere description, much less a photograph.

If any reader IS willing to help unravel the real mystery of this DeMaray line, any information received would be joyously acknowledged and shared with other Seibel devotees.

Attached to this group—but certainly not as an afterthought—is a well-designed series of tea kettles. Highly useful and strikingly designed, these teakettles were produced for the SFC Association in Japan, and are prime examples of a perfect fit for their stated function.

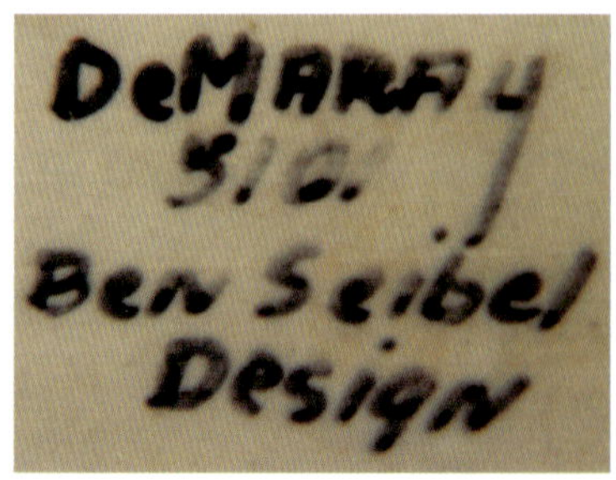

The handwritten (?) identification of my one DeMaray piece.

The low individual casserole. The cover does not fit very well, and the finial does not allow for ease of removal. Can any collector date this item for us? Price: $10-12.

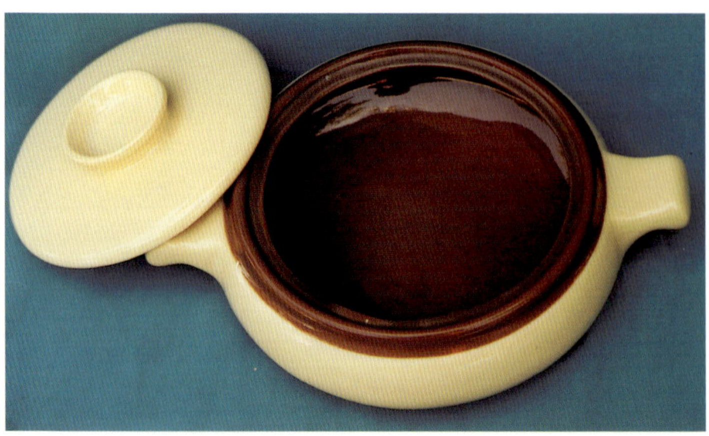

A favorite utilitarian pitcher. It would be used often except for its comparative rarity. This piece is 6.50" high. Please notice the spout—perfectly designed for accurate pouring. This stoneware came only in this handsome orange/sandstone finish. Price: $30-40.

The box—quite a collectible also.

The bottom of the Bubble Pot. Clearly Japanese produced and Seibel designed.

The SFC teakettle comes in two known version—and there may be others: the very popular *Bubble Pot*, and the less known *Whistle Pot*. Both are pure Mid-Century-Modern joys: graceful in shape, perfect in balance, neat, clean, and crisp in outline. The two problems with which a metal teakettle might snare the unwary are (1) it gets too hot to hold and (2) it becomes too heavy when filled with water—boiling water—to safely lift. Ben Seibel designed his teakettle so well that these dangerous possibilities are eschewed.

And what a Fiesta-like selection of color graces the *Bubble* and *Whistle* pots: clear primary colors in red, green, sunflower yellow, delft blue, and glossy rich black: color with meaning.

The *Bubble Pot* has a shorter spout, an attached lid easily maneuvered by a hinge on the handle. The *Whistle Pot* is more traditional with a detachable lid topped by a large, easily grasped, low finial, and a longer, more slender spout. Both handles easily fit the hand, and both pots sit securely and safely on the burner—no tipping here.

A Ben Seibel collection is not complete without an example of both these teakettles! The designs mentioned in this section could be said to be linked together by one condition: outside of the area of the avid Ben Seibel collector they are relatively unknown. DeMaray pieces remain a mystery, *Royal Haeger Stoneware* is only slightly better known, *Tempron*, and its connection to Gilley, Inc. has not yet been fully explored, and the Gilley *Town House China*, while more recognized, is still elusive and shadowy to the general public. And who would have believed such practical and useable items as the SFC teakettles could colorfully grace our contemporary stove tops?

Certainly, more research is needed. This book should be regarded as a living, unfinished, and growing resource. Penciled notes and comments in the margins, inserted jottings and opinions, questions rapidly scrawled or painstakingly penned, will, over the years, greatly enhance the value of any collectible book. At this juncture, the readers can contribute magnificently to the subject of Ben Seibel Tableware.

Two shakers: these are sturdy pieces measuring 4.25" high standing on a base nearly 2.50" round. Both have the same number and size of holes, so it is thought they are both salt shakers. Seibel usually carefully distinguished between the pepper and the salt. Price: (set) $15-18.

DeMaray tumbler (#5302). Price: $40-45.

The teakettle itself. A perfectly designed piece. Notice there is no need for a finial because the lid is raised from the handle. Beautifully balanced, safe, and easy to use. Price: $25-30.

The Function of Form

Now that the reader is nearing the end of this account of the tableware designs of Ben Seibel, questions must arise regarding the comparative value of each individual line. How do they compare one to the other? Not in the terms of collector popularity, but how the designed form of each line fulfills its stated or implied function.

A number of individual pieces in a number of modern tableware shapes are exceptionally dramatic in form but tend to fall short in useful functionality. This problem rarely appeared in older dinnerware, although a non-functioning item was occasionally offered to the public. Usually this errant piece disappeared quickly. A very well known example of this event is the *Fiesta* covered onion soup. It was a charming little piece, and, as we all know, in great demand among today's collectors, yet did not fulfill its function. Really, a cover has no place perched upon an onion soup bowl, and the bowl itself must be able to undergo a bout beneath the broiler to crisp and melt the topping of toast and cheese. To place a cover on such a delightful melted mixture would "soggy" it all up. A real mess!

As a matter of curiosity, I have read many recipes for onion soup and all require this moment of truth under the broiler. To serve onion soup—true onion soup—in the *Fiesta* bowl, one would have to do the broiler business in a simple oven safe utensil, then scoop all the contents out and rearrange in the *Fiesta*—with a complete loss of presentation. Alas, hardly worth the effort. So this little piece, so popularly displayed on the shelves of modern collectors, was cancelled. It was a nicely formed little covered bowl that simply did not meet its stated function. Presto! Gone!

The desire for the stretched and sculptural look caused some Mid-Century-Modern ceramic designers to go to such lengths as to render a number of their shapes nearly impossible to use. Because of the stature of these designers, and the desire of the public for "anything new," a good number of these designs were produced, marketed, and accepted by the consumers—accepted not because the form complied with the function, but simply because that form was attractive, elegant, and modern.

A digression: the powerful, but perplexing, designer known as Erte has been mentioned before within these pages. Born in St. Petersburg, Russia, as Romain de Tirtoff in 1892, he was the *enfant terrible* within his family. Fleeing Russia at the age of nineteen, he settled in Paris and over the years became a noted fashion, stage, and ceramic designer. His *nom de plume* (Erte) was devolved from the French pronunciation of his initials, "R.T." In 1925, at the invitation of Louis B. Mayer, he traveled to Hollywood to design costumes for the motion pictures. While his costume designs were fabulously beautiful, they were functionally disastrous: the actresses could walk slowly and deliberately when dressed in an Erte costume, but any type of sustained acting or inspired movement was impossible. Erte left Hollywood within the year.

Here I feel that explanation is necessary. I rarely fault a shape itself—some dinnerware shapes are extremely beautiful, absolutely stunning in their sculptural essence, even becoming works of individual art. But when this beautiful piece of art cannot—because of its form—carry out it stated function, then something is amiss! Or am I wrong? Do we simply worship a fantastically lovely teapot that (1) dribbles incessantly when the hostess attempts to pour, or (2) is so heavy when filled with tea that a lady wrestler is needed to heave it from the table? This is a clear case of an exalted form dominating any possible function.

And what about those graceful, elegant, shallow and wide champagne glasses that allow all the expensively acquired bubbles to dissipate before the second sip. And if a designer adds a hollow stem under the flat bowl, the glass becomes a horror to clean beside the loss of all those snappy little bubbles! Glassware designers create this type of item over and over, and the public buys over and over. Is this marketing hype or a misplaced sense of fashion?

It is not particularly easy to create a stunning form that functions just as beautifully. This is where the genius of the great industrial designer bubbles forth to give the consumer the tulip-shaped champagne glass, the lidless onion soup bowl built to stand the heat, or the perfectly arched handle that makes "teapot lifting" a delight rather than a drag!

Unfortunately, even these great designers sometimes create a beautiful form that does not really function, and we must accept the form (because we admire the designer?) and forgo adequate functioning. I admire the prodigious talents of the Mid-Century-Modern designer Eva Zeisel, but she has made mistakes. In the surprising and delicately balanced Hallcraft line titled *Tomorrow's Classic*, Mrs. Zeisel created a gravy boat. This piece was conceived, possibly, to reflect the shape of the low candleholder, and while the curved "handles" of the candleholder fulfill its function, these same styled handles severely restrict the use of the gravy boat—as a gravy boat. The shape works fine as a candy basket or a large nut dish—in fact I have seen this piece labeled as a basket—many times but the function fades somewhat when the diner attempts to ladle gravy from beneath the arches. Two lovely, very similar shapes: one working well in tune with its function, the other awkwardly applying itself laboriously to fulfill its function.

Is all this ruminating beyond the interest of most collectors? Perhaps, but it is sincerely hoped not! A mere collector gathers and displays, and if this person has money and connections, the gathering and displaying become unappetizingly easy. However, when the collector stretches his imagination, expands his interests, and moves into the realm of the researcher, his enjoyment explodes. Then, if this collector-researcher becomes an educated critic: a critic whose admiration for a favorite designer does not becloud the truth that this designer made some mistakes. Collector-Researcher-Critic: ah, there is the perfect combination.

Once, long years ago, when I was struggling with a university course in epistemology—the nature of knowledge—the Benedictine monk who was guiding our investigations posed a very interesting challenge.

Try, he demanded, to reduce an item to its essence within a few words.

What this learned professor asked of the class was to describe a thing in its simplest terms, i.e. what makes a plate a plate, or a water tumbler a water tumbler? Try it! You will find it harder than it seems.

One can also attempt this reduction in the area of writing. Read a paragraph and then reduce it to a few words that contain its essence. This is called constructing a *précis*. In both cases, there is an attempt to reduce the item or the paragraph to its basic condition. The successful designer needs to understand true essence of an object before any creative work can begin.

What makes an admirable candleholder, falls short as a gravy boat.

So how does an industrial designer such as Ben Seibel chose the best form to fulfill a particular item's function? And can this chosen form be termed its "essence?" After having looked at all the known creations designed by Ben Seibel—one after another like the treasured shapes they are—which one taken as a whole illustrates the best form?

What about the teapot, or what is euphuistically called today "a beverage server?" What are the basic "essences" from which the ceramist can create or build his/her server? (1) A hollow shape to hold the liquid, (2) an opening whereby the liquid is poured into this hollow shape, (3) some type of hole through which the liquid can be directed into a smaller shape (the cup), and (4) some type of handle by which the hollow shape can be lifted. Basically this is all that is required. The opening for pouring liquid INTO the shape does not need a cover, but the desire to keep the liquid hot, or cold, or sanitary makes this cover a desirable adjunct. From this the designer advances and builds: the end result might be crudely created but magnificently functional—the little round and brown stoneware teapot of English fame—or artistically perfect but dreadfully dysfunctional.[1]

Let us pass over the teapots and start with the samovars—those monumental pieces that tend to dominate all space around them. These pieces are one of Ben Seibel's favorites: he used them wherever he could. The traditional definition of a "samovar" does not fit into Seibel's modern conception. It was a term used to refer to a large metal urn with a spigot used to boil water for tea. The hostess places some of the very strong tea mixture—usually from a china teapot settled warmly on the top of the samovar—into a teacup and dilutes it with boiling water drawn from the samovar's spigot. *Voila*! Your cup of tea!

Seibel's conception was very different—even with the occasional remaining spigot. The Seibel samovar was simply a large, impressive beverage server. So large was this server that drawing off the liquid needed another method other than ordinary hand pouring. Thus arises the need for the spigot or the swinging cradle. If a spigot was used, it needed to be at the bottom of the server, and thus the server needed to be elevated from the table. *Ergo*: the stand. And because there was so much liquid inside the "samovar," it needed to be kept hot (if it were a hot liquid): thus within the stand some source of heat—usually a votive candle.

The *Raymor Modern Stoneware* swinging coffee pot with its extremely breakable cradle might be considered a forerunner of a type of "samovar"—or, perhaps, Seibel's concept of a samovar. To claim this is a stretch, I will admit, but a germ of a "samovar" is present: the idea of placing a heavy beverage server in some type of "cradle" to allow for easier use. Again, please remember, we are discussing how Seibel conceived his samovars, not the traditional Russian piece. When the Roseville Raymor ceramic coffee pot cradle proved predisposed to shatter, Seibel reverted to the cast iron stand. Certainly not as charming or so picturesque, but much more satisfyingly practical (i.e. functional.) The "cradle," the "stand," and the "warmer" entered the Seibel lexicon at this time and really never entirely disappeared.

Seibel was probably working on *Country-Time* during the same period as he was Roseville Raymor: both lines appeared in 1952. Thus he transferred his delight in a huge, swinging pot from one unto the other. *Country-Time's* coffee samovar (the official name) is a monstrous piece! Holding twenty-eight cups, it swings on an iron framework, its direction propelled by a folding iron frame handle attached to two "nubbins" fore and aft. The base squared into a grid-iron of construction. To pour a beverage from the spout of this creation is chancy, and to pour it gracefully and without spilling comes as a gift of the gods of dinnerware and ceramics. I have tried it, and I know. With deliberation and pre-party study, such a "pouring" is possible, yet which hostess (or host for that matter) would take the time to learn? No, it was a "fun" line, quirky with a joyous quality that did not mind spills and dribbles. A mightily impressive basketball of a samovar, but it was awkward to control.

With Iroquois' *Informal* Seibel got wiser. Since the function was not up to the form in his first two "samovar" attempts, he tried again but this time utilized the spigot. Again large, rotund as the Pfaltzgraff samovar, but here Seibel placed it, heavily but sedately, seated immoveable on a gracefully arched sturdy stand. The effect is that of a basketball balancing upon a duchess' *tabouret*.[2] This samovar is a perfect picnic or buffet table server; it can be imagined the spigot gushed more cold drinks—ice tea, lemonade, or, alas, even perhaps a fountain of gin and tonic—than hot coffee. It was amusingly shaped and performed its function with humorous aplomb.

In the 1960s, Seibel adapted the Iroquois samovar for Forum International *Stoneware*: he stretched it a little, pinched it decorously, added handles for more artistic interest, but it still was bulbous and needed a spigot. More elegantly conceived than the *Informal* example, the Forum International *Stoneware* verges on usable sculpture. This samovar has always been a favorite Seibel piece.

However, when the collector reaches the seventies designs, he will find a lean, tall, and stark Mikasa *Duplex* samovar. Stovepipe tall—perhaps not in perfect harmony—this samovar is pure utilitarian: all function with little exciting form.

Now the inquiring collector can never forget each manufacturer held the final decisions on each of these samovars, yet the weight of the Seibel prestige carried much before it. By tracing the samovars, the teapots, the sugar and creamer sets (these are always viewed as a "couple"), or the casseroles, the shaker sets, shape by shape, line by line, year by year, the critical collector can trace the development—forth or back—of the Seibel genius.

Erté's design for a "balloon" dress has a very interesting and attractive form, but one can hardly imagine Mary Pickford wearing this to fight off a movie villain. *Copyright Sevenarts, Ltd. Courtesy of Mark Schachner and the Erte Museum of Fashion and Theatre Designs.*

As the years accumulated, the designer relied on the past, remembers the past. I can hear Mr. Ben Seibel saying to himself: "Well, that worked in 1958, let's try the same idea again, but with these changes." And out comes the drawing pencils and a new design develops but still basically rooted in the past.

This necessary connection with the past enriches with remembrances the lives of the no-longer-young. It can be our only hope for sanity, and these links must be cherished. It is amusing, as an old man, to see the earnest, brash and rash opinions of some youthful twenty-year-olds. Their complacent arrogance toward the elderly is humorously entertaining when viewed from afar. These youth have the answer to every problem, they know all the truths, they know all that is worth being known, and they are inflexible in their assumed perfection. Yet, with the passage of the years, these once arrogant young people slowly realize how little they know of the truly important things of life, and then it is often too late. So too, as he grew older, did Ben Seibel eschew the understandable arrogance and experimentation of the young. He mellowed, and while never failing to follow an exceptional approach to design, he grew more practical, more conservative, and gentler.

Ben Seibel made a number of mistakes, and surely he would be willing to admit to them. He erred in his design for some finials: they became impossible to grasp for the sense of "stackibility." Also, the weightiness of some pieces is excessive. At times it does seem the form is more vital than the function. It is as if Seibel put more value on beauty of line rather than functional utility. This philosophy is easily understood, and accepted. While gazing at the lovely form of his *Contempora* teapot, does the collector really worry that the devilishly cute little spout can have a hard time handling the function of pouring tea? I do not think so.

In some cases Seibel doted on functionality. The simple yet charmed invention of the "raised" saucer well! Here the cup—with a recessed base—fits securely over the well, locking it securely in place.

Should the collector wonder why Seibel put two dimpling spouts on a number of his faststand gravy boats when pouring out the gravy was absolutely impossible? I do not think so. His best design in this area is the gravy with the stick handle. Here the user's thumb is safe from the hot sauce—not really so if the "handles" in *Contempora* and *Roseville Modern Stoneware* gravies are taken seriously!

Great industrial designers have always been firstly great artists, and secondly, functionalists.[3] We either accept the premise that artistry and form was, to them, more vital than plebian functionality, or we use the pretty little dinnerware sets conjured up by clever nonentities for such mega-stores as Wal-Mart™ or K-Mart™. Perhaps we should admire the great designers for their decisions?

End Remarks

Well, there it is! We have, you and I, spent some hours together. As the author, my hopes are that you enjoyed my observations, comments, and, interspersed, as they are, my feelings. It is hoped also that these "feelings" never get in the way of information. There is one expression that was a favorite of my grandfather—a rather cynical Victorian gentleman of inflexible beliefs. He used this saying constantly—almost to boredom. It went: "what goes around, comes around." And, he simply meant, a person reaps what he sows!

The information "sown" within the pages of this book was for me as true and as honest as possible. When a bit of knowledge has escaped me, I have said so, and throughout the pages have often requested help from you, the readers. This book is one of the first written about the genius of Ben Seibel, but it will not be the last. There is certainly much more to learn, and much more to write about. One author's insights and interests can be at variance with another's, yet the two of them—divergent as they may be—taken together, present a clearer, more rounded, and complete picture of the subject. Often authors forget—and I also fall prey to this condition—that we are here to honor Ben Seibel, not ourselves. Ben Seibel is "what it is all about!"

If among some sections there are moments of "sharpness," I request understanding. I truly have meant not to embarrass or agitate anyone. "Sharpness" comes with age, disappointment, and frustration, and all of us have experienced frustrating disappointments, and everyone, even today's beautiful, energetic youth, will soon fall victim to age: it can not be escaped.

It takes the perspective of age to stand aside and view all the contentious squabbling between members of a group who really have the same aims—and say: "Look here, my friends, and fellow collectors, all our misunderstandings deal with dishes. When we stand back and clearly view the problems of the world and our various roles within it, are dishes really worth our silly struggles?"

How easy to say from one whose life might be measured in months—dependent upon the vagaries of nature or the will of greater powers. A dish might be a beautiful object, but how much more beautiful is the respect of one's fellow human beings.

So it is wished my words have been read with understanding and appreciation. They are but a modest beginning.

Richard G. Racheter
St. Petersburg, Florida
January 1, 2003

Endnotes

Introduction

1. This list appears just as it was received with no editing.

2. These words are being written during an unusually hot and muggy October of 2001.

3. This article appeared in *Today's Collector*, October 1997. Edited by Steve Ellingboe. The article was impressively presented, but since I still had a great deal to learn about Ben Seibel, mistakes were made. I called Seibel "a forgotten American ceramic artist" which was, of course, not quite true!

Random Thoughts Regarding American Tableware

1. Made by the Homer Laughlin China Company, East Liverpool, Ohio. Produced from about 1899 until about 1910. One of the largest tableware sets produced in the United States.

2. Also a product of the HLC, consisting of approximately seventy-eight items and produced from 1906 until around 1915. It is believed not to have been popular with the public.

3. HLC: Eighty-three pieces—although this is not exact, as *Seneca* is sometimes not marked. Also advertised in the Sears catalog beginning in 1901.

4. HLC: Selection of sixty-eight pieces and in production from 1906 until the end of the 1920s. This is one of the easiest ornate shapes to locate.

5. HLC: Seventy-eight individual pieces dating from 1905 until 1916. It appeared in the Sears catalog of 1906.

6. Produced by Edwin M. Knowles China Company, Chester, West Virginia. It consisted of eighty-one pieces. The line included twelve sizes of platter, six jugs holding from one pint to eight pints, three covered dishes, two casseroles, five nappies (open vegetable bowls) from seven to eleven inches round, plus numerous specialty items.

7. Manufactured by The Knowles, Taylor, Knowles China Company, East Liverpool, Ohio. It contained a mere seventy-two separate pieces: nine platters, but three fruit dishes, plus the usual items thought necessary for the middle-class dining experience.

8. Vodrey Pottery Company, East Liverpool, Ohio, in production in 1913. Fifty some pieces, the number of individual items was slowly dwindling.

On Defining Terms

1. Admittedly a stretch, but the collector cannot disregard the trivet.

2. See sections on these two patterns.

Freelance Designers and Mid-Century-Modern

1. This lofty category of female singer no longer exists. It ceased with the virtual operatic retirement of Maria Callas in the mid-1960s.

2. Granted that Mr. Schreckengost did manage to design *Epicure* (1955), this curvaceous and lovely solid glazed line never had the chance to draw HLC into the MCM camp. *Epicure*, sincerely beloved by the most refined of HLC collectors, simply is too rare. The *Kennilworth* coffee bottle is pure Mid-Century-Modern, but again relatively unknown and quite scarce.

***Contempora* by Steubenville**

1. Most dealers when describing this color use the common term "Fawn." Imagine how pleasing it was to see the official term "Faun" used by Herb Fogliano of *Fiftysdish*. There may be others who use the exact spelling, of course, but these have yet to be noted.

2. The sgraffito lines on the outside of the *Contempora* gravy cause it to appear darker, but comparing the interiors, the collector realizes that the name does matter: *American Modern's* Granite Gray is "harder" than *Contempora's* Mist Gray.

3. The official Steubenville numbers were taken from an advertisement. Those numbers not given were missing from the brochure.

Raymor Modern Stoneware

1. The Wisconsin Pottery maintains this interesting web site at http://www.Wisconsinpottery.org/Roseville

2. These brighter glazes seemed not to have been very stable. They range from quite spectacular color to the almost muddily mundane. Good examples can command very high prices. For example, a robin's egg blue celery and olive dish can be priced as high as $225.

3. The lid for the creamer is one of the most difficult pieces to locate–almost impossible in good condition.

4. The mug can be found in two versions: short handled and long handled. Collectors prefer the latter.

5. The plates are measured from the rounded, not the handled (blunt point) sides.

6. A study of the restyled pieces has yet to be completed. There is confusion as to exactly which pieces were (1) restyled and sold in new glazes; (2) restyled and sold in the original glazes; and (3) NOT restyled but still appear in the new glazes. The known new glazes are chartreuse and robin's egg blue.

7. If any reader has compiled lists touching on the three categories noted in the endnote above, perhaps they would share these findings. I have seen (1) dinner and bread & butter plates in a slate blue, (2) bread & butter plates in terra cotta, and (3) dinner plate, lug soup bowl, coffee pot, celery/olive, divided vegetable, covered ramekin, and butter dish cover in robin's egg blue.

8. When offered for sale by private individuals these "unobtainable" pieces are priced astronomically, i.e. fruit basket in autumn brown: $650.00; in frogskin: $995.00; swinging coffee pot with ceramic saddle: $795.00; with wrought iron stand: $595.00. What average Roseville Raymor collector could or would part with sums such as these?

9. Occasionally butter has seeped under the glaze and stains the base of the butter dish. Never purchase one of these expensive pieces without a thorough examination.

10. Sir Cecil Beaton (1904-1980) received his second Academy Award as general production designer for *My Fair Lady* (1964). His sequence known as the "Black and White Ascot" is one of the highlights in the non-use of cinematic color. This musical was based upon George Bernard Shaw's delightful play *Pygmalion*.

11. Not all the stands are stark. Several have been seen obviously not meant to function as a warmer, but as an elegant wooden frame to hold two, three, four of the smaller double-handled bean pots off the table in a low metal sling. Since these frames come in a variety of forms, it is hard to tell exactly who manufactured them. The important point is they are quite beautiful.

Pfaltzgraff's *Country-Time*

1. The dates of introduction for the three early Raymor lines all appear to be between 1950 and 1953. *Contempora* is placed in 1950, *Country-Time* as circa 1952, and *Raymor Modern Stoneware* early in 1953. If this is the correct sequence, then *Country-Time* is the second Seibel line, but I have taken a loosely applied prerogative—because of the obvious design similarities—and followed *Contempora* with Roseville Raymor. I am sorry if this offends any collectors. Then too, as it must be stressed, the production date of a tableware line has nothing to do with its design date. RMS could have been designed in 1952 or 1951, and not produced until 1953.

2. During these years, Ben Seibel developed a life-long friendship with Irving Richards who held an important position at Raymor.

3. These numbers do not appear on the pieces.

4. Pieces marked with (S) have metal stands and warmers.

5. This cup is often called a "mug."

6. The grill plate was officially called a "Bar-B-Q" plate.

7. The meat platter and the cheese and relish tray had wooden inserts.

8. In my collection there are examples of designs being stamped inaccurately, or evidence of slipping and sliding. The "snowflake" seems more liable to this problem.

The Iroquois China Company/Ben Seibel Connection

1. The Jenfred line of brass and other metal items included candleholders, candy bowls, trays, and shaker sets that could be considered "tableware." Jenfred ware was a product of LEVCO Metal Finishers, Inc. of Long Island City, New York, and distributed by Richards Morgenthau & Company of New York City and Chicago. This company also distributed Raymor products.

2. Duke, Harvey. *Official Price Guide to Pottery and Porcelain.* 8th ed. New York: House of Collectibles, 1995, p. 346.

3. These e-mail conversations took place the summer of 1997.

4. The years 1952 and 1954 have both been mentioned as the date when *Interplay* first appeared.

5. The readers again are asked to remember that, except for Pfaltzgraff's *Country-Time*, the first designs of the Seibel/Raymor connection did not accomplish their goals. Thus, while they later became fascinating pieces of dinnerware for collectors, and while they were critical successes at the time of their introduction, they were labeled—in the 1950s—as commercial failures.

6. A philosophical resemblance versus a physical resemblance, i.e. the former might be the repeat appearance of a small footed fruit compote, the latter would involve the simple fact that a finial in one line would be physically repeated in another.

7. *Impromptu* was introduced to the ceramic critics in January 1956, thus Seibel must have had some months prior to work on it.

8. A dark gray solid glaze has also been reported, but this has never been personally seen.

9. These pieces differ between the two lines.

Impromptu and its Library

1. Those items in italics were no longer available in 1965.

2. Some unofficial lists include two soups: coupe and lug.

3. This is a rather bold statement that I might regret. The person compiling the *Impromptu* list was also working on one for *Informal*. Perhaps there has been mild confusion between the two listings?

4. In fact, the only mug seen belongs to the *Informal* line, but the drawing on a later *Impromptu* advertising sheet shows the mug is the same in each. This raises to three the number of shared pieces: ashtray, cheese dish, and coffee mug.

5. It is useful to remember that Seibel was working on *Informal* at this same time—at least in his imagination or preliminary drawings. Perhaps he wished to try out a version of the *Informal* cup and saucer.

6. In mid-2002, this question was answered by the appearance of the treatment Fjord on both cup/saucer sets.

7. *Country-Time*, produced by Pfaltzgraff, is a unique shape—it bears no resemblance to any other dinnerware. Presently Raymor's involvement is being questioned.

8. Due to the existence of an Iroquois China Company press release (January 1956), it is known that the name "Chrysanthemums" was changed to "Pompon" before, or shortly after, it was offered for sale.

9. This phrase was taken from a news release (January 1965) issued by Alfred Auerbach Associates, a New York City based advertising firm. The prose of these releases tends to be effusive.

10. Well into my research, an advertising brochure or announcement was discovered that listed the seven original treatments on the soon-to-be-released *Impromptu*. Chrysantheums did not appear, but PomPon did. Thus it is believed there was a name change BEFORE the actual introduction.

Informal Cookware and its Library

1. Technically, only three pieces of *Informal* were actually cookware: Dutch oven, fry pan, and sauce pan, but they lent their name to the entire line. They most certainly could be used in oven and on top of the stove. There were, however, careful suggestions and instructions written on the bottom of these pieces: some cautioning regarding the need for asbestos pads.

2. Ben Seibel was never one to let a good design go wanting. On December 6, 1966, he introduced a line of tables and stools named *Pivotal* that reused this double triangle or pyramid shape. The furniture name itself was reused to become the most delicate and refined of his important late 1970s Mikasa dinnerware lines.

3. As explained later in this section, the lazy susan relish set ceased production by 1965, perhaps even earlier, and thus there is a potent possibility that it exists in only the first four treatments.

4. There is some unsolved confusion about the placement of the heraldic motif on the dinner plate. Both patterns, Teuton and Thane, appear on *Informal* and the more stately *Inheritance*. The plate illustrated in the Harvey Duke book (*The Official Price Guide to Pottery and Porcelain*, 8th edition, p. 351) is *Inheritance*: the device is large and single and centered boldly. This led me to believe the size and placement on this device changed according to the line of dinnerware. It does not! After seeing photographs of Inheritance dinner plates bearing both Thane and Teuton, one learns the treatment is exactly the same—a controlled scattering of the motif. I cannot explain the Thane/Teuton black and white photograph in Mr. Duke's book. Perhaps it is an early and rare version.

5. After this first original brochure, the samovar and stand were no longer classified as cooking items.

6. Please remember, just as with *Impromptu*, this butter dish is not marked *Informal*, but merely "Iroquois China."

7. One of the charms of my favorite Mikasa/Seibel tableware shape, *Potter's Art*, is that the gravy has a handle and can be expertly poured with no stress or anxiety.

***Inheritance*: A Dinnerware Line Set Apart**

1. Iroquois did put together a tea set that included the teapot on its stand, the sugar and creamer on the serving tray. This might have been considered a "gift set."

2. The reader must remember it is 1959, when only women were supposed to be interested in dinnerware. Today a good majority of the serious collectors of Ben Seibel tableware designs are men. Is this sexism in reverse?

3. Early *Inheritance* was divided into three categories: Sheer White; Group I: Baroque, Su-Shi, Knollwood, Gold Band, Platinum Band; Group II: Cotillion, Grecian Gold. Sheer White and Group I were priced at the same level as *Impromptu* and *Informal*. Group II was priced slightly more. For all its glamour, *Inheritance* was very affordable.

4. A careful reading of all these press releases allows the collector to pinpoint the exact public introduction of *Inheritance*: September 1959.

5. *Official Price Guide to Pottery and Porcelain*, 8th ed., p.351.

***Intaglio*: The Fourth and Last of Seibel/Iroquois Partnership**

1. The date of *Intaglio*'s introduction has been given variously as 1962 and 1964. The date of this press release and the use of the phrase "new *Intaglio* collection" seems to prove 1964 was the date.

2. The saucer is also always undecorated white and has no debossment.

3. In my opinion, there is a plump, very matronly quality about this shape: gently rounded, hardly delicate, but still feminine as a favored aunt: not glamorous Auntie Mame, nor Dorothy's stern Aunt Em, but perhaps Scarlet's vague and vaporous Aunt Pittipat?

The Mikasa/Seibel Connection: Including a Study of Five Mikasa Catalogs

1. On page 7 of the 1978 catalog, Mr. Ohtake, a Japanese artist, is given credit for the "original designs" on Natural Beauty. This could mean that Seibel designed the shape and Mr. Ohtake the treatments.

2. It is now accepted that *Mexicana* was produced before *Duplex*

3. These figures come from the cash receipts ledger now housed in the Siebel archives at Syracuse University Library.

4. Almost continuous efforts were made to contact Mikasa at its Secaucus, New Jersey headquarters, but to no avail!

Mikasa *Duplex*: Considered the Most Available and its Library

1. No other proof is needed that America's dining habits had changed drastically since the 1950s. Mikasa belongs firmly in the 1970s: the years when women were becoming disenchanted by housewifery and were seeking interests outside the home. Simplicity was not a foible but a necessity.

2. The number of *Duplex* treatments continues to grow. When my personal collection of plates reached to thirty-six a few years ago, it was believed that was all that there was to be had. What a ridiculous belief! Four more were added, and when the Mikasa catalogs were studied (see Introduction to Mikasa) another four were discovered—for a grand total of forty-seven. Has the end been reached?

3. Some collectors will disagree with this statement.

4. Rather than list all the treatments in this section, the reader is asked to study them in the following chapter: Duplex: The Library of Treatments.

5. It must not be assumed that 1971 was the introductory year for *Duplex*. Some of these twenty-one treatments could have appeared as early as 1969 or 1970.

6. Granted, this is a curious definition. What is meant is a completely symmetrical, circular pattern either filled or edging the well.

***Pivotal*: Library of Treatments**

1. There is in my possession, one soup bowl with a grayer matte finish—more like a moss green. The stamp has the name Pivgreen with a number 5014. I have placed this treatment on the list. Does any reader have a plate stamped "Pivgreen"?

***Potter's Art* and its Library**

1. *Potter's Art* appeared in the Mikasa catalogs in

the mid-1970s, after both *Duplex* and *Pivotal*.

2. Seibel conceived of the Pfaltzgraff *Country-Time* gravy and butter warmer with a handle. He returned to the concept some twenty years later with *Potter's Art*. Even though it is eminently useful, he does not seem to have favored the handled gravy.

3. Casserole of tripe.

4. Casserole of white beans baked with meats.

5. Rabbit stewed in white wine sauce.

6. The title is another proof of Ben Seibel's ultimate aim for this line of tableware.

7. Not necessarily ceramic. Seibel did not fully understand the beauty and practicality of warmer stands until *Impromptu*, and then stands—not always warmers—appeared with regularity, and in a wide variety of materials.

8. These five belong to the PF09—series and use the *Discovery* cup and saucer.

9. PF850 is not named and was called "regular" merely for identification. It provides the hollowware for Country Cabin.

Mexicana: Library of Treatments

1. According to the excellent book *The Color Compendium*, by Augustine Hope and Margaret Walsh (New York: Van Nostrand Reinhold, 1990), this term is "loosely applied by paint manufacturers to a variety of greens, including emerald green, Verona green (glauconite), and chrome green, named for Paolo Veronese (1528-88), a Venetian painter. Here, naturally, it means "Parrot Green."

2. Lee Russell, a very perceptive collector, must be thanked for the list in this form.

3. The name of this treatment was obtained from a very dark copy of a small advertising slip for *Mexicana* plate patterns. The name and number could be discerned, but the actual pattern was impossible to see.

4. My listing and photographs (black and white) of twelve *Mexicana* treatments lists this as Cero Gorde. A few collectors insist that this name is not Spanish and the name should be Cerro Gordo. The choice becomes the reader's.

5. This is a very doubtful name for a *Mexicana* treatment, but since I have heard it a few times, it is included here. It has never been seen or mentioned in any official Mikasa listing. It is a very wan possibility.

Mikasa/Seibel Clones: Many Questions, Few Answers

1. Please read the section on the Mikasa catalogs.

2. This exact same technique—washing the insides of teacups, creamers, etc. with a matching tint—is followed in some of the *Duplex* clones

3. The *Discovery* cup and saucer appears in the five *Potter's Art* treatments known arbitrarily as the PF09—series.

4. The two treatments labeled as *Potter's Art* in the 1977 Mikasa catalog were Wind Blown and Birch Lane: neither were shown with an official number. Since the latter depicted thin wispy twigs sprouting large round blossoms—a characteristic design on *LifeStyle* plates—this treatment was placed here. It could logically be (PG008), but the urge to number it so will be suppressed.

5. Might the appearance of the *Duplex* sugar and creamer set in *Majorca* advance the proposition that Seibel created the latter line?

6. These three are only decorated with colored bands.

7. These four have decorated saucers.

8. These four have decorated saucers.

Kasuga/*Virrastone*

1. When a man (and it usually is a man) eats a slice of raw blowfish sushi, he reinforces his trust in the cook who prepared the dish. Raw blowfish, incorrectly cleaned, is deadly poisonous.

2. Even though called a soup "plate," this piece is really a 7" bowl.

3. Originally sold as a pair.

4. A collector finding new uses for standard items in a dinnerware set is to be commended.

5. All the broad-based pieces (coffee pot, jug, and creamer) need to be very stable as they are holding liquid.

The Forum International Family

1. Perhaps the "quiche dish" is not as fanciful as first thought—especially if advertising copy shows these triangular inserts used to serve salad.

2. Some dark solid green pieces have been seem marked "Stoneware, Original, Japan, Oven Proof." These are thought to be marketed by the Japanese as alternatives to the true Forum International *Stoneware*.

3. One collector has informed me that a ladle accompanied the spoon and fork.

The Forum International Family: Stoneware

1. Some dark solid green pieces have been seen marked "Stoneware, Original, Japan, Oven Proof." These are thought to be marketed by the Japanese as alternative competitors to the true *Forum International Stoneware*.

Oneida Melmac

1. It is vital to remember these two colors. When any of these pieces, modified by loss of cover or handle, appear in any other color, they belong to a regular set.

2. I apologize if I seem to return to the question of *Interplay*.

3. The saucer occasionally appeared in a solid glaze.

4. Advertising brochure: Oneida Premier, a New Era of Splendor in Melamine Dinnerware (n.d.).

Fostoria Glassware

1. 1972, Design Department Manager. When Marvin Yutzey retired in 1977, Mr. Saffell became Director of Design.

2. Ms. Olert, involved in the bridal market, was appointed to the newly created position of Production Development Coordinator. She added a woman's touch to what was basically a woman's market.

3. These are the official Fostoria identification numbers.

4. These are names of etchings.

5. There is no direct proof regarding *Festive*—only assumptions.

6. Jon Saffell identifies *Facets* as giftware.

7. Mr. Saffell uses the term "tableware" to describe *Gourmet*.

8. The terms "clear glass" and "no optics" need clarification. An "optic" is an indentation in the glass often used for a decorative affect. "No optic" means the glass is free of any indentations. "Clear glass" does not mean "crystal." Clear glass can be in any color, just simply free of any optic indentations. However, remember, optics are NOT etchings. The patterns are:

Regular optic: a series of slight straight lines top to bottom.

Narrow optic: same as above but arranged more closely.

Spiral optic: curving lines running from top to bottom.

Looped optic: a series of draped loops.

Dimpled optic: scattered indentations.

Niagara optic: wavy lines going from top to bottom.

No optic: absolutely clear.

The first and the last are the most common

9. The *ying* and *yang* effect in design technically is limited to the use of white (the passive feminine *ying*) contrasting with black (the aggressive masculine *yang*). Nevertheless modern interpretation of this effect can sometimes be stretched to consist of any light/dark contrast, i.e. pale pink with dark maroon.

10. Please be aware there are TWO Fostoria lines named *Raidance* (2700) (1956-1957) designed by Raymond Loewy and *Raidance* (3113) (1981-1982). The former is a full dinnerware line, the latter a stemware line of only six pieces. It is not known why Fostoria reused the name.

Miscellaneous Ben Seibel Not To Be Missed

1. Although most of the frames were ironware some examples were offered in polished brass.

2. Whenever necessary—to be heated or for hot foods—the "glassware" was Pyrex.

3. Official numbers for casseroles are sometimes used more than once.

The Function of Form

1. My grandmother once owned and loved a Wedgwood green teapot, yet whenever she used it—and this was rarely—the front had to be fitted with a hand-crocheted "bib" to absorb the succession of dreadful dribbles. I own it still, but the bibs have disappeared.

2. Louis le Grand, Sun King of France (1643-1715), to control his potentially fractious nobles devised many "honors" that were meaningless and even cumbersome. He announced that only duchesses (nobility's highest rank) could sit in the presence of royalty. He then gave these august ladies *le tabouret*, a small, low stool upon which they could seat themselves, balanced precariously. Inconvenient, indeed, but once granted, these little stools became *la place d'honneur*.

3. The pull between form and function is the agonizing bane of most ceramic and/or glassware designers. Their artistry must be tempered by practicality. My grandfather had a saying that certainly was opinionated: "All veterinarians are frustrated medical doctors." I doubt if this is really true, but if it is, then do all Wrights, Schreckengosts, Zeisels, and Seibels yearn to be Rodins and Brancusis?

Selective Bibliography

Bones, Frances. *Fostoria Glassware, 1887-1982: Identification and Values*. Paducah, KY: Collector Books, c. 1999.

Cunningham, Jo. *The Collector's Encyclopedia of American Dinnerware*. Paducah, KY: Collector Books, c. 1982, 1992.

_____. *Homer Laughlin: A Giant Among Dishes, 1873-1939*. Atglen, PA: Schiffer Publishing, Ltd., 1998.

_____. *Homer Laughlin China, 1940s & 1950s*. Atglen, PA: Schiffer Publishing, Ltd., 2000.

Duke, Harvey. *Official Price Guide to Pottery and Porcelain*. 8th ed. New York: NY: House of Collectibles, c. 1995.

Gonzales, Mark. *Collecting Fiesta, Lu-Ray & Other Colorware*. Gas City, IN: L-W Book Sales, c. 2000.

Kerr, Ann. *Fostoria: an identification and value guide of pressed blown & hand molded shapes*. Paducah, KY: Collector Books, c. 1994, 1997.

_____. *The Collector's Encyclopedia of Russel Wright Designs*. Paducah, KY: Collector Books, c. 1990.

Lehner, Lois. *Lehner's Encyyclopedia of U.S. Marks on Pottery, Porcelain & Clay*. Paducah, KY: Collector Books, 1988.

Long, Milbra and Emily Seate. *Fostoria Stemware: the Crystal for America*. Paducah, KY: Collector Books, c. 1995, 1998.

_____. *Fostoria Tableware, 1944-1986: the Crystal for America*. Paducah, KY: Collector Books, c. 1999.

Piña, Leslie. *Pottery: Modern Wares, 1920-1960*. Atglen, PA: Schiffer Publishing, Ltd., 1994.

Pratt, Michael. *Mid-Century Modern Dinnerware*. Atglen, PA: Schiffer Publishing, Ltd., 2002.

Spours, Judy. *Art Deco Tableware: British Domestic Ceramics, 1925-1939*. New York, NY: Rizzoli, 1988.